JOURNAL FOR THE STUDY OF THE NEW TESTAMENT
SUPPLEMENT SERIES
29

Executive Editor, Supplement Series
David Hill

Publishing Editor
David E Orton

JSOT Press
Sheffield

24.61

ABRAHAM IN GALATIANS

Epistolary and Rhetorical Contexts

G. Walter Hansen

Journal for the Study of the New Testament
Supplement Series 29

Published by JSOT Press
JSOT Press is an imprint of
Sheffield Academic Press Ltd
The University of Sheffield
343 Fulwood Road
Sheffield S10 3BP
England

Printed in Great Britain
by Billing & Sons Ltd
Worcester

British Library Cataloguing in Publication Data

Hansen, G. Walter
    Abraham in Galatians
    1. Bible. N.T. Galatians Critical studies
    I. Title   II. Series
    227'.406

    ISSN 0143-5108
    ISBN 1-85075-171-4

CONTENTS

PREFACE

This study is a modification of my doctoral dissertation accepted by Wycliffe College and The Toronto School of Theology of The University of Toronto in 1985.

I am grateful for the exemplary scholarship, perceptive criticisms, and gracious friendship of Professor Richard N. Longenecker, who served as director of the dissertation. The hours spent with him in personal consultation over my work contributed substantially not only to the completion of this study but also to the quality of my life.

Professor John C. Hurd, Jr. also deserves special thanks for the valuable insights which were gained in his seminar on the structure of Paul's letters.

During my two years at Tyndale House in Cambridge, my research colleagues challenged me to consider new perspectives. Murray Harris and John Barclay were especially helpful. Discussion with my colleagues at Fuller Theological Seminary in Pasadena and Trinity Theological College in Singapore has continued to clarify my thinking.

The generosity and encouragement of my parents, Ken and Jean, enabled me to concentrate on this project. Their life together is an eloquent witness to the reality of freedom in Christ.

My deepest gratitude is expressed to my wife, Darlene, for her love enabled me to work with joy and confidence. And my children, Nathaniel, Jonathan, and Linnea, also contributed to this work, for precious times with them cleared my mind and refreshed my heart.

SOLI DEO GLORIA

ABBREVIATIONS

Periodicals, Reference Works, and Serials

AGJU	Arbeiten zur Geschichte des antiken Judentums und des Urchristentums
AnBib	Analecta biblica
ATR	*Anglican Theological Review*
AusBR	*Australian Biblical Review*
BAG	W. Bauer, W.F. Arndt, F.W. Gingrich, and F.W. Danker, *Greek-English Lexicon of the New Testament and Other Early Christian Literature*
BDF	F. Blass, A. Debrunner, and R.W. Funk, *A Greek Grammar of the New Testament*
BEvT	Beiträge zur evangelischen Theologie
BFCT	Beiträge zur Förderung christlicher Theologie
Bib	*Biblica*
BJRL	*Bulletin of the John Rylands University Library of Manchester*
BTB	*Biblical Theology Bulletin*
BWANT	Beiträge zur Wissenschaft vom Alten und Neuen Testament
BZ	*Biblische Zeitschrift*
BZNW	Beihefte zur *ZNW*
CBQ	*Catholic Biblical Quarterly*
ConBNT	Coniectanea biblica, New Testament
CQ	*Church Quarterly*
CTM	*Concordia Theological Monthly*
DBSup	*Dictionnaire de la Bible, Supplement*
EstBib	*Estudios biblicos*
EvQ	*Evangelical Quarterly*
EvT	*Evangelische Theologie*
ExpTim	*Expository Times*
FRLANT	Forschungen zur Religion und Literatur des Alten und Neuen Testaments

FS	Festschrift
HeyJ	*Heythrop Journal*
HKNT	Handkommentar zum Neuen Testament
HNT	Handbuch zum Neuen Testament
HR	*History of Religions*
HSM	Harvard Semitic Monographs
HTKNT	Herders theologischer Kommentar zum Neuen Testament
HTR	*Harvard Theological Review*
HTS	Harvard Theological Studies
HUCA	*Hebrew Union College Annual*
ICC	International Critical Commentary
IJT	*Indian Journal of Theology*
Int	*Interpretation*
JBL	*Journal of Biblical Literature*
JES	*Journal of Ecumenical Studies*
JETS	*Journal of the Evangelical Theological Society*
JJS	*Journal of Jewish Studies*
JQR	*Jewish Quarterly Review*
JR	*Journal of Religion*
JSJ	*Journal for the Study of Judaism in the Persian, Hellenistic and Roman Period*
JSNT	*Journal for the Study of the New Testament*
JSS	*Journal of Semitic Studies*
JTS	*Journal of Theological Studies*
KD	*Kerygma und Dogma*
LCL	Loeb Classical Library
MeyerK	H.A.W. Meyer, Kritisch-exegetischer Kommentar über das Neue Testament
MNTC	Moffatt NT Commentary
MTZ	*Münchener theologische Zeitschrift*
NIDNTT	*The New International Dictionary of New Testament Theology*
NKZ	*Neue kirchliche Zeitschrift*
NovT	*Novum Testamentum*
NovTSup	Novum Testamentum, Supplements
NTS	*New Testament Studies*
PTMS	Pittsburgh Theological Monograph Series
RelSRev	*Religious Studies Review*
RevThom	*Revue thomiste*

RSR	*Recherches de science religieuse*
SBLASP	Society of Biblical Literature Abstracts and Seminar Papers
SBLDS	SBL Dissertation Series
SBLMS	SBL Masoretic Studies
SBLSCS	SBL Septuagint and Cognate Studies
SE	*Studia Evangelica*
SJLA	Studies in Judaism in Late Antiquity
SJT	*Scottish Journal of Theology*
SNTSMS	Society for New Testament Studies Monograph Series
SPB	Studia postbiblica
ST	*Studia theologica*
Str-B	Strack and Billerbeck, *Kommentar zum Neuen Testament*
STVP	Studia in Veteris Testamenti pseudepigrapha
TDNT	G. Kittel, ed. *Theological Dictionary of the New Testament*
TF	*Theologische Forschung*
THKNT	Theologischer Handkommentar zum Neuen Testament
TLZ	*Theologische Literaturzeitung*
TQ	*Theologische Quartalschrift*
TSK	*Theologische Studien und Kritiken*
VT	*Vetus Testamentum*
WTJ	*Westminster Theological Journal*
WUNT	Wissenschaftliche Untersuchungen zum Neuen Testament
ZAW	*Zeitschrift für die alttestamentliche Wissenschaft*
ZNW	*Zeitschrift für die neutestamentliche Wissenschaft*
ZST	*Zeitschrift für systematische Theologie*
ZTK	*Zeitschrift für Theologie und Kirche*

Dead Sea Scrolls

CD	Cairo Damascus Document
1QpHab	*Pesher on Habakkuk* from Qumran Cave 1
1QM	*Milhamah* (*War Scroll*)
1QIsa	Copy of Isaiah from Qumran Cave 1
1QapGen	*Genesis Apocryphon* of Qumran Cave 1

Works of Philo

Abr	*De Abrahamo*
Cher	*De Cherubim*
Cong	*De Congressu quaerendae Eruditionis gratia*
Heres	*Quis Rerum Divinarum Heres*
Immut	*Quod Deus immutabilis sit*
Leg All	*Legum Allegoriae*
Migr	*De Migratione Abrahami*
Mut	*De Mutatione Nominum*
Post	*De Posteritate Caini*
Praem	*De Praemiis et Poenis*
Qu Gen	*Quaestiones et Solutiones in Genesin*
Spec Leg	*De Specialibus Legibus*
Virt	*De Viritutibus*

Works of Josephus

Ant	*Antiquitates Judaicae*
Ap	*Contra Apionem*

Rabbinic Works

References to tractates in the Mishna, Tosephta, Babylonian Talmud, and Jerusalem Talmud are signified by the letters *m*, *t*, *b*, or *y* respectively.

Bikk.	*Bikkurim*
B. Kam.	*Baba Kamma*
B. Mes.	*Baba Mesia*
Kidd.	*Kiddushin*
Ned.	*Nedarim*
Sanh.	*Sanhedrin*
Pirqe R. El.	*Pirqe Rabbi Eleizer*
Pesiq. R.	*Pesiqta Rabbati*
Gen. Rab.	*Genesis Rabbah*
Lev. Rab.	*Leviticus Rabbah*

Collections of Papyri

B.G.U.	*Ägyptische Urkunden aus den Staatlichen Museen zu Berlin, Griechische Urkunden*
P. Baden	*Veröffentlichungen aus den badischen Papyrus-Sammlungen*
P. Cairo Zen.	*Catalogue général des antiquités égyptiennes du Musée du Caire: Zenon Papyri*
P. Cornell	*Greek Papyri in the Library of the Cornell University*
P. Ent.	Εντεύξεις. *Requêtes et plaintes adressées au roi d'Egypte au IIIe siècle avant J.C.*
P. Fay	*Fayum Towns and their Papyri*
P. Giss.	*Griechische Papyri im Museum des Oberhessischen Geschichtsvereins zu Giessen*
P. Grenf. I	*An Alexandrian Erotic Fragment and other Greek Papyri chiefly Ptolemaic*
P. Harr.	*The Rendel Harris Papyri of Woodbrooke College, Birmingham*
P. Herm.	*Studien zur Paläographie und Papyruskunde*
P. Lips.	*Griechische Urkunden der Papyrussammlung zu Leipzig*
P. Lond.	*Greek Papyri in the British Museum*
P. Mich.	*Papyri in the University of Michigan Collection*
P. Merton	*A descriptive catalogue of the Greek papyri in the collection of Wilfred Merton*
P. Oxy.	*The Oxyrhynchus Papyri*
P. Princ.	*Papyri in the Princeton University Collections*
P. Ryl.	*Catalogue of the Greek Papyri in the J. Rylands Library, Manchester*
P. Tebt.	*The Tebtunis Papyri*
S.B.	*Sammelbuch griechischer Urkunden aus Ägypten*

INTRODUCTION

Since the gospel according to Paul is the fulfillment of the Abrahamic promise, it is not surprising that discussion of major themes in Paul's theology so often turns to an analysis of his interpretation of the Abraham story. In fact the decade of the 80's is marked by a series of articles and monographs which focus to one extent or another on Paul's use of the Abraham story in Galatians.[1] These recent studies attempt to explain Paul's use of the OT by defining the theology of the troublemakers in Galatia, by describing the portraits of Abraham in Jewish literature, or by delineating the Jewish principles of exegesis employed by Paul. Valuable insights have been gained by these lines of investigation.[2]

As helpful as these different approaches are, however, far from moving scholars toward consensus, such contextual and historical studies have been used to develop contradictory theories regarding the purpose and meaning of Paul's interpretation of the Abraham story. For example, the use of Gen. 15.6 in Gal. 3.6 is seen by some as a '"proof text" which establishes the Pauline thesis that justification and santification occur by faith';[3] whereas others claim that Paul used Gen. 15.6 'to support his doctrine of the inclusion of uncircumcised Gentiles, not to separate man's faith from his works;'[4] and still others assert that Paul's major theological concern in the use of this text is 'not the justification of individuals by their faith, but the justification of the legitimacy of his apostleship'.[5]

One reason for these conflicting interpretations is the lack of sufficient attention given to a fundamental issue. Little attention has been given to the structure of the letter and to the development of Paul's argument. Robert Funk's challenge is still appropriate: '. . . with respect to critical literary questions the situation is far from satisfactory. A breakthrough is urgently needed in this sphere, if for no other reason than that the discussion tends to stall always at the same points and wear itself out on the same insoluble issues'.[6]

The analysis of the structure of Galatians requires, first of all, that the letter be read as a letter. Since it is a Greek letter, it needs to be read in the light of the Greek letter tradition. John L. White has shown how the standard forms of Greek letters are reflected in Paul's letters.[7] Yet in his analysis of Galatians he fails to use the forms that he has discovered.[8] At the 1973 SBL Seminar on Paul, Nils Dahl made the suggestion in an unpublished paper that Paul's letter to the Galatians is similar to rebuke–request letters in the Greek letter tradition.[9] This observation that there is a rebuke (1.6)-request (4.12) structure in Galatians challenges the traditionally accepted perspective that 3.1–4.31 is one continuous section, an unbreakable chain of arguments. For if Dahl's suggestion is valid, then Paul's use of the Abraham story in 4.21-31 follows a major turning point in the letter. Our work in chapter one seeks to demonstrate the validity of Dahl's suggestion and to show how it sheds fresh light on Paul's differing use of the Abrahan story in 3.6-29 and in 4.21-31. On the one hand, Paul's exposition of the Abraham story in 3.6-29 serves in a parallel way with the autobiographical section as substantiating his rebuke for his Galatian converts' desertion from the gospel and their foolishness about the meaning of the gospel. On the other hand, Paul's application of the Hagar–Sarah story in 4.21-31 serves as scriptural support for his ethical imperatives.

Chapter two is taken up with rhetorical analyses of Galatians. Galatians has already been analyzed in terms of its rhetorical structures by Hans Dieter Betz.[10] But Betz himself confesses bewilderment when he tries to analyze the rhetorical structure of chapters 3 and 4.[11] Betz failed to observe that there is a significant rhetorical shift at 4.12 from forensic rhetoric to deliberative rhetoric. My analysis seeks to show how the function of the Abraham argument in chapter 3 differs from the rhetorical function of the Hagar–Sarah allegory in chapter 4. Paul first uses the Abraham argument (3.6-29) to accuse the Galatians of foolish adherence to a false gospel. Then he turns from accusation of past misbehavior and supports his call to a specific course of future action with the Hagar-Sarah allegory (4.21-31).

In chapter 3 two issues are discussed. First, Bligh's extensive structuring of Galatians in terms of chiasmus is evaluated.[12] While Bligh has overstated his case, nevertheless he has pointed to a significant conceptual and verbal pattern in Paul's style of argument. And our work in this area highlights a chiastic pattern in Gal. 3.1–

4.11 which helps us in tracing out the steps of Paul's Abraham argument. Our outline of this chiastic pattern shows that the discussion of justification by faith and the place of the law is set within the context of references to the experience of the Spirit in the Galatian community and the inclusion of the Gentiles. Such a context indicates that the argument for justification by faith apart from works of the law functions as a defense of the inclusion of Gentile believers and as a rationale for their experience of the Spirit.

Second, in chapter 3 a recent use of the so-called 'new rhetoric' in the rhetorical analysis of Paul's letters is also discussed. Wilhelm Wuellner[13] and Folker Siegert,[14] using Chaim Perelman's description of rhetorical techniques[15] in their analyses of Paul's argumentation in Romans, suggest a helpful method for the detection of various rhetorical techniques which Paul employs. To date this method has not been used in the analysis of Paul's polemical use of the Abraham story in Gal. 3-4. In our application of the method, rhetorical techniques such as arguments from authority, by definition, by dissociation, by enthymeme, and by transitivity are defined in chapter 3 as a basis for explaining Paul's argumentation in Galatians.

Part I of this study, therefore, evaluates these methods of epistolary and rhetorical analysis, modifying them in important respects and applying them to Paul's central argument in Galatians.[16] Part II is an exegetical analysis of Paul's use of the Abraham story in Gal. 3-4 in the light of the results of our epistolary and rhetorical analyses in Part I. A fresh understanding of the structure and meaning of Gal. 3-4 is gained by integrating the methods of epistolary and rhetorical analysis.

In the conclusion of this study some significant implications which relate to broader theological issues in Pauline theology are set forth. From the perspective of our literary analyses and exegetical work we can see how Paul's doctrine of justification by faith serves as the logical basis for his Gentile mission, why Paul's critique of the opponents' theology should not be construed as a general attack on Judaism, and how the convenantal structure of Paul's ethics relates the response of faith to obedience to the divine will. Although in-depth exploration of these issues is beyond the scope of this work, it is important to see how Paul's interpretation of the Abraham story functions as a substructure of Pauline theology.

PART 1

EPISTOLARY AND RHETORICAL ANALYSES

CHAPTER 1

EPISTOLARY ANALYSIS

1. *The Genre of Galatians*

The first step in any literary analysis of Galatians is the consideration of its genre: What type of letter is it? Many approaches have been made and answers given, but I propose to follow W.G. Doty's two guidelines: that generic definition should (1) 'demonstrate how some literary works are similar', and (2) 'focus upon formal, structural composition of the literary work rather than on thematology'.[1]

Deissmann's Private Letter Thesis

Adolf Deissmann's answer to the question regarding the genre of Paul's letters set the stage for all subsequent discussion. In the light of his study of Hellenistic papyrus letters, he made a sharp distinction between (1) the real, private, non-literary *letter*, and (2) the artificial, public, literary *epistle*. According to Deissmann, 'the letters of Paul are not literary; they are real letters, not epistles; they were written by Paul not for the public and posterity, but for persons to whom they were addressed'.[2] Paul's letter to the Galatians, in fact, was characterized by Deissmann as 'the offspring of passion, a fiery utterance of chastisement and defense, not at all a treatise "De lege et evangelio", the reflection rather of genius flashing like summer lightning'.[3]

Deissmann's emphasis on Paul's letters as real letter (*wirkliche Briefe*) written to specific people in response to specific occasions is generally recognized as valid. Sykutris in his survey of ancient epistolography concurs with this emphasis:

> Als Paulus aus Ferne an die Gemeinden schrieb, hat er gewiss keine Literatur machen wollen. Er teilte ihnen schriftlich mit, auf Grund der konkreten Verhältnisse der Adressgemeinde, was er ihnen sagen würde. In daher ist Deissmanns These, der die

paulinischen Briefe mit den Privatbriefen gleichsetzt, zwar als Reaktion gegen die theologische Auffassung, die darin Abhandlungen über das Dogma zu sehen gewohnt war, sehr richtig.[4]

Paul Wendland's analysis of the literary form of Paul's letters also underscores the fact

> dass sie ursprünglich nicht Literaturprodukte im strengsten Sinne gewesen sind, sondern wirkliche Briefe, entsprungen aus der Sorge des Apostels für seine Gemeinden, bestimmt sie zu beraten und zu leiten, durchflochten von einer Fülle der Beziehungen auf die konkreten Verhältnisse des Verfassers.[5]

This distinction between real letters and literary treatises was not entirely new with Deissmann. The ancient theorist Demetrius warned that the heightening of the literary style 'should not be carried so far that we have a treatise in place of a letter' (σύγγραμμα εἶναι ἀντ᾽ ἐπιστόλες).[6] 'Non-real' letters (i.e., literary treatises in letter form), which are not written in response to a specific occasion in the context of a real addressor–addressee relationship,[7] may have some superficial resemblance to real letters. They are not, however, trustworthy guides for the analysis of the structures of real letters since the epistolary forms of 'non-real' letters serve as merely external brackets and are not integrally related to the content of the letter.

Certainly Paul's letter to the Galatians is a real letter. It was written in the context of a specific situation and a very personal relationship, and it should, therefore, be analyzed in the light of similar, real letters—i.e., letters in which the epistolary forms serve the purpose of genuine communication from the sender to the recipient, rather than function merely as literary forms. For this reason it is entirely appropriate to use the epistolary forms of 'real' Hellenistic letters of the day as a basis for understanding the epistolary structure of Galatians.[8]

As important as it was, however, subsequent literary analyses—both of Greek papyrus letters and of the Pauline letters—have brought to light at least four ways in which Deissmann's thesis needs to be modified. First, Deissmann's classification of Paul's letters as 'private' letters, as opposed to 'public' letters, needs qualification by the recognition that, in the words of Stykutris, 'die Grenzen zwischen dem literarischen und dem Privatbrief können nicht scharf gezogen werden'.[9] Doty develops a spectrum of letter types ranging from the 'more private' letters to the 'less private letters',[10] and classifies Paul's letters as being 'more private' in type.[11] But this classification needs to be balanced by Stykutris' reminder that Paul's writing 'war nicht privaten Ansprachen gleich; es war viel mehr'.[12] This 'more than' private character of Paul's letters is correctly assessed in Paul Wendland's comment: 'Paulus redet in den Gemeindebriefen nicht als Privatperson, sondern als Seelsorger und Leiter der Gemeinde. Die Betonung des Apostolates im Eingang schon gibt den Briefen eine besondere Bedeutung'.[13] The emphasis on apostleship is especially prominent in Paul's letter to the Galatians (1.1, 15, 16; 5.2). Also, the address ταῖς ἐκκλησίαις τῆς Γαλατίας indicates the somewhat public, at least circular, nature of this letter.

At the same time, however, Paul's letter to the Galatians should still be classified as a 'more private' type—as opposed to (1) literary essays, which adopted an epistolary form but were written for an unspecified, universal audience, and (2) official letters, which were not written in the context of a personal relationship.[14] Galatians is a highly personal letter written within the framework of an immediate relationship to a specific group of people, not to society at large. However inclusive the designation αἱ ἐκκλησίαι τῆς Γαλατίας is, it still was meant as an exclusive reference to a relatively small minority group in the Greco-Roman world. Therefore, although the private/public distinction needs more careful definition when applied to his letters, Paul's letters are, nevertheless, more comparable to the private papyrus letters of the Hellenistic period.

A second defect that has come to light with respect to Deissmann's thesis concerns his conception of Paul's letters as being non-literary letters, lacking form or structure except for a few stereotyped conventions in the salutations and closings. Recent form analyses have demonstrated the existence of many structural features in both the common, private papyrus letters and the Pauline corpus. There is, of course, a wide range of literary styles in real letters, from chaotic and artless scribbles to polished and artistic productions. Nevertheless, there are epistolary (i.e., literary) conventions which can be observed both in the common Greek letters of the day and in Paul's letters.[15]

Paul's letter to the Galatians is well described as 'the offspring of passion, a fiery utterance of chastisement and defense'.[16] But to recognize the spontaneous, passionate nature of the letter does not justify ignoring the various epistolary conventions and formulae to be found in the Hellenistic papyrus letters—conventions and formulae to be found not only in the opening and closing, but also in the body of the letters. Because of the demonstrated similarity of such structural elements in Paul's letters *vis-à-vis* the private Hellenistic letters, it is perfectly valid for J.L. White to assert that 'the common letter tradition, though certainly not the only tradition on which Paul depends, is the primary literary *Gattung* to which Paul's letters belong'.[17]

In opposition to Brinsmead's assertion that the 'papyri give us no help in understanding the overall structure of Paul's letters',[18] I will attempt to demonstrate in this chapter that Paul's use of such epistolary conventions as found in the private Greek papyrus letters is, indeed, a very helpful guide to the structure of his letter to the Galatians. Brinsmead criticizes Deissmann's distinction between 'literary' and 'non-literary', which he insists 'breaks down, both for the pagan Greco-Roman letters and for later Christian letters'.[19] But he implies that Deissmann was correct in his judgment that 'the Pauline letters at least will continue to be conceived as salutation, thanksgiving, and closing, with virtually anything in any order thrown in between'.[20] However, Deissmann's distinction between 'literary' and 'non-literary' breaks down, not because of the formlessness of structure in the body of ancient letters, but precisely because of the widespread use of epistolary conventions and literary forms throughout Paul's letters and private, Hellenistic letters. And an awareness of these literary forms enables us to move beyond Deissmann's theory that Paul's letters were chaotic and unstructured, except for their salutations, thanksgivings, and closings.

A third way in which Deissmann's thesis needs modification concerns his simple letter/epistle classification, which needs to be expanded by an acknowledgment of the wide variety of common, real letters in the Greek papyri. Τύποι Ἐπιστόλικοι, an ancient handbook on epistolary theory (dated between 200 BC and AD 50), provides descriptions of twenty-one types of letters with an example of each type. This list is expanded in Ἐπιστολιμαῖοι Χαρακτῆρες (dated between the fourth and sixth centuries AD) to 41 specific types—e.g., letters of friendship, recommendation, request, information, instruction, consolation, praise, thanksgiving, accusation, apology, introduction, interrogation, invitation, rebuke, etc. There is even a 'mixed letter' type.[21]

Recent study of diverse letter types enables us to develop a complex generic matrix for the purpose of classifying Paul's letters. Of course, none of Paul's letters are pure models of the types described in the handbooks and as illustrated in the papyri. But an examination of the purpose, mood, style, and structure of each of Paul's letters provides a basis for classifying it according to then existing categories of Hellenistic letters. It is illuminating, in fact, to note the resemblance of Philemon to a letter of recommendation; of 1 Corinthians to a letter of response and instruction; of Philippians to a letter of thanksgiving; and, as here suggested, of Galatians to a letter of rebuke and request.[22] In what follows, I intend to demonstrate that a comparison of Galatians to Hellenistic rebuke-request letters provides significant insights into the structure of the body of Paul's letter to his Galatian converts.

A fourth weakness in Deissmann's thesis regarding the genre of Paul's letters is his classification of them solely on the basis of his letter/epistle distinction. This oversimplification has been modified, to some extent, by the analyses of other literary traditions in Paul's letters, such as diatribe, paraenetic material, hymns, kerygmatic formulae, and midrashic material.[23] Thus, although the real, private Hellenistic letter tradition is 'the primary literary *Gattung* to which Paul's letters belong',[24] it is necessary to develop something of a multiple classification procedure to account for Paul's eclectic use of other literary traditions.

Betz's and Brinsmead's Apologetic Letter Thesis
Hans-Dieter Betz and Bernard Brinsmead dismiss the common Hellenistic papyrus letter tradition as an appropriate genre for understanding the overall structure of Galatians, arguing instead for what they call the 'apologetic letter genre',[25] Betz points to Plato's *Epistle 7* as the original literary precedent for this genre, citing as well Isocrates' *Antidosis*, Demosthenes' *De Corona*, Cicero's *Brutus*, and Libanius' *Oratio*. He admits, however, that 'the subsequent history of the genre is difficult to trace since most of the pertinent literature did not survive'.[26] Neverthlesss, Betz quotes with approval Arnaldo Momigliano's remark that 'one vaguely feels the Platonic precedent in Epicurus, Seneca, and perhaps St. Paul'—adding with confidence the assertion that 'the cautious "perhaps" is no longer necessary'.[27]

The basis for such a confidence in classifying Galatians is, however, severely shaken by a comparison of the autobiographical-apologetic essays cited by Betz with Galatians. For there is a fundamental and important difference between them. The so-called 'apologetic letters' are not real letters. R.G. Bury, in his introduction to Plato's *Letter 7*, observes

> [It is] probable that not only is this letter an 'open' letter addressed rather to the general public than to the parties named in the superscription, but that the superscription itself is merely a literary device. The letter was never meant to be sent to Sicily at all. . . so that what Plato is doing in this letter is to indulge in a literary fiction which enables him to publish in epistolary form what is at once a history, an apology, and a manifesto.[28]

Likewise, Isocrates' *Antidosis* is not a letter at all. Isocrates' stated intention for the work is that it be a composition of 'a discourse which would be, as it were, a true image of my thought and of my whole life'.[29] So he sought to dissipate the prejudice against him by publishing this discourse in the form of a defense in court. His defense clearly echoes Socrates' as recorded by Plato in the *Apology*.[30] Yet *Antidosis* is more discursive than strictly a defense appropriate to a judicial proceeding, for, as Isocrates points out, 'some things in my discourse are appropriate to be spoken in a courtroom, others are out of place amid such controversies, being frank discussions about philosophy'.[31] Demosthenes' *De Corona* is also hardly to be compared to a real letter, being a speech delivered on August 330 BC before a jury of more than five hundred Athenian citizens. As C.A. Vance, who translated this speech for the Loeb Classical Library, says: 'the unremitting attention of the jury is secured by the alteration of passages of narrative with rhetorical argument, and of defence with retort; passages of lofty eloquence are distributed throughout the narration'.[32] Also, it needs to be said that Cicero's *Brutus* is a lengthy defense of his oratorical stance by means of a review of the Roman practice of oratory,[33] and Libanius' autobiography, *Oratio 1*, is a direct imitation of Isocrates' *Antidosis*[34]— with neither being comparable in either form or content to Galatians.

These examples are unable to serve as precedents for a real letter genre or as a source for illuminating the epistolary structure of Galatians.[35] The classification of Galatians as an 'apologetic letter' is more a reference to the rhetorical genre of Galatians than to its epistolary genre. Indeed, Galatians can be classified and analyzed in terms of literary rhetoric, and the elements of autobiography, apology, and self-defense are important factors to consider in any rhetorical analysis of the letter.[36] But the rhetorical analysis of Galatians should not be confused with or replace attempts to define its epistolary genre and describe its epistolary structure. Betz, of course, believes that the epistolary framework of Galatians can be easily removed 'as a kind of external bracket for the body of the letter',[37] so that what is left is rhetoric, or an 'apologetic speech'— which Betz and Brinsmead then analyze in light of the rules for forensic speech as found in the classical, rhetorical handbooks. Their rhetorical analysis of Galatians has value, and will be evaluated in the next chapter. My point here, however, is that neither Betz nor Brinsmead has given sufficient attention to an epistolary analysis of Galatians. They have too quickly concluded that 'the epistolary nature of Galatians has little consequence for the structure of its contents'.[38] Their lack of attention to the epistolary nature of Galatians has caused them to overlook many significant epistolary conventions which serve as indicators for the structure of the entire letter.

2. The Structure of Galatians

As to epistolary genre, I have proposed that Galatians should be classified as a 'real', 'more private', 'rebuke–request' letter. Here I propose to demonstrate how an analysis of Galatians in light of the literary conventions of this genre clarifies the structure of Paul's entire Galatian letter.

Conventional Epistolary Formulae
Analyses of Hellenistic papyrus letters have produced a substantial list of conventional epistolary formulae.[39] While it is not within the scope of our study to examine in detail the use of these formulae in the Greek letter tradition, it is necessary for our purpose to summarize the findings of those who have done this research. Thus the formulae listed below are some of the most significant epistolary conventions that appear frequently in the Hellenistic papyrus letters. Their appearance here is because of their use, with some modifications, by Paul. In most cases I have illustrated the epistolary conventions by quoting phrases from papyrus letters. Additional examples may be found in the secondary sources noted.

Opening formula[40]
1. Sender (nominative)—Addressee (dative) -
   relation (e.g., ἀδελφῷ—χαίρειν)
   or Addressee—Sender—χαίρειν
2. *Closing formula*
   P. Merton 80 ἐρρῶσθαι σε εὔχομαι
3. *Thanksgiving formula*[41]
   B.G.U. 816 πάτερ εὐχαριστῶ πολλὰ Ἰσιδώρω
   τῷ ἐπιτρόπω, ἐπεὶ συνέστοκέ
4. *Prayer formula*
   P. Mich. 209 πρὸ μὲν πάντων εὔχομε σαι ὑγειένειν καὶ
   προκόπτειν, ἅμα δὲ καὶ τὸ προσκύνημά σου ποιοῦμε
   ἡμερησίως παρὰ τοῖς πατρῴες θεοῖς
5. *Joy expression*[42]
   P. Giss. 21.3 λιὰν ἐχάρην ἀκούσασα ὅτι
6. *Astonishment-rebuke formula*[43]
   P. Oxy. 113.20 Θαυμάζω πῶς
7. *Expression of grief or distress*[44]
   B.G.U. 449.4 ἀκούσας ὅτι νωθρεύη ἀγωνίουμεν
8. *Reminder of past instruction*[45]
   P. Mich. 202.3 ὡς ἠρωτηκά σε
9. *Disclosure formulae*[46]
   P. Giss. 11.4 γινώσκειν σε θέλω ὅτι
   P. Mich. 28.16 γνώριζε οὖν
   P. Oxy. 1219.1 ἀλλὰ οἶδα ὅτι
10. *Request formulae*[47]
    B.G.U. 846.10 παρακαλῶ σαι μήτηρ διαλάγητι μοι
    P. Mich. 209 ἐρωτηθεὶς οὖν, ἀδελφέ, τάχιον μοι γράφιν
    P. Ent. 82.6 δέομαι οὖν σου, βασιλεῦ, εἴ σοι δοκεῖ
11. *Formulaic use of the verb of hearing or learning*[48]
    P. Tebt. 760.20 ἀκούσας δὲ τὰ κατὰ τὸν πτολεμαῖον
    ἐλυπήθην σφόδρα
    P. Oxy. 930.4 ἐλοιπήθην ἐπιγνοῦσα παρά
12. *περί with the genitive*[49]
    P. Oxy. 1220.23 καὶ περὶ τῶν χωρίων
13. *Notification of a coming visit*[50]
    P. Oxy. 1666.11 Θεῶν οὖν βουλομένων, πρὸς τὴν ἑορτην...
    πειράσομαι πρὸς ὑμᾶς γενέσθαι...
14. *Reference to writing*[51]
    P. Mich. 36.1 ἔγραψάς ἡμῖν ὅτι

15. *Verbs of saying and informing*[52]
    P. Oxy. 932.3 ἐρῖ σοι δὲ Ἀπολινάρις πῶς
    P. Fay. 122.14 καὶ δηλωσόν μοι πόσαι ἐξέβησαν ἵνα εἰδῶ
16. *Expression of reassurance*[53]
    P. Mich. 206.11 τοῦτο μὴ νομίσῃς ὅτι
17. *Responsibility statement*[54]
    P. Aml. 143.2 μὴ ἄμελήσῃς ἐν τῇ αὔριον ἀπαντῆσαι πρὸς ἡμᾶς
18. *The use of the vocative to indicate transition*[55]
    P. Mich. 206.4 φανερόν σοι ποιῶ ἀδελφέ

These epistolary conventions are most often used in Hellenistic letters for purposes of introduction, closing, or transition. T.Y. Mullins clarifies their function as follows:

> Simply reading through a great many letters from the non-literary papyri suggests a general principle: *the use of one form tends to precipitate the use of others with 'it.* Thus, right in the middle of P. Oxy. 1070 there is a pause where the writer inserts a greeting; immediately, he adds a thanksgiving. But behind the general principle lies the nature of these forms as they are used in letters. *They almost always punctuate a break in the writer's thought.* The opening is a sort of warm-up for the main issue and provides a convenient clustering place for matters less important than the main issue (but not necessarily introductory to it). The closing constitutes the final communication and is a natural clustering place for matters of minor importance which the writer wants to add before breaking off. But in a letter of any considerable length there will be places where a writer will pause and break the flow of his thought for a moment. He may mark such places with epistolary forms whose relevance to the main subject matter will vary according to the way the writer thinks and expresses himself.[56]

Thus clustering of epistolary formulae in Galatians should be viewed as strong evidence for a significant break or turning point in the letter.

An analysis of the structure of Paul's letters indicates that he makes use of much of the conventional phraseology found in private Greek letters of his day, but modifies many of the phrases to suit the circumstances and purposes of his letters.[57] For example, the thanksgiving which follows the salutation in most of Paul's letters is in line with Hellenistic epistolary style,[58] but seems also to reflect

primitive Christian liturgical style.[59] Robert Funk concludes his
review of analyses of Paul's letters as follows:

> The preceding observations permit us to posit the following
> working hypothesis concerning the substructure of the Pauline
> letter form: (1) salutation (sender, addressee, greeting); (2) thanks-
> giving; (3) body with its formal opening, connective and transitional
> formulas, concluding 'eschatological climax' and travelogue; (4)
> paraenesis; (5) closing elements (greetings, doxology, benediction).
> It should be emphasized that these elements are subject of
> variation in both context and order, and that some items are
> optional, although the omission of any one calls for explanation. It
> is put this way around on the view that Paul is not rigidly folowing
> an established pattern, but is creating his own letter form—in
> relation, of course, to the letter as a literary convention. If he has
> molded this particular pattern out of the circumstances of his
> apostolic ministry and on the basis of his theological understanding,
> he seems to follow it without conscious regard to its structure. It is
> just the way he writes letters. It is only in this sense that we can
> legitimately speak of 'form'.[60]

And in his application of this hypothesis to Galatians, Funk observes
that

> all the elements are present in Galatians save for the thanksgiving,
> which, as nearly all commentators agree, has its special explanation;
> the greeting in Galatians, on the other hand, is combined with a
> doxology, perhaps as a substitute for the customary thangsgiving.
> The order is somewhat modified: The travelogue-surrogate falls
> within the body of the letter (4.12-20), and the eschatological
> climax, if it be such, comes at the end of the paraenesis (6.7-
> 10).[61]

The epistolary structure of Galatians can be described in greater
detail by considering the specific form and function of the epistolary
formulae in the letter. The following list is derived from a
comparative study of conventional epistolary phrases in the papyrus
letters and phrases in the other Pauline letters similar to those found
in Galatians.

Epistolary formulae and other indicators of the epistolary structure

| 1.1 | Παῦλος. . .ταῖς ἐκκλησίαις τῆς Γαλατίας | salutation |
| 1.3 | χάρις ὑμῖν καὶ εἰρήνη | greeting |

1.6	Θαυμάζω ὅτι	rebuke formula
1.9	ὡς προειρήκαμεν καὶ ἄρτι πάλιν λέγω	reminder of instructions
1.11	Γνωρίζω γὰρ ὑμῖν ἀδελφοί	disclosure formula
1.13	Ἠκούσατε γάρ	disclosure formula
3.1	ᾮ ἀνόητοι Γαλάται	vocative—rebuke
3.2	τοῦτο μόνον θέλω μαθεῖν ἀφʼ ὑμῶν	formulaic verb of learning
3.7	Γινώσκετε ἄρα ὅτι	disclosure formula
3.15	Ἀδελφοί...λέγω	vocative—verb of saying
3.17	τοῦτο δὲ λέγω	verb of saying
4.1	Λέγω δέ	verb of saying
4.11	φοβοῦμαι ὑμᾶς	expression of distrust
4.12	ἀδελφοί δέομαι ὑμῶν	request formula
4.13	οἴδατε δὲ ὅτι	disclosure formula
4.15	μαρτυρῶ γὰρ ὑμῖν ὅτι	disclosure formula
4.19	τέκνα μου	vocative
4.20	ἤθελον δὲ παρεῖναι πρὸς ὑμᾶς	apostolic *parousia*
4.21	Λέγετέ μοι	verb of saying
4.28	ὑμεῖς δὲ ἀδελφοί	vocative
4.31	διὸ ἀδελφοί	vocative
5.2	Ἴδε ἐγὼ Παῦλος λέγω ὑμῖν ὅτι	motivation for writing
5.3	μαρτύρομαι δὲ πάλιν	disclosure—attestation
5.10	ἐγὼ πέποιθα εἰς ὑμᾶς ἐν κυρίῳ ὅτι	confidence formula
5.11	ἐγὼ δὲ ἀδελφοί	vocative
5.13	Ὑμεῖς γὰρ ἀδελφοί	vocative
5.16	Λέγω δέ	verb of saying
6.1	Ἀδελφοί	vocative
6.11	Ἴδετε πηλίκοις ὑμῖν γράμμασιν ἔγραψα	autographic subscription
6.16	εἰρήνη ἐπʼ αὐτοὺς καὶ ἔλεος	benediction
6.18	Ἡ χάρις...ἀδελφοί	grace wish—vocative

It is particularly important to note that these epistolary formulae in Galatians are not evenly distributed throughout the letter, but appear in clusters. Their distribution can be seen on the graph which follows (where 1 mm equals one verse; each / represents an epistolary formula)—though, of course, such a graph cannot indicate the significance of each formula.[62]

The distribution of epistolary conventions in Galatians

1	2	3	4	5	6

‖‖ ‖‖   ‖‖ ‖   ‖‖‖‖‖ ‖ ‖ ‖‖‖ ‖ ‖‖

The distinction between those sections that contain a heavy concentration of epistolary formulae and those that contain relatively few significant formulae can be further diagrammed as follows:

Sections with epistolary formulae		*General, thematic sections*
1.1-13	salutation, astonishment-rebuke, disclosure statement	
		1.13-2.21 autobiography
3.1-7	vocative, rebuke questions, disclosure statement,	
		3.7-4.10 argument from Scripture
4.11-20	expression of distress, request formula, disclosure formulae, travelogue and visit wish	
		4.21-30 allegory from Scripture
4.31-5.12	vocative, summary appeal, 'official' decision, attestation, expression of confidence	
		5.13-6.10 paraenesis
6.11-18	autographic subscription benediction	

So it is possible to argue that those sections with epistolary formulae, together with other indicators of epistolary structure, provide a basis for outlining the entire letter.

The Salutation

The opening section, 1.1-13 begins with a salutation, 1.1-5. All the standard elements of sender, addressee, and greetings are present, as well as theological statements concerning apostleship, christology, and soteriology, which reflect central themes of the letter.

After the salutation, Paul's letters usually have a thanksgiving prayer section (εὐχαριστῶ τῷ θεῷ μου πάντοτε περὶ ὑμῶν [1 Cor 1.4 cf. 1 Thess. 1.2; 2 Thess. 1.3; Phil. 1.3; Rom. 1.8; Philem 4; Col. 1.3]). Paul Schubert, in his study of the Pauline thanksgivings, concludes that 'the function of the epistolary thanksgiving in the papyrus letters is to focus the epistolary situation, i.e., to introduce the vital theme of the letter'.[63] And the thanksgiving-prayer sections in Paul's letters serve this same function: they 'tend to "telegraph" the content of the letter'.[64]

In Galatians, however, θαυμάζω takes the place of εὐχαριστῶ and basically fulfils the same function of introducing the theme of the letter.

The Rebuke Section

A major turning point in Galatians is introduced by the word θαυμάζω, a conventional term in the Greek papyrus letters (iii BC— AD iv)[65] used to express astonishment, rebuke, disapproval, and disappointment. T. Mullins says that a letter writer who uses θαυμάζω 'is rebuking, even scolding the addressee. He is not using θαυμάζω in its common meaning; he is using it ironically, often sarcastically. He is not really astonished; he is irritated. This ironical use is an essential element in the form. It should be called "ironic rebuke"'.[66] Mullins' point on the use of θαυμάζω as a common expression of rebuke is confirmed by a study of its appearance in the papyri letters. But his denial of surprise or astonishment in the term is an overstatement. True, in some letters the author does not appear to be really surprised, only irritated; in others, however, the author seems to be genuinely surprised as well as displeased.[67] And insofar as the surprise is genuine, it is not essential to attribute irony to the form. It is more accurate, therefore, simply to call θαυμάζω an 'astonishment-rebuke' formula.

The θαυμάζω sections in Greek letters often include such features as: a statement of the cause for the astonishment-rebuke; a reminder of previous instructions which have not been carried out; rebukes for foolishness, negligence, or a change of mind; expressions of distress; rebuking questions; and summons to responsibility. The θαυμάζω section is almost always followed by a request formula and an appeal to the addressees to some action which will remedy the disappointing, distressing situation. This request is sometimes followed by further instructions.

The twelve θαυμάζω letters which follow have been selected to illustrate these features.

B.G.U. 850.1-6 AD 76

1	Χαιρήμων Ἀπολλωνίωι	salutation
	τῶι φιλτάτωι χαίρειν	greeting
	Θαυμάζω ἐπὶ τῆι ... ντα	rebuke
	ξία σου καίτοι ἐμοῦ σε πολλά	
5	ἐρωτήσαντος παρακληθεὶς	request
	οὖν ἄδελφε ἄνελθε πρός	vocative—imperative

P. Baden 35.1-11 AD 87

1	Ἰοάννη Ἐπαγάθο τῶ εἰδίο	salutation
	πλεῖστα χαίρειν	
	οὐ καλῶς ἐπόισας ἅπαντα	rebuke for change of mind
	ὑπαλλάξας	
	καὶ παραβάς σου τὴν	
	συνταγὴν	
	και ἐπιδεξαμένην με κυρίαν	
	εἶναι	
5	δραχμῶν καὶ τὸν τόκον ἀρὲς	
	κεφάλα ιον με	
	ἰχσέσσθαι θαυμάζω πῶς τὴν	rebuke formula
	πίστιν	
	σου ἤλλαξαι μὴ μ ἀνακάσης	rebuke for change of faith
	οὖν θέλω ποιῆσαι καὶ ἐπὶ	request
	τόπων	
	διατρέψαι σε μηδὲ ἐπιστολ-	
	ειδίου	
10	μέκαπα ὁ τόκος σῆμα ἐστιν	
	τοῦτο ἀγνομοσύνης	rebuke for foolishness

P. Mich. 209.1-13, 26 AD ii

1	Σατορνῖλος Σεμπρωνίῳ τῷ	salutation
	ἀδελφῷ	
	καὶ κυρίῳ πλεῖστα καίρειν	greeting
	πρὸ μὲν πάντων εὔχομε σαι	prayer
	ὑγειένειν καὶ	
	προκόπτειν ἅμα δὲ καὶ τὸ	
	προσκύνημά	
5	σου ποιοῦμε ἡμερησίως παρὰ τοῖς	
	πατρῶες	
	θεοῖς θαυμάζω ἄδελφε	rebuke formula
	δευτέραν ἐπιστολὴν	
	αὕτη ἣν ἔπεμψά σοι ἀφ᾽ ἧς	cause for rebuke
	ἐγανάμην	

ἰς οἶκον καὶ οὐδεμίαν
ἀντιφώνησίν μοι
ἔπεμψας Ἐρωτηθεὶς οὖν   request formula
ἄδελφε τάχιόν
10 μοι γράφιν περὶ τῆς σωτηρίας
σου εἴνα κἀγὼ
ἀμεριμνότερος διάγω οἶδας   distress / disclosure
γὰρ ἄδελφε
ὅτι οὐ μόνον ὡς ἀδελφόν σε
ἔχω ἀλλὰ
13 Καὶ ὡς πατέρα καὶ κύριον καὶ
θεόν
26 Ἐρρῶσθαι σαι εὔχομαι   closing health wish
ἄδελφε κυριώταται

Saturnilus to Sempronius, his
brother and lord, very many
greetings. Before all things I
pray for your health and suc-
cess; at the same time I also make
daily obeisance for you before
our ancestral gods. I wonder
brother—this is the second letter
which I have sent to you since I
came home, and you have written
me no reply. I therefore ask
you, brother, to write to me at
once about your well-being,
that I too may be less troubled.
For you know, brother, that I
regard you not only as a brother
but also as a father and lord and
god. ... I pray for your health,
lordly brother.

P. Merton 80.1-15 AD ii

1   Ἀχιλλᾶς Ἀπολλωνίῳ τῷ   salutation
πατρὶ
χαίρειν   greeting
Θαυμάζω πῶς τοισούτων   rebuke formula
ἀνελυόντων μετὰ
καὶ κτηνῶν κενῶν οὐκ   cause for rebuke
ἔπεμψας
5   Σαραπάμμωνα εἰδὼς ὅτι χρία
αὐτοῦ

ἐστὶν ἐνθάδε μέχρι νῦν οὐδίς
σε
ἐπεζήτεσε ὁ ἀναδούς μοι τὸ
ἐπιστόλιον ἀνέφαινε λέγων ὡς
ἐκπλέκη Ἄρειος δοὺς τὰ   disclosure formula
κολλημάτα
10   τῷ βασιλικῷ οὐκ ἐπόησε αὐτὰ
ἐπισταλῆναι Διὼ γράφω σοι
ἵν εἴδης συ εἴ τι δεόν ἐστὶ τί
πράξης
εἰδὼς ὅτι εἰ μὴ συ παραγένῃ   disclosure formula
λύσιν
οὐ λαγχάνι τοῦτο Διὼ μὴ   summons to responsiblity
ἀμελῆς

Achillas to his father Apollonius,
greeting. I am surprised that
when so many have come up
country and that with beasts
unladen, you have not sent
Sarapammon, for you know
there is need of him here. Up to
the present no one has enquired
after you. The man who handed
me the letter declared in so
many words that Arius will get
you out of it, having given the
rolls to the royal scribes; he did
not have them sent. So I am
writing to you in order that you
may know, if there is anything
necessary, what you are to do;
for you know that, if you are
not present, this affair finds no
solution. So do not neglect
this.

P. Oxy. 113.19-24 AD ii

19   περὶ ὧν σοι γεγράφειν διὰ   prior instructions
Κορβόλωνος
20   πέμψαι μοι θαυμάζω   rebuke formula
πῶς οὐκ ἐδικαίωσάς μοι πέμψαι   cause for rebuke
καὶ
ταῦτα ἐμοῦ χρήζοντος εἰς
ἑορτήν

Ἐρωτηθεὶς ἀγόρασόν μοι   request formula
σφραγῖδα ἀργοῦν
24 καὶ τάχειόν μοι πέμψον   imperative

I wonder that you did not see
your way to let me have what I
asked you to send by Corbolon,
especially when I wanted it for
a festival. I beg you to buy me a
silver seal and send it to me
with all speed.

P. Ryl. 235.6-14 AD ii

6 ἐθαύμασε δὲ πῶς διὰ Λυπέρκου   rebuke formula
οὐκ ἐδήλωσάς μοι   cause for rebuke
περὶ τῆς εὐρωστίας σου καὶ
πῶς
διάγεις ἵνα καὶ ἡμεῖς
10 περὶ σου ἀμερίμνως διάγωμεν   expression of distress
ἀλλὰ οὐ πρώτως σου
τὸ εἰκαῖον μανθάνομεν Διὸ   rebuke for foolishness
μέμνησο καὶ ἡμῶν κἂν πάνυ   imperative
14 τινὰ ἀλλὰ πράττῃς

I was surprised that you did not
inform me through Lupercus of
your good health and how you
are in order that we too may be
free of care about you, but it is
not the first time that we learn
of your heedlessness. Therefore,
bear us in mind even if you are
engaged in quite other pursuits.

P. Oxy. 3063.11-16 AD ii

11 Θαυμάζω εἰ χρεία ἐστὶ τριῶν   astonishment-rebuke
ζευγῶν εἰς ἐπαντλησμὸν τῆς ἐν
Χαλώθει
ἀμπέλου εἰς ὀλίγον περιεστα-
μένης οὐ γὰρ
τῆς τειμῆς ἐστιν τοῦ περισσοῦ
ζεύγους ὡς τῶν
15 τροφῶν καὶ τῆς ἄλλης δαυπάνης
εἰ δέ γε σὺ δοκεῖς
χρείαν εἶναι διάπεμψαι τὴν   imperative
ἐπιστολήν μου

38   *Abraham in Galatians*

I find it surprising if it needs
three pair of oxen to water the
vineyard at Chalothis, which
hasn't come to much. It isn't so
much a matter of the cost of the
extra pair, as of their feed and
other expenses. But if you think
it's needed, send on my letter
. . .

P. Oxy. 2728: 1-10 AD iii–iv

1	Καπιτωλῖνος Σαραπάμμωνι	salutation
	ἀδελφῷ	
	Χαίρειν πρὸ μὲν πάντων	greeting
	εὔχομαί σου τὴν ὁλοκληρίαν	prayer
	μετὰ τῶν	
	τέκνων σου ἅμα τῇ συμβίῳ	
	σου	
5	παρὰ τῷ κυρίῳ θεῷ θαυμάζω	rebuke formula
	πῶς καὶ νῦν τοῦ Ὡριγένους	
	ἐρχομένου	
	πρὸς ἐμὲ οὐδέν μοι ἐδήλωιας	cause for rebuke
	περὶ οὐδενός	
	ἐπίσταμαι ὅτι πολλὰ βαροῦμαί	
	σε ἀποταγῇ μέρος	
	σιγὴ γὰρ παρὰ φιλοσόφοις ἀπό-	
	κρισις μὴ οὖν	
10	Κἀγὼ δύναμε μὴ ἀποκρίνασθαι;	rebuking question

Capitolinus to Sarapammon,
his brother, greeting. Before all
I pray for your health with that
of your children and your wife
before the lord god. I am surprised
that even now when Horigenes
comes to me he let me know
nothing about any thing. I know
that I weigh heavily upon you.
Let part be set aside. For among
philosophers silence is an answer.
Could not I refuse to answer?

P. Oxy. 123.1-9 AD iii

1	κυρίῳ μου υἱῷ Διονυσοθέωνι	salutation
	ὁ πατὴρ χαίρειν	greeting

εὐκαίρη τις καὶ νῦν τοῦ ἀνερχο-
μένου πρὸς ὑμᾶς
ἀναγκαῖον μοι ἐγένετο προσαγο-
ρεῦσαι ὑμᾶς
5 πάνυ θαυμάζω υἵε μου μέχρις   rebuke formula
σήμερον γράμματά
σου οὐκ ἔλαβον τὰ δηλοῦντα   cause for rebuke
μοι τὰ περὶ τῆς
ὁλοκηρίας ὑμῶν κἂν δέσποτά   imperative
μοι ἀντίγραψόν
μοι ἐν τάχει πάνυ γὰρ θλείβομαι   distress
διότι
οὐκ ἐδαξάμην σου γράμματα

To my son, master Dionysotheon,
greeting from your father. As an
opportunity was afforded me by
some one going up to you I
could not miss this chance of
addressing you. I have been
much surprised, my son, at not
receiving hitherto a letter from
you to tell me how you are.
Nevertheless, sir, answer me
with all speed, for I am quite
distressed at having heard nothing
from you.

P. Cornell 52.1-12 AD iii

1 κυρίῳ μου ἀδελφῷ Ἀμμωνιανῷ   salutation
Γερόντιυς χείρειν   greeting
ἐν τῇ χθὲς ἦλθον εἰς τὴν
Τακόνα καὶ ἐσχόλασα
τῇ καταστάσει τῶν ἄλλων λι-
τουργιῶν ἵνα
5 δυνήθη ἡ ἀπαίτησις προχωρῆσαι   rebuke formula
Θαυμάζω
δὲ πῶς οὐδείς μοι ἤνεγκε γράμ-   cause for rebuke
ματά σου
καὶ ἀθυμῶ τούτου ἕνεκα ἐπειδὴ
οὐκ οἶδα
πῶς διάκειται ἡ οἰκία ἡ τὰ καθ᾽
ἡμᾶς καὶ
κατὰ τὴν πόλιν σπούδασον οὖν   imperative
ἔχων πολλοὺς

10   ἐρχομένους εἰς τὴν τακόνα ἢ
      τοῦ κονδουκτορίου
      ἢ τῆς κώμης ἀντιγραψαί μοι   imperative
      περὶ
      πάντων περὶ δὲ τῶν ἀπαιτησέων
      ἐάν

To my lord and brother, Ammon-
ianus from Gerontius, greeting.
Yesterday I came to Taconda
and engaged in the induction of
the other liturgical officials in
order that the tax collection
could proceed. I wonder that no
one has brought me a letter
from you, and I am disturbed
because of it, since I do not
know either how the household
is or how affairs are going with
us in the city. Hasten therefore
to write back to me on all
matters, since you have persons
either of the postal service or of
the village who are coming to
Tacona. As to the tax collections,
if. . .

P. Oxy. 1223.1-22, 33-37 AD iv

1   κυρίῳ μου ἀδελφῷ Ὠριῶνι   salutation
     Ἑρμείας
     Θαυμάζω εἴπερ ὁ ἀποστελλου-   rebuke formula
     μενος
     πρὸς σε τὸ πλοῖον τὸ   cause for rebuke
5   τοῦ γεούχου καταλαμβάνει
     παρὰ σοί πλὴν ἐὰν διὰ
     ἀμέλιαν τινὰ καταλάβῃ   rebuke for negligence
     σπούδασον πάραντα τὸν
     ναύτην ἐπὶ τὴν πόλειν
10   ἅμα τῷ πεμφθέντι συμμάχῳ   imperative
     ἐκπέμψαι ἀλλ᾽ ὅρα μὴ
     ἀμελήσῃς ἢ καὶ εὐδία ἐστὶ   summons to responsibility
     καὶ τὸ πλοῖον ἀνενέγκε οὐ
     δύναται ἐν τῇ σήμερον
15   αὐτὸς ὁ ναύτης ἀπαντήσῃ
     πρὸς χιρογραφίαν οὐκ ὀλίγως

γὰρ ἐνοχλούμεθα ἐὰν δὲ ἀμελ-   expression of distress
ήσῃς
ὁ οἶκος ἡμῶν περιστάσι
κοινωνεῖν μέλλει διὰ τὴν
20 ἀπουσίαν τοῦ γεούχου ὑπὸ
τοῦ
φορτικοῦ Ἀμμωνίου σπεκουλά-
τορος
22 καὶ τοῦ ἐπαρχικοῦ
33 μὴ ἀμελήσῃς   summons to responsibility
ἐν τῇ σήμερον τὸ πλοῖον
ἢ τὸν ναύτην ἀποστῖλαι
ἐρρῶσθαί σε εὔχομαι   closing health wish
37 πολλοῖς χρόνοις ἄδελφε

To my lord and brother, Horion, from Hermias. I am surprised if my messenger finds the boat of the landlord with you; if, however, owing to some carelessness he finds it there, make haste to send the sailor to the city at once with the attendant whom I have sent. See that you do not neglect this. If it is calm weather, and he cannot bring back the boat today, let the sailor himself return in order to make a bond, for I am worried not a little. If you neglect it, our house is likely, owing to the absence of the landlord, to be brought to a critical pass through the tiresome Ammonius, the speculator and the praefect's assistant. . . [additional instructions]. Do not neglect to send the boat or the sailor today. I pray for your lasting health, brother.

P. Herm. 11.1-19 AD iv

1 Μέγας Ὀλυμπίῳ χαίρειν   salutation
Θαυμάζω πῶς   rebuke formula
ἐπελάθου τῶν ἐμῶν   cause for rebuke
ἐντολῶν ὧν πολλάκις   prior instruction

5   σοι κατ' ὄψιν
    ἐνετειλάμην περὶ τοῦ
    συνεχῶς μοι δηλῶσαι
    πρῶτον μὲν
    περὶ τῆς σωτηρίας σου
10 ἔπειτα περὶ πάντων
    ὧν ἔπραξας ἐν Σαρβιττίῳ
    εἰδὼς ὅτι οὐ μικρῶς   disclosure formula
    ἀγωνιῶ καίτοι γε πολλῶν   expression of distress
    κατερχομένων
15 πρὸς ἐμὲ κἂν νῦν οὖν
    πάντα ὑπερθέμενος γράψον   imperative
    μοι περὶ πάντων τῶν
    κατά σε καὶ ἀσφαλῶς πάντα
    ποίει

Megas to Olympius, greetings. I
wonder how you have forgotten
my instructions, which I often
gave you when I was with you,
about keeping me informed all
the time, first as to your well-
being and then about all your
doings at Sarbittium, knowing
as you did that I am in great
distress. Yet when many are
coming down my way, now at
least write to me about everything concerning yourself and
conduct all your business safe-
ly.

The correspondence between these features of the Θαυμάζω
letters and similar features in Galatians can be observed in the
following chart:

Features of Θαυμάζω *letters*		*Galatians*	
1.	astonishment–rebuke formula	Θαυμάζω ὅτι	1.6
2.	the cause of rebuke	ταχέως μετατίθεσθε	1.6
3.	reminder of previous instruction	ὡς προειρήκαμεν	1.9
4.	rebuke for foolishness	Ὦ ἀνόητοι	3.1
		οὕτως ἀνόητοί ἐστε	3.3
5.	rebuke for negligence	πῶς ἐπιστρέφετε	4.9

6.	rebuke for change of mind	μετατίθεσθε	1.6
		ἐπιστρέφετε	4.9
7.	expression of distress	φοβοῦμαι ὑμᾶς	4.11
		ἀποροῦμαι ἐν ὑμῖν	4.20
8.	rebuking questions	five rebuking questions	3.1-5
		πάλιν ἄνωθεν δουλεύειν θέλετε;	4.9
9.	request formula	ἀδελφοί, δέομαι ὑμῶν	4.12
10.	appeal to action	γίνεσθε ὡς ἐγώ	4.12
11.	further instructions	imperatives	4.27, 31; 5.1f

This correspondence of characteristic elements in the Θαυμάζω letters with similar elements in Galatians sheds new light on the epistolary structure of Galatians. After the salutation, Paul begins the body of his letter with a conventional expression of rebuke (1.6a), a statement about the cause for his rebuke (μετατίθεσθε ἀπὸ τοῦ καλέσαντος ὑμᾶς ἐν χάριτι εἰς ἕτερον εὐαγγέλιον [1.6b]), and a reminder of previous instructions (ὡς προειρήκαμεν καὶ ἄρτι πάλιν λέγω εἴ τις ὑμᾶς εὐαγγελίζεται παρ᾽ ὃ παρελάβετε ἀνάθεμα ἔστω [1.9]). Later he restates the rebuke in the form of questions in 3.1-5 and 4.8-10, and adds rebukes for foolishness (3.1, 3) and negligence in not following the knowledge they had (4.9). The first rebuke regarding a change of mind in 1.6 is restated in 3.3 and 4.9. And expressions of distress in 4.11, 20 communicate Paul's reaction to this change.

These features common to Θαυμάζω sections are closely related to the other epistolary formulae in Galatians. For after his opening rebuke of 1.6-9, Paul uses two disclosure formulae. The first (Γνωρίζω γὰρ ὑμῖν ἀδελφοὶ τὸ εὐαγγέλιον) introduces his basic thesis statement of 1.11-12 regarding the nature (οὐκ ἔστιν κατὰ ἄνθρωπον) and origin of his gospel (οὐ δὲ γὰρ ἐγὼ παρὰ ἀνθρώπου παρέλαβον αὐτό, οὔτε ἐδιδάχθην ἀλλὰ δι᾽ ἀποκαλύψεως Ἰησοῦ Χριστοῦ). The second disclosure statement, which is a formulaic use of the verb of hearing (Ἠκούσατε γάρ), introduces Paul's autobiography in 1.13–2.21.

The rebukes for foolishness and the rebuking questions of 3.1-5 are combined with the transitional use of the vocative (Ὦ ἀνόητοι Γαλάται, v. 1), a request for information by the use of the verb of learning (θέλω μαθεῖν ἀφ᾽ ὑμῶν, v. 2), and a disclosure formula (Γινώσκετε ἄρα ὅτι, v. 7) which draws a conclusion from the introductory OT citation of Gen. 15.6 in 3.6 and also provides a transition to the extended argument from Scripture in 3.6–4.10. The following outline of the Θαυμάζω-rebuke section of Galatians is derived from this analysis of the features common to Θαυμάζω letters and the epistolary conventions related to these features.

I. Salutation 1.1-5

II. Rebuke Section 1.6–4.11

  A. Rebuke for deserting the gospel 1.6–2.21
    1. Expression of rebuke 1.6–2.21
      Rebuke formula and statement of cause 1.6
      Θαυμάζω ὅτι οὕτως ταχέως μετατίθεσθε
      Reminder of instructions 1.9
      ὡς προειρήκαμεν, καὶ ἄρτι πάλιν λέγω
    2. Disclosure of central thesis 1.11-12
      Disclosure formula 1.11
      Γνωρίζω γὰρ ὑμῖν ἀδελφοί
    3. Disclosure of Paul's autobiography 1.13–2.21
      Formulaic use of verb of hearing 1.13
      Ἠκούσατε γὰρ τὴν ἐμὴν ἀναστροφήν
  B. Rebuke for foolishness about the gospel 3.1–4.10
    1. Expression of rebuke 3.1-5
      Transitional use of vocative 3.1
      Ὦ ἀνόητοι Γαλάται
      Formulaic use of verb of learning 3.2
      τοῦτο μόνον θέλω μαθεῖν ἀφ᾽ ὑμῶν
      Rebuking questions 3.1-5
    2. Disclosure of Scriptural teaching 3.6–4.7
      Disclosure formula 3.7
      γινώσκετε ἄρα ὅτι
    3. Expression of rebuke 4.8-11
      Rebuking question for negligence and change of 4.9
      mind
      πῶς ἐπιστρέφετε πάλιν ἐπὶ τὸ ἀσθενῆ
      Expression of distress 4.11
      φοβοῦμαι ὑμᾶς

The Request Section

Gal. 4.12-20 contains a cluster of five epistolary conventions: a request formula (4.12); two disclosure formulae (4.13, 15); the vocative (4.12); and a reference to an apostolic visit (4.20). Such a cluster of phrases—combined with an expression of distress in 4.11

and the transitional use of the verb of saying in 4.21—suggests that this section is a significant turning point in the letter. As Mullins has observed, when such forms are combined in a letter 'they almost always punctuate a break in the writer's thought'.[68] John Hurd also notes in his study of the structure of 1 Thessalonians that 'Paul had a tendency to pair his transitional sentences at significant turning points in his writing'.[69]

The significance of this cluster of epistolary formula in Gal. 4.12-20 is further emphasized by a study of the form and function of these phrases. The request formula of 4.12 (γίνεσθε ὡς ἐγώ, ὅτι κἀγὼ ὡς ὑμεῖς, ἀδελφοί, δέομαι ὑμῶν) can be analyzed in terms of the three basic elements of the petition as a literary form: (1) the background, (2) the petition verb, and (3) the desired action.[70] John White, based on his study of letters of petition among the papyri, writes that 'the body of the letter of request divides into two parts, the background and the request'.[71] He also notes that certain conventional phrases are used in the background section to strengthen the request: 'the disclosure formulae, the wonder element (introduced by Θαυμάζω, 'I am amazed . . .', or a similar expression).[72] As we have observed, a θαυμάζω-rebuke section in a papyrus letter almost always serves as the background for a request formula and an imperative, or simply for an imperative.

An analysis of request formulae in Paul's letters indicates that Paul's requests are prefaced by a background section which prepares the way for the request. C.J. Bjerkelund concludes a careful study of the request formulae in Philemon and 1 and 2 Thessalonians with the comment that 'in den drei paulinischen Briefen, die wir bisher analysiert haben, meinen wir auf eine deutliche εὐχαριστῶ-παρακαλῶ (ἐρωτῶ) Struktur gestossen zu sein'.[73] And he argues that this same εὐχαριστῶ-παρακαλῶ structure can be observed in 1 Corinthians and Romans.[74] The structure, however, is somewhat modified in 2 Corinthians. 'Dennoch ist der Versuch des Apostels, an der εὐχαριστῶ-παρακαλῶ Struktur festzuhalten und sie in die Briefsituation einzupassen durch den gesamten 2Kor hindurch spürbar'.[75] In this 'danke-bitte' letter structure, Paul prepares the way for his request in the thanksgiving section—which may, therefore, also be labeled a background section.

Carl Bjerkelund goes on to suggest that whereas in most of Paul's letters there is a εὐχαριστῶ-παρακαλῶ structure, in Galatians παρακαλῶ would be completely out of place.[76] The δέομαι formula in 4.12, which is equivalent to the usual παρακαλῶ formula, is a more fitting choice of words following the sharp tone set by θαυμάζω at the beginning of the letter. Bjerkelund, in fact, argues that the θαυμάζω—δέομαι structure of Galatians reflects the tension and estrangement which existed when Paul wrote this letter.[77] Likewise, Mullins says that 'used by itself δεῖσθαι indicates a definite degree of dignity or of formality beyond the other verbs of petition'.[78] And Mullins disagrees with Lightfoot and Burton's attempt to interpret δέομαι in 4.12 as a tender and affectionate appeal; rather, he suggests that Paul's use of δέομαι here is 'probably to be interpreted as more forensic than fond'.[79]

So in light of the normal function of background sections in Greek papyrus letters and the Pauline corpus, and in view of the request formula of 4.12 as it relates to the tone of the letter set by the rebuke formula of 1.5, it is appropriate to view the entire first half of Paul's letter to the Galatians introduced by θαυμάζω ὅτι (1.6–4.11) as the background section to the request of 4.12.[80]

The imperative γίνεσθε ὡς ἐγώ of 4.12, which expresses the desired action, should, therefore, be interpreted within the context of this rebuke–request structure. Paul's appeal to his Galatian converts to imitate him follows a background section in which he provides an extended autobiographical account of his own loyalty to the truth of the gospel (1.13–2.21) and a scriptural exposition of the benefits of the law-free gospel (3.6–4.7). So Paul is requesting the Galatians to: Become as I am—viz., loyal to the truth of the gospel (2.5, 14), dead to the law (2.19), no longer under the law (3.25), living by faith in Christ (2.20), and, therefore, not nullifying the grace of God (2.21) and incurring the curse of the law upon those who live by the works of the law (3.10), but enjoying all the benefits of the gospel (the Spirit, righteousness, the blessing, sonship, inheritance [3.6–4.7]) by faith in Christ. The autobiographical account of Paul's own loyalty to the truth of the gospel and the scriptural exposition of the meaning of the gospel serve (1) to intensify the rebuke by pointing out the failure and folly of the Galatians, and (2) to prepare for the basic request by illustrating and expounding the way which they should take.

The words ὅτι κἀγὼ ὡς ὑμεῖς of 4.12, which serve as the basis for the command, point back to the dramatic before and after portrayals (note the use of ποτε in 1.13 and 23) that Paul gives of himself elsewhere in the letter—viz., that as a result of his call by grace (1.15) to evangelize the Gentiles (1.16) he became free from a zealous attempt to keep the Jewish traditions (1.13-14) and was determined not to rebuild that old life (2.18), for through the law he had died to the law in order that he might live to God (2.19). The irony of the situation in Galatia, as Paul saw it, was that Galatian Christians were deserting their call by grace (1.6) in their attempt to keep the Jewish laws. So Paul rebukes them and requests them to be like him (i.e., free from the law) for in his evangelistic mission to them he became like them (i.e., free from the law).

It is important to note that γίνεσθε ὡς ἐγώ is the first imperative to appear in the letter to the Galatians. And the carrying out of this request is the chief concern of the rest of the letter. But before Paul spells out the implementation of this request through a series of imperatives,[81] he supports this initial request with further autobiographical statements (4.13-20). The autobiographical statements are introduced by two disclosure formulae: οἴδατε δὲ ὅτι (4.13) and μαρτυρῶ γὰρ ὑμῖν ὅτι (4.15).[82] There are other examples in the Greek papyrus letters and Paul's letters of the request formula being followed immediately by a disclosure formula (cf. P. Mich. 209.10-11; 1 Thess. 4.1-2; 1 Cor. 16.15). Here, it appears, the disclosure formulae are used to remind the Galatians of the close relationship which they and Paul enjoyed before their departure from the gospel. And Paul's account of their previous welcome (as if he were Christ Jesus) and their willingness to give him their own eyes adds great force to his request for renewed identification and imitation. His request that they imitate him is also intensified by the vocative τέκνα μου (4.19), which presents Paul as a mother in labor with unborn children.

This autobiographical section is concluded with an expressed desire to visit the Galatian churches: ἤθελον δὲ παρεῖναι πρὸς ὑμᾶς ἄρτι (4.20). Robert Funk has analyzed the structure of the sections of Paul's letters which contain similar 'travelogues'[83] and concludes that the travelogue is only one aspect of a larger feature which may be called 'the apostolic *parousia*': 'Paul regarded his apostolic presence to his congregation under three different but related aspects at once: the aspect of the letter, the apostolic emissary, and his own personal presence'.[84] So while Funk acknowledges that Paul's reference to his presence in Galatia (4.20) lacks somewhat with regard to form, he insists that 'it nevertheless functions structurally in a way comparable to the apostolic *parousia* in the other letters'.[85]

The only importance Funk sees in this apostolic *parousia* feature of Galatians is that it provides evidence that Galatians was written late in Paul's travels, at a time when there was not an opportunity to visit or even to send an emissary. 'It was written at the time he had already set his face to the west. Surely nothing less than that would have prompted him to turn away with a mere wish that he could be there now!'[86] That may be so. More important for our purposes, however, is the recognition that Paul's wish to be present is structurally one element of an 'apostolic *parousia*' formula and that such an 'apostolic *parousia*' formula often appears at a turning point in Paul's letters.[87] Here in Galatians, Paul says that if he were present he would change his voice (4.20). In fact, his tone does change. Although he expresses severe judgment upon those who have infiltrated the Galatians and led them astray, he no longer speaks with such a harsh, rebuking tone toward the Galatians themselves. From this point on his tone is one of urgent request rather than harsh rebuke.

We conclude, therefore, that 4.12-20 is a major turning point in the structure of Galatians. The request formula followed by disclosure formulae, the vocative, and, finally, a desire for apostolic presence all combine to indicate a major transition in Paul's mood and the direction of thought. Paul follows this in 4.21-31, then, with his allegorical treatment of Hagar and Sarah—with the transition to this new section being the coupling of two conventional epistolary expressions: the statement of desire for apostolic presence (4.20) and a verb of saying (4.21).[88]

Many exegetes have attempted to explain the difference between Paul's use of the Abraham story here and his exposition on Abraham in 3.6-29.[89] We propose, however, that the difference itself is another line of evidence in support of our view that a major transition has taken place at 4.12. The function of this allegory is clarified by seeing its place within the structure of the letter. Beginning at 4.12 Paul has turned from rebuke to request. His initial imperative of 4.12 is now spelled out by quoting imperatives from the law itself: εὐφάνθητι (4.27 from Isa. 54.1) and ἔκβαλε (4.30 from Gen. 21.10). The allegory simply sets up the typological setting for these imperatives. And the 'punch line' of the allegory is to command the Galatians through the law—for since they want to be under the law, Paul challenges them to listen to the law (4.21)—to 'cast out the bondwoman and her son' (4.30; Gen. 21.10). Thus the allegory is

Paul's first step in explaining the meaning of his general request, 'Become as I am'. It gives him an indirect way to say what he will later say in a very direct way: that the Galatians are free (4.21, 31; cf. 5.1, 13) and that Scripture itself says that the bondwoman and her son should be cast out (4.30; cf. 5.4, 12). Paul is using OT texts here as a scriptural basis for his own appeal.

The conclusion and application of the allegory is signaled by a conjunction and vocative, διό, ἀδελφοί (4.31), and, so, the transition is made from a scriptural basis to Paul's own personal, apostolic appeal in 5.1-13. The request of 4.12 to imitate Paul in his stand is now restated: στήκετε οὖν καὶ μὴ πάλιν ζυγῷ δουλείας ἐνέχεσθε (5.1). Further motivation for a positive response to this appeal is given by a series of declarations which could almost be called Paul's own 'apostolic decrees'.

Certainly the declaration Ἴδε ἐγὼ Παῦλος λέγω ὑμῖν ὅτι ἐὰν περιτέμνησθε Χριστὸς ὑμᾶς οὐδὲν ὠφελήσει of 5.2 stands out in bold relief as the ultimate authoritative statement of the letter. Stirewalt suggests that this statement should be viewed as 'the decision' of an official letter in response to a delegation from the Galatian churches which has asked Paul whether they ought to undergo circumcision.[90] Admittedly, some elements of Stirewalt's suggestion are highly conjectural.[91] Yet it is apparent that Paul underscores the authoritative nature of this statement by his bold introduction (Ἴδε ἐγὼ Παῦλος λέγω ὑμῖν) and by the attestation and restatement of this command in 5.3 (μαρτύρομαι δέ).

White views the declaration of 5.2 as the first body-closing formula of Galatians, and speaks of it as 'the motivation for writing-responsibility formula'.[92] The usual function of such a formula, White observes, is to repeat the occasion for writing and to lay the basis for future correspondence. Thus, when the addressor expects a response, he employs a 'responsibility' phrase.[93] And since Gal. 5.2 is Paul's declaration of his basic decision regarding the Galatian crisis which motivated him to write his letter, White views it as Paul's first body-closing formula. But this formula cannot be considered as a body-closing formula per se, since, as I will attempt to show, the ethical section of Galatians (5.13-6.10) is also part of the body of the letter.[94]

The statement of 5.10, ἐγὼ πέποιθα εἰς ὑμᾶς ἐν κυρίῳ ὅτι οὐδὲν ἄλλο φρονήσατε, is labelled a 'confidence formula' by White.[95] The letter has now come full circle and Paul is confident that its purpose will be fulfilled. He began in 1.6 by expressing his astonishment about the rebuke of their change of mind (μετατίθεσθε). Now he expresses his confidence that they will not change their minds (οὐδὲν ἄλλο φρονήσετε).

Thus to bring together much of what we have said so far, the way in which the request section is parallel to the rebuke section—and the way in which the development of Paul's thought in Galatians should be seen, as indicated by the structure of the letter—can be diagrammed as follows:[96]

1.6	rebuke:	4.12	request:
	Θαυμάζω οὕτως ταχέως μετατίθεσθε ἀπὸ τοῦ καλέσαντος ὑμᾶς ἐν χάριτι		Γίνεσθε ὡς ἐγώ, ὅτι κἀγὼ ὡς ὑμεῖς, ἀδελφοί, δέομαι ὑμῶν
1.13	Disclosure of autobiography:	4.13	Disclosure of autobiography
	Γνωρίζω γὰρ ὑμῖν ἀδελφοί		οἴδατε δὲ ὅτι
	Ηκούσατε γάρ		μαρτυρῶ γὰρ ὑμῖν ὅτι
3.7	Disclosure of Scripture:	4.21	Appeal through Scripture
	γινώσκετε ἄρα ὅτι		Λέγετέ μοι, ὁ ὑπὸ νόμον θέλοντες εἶναι, τὸν νόμον οὐκ ἀκούετε;
4.9	Rebuking question:	5.1	Requested action:
	πάλιν ἄνωθεν δουλεύειν θέλετε;		μὴ πάλιν ζυγῷ δουλείας ἐνέχεσθε
4.11	Expression of distress:	5.10	Expression of confidence:
	φοβοῦμαι ὑμᾶς μή πως εἰκῇ κεκοπίακα		ἐγὼ πέποιθα εἰς ὑμᾶς ἐν κυρίῳ ὅτι οὐδὲν ἄλλο φρονήσετε

The Paraenetic Section

Paul's expression of confidence that the purpose of his letter will be accomplished seems to set him free to give some specific advice regarding the responsible use of Christian freedom in 5.13–6.10. Our analysis of the structure of Galatians suggests that the long debate regarding just where the paraenetic section of Galatians begins must now be concluded in favor of 5.13 as marking that beginning.[97] Up to this point, Paul has been providing motivation for a positive response to his urgent request for a radical commitment to the gospel of freedom in Christ. The autobiographical statements (4.13-20), the allegorical exposition of the law (4.21-31), and the apostolic decisions of Paul (5.1-12) are all intended to motivate the Galatians to be as Paul is—viz., dead to the law and free in Christ. Now that he is confident (5.10) of their commitment to his position, he moves on to list certain ethical implications of true freedom in Christ (5.13-6.10). If paraenesis is defined as 'the giving of rules or directions for proper thought and action in daily living in a form which permits a wide applicability of the teachings', then 5.13 marks the beginning of the paraenetic section.[98]

But though the ethical instructions of this section permit wide applicability, it is doubtful that the *topos* form (i.e., 'self-contained, unitary teachings which have but a loose, and often an arbitrary, connection with their context'), as used in Stoic-Cynic itinerant preaching, should be ascribed to this paraenetic section.[99] True, 5.13-6.10 contains a series of brief exhortations, general rules of conduct, discussions of specific topics, lists of vices and virtues, and traditional materials such as quotations and proverbial sayings. Yet it is also clear that these items are woven together by the main themes of the entire letter. Thus the emphasis on freedom, the spelling out of a new relationship to the law, and the contrast between the flesh and the Spirit are all themes which must be seen as intimately related to the larger context of the letter.[100]

The structure of the paraenetic section itself is clearly indicated by conventional epistolary signals. The section is introduced by the phrase ὑμεῖς γὰρ ἐπ᾽ ἐλευθερίᾳ ἐκλήθητε ἀδελφοί (5.13). Two minor transitions are marked by λέγω δέ (5.16) and ἀδελφοί (6.1). The conclusion is identified by the double conjuction ἄρα οὖν (6.10).[101]

The Subscription

The autographic letter conclusion begins with the phrase Ἴδετε πηλίκοις ὑμῖν γράμμασιν ἔγραψα τῇ ἐμῇ χειρί (6.11).[102] The debate regarding how much of Galatians was actually written in Paul's own hand is reviewed by Gordon Bahr.[103] Bahr begins his review of this controversial point with a survey of subscriptions in common Hellenistic letters and concludes with a helpful description of the function of the subscription. As Bahr points out, the subscription was more than a signing of the addressor's name. It was also a summary of the body of the document. By giving such a summary, the signator made the contents of the body of the document his own and bound himself to the stipulations of the letter. Normally the subscription only repeated the cardinal points in the body of the document. In certain cases, however, the subscription became a rather long and detailed summary.[104]

On the basis of this study of the function of the subscription in contemporary literature, Bahr argued that the subscription of Galatians was not simply 6.11-18, nor did Paul write the whole letter. Rather, according to Bahr, 5.2 marks the beginning of the subscription.[105] But when the evidence which Bahr presents regarding the function of the subscription as a final summary is interpreted in the light of our analysis of Galatians' literary structure, we must, I believe, hold that the subscription begins at 6.11.[106] The summary does not begin at Gal. 5.2; rather, 5.2 states a solemn decision regarding the central issue of the Galatian crisis. It is 6.11-18 that contains the summary of the cardinal points of the letter. The denunciation of the intruders (6.12-13); the autobiographical statement of personal loyalty to the cross of Christ (6.14), with the mention of the *stigmata* as evidence of that loyalty (6.17); the reminder that circumcision means nothing whereas the new creation means everything (6.15)—all these repeat and underscore the main themes of the letter.[107]

The first benediction (6.16), the second benediction (6.18), the appellation (ἀδελφοί), and final 'Amen' all suggest that, whereas Paul began his letter with an ironic rebuke and conditional curse, he closes it with confidence that his request will be well-received by his Galatian converts.

Summation
Now that the significant structural features of 4.12-6.18 have been reviewed, the outline of the epistolary structure of Galatians can be completed.

I. Salutation 1.1-5

II. Rebuke section 1.6-4.11
  A. Rebuke for deserting the gospel 1.6-2.21
    1. Expression of rebuke 1.6-10
        Rebuke formula and statement of cause 1.6
        Θαυμάζω ὅτι οὕτως ταχέως μετατίθεσθε
        Reminder of instruction 1.9
        ὡς προειρήκαμεν καὶ ἄρτι πάλιν λέγω
    2. Disclosure of central thesis 1.11-12
        Disclosure formula 1.11
        Γνωρίζω γὰρ ὑμῖν ἀδελφοί
    3. Disclosure of Paul's autobiography 1.13-2.21
        Formulaic use of verb of hearing 1.13
        Ηκούσατε γὰρ τὴν ἐμὴν ἀναστροφήν
  B. Rebuke for foolishness about the gospel 3.1-4.11
    1. Expression of rebuke 3.1-5
        Transitional use of vocative 3.1
        Ὦ ἀνόητοι Γαλάται
        Formulaic use of verb of learning 3.2
        τοῦτο μόνον θέλω μαθεῖν ἀφ᾽ ὑμῶν
        Rebuking questions 3.1-5
    2. Disclosure of Scriptural teaching 3.6-4.7
        Disclosure formula 3.7
        γινώσκετε ἄρα ὅτι
    3. Expression of rebuke 4.8-11
        Rebuking question for negligence
        and change of heart 4.9
        πῶς ἐπιστρέφετε πάλιν ἐπὶ τὰ ἀσθενῆ
        Expression of distress 4.11
        φοβοῦμαι ὑμᾶς

III. Request section 4.12-6.10

  A. Personal appeal 4.12-20
    1. Request for imitation 4.12
        Request formula 4.12
        ἀδελφοί, δέομαι ὑμῶν
    2. Disclosure of autobiography 4.13-19
        Disclosure formulae 4.13
        οἴδατε δὲ ὅτι / μαρτυρῶ γὰρ ὑμῖν ὅτι
        vocative 4.19
        τέκνα μου

3. Wish for personal visit 4.20
    statement of apostolic parousia 4.20
    ἤθελον δὲ παρεῖναι πρὸς ὑμᾶς ἄρτι
B. Scriptural appeal 4.21-4.31
    1. Appeal to the law 4.21-30
        Formulaic use of verb of saying 4.21
        Λέγετέ μοι οἱ ὑπο νόμον θέλοντες εἶναι
    2. Conclusion from the law 4.31
        vocative 4.31
        διό, ἀδελφοί 4.31
C. Authoritative appeal 5.1-12
    1. Decision 5.2
        motivation for writing formula 5.2
        Ἴδε ἐγὼ Παῦλος λέγω ὑμῖν ὅτι
    2. Disclosure of consequences 5.3-9
        Disclosure formula 5.3
        μαρτύρομαι δὲ πάλιν
    3. Confidence statement 5.10
        Confidence formula 5.10
        ἐγὼ πέποιθα εἰς ὑμᾶς ἐν κυρίῳ ὅτι
D. Ethical appeal (paraenesis) 5.13-6.10
    Vocative
    Ὑμεῖς γὰρ ἐπ᾽ ἐλευθερίᾳ ἐκλήθητε ἀδελφοί
    Ἀδελφοί
IV. Autographic Subscription 6.11-18

CHAPTER 2

RHETORICAL ANALYSIS A: GENRE AND STRUCTURE

1. *Methodology*

Paul specifies his primary, apostolic task as the preaching of the gospel (Gal. 1.16). So when he writes, it is not surprising that he writes as a preacher. His letter, though a real letter comparable to rebuke-request letters of the Hellenistic letter tradition, is nevertheless similar in many ways to oral speech.[1] As Hans Hübner observes, 'Die Kombination von (literarischer) Rede und Brief im Gal wird von daher verständlich, dass Paulus Apostel war und als solcher, sofern er schreibt, "redend schreibt"'.[2] In terms of an Aristotelian definition of rhetoric, Galatians is an example of the 'art of discerning the possible means of persuasion'.[3] For this reason, our epistolary analysis must be supplemented by a rhetorical analysis of Paul's argumentation in Galatians.[4]

Rhetoric has been used a a pejorative term ever since Plato's critique of it in *Gorgias*.[5] It has been negatively regarded as ornamental speech for its own sake, manipulation of emotions, and based upon opinion and appearance instead of truth and reality.[6] Our use of the term, however, is meant simply as a descriptive reference to argumentative discourse.

It is, of course, beyond reasonable doubt that Paul's argumentation, in one degree or another, was shaped by the dominant influence of Hellenism and, in particular, Hellenistic rhetoric. Although Paul may not have received a formal education in classical rhetoric in a Greek school, he would certainly have been exposed to popular rhetorical practice in his culture.[7] According to Dibelius, 'it is certain that that kind of popular rhetoric had merged into the eloquence that was practised in the Greek speaking congregations of the synagogues'.[8] Hengel's studies have shown that even Palestinian Judaism was permeated by the influence of Hellenistic rhetoric.[9] As E.A. Judge says, 'Paul would have had the opportunity of a Greek education even in Gamaliel's school at Jerusalem'.[10] This assertion is confirmed by D. Daube's evidence that the formation of Hillel's rules of interpretation was influenced by Hellenistic rhetoric.[11] Thus it is reasonable to assume that Paul employed the art of Hellenistic rhetoric in the development of his argument in Galatians. The extent of correspondence which Betz has shown between Paul's argumentation and classical rhetoric supports this assumption.[12]

Our primary purpose in analyzing Paul's argumentation, however, is not to demonstrate the extent to which Paul was influenced by the forms of Hellenistic rhetoric. Thus it is important to distinguish between the use of the classical rhetorical handbooks in our analysis and a kind of source-critical analysis which would seek to examine Paul's literary dependence on these handbooks. In spite of his assertion about the originality of Paul's argumentation,[13] Betz often appears to be engaged in such a source-critical analysis. He quotes at length from the ancient rhetorical handbooks to demonstrate that Galatians is structured in accordance with the requirements of classical rhetorical theory, and is constantly concerned to show the influence of Greco-Roman rhetorical theory on Paul's argumentative discourse. According to Betz, the structure of Paul's argument is best understood by observing how Paul 'conforms' to the requirements of the handbooks of Aristotle, Cicero, Quintilian, and others.[14] Betz's frequent use of such terms as 'conforms', 'follows', and 'obeys' to depict Paul's relationship to classical rhetorical conveys the impression that it is his purpose to demonstrate Paul's direct, even conscious, dependence upon classical rhetoric in the development of his argument.

Without denying the importance of the role which Hellenistic rhetoric must have played in the formation of Paul's argument, I intend to use the parallels which are applicable from the rhetorical handbooks simply as descriptive tools.[15] Classical rhetoric was, after all, based upon an inductive description of the elements of persuasive speech.[16] Although the classical rhetoricians wrote in a doctrinaire, prescriptive tone, they nevertheless clearly stated their purpose and method to be descriptive. Quintilian affirms that 'it was then nature that created speech, and observation that originated the art of speaking. Just as men discovered the art of medicine by observing that some things were healthy and some the reverse, so they observed that some things were useful and some useless in speaking, and noted them for imitation or avoidance'.[17]

The descriptive value of the system developed by the classical rhetoricians is highly regarded by many recent rhetorical critics.[18] George Kennedy, for example, emphasizes the universal applicability of Greek rhetoric:

> Though rhetoric is colored by the traditions and conventions of the society in which it is applied, it is also a universal phenomenon which is conditioned by basic workings of the human mind and heart and by the nature of all human society. Aristotle's objective in writing his *Rhetoric* was not to describe Greek rhetoric, but to describe this universal facet of human communication. The categories he identifies are intended to exhaust the possibilities, though the examples of them which he gives are drawn from the specific practice of Greek city state. It is perfectly possible to utilize the categories of Aristotelian rhetoric to study speech in China, India, Africa, and elsewhere in the world, cultures much more different from Greek than was Palestine in the time of the Roman empire. What is unique about Greek rhetoric, and what makes it useful for criticism, is the degree to which it was conceptualized. The Greek gave names to rhetorical techniques, many of which are found all over the world.[19]

Since the classical rhetoricians were quite thorough in their work of observing and systematizing almost every conceivable feature of argumentation, it is not surprising that many of the features of Pauline argumentation are described in their handbooks.

Our experiment in the practice of rhetorical analysis will follow four stages:[20] in this chapter we will seek (1) to determine the species or genre of rhetoric represented by Galatians, and (2) to describe the arrangement of material or the structure of the argument. The next chapter is an attempt (3) to delineate one device of style and (4) to outline various rhetorical techniques employed by Paul.

2. *The Rhetorical Genre*

Three species of rhetoric are described in the classical tradition:[21] (1) *forensic* rhetoric is addressed to the jury or judge with the goal being to defend or accuse someone regarding past actions; (2) *deliberative* rhetoric is addressed to the public assembly in order to exhort or dissuade the public regarding future actions; and (3) *epideictic* rhetoric is addressed to spectators in order to affirm communal values by praise or blame. These three rhetorical genre seek different kinds of judgment from the audience. Forensic: Is it just? Deliberative: Is it expedient? Epideictic: Is it praiseworthy?

In Betz's opinion, the letter to the Galatians presupposes the situation of the law court:[22] the addressees are the jury; Paul is the defendant; and the intruders are the accusers. The goal of Paul is a defense of himself (a self-apology) and his gospel against the attack of the intruders. Seen in this light, the letter is classified by Betz as an example of forensic rhetoric.

Betz's classification of Paul's argument in Galatians within the forensic genre has been challenged by a number of critics of his work. David Aune claims that 'in terms of ancient rhetoric, Paul turns from forensic oratory in Gal. 1–2 to deliberative oratory in Gal. 3–4'.[23] G. Kennedy asserts that 'Galatians is probably best viewed as deliverative rhetoric'.[24] In his view, 'the exhortation of 5.1–6.10 is strong evidence that the epistle is in fact deliverative in intent'.[25] The problem which Betz has in locating any reference to exhortation in the classical definition of forensic rhetoric[26] is addressed by Kennedy's reference to Quintilian's statement that exhortation and dissuasion are two forms of deliberative rhetoric.[27] Betz's overemphasis on the presence of narrative as a feature of forensic rhetoric and his neglect of the use of exhortation as a form of deliberative rhetoric have caused him, according to Kennedy, to destroy the interpretation of the argument.[28] 'What Paul is leading to in chapters 1–4 is the exhortation of chapters 5–5'.[29] Kennedy goes on to explain:

> The basic argument of deliberative oratory is that an action is in the self-interest of the audience, or as Quintilian prefers to put it, that it is right (8.3.1-3). That is the pervasive argument of Galatians. The Christian community should not observe Jewish law and should not practice circumcision, which is now not only unnecessary, but wrong. Conversely, Christians should love one another and practise the Christian life. The letter looks to the immediate future, not to jdugment of the past, and the question to be decided by the Galatians was not whether Paul had been right in what he had said or done, but what they themselves were going to believe and do.[30]

So it is necessary to modify Betz's analysis by observing that Galatians contains features of deliberative rhetoric, such as are to be found particularly in the exhortation section. This observation, however, does not necessarily rule out the forensic aspects of the argument. Betz bases his determination of the forensic genre primarily on the first half of Galatians (chs. 1–4), with particular emphasis on the narrative. Kennedy, on the other hand, bases his determination of the deliberative genre primarily on the last half (chs. 5-6) with special emphasis on the exhortation. The truth of the matter, it seems, is to admit with Aune that there is a mixture of the forensic genre and deliberative genre in Paul's Galatians' argument. W.J. Brandt in clarification of the Aristotelian division of rhetoric into deliberative, forensic, and epideictic, observes that the classical definitions of these species of argumentation proved to be too narrow: 'In the long run, the deliberative, the forensic, and the epideictic could not be kept apart'.[31] And Paul's mixture of forensic and deliberative features is an illustration of Brandt's assessment.

Indeed, Gal. 1.6-4.11 has the characteristics of forensic rhetoric: Paul *defends* himself against accusations (1.10);[32] at the same time, he *accuses* his opponents of perverting the gospel of Christ (1.7). Paul's strong denials (1.1, 11-12, 16-17, 19-20, 22; 2.5, 6, 17, 21) and the development of his autobiography (1.13-2.21) to support these denials make the courtroom image a feasible backdrop for this section of the argument.[33] It should be noted, however, that the roles of the participants in this courtroom cannot be so easily assigned as Betz suggests.[34] Paul is at times the defendant, but he is also the accuser-prosecutor as he makes his charges against the intruders and the Galatians. The Galatian believers are in some respects the jury called upon by Paul to acquit him of all charges and condemn the intruders. But the Galatians also stand on trial themselves, accused of desertion. They are not the jury but the accused when Paul interrogates them directly (3.1-5; 4.9-10) and charges them with turning away from faith in Christ and the experience of the Spirit to works of the Law and τά ἀσθενῆ καὶ πτωχὰ στοιχεῖα (4.9). As demonstrated in our epistolary analysis, these rebuking questions form a parenthesis for the arguments in 3.6-4.7. Hence in this context the Abraham story in 3.6-29 serves as evidence from the Torah which Paul provides to support his legal case against the accused,—i.e., the intruders, of course, but also the Galatians who have been 'bewitched' (3.1) by them. Thus Gal. 1.6-4.11 may be appropriately classified within the forensic rhetorical genre.

In Gal. 4.12-20, however, a major rhetorical shift occurs. There are here still some elements of forensic rhetoric to be observed in the accusations made against the intruders (4.17; 5.7-12; 6.12-13) and in the statements of self-defense (4.13-16; 5.11; 6.14, 17). But the dominant tone is deliberative rather than forensic. Paul is no longer so much concerned to accuse or defend as he is to persuade the Galatian believers to adopt a certain course of action.[35] He begins his appeal to this new course of action in 4.12: Γίνεσθε ὡς ἐγώ, ὅτι κἀγὼ ὡς ὑμεῖς, ἀδελφοί, δέομαι ὑμῶν. Here is a significant shift to the imperative mood. Paul even says that he wishes he could be present with the Galatians and change his tone of voice (4.20). Perhaps his expressed desire to change his tone should be interpreted in rhetorical terms as a signal that he has indeed changed from accusation and defense to exhortation, i.e., from forensic to deliberative rhetoric.[36] Paul's appeal to a new course of action (4.12) is then supported by the command from the Abraham story to 'cast out the slave and her son' (4.30), clarified by authoritative decrees to stand in freedom (5.1-12), and defined in specific terms in the ethical exhortation to walk in the Spirit (5.13-6.10). Betz accurately labels 5.1-6.10 as *exhortatio*.[37] Exhoration, however, is characteristic of deliberative rhetoric, not forensic rhetoric.[38]

Deliberative rhetoric seeks to exhort or dissuade an audience regarding future actions by demonstrating that those actions are expedient or harmful.[39] Paul points to the harmful effects of the actions which he seeks to dissuade the Galatian believers from following: obligation to the whole law (5.3), severance from Christ and grace (5.4), exclusion from the kingdom of God (5.21), and a reaping of corruption (6.8). He underscores the expediency of the course of action which he has exhorted them to follow in the promise of the harvest of eternal life (6.8) and in the benediction upon all those who walk according to 'this canon' (6.16).

Betz's attempt to interpret the entire letter as an example of forensic rhetoric hindered him from detecting the important rhetorical shift in Paul's argument at 4.12. Our analysis of the cluster of epistolary conventions in Gal. 4.12-20 suggests that this section is a major turning point in the letter. Now, in the light of the evidence for the sift from forensic to deliberative rhetoric, this section appears to be a major turning point in the argument as well. Our interpretation of Paul's use of the Abraham story will be guided by this perspective on his use of forensic and deliberative rhetoric and his shift from one to the other.

3. *The Structure of the Argument*

The basic structure of a speech, as developed by the classical rhetoricians, consists of six parts:[40] (1) the *introduction* (*exordium*), which defines the character of the speaker (*ethos*) and the central issue that he addresses; (2) the *narration* (*narratio*), which is a statement of facts related to the issues of the case; (3) the *proposition* (*propositio*), which states the points of agreement, disagreement, and the central theses to be proved; (4) the *confirmation* (*probatio*), which develops the central arguments; (5) the *refutation* (*refutatio*), which is a rebuttal of the opponents' arguments; and (6) the *conclusion* (*peroratio*), which summarizes the case and evokes a sympathetic response.

The Structure of the Argument according to Betz
Betz uses the Latin terms of classical rhetoric to outline Galatians as follows:[41]

I.	Epistolary Prescript	1.1-5
II.	*Exordium*	1.6-11
III.	*Narratio*	1.12–2.14
IV.	*Propositio*	2.15-21
V.	*Probatio*	3.1–4.31
VI.	*Exhortatio*	5.1–6.10
VII.	Epistolary Postscript (*Peroratio*)	6.11-18

Generally, of course, as Betz lays it out Galatians appears to correspond fairly well to the arrangement advocated in the classical rhetorical handbooks. In his detailed analysis, Betz offers numerous parallels from the handbooks as evidence that each part of the argument in Galatians 'conforms to the form, function, and requirements' prescribed by the handbooks. The following list of the major features in Betz's analysis of Paul's argument for which he cites parallels from classical rhetoric indicates the extent of the correspondence that he finds.

Exordium (1.6-11)
(1) *The expression of astonishment*: 'I am astonished . . .' (Gal. 1.6)
Cicero 'recommends the expression of astonishment and perplexity as one of the means to regain the goodwill of an audience which has been won over by the opposition' (Betz, p. 45;[42] cf. Cicero, *De inv.*, 1.17.25).

(2) *The mixture of 'direct opening' and 'subtle approach'*
The 'direct opening' is used to address a receptive audience (*Rhet. ad Her.* 1.4.6). The 'subtle approach' is used when the audience has been won over by the opponent (*Rhet. ad Her.* 1.6.9). Betz says that Paul combines both approaches since the Galatians are receptive to him and yet they have almost been won over (Betz, p. 45).

(3) *The discussion of adversaries*

The way in which Paul 'discredits his adversaries by using the language of demagoguery' (Betz, 45) is compared to the advice in *Rhetorica ad Herennium*: 'from the discussion of the person of our adversaries we shall secure goodwill by bringing them into hatred, unpopularity, or contempt' (1.5.8).

(4) *The use of threats*

Quintilian's discussion of the use of threats to frighten and persuade the judge or jury (4.1.20-22) is used by Betz to explain Paul's use of the curse in the *exordium* (Betz, p. 46).

(5) *The statement of the 'causa'*

The function of the *exordium* to state the central issue of the case (*Rhet. ad Her.* 1.4.7) is fulfilled by Paul's reference to the Galatians' desertion from the gospel and the intruders' perversion of the gospel (Betz, p. 46).

(6) *The transition to the next section*

The rhetoricians required that there be a smooth transition between the *exordium* and *narratio* which concludes the *exordium* and is in harmony with the beginning of the *narratio* (Quintilian 4.1.76-79). 'Verses 10-11 meet these requirements very well' (Betz, p. 46).

Narratio (1.12–2.14)

(7) *The position of the narratio*

'As the Greco-Roman rhetoricians recommend, Paul's *exordium* is followed by the "statement of facts" (*narratio*)' (Betz, 58; cf. Quintilian 4.2.9).

(8) *The purpose of the narratio*

Cicero defines one type of narratio as that 'which contains just the case and the whole reason for the dispute' (*De inv.* 1.19.27). Betz states that this type applies to the *narratio* (1.12-2.14) in Galatians (Betz, p. 58).

(9) *The qualities of the narratio*

Most rhetoricians listed three necessary qualities for the *narratio*: 'it should be brief, clear, and plausible' (Cicero, *De inv.* 1.20.28). Betz attempts to show how Paul's *narratio* possesses these virtues (Betz, p. 59).

(10) *The subdivision of the narratio*
Quintilian recommends the division of the *narratio* into subsections (4.2.47-51). 'It is apparent that Paul follows this recommendation' (Betz, p. 61).

(11) *The use of denials and the narratio*
The *narratio* should deal with the facts which make denials plausible (Quintilian 4.2.1-11). There are strong denials in Galatians (1.11-12, 20; 2.17-21) supported by the facts of the *narratio* (Betz, p. 59).

(12) *The assignation of reasons and motives for the facts*
Quintilian requires that the *narratio* be made credible by assigning reasons and motives for the facts (4.2.52). 'Again Paul's *narratio* seems to obey the main rules of theory' (Betz, 61). The motivation for the main events is provided by the account of the revelations received by Paul (1.15-16; 2.1-2).

(13) *The characterization of the persons involved*
The *narratio* is also made credible when the persons involved are characterized in keeping with the events described (Quintilian 4.2.52). Paul does this by the use of such phrases as 'the false brothers' (2.4), οἱ δοκοῦντες (2.6), and, in 2.11-14, the 'hypocrisy' of Cephas, Barnabas, and the other Jews (Betz, p. 61)

(14) *The conclusion of the narratio*
Nearly all the classical rhetoricians ruled that the *narratio* should 'end where the issue to be determined begins' (Quintilian 4.2.132). According to Betz, Paul's formulation of the dilemma faced by Cephas (2.14) poses the very same question which confronts the Galatians: 'why do you compel the Gentiles to judaize?' (Betz, p. 62).

Propositio (2.15-21)

(15) *The summation of the narratio*
The *propositio* should summarize the legal content of the *narratio* by stating the points of agreement and disagreement with the opponents (*Rhet. ad Her.*). Betz interprets Gal. 2.15-16 as the point of agreement and 2.17-18 as the point of disagreement (Betz, p. 114)

(16) *The statement of a thesis*

The *propositio* also stands at the beginning of the *probatio*. It should be a concise statement of the thesis or theses to be elaborated and defended in the *probatio* (Quintilian 4.4.1). In his exposition of Gal. 2.19-20, Betz outlines four theses which he calls 'dogmatic abbreviations' (Betz, p. 114)

Probatio (3.1-4.31)

(17) *The diversity of arguments*

The *probatio* was not to be an inescapable system of syllogisms. Quintilian's dictum was 'to diversify by a thousand figures' (Quintilian, 5.14.32). Betz explains that 'the frequent interruption of the argumentative sections by dialogue, examples, proverbs, quotations, etc. . . is in conformity with the requirements of Hellenistic rhetoric' (Betz, p. 129).

(18) *The question of quality*

The argument should differentiate between the 'fact' of a certain act and the 'quality' of that act (Quintilian 3.6.79). In the case of Galatians the 'fact' is the founding of the Galatian churches. The question of 'quality' is whether that act of founding the churches was done rightfully or 'in vain' (Betz, p. 129)

(19) *The interrogation of witnesses*

The interrogation of witnesses produces compelling evidence for the case (Aristotle, *Rhetoric*, 1.15.15; Quintilian 5.7.1). Paul uses the interogation of witnesses (3.1-5) to present the undeniable evidence of the gift of the Spirit (Betz, p. 129).

(20) *Examples*

The use of examples in argumentation was treated by the classical rhetoricians (Quintilian 5.11.6). Paul uses the historical example of Abraham (Betz, p. 137), the simile of the human covenant (Betz, p. 154), and the allegory of Hagar and Sarah (Betz, p. 239).

(21) *Proof from Scripture*

The use of the precepts of wise men (Quintilian 5.11.36-42) and divine oracles (Quintilian 5.5.1-2) is recommended. Betz views Paul's use of Scripture as his conformity to this guideline.[43]

(22) *The argument from friendship*
The 'rhetorical character' of Gal. 4.12-20 is explained by Betz as 'a
string of topoi belonging to the theme of 'friendship' (περὶ φιλίας)'.
He states that 'a personal appeal to friendship is entirely in
conformity with Hellenistic style, which calls for change between
heavy and light sections'. Betz cites parallels from the Stoic diatribe
literature, epistolary literature, and the literature of Hellenistic
Judaism (Betz, p. 221).

Exhortation (5.1-6.10)
As we have already noted, Betz is not able to cite parallels to the
paraenetic section (5.1-6.10) from the classical rhetorical handbooks.
He turns instead to the Hellenistic philosophical letters and diatribe
literature (Betz, p. 254).

Peroratio (6.11-18)

(23) *The recapitulation*
One purpose of the *peroratio* was to sum up the main points of the
case (Quintilian 6.1.1-2). Paul's summary statement on circumcision and the cross fulfills this purpose (Betz, p. 313).

(24) *The appeal to the emotions*
The *peroratio* was also considered to be the place to make a strong
emotional impression on the audience. The *indignatio* is a passage
which arouses hostility against the opponents and the *conquestio*
arouses the pity of the audience (Cicero, *De inv.* 1.55.106). Betz
interprets Paul's denunciation of his opponents (6.12-13) and his
display of the 'mark of Jesus' (6.17) in the light of these rhetorical
conventions (Betz, pp. 314, 317).

The following table summarizes some of the most significant
parallels between the prescription of classical rhetoric and Paul's
argumentation in Galatians.

	Parallels from classical rhetoric	*reference in handbook*	*in Gal*	*in Betz*
1.	expression of astonishment	Cicero, *De inv.*, 1.17.25	1:6a	45
2.	direct/subtle approach	*Rhet. ad Her.* 1.4.6;1.6.9	1:6-11	45
3.	discussion of adversaries	*Rhet. ad Her.* 1.5.8	1:7	45
4.	use of threats	Quintilian, 4.1.20–22	1:8-9	46
5.	statment of *causa*	*Rhet. ad Her.* 1.4.7	1:6-7	46
6.	transition	Quintilian, 4.1.76–79	1:10-11	46
7.	position of *narratio*	Quintilian, 4.2.9	1:12–2:14	58

8.	purpose of *narratio*	Cicero, *De inv.* 1.19.27	1:12—2:14	58
9.	brief, clear, plausible	Cicero, *De inv.* 1.20.28	1:12–2:14	59
10.	subdivision of *narratio*	Quintilian, 4.2.47-51	1:12–2:14	61
11.	conformation of denials	Quintilian, 4.2.1-11	1:10–2:21	59
12.	assignation of motives	Quintilian, 4.2.52	1:16–2:2	61
13.	characterization of persons	Quintilian, 4.2.52	2:4,6,11–14	61
14.	conclusion of *narratio*	Quintilian, 4.2.132	2:14	62
15.	summation of *narratio*	*Rhet. ad Her.* 1.10.17	2:15–18	114
16.	statment of thesis	Quintilian, 4.4.1	2:19–20	114
17.	diversity of arguments	Quintilian, 5.14.32	3:1–4:31	129
18.	question of quality	Quintilian, 3.6.79	3:1–5	129
19.	interrogation of witnesses	Aristotle, 1.15.15	3:1–5	129
20.	examples	Quintilian, 5.11.6, 32-35	3:6, 15; 4:22	137
21.	precepts, divine oracles[44]	" 5.11.36-42;5.5.1-2	3:6–14	371
22.	friendship argument	Epictetus, Seneca, *et al.*	4:12–21	221
23.	recapitulation	Quintilian, 6.1.1-2	6:11–18	313
24.	appeal to emotions	Cicero,*De inv.*, 1.55.106	6:12–17	314

At least fourteen of the parallels which Betz quotes from classical rhetoric appear to be fairly accurate descriptions of certain features of Paul's argument: his use of an expression of astonishment (1),[45] the discussion of his adversaries (3), the statement of the *causa* (5), the transition (6), the subdivision of the *narratio* (10), the support of denials (11), the assignation of reasons and motives for major events (12), the characterization of persons (13), the statement of a proposition to be elaborated and defended in the *probatio* (16), the diversity of arguments (17), the interrogation of witnesses (19), the use of examples (20), the recapitulation (23), and the appeal to the emotions (24).

Some of these features in Paul's argument, however, are also common epistolary conventions: (1) (10), (23), (24).[46] Although the parallels from classical rhetoric illuminate the argumentative function of these features, Paul's use of them may be explained on the basis of common epistolary practice as well as in terms of rhetorical prescriptions.

Furthermore, there are features in Paul's argument that are also common features in the rhetoric of the OT: the use of curses (4) is an essential part of the covenant form;[47] the appeal to 'revelation' (12) as the motivation for prophetic ministry is a common element in OT literature;[48] the characterization of persons (13) as 'false' (2.4) and as hypocrites (2.13) occurs in the OT;[49] the use of historical examples (20), especially the example of the history of Israel beginning with Abraham, is, of course, a prominent element in OT literature;[50] and the quotation of the precepts of wise men and divine oracles (21) is commonplace in the OT.

It need also be said that some of the parallels which Betz quotes from classical rhetoric have questionable applicability to features of Paul's argument. For example, in what sense is Paul's harsh characterization of his adversaries and repetition of the curse a 'subtle approach' (2)? Does Paul's *narratio* contain 'just the case and the whole reason for the dispute' (8)?[51]

In sum, our review of the parallels between classical rhetoric and Paul's argument in Galatians indicates that, even though Betz may have overstated his case at some points, he has nevertheless provided sufficient evidence to indicate the influential role of Hellenistic rhetoric in the formation of Paul's argument and the beneficial role of classical rhetorical theory in the analysis of Paul's argumentation. Since our interest is in the rhetorical function of the Abraham story, we will concentrate on one major benefit and on one significant defect in this use of classical rhetorical handbooks in the analysis of Galatians.

A Benefit: The Unity of the Argument
In our study of Paul's use of the Abraham story, it is helpful to observe how Betz's rhetorical analysis illuminates the unity of the entire Galatians argument. This unity is highlighted in the following synopsis of the development of Paul's argument in the light of the categories of classical rhetoric.

In Paul's *exordium* (1.6-12), the central issue of the dispute is defined: the Galatians are deserting from the gospel which Paul preached (1.6; cf., 3.1-5; 4.9) under the influence of certain troublemakers who are perverting that gospel (1.7; cf., 3.1; 4.17; 5.7-10; 6.12-13). It becomes clear in the course of the argument that their perversion of the gospel includes their attempt to force Gentile Christians to judaize by requiring the acceptance of Jewish ritualism (4.10) and circumcision (5.2, 3; 6.12-13). Paul underscores his anathema on all who preach such a perverted gospel (1.8-9).

The *narratio* (1.13-2.14)[52] does not recount the facts directly related to the history of the situation in Galatia.[53] But it does set forth facts which have a direct bearing on the case.[54] Paul's autobiography is a defense of the gospel which he preached.[55] Seen in this light, it is just as much part of the 'proofs' (*probatio*) as chapters 3-4.[56] The main purpose of Paul's entire argument is to persuade the Galatians to reaffirm their adherence to his gospel, i.e., the gospel to the Gentiles ('the gospel of uncircumcision').[57]

Paul's gospel was not received through Jewish traditions (1.13-14) or the traditions of the Jerusalem church (1.17-24); it was received by divine revelation (1.12, 16). Paul was called by God to preach this gospel to the Gentiles (1.16; 2.8-9) and so he did (1.21-24; 2.2). He resisted anyone who detracted from the 'truth of the gospel'—whether 'false brothers' in Jerusalem (2.3-5) or Peter himself in Antioch (2.11-14). 'The gospel of uncircumcision' which he preached, although not derived from the Jerusalem church, elicited the approval of the churches in Judea (1.22-24) and was confirmed by the 'pillars' of the church in Jerusalem (2.6-10). These are the essential points which Paul makes in his *narratio* in rebuke of the Galatian believers for their disloyalty to the gospel (1.6), to refute any suggestion that he had compromised the gospel in his attempt to please men (1.10; 5.11), to deny any hint that his apostolic mission and gospel were derived from and subject to the Jerusalem church (1.11-17), and to provide a basis for his appeal to the Galatians to be as loyal to the gospel as he had been (4.12). As Betz suggests, the *narratio* ends with a rebuking question addressed to Peter which, in fact, relates directly to the central issue of the dispute in Galatia: πῶς τὰ ἔθνη ἀναγκάζεις ἰουδαΐζειν; (2.14).[58]

The *propositio* (2.15-21) functions as a summary of the preceeding *narratio* section and as an introductory thesis statement to be elaborated in the following *probatio* section. Paul moves from his rebuke of Peter for his hypocritical departure from the truth of the gospel (2.14) to a basic definition of the truth of the gospel[59] in judicial (2.15-18) and participatory (2.19-20) terms.[60] Betz observes that in 2.16 'Paul has succinctly introduced the two major types of evidence he his going to use in the *probatio* section (3.1-4.31): eyewitness evidence ('we have come to believe' [v. 16b]) and proof from Scripture'.[61] The concept of 'justification by faith in Christ, not by works of the law' (2.16) is elaborated in 3.6-29. The meaning of 'death through the law to the law' (2.19a) is expanded in 3.13. The statement regarding crucifixion with Christ (2.19b) is echoed in the *exhortatio* (5.24) and in the *peroratio* (6.14). As Betz points out, 'the doctrine of the indwelling Christ [2.20a] is developed in the *probatio* section in those sections which deal with the Spirit (3.2-5; 4.6 especially) and in the *exhortatio* section in the passages dealing with 'life in the Spirit' (especially 5.5, 16, 17, 18, 22-23, 25; 6.1, 8)'.[62] The full interpretation of the thesis regarding the expression of the Christ-life through faith (2.20b) 'is to be found in the entire *probatio* section (3.1-4.31) and in the *exhortatio* section (5.1-6.10)'.[63]

The form of the *propositio* as seen in the light of the classical rhetorical handbooks sets forth the central issue of the Galatian dispute regarding the nature of the gospel in terms of (1) the point of agreement (2.15-16), (2) the point of disagreement (2.17-18), and (3) the major thesis to be demonstrated (2.19-21).[64] The point of agreement is a summary of the doctrine of justification by faith, which is not only presented as the logical conclusion that should be derived from the *narratio* but is also the premise for the *probatio*. The citation of Gen. 15.6 in Gal. 3.6 is a biblical restatement of this point of agreement.[65] The point of disagreement spells out the implications of the point of agreement: rebuilding distinctions between Jews and Gentiles on the basis of the law is a denial of the truth of the gospel.[66] The truth of this implication stands as the conclusion (3.28-29) of the Abraham argument (3.6-29). The thesis that Christ's death, not the law, is the basis of righteousness and life (2.19-21) is the focal point of the contrast between faith and law in the Abraham argument.[67]

The *probatio* (3.1-4.31) presents a series of arguments in defense of the gospel (which equals the promise, cf. 3.8). The two major lines of evidence are (1) the Galatians' own experience of the Spirit after they heard Paul's proclamation of Christ crucified (3.1-5; 4.6) and were baptized (3.26-29), and (2) the exposition of Scripture (3.6-25; 4.21-31).

In the *exhortatio* (5.1-6.10) 'Paul applies his dialectic of "indicative" and "imperative"'.[68] Each of the three parts of the paraenetic section (5.1-12; 5.13-24; 5.25-6.10) begins with a restatement of the 'indicative' of salvation, which sums up what the reader has been told since the beginning of the argument regarding the nature of the gospel. The 'indicative' of the gospel is freedom—Τῇ ἐλευθερίᾳ ἡμᾶς Χριστὸς ἠλευθέρωσεν (5.1). This freedom was made possible by the cross of Christ (1.4; 2.20; 3.1, 13; 4.5); it was experienced in the gift of the Spirit (3.1-5; 4.6); it includes liberation from slavery under the law and sin (2.19; 3.13, 23-25; 4.1-10) and from the 'elements of the world' (1.4; 4.3, 9). 5.1 'sums up the logic which relates the argumentative section of the letter (in principle including the whole of 1.6-4.31) with the paraenetical section (5.1-6.10)'.[69]

The *peroratio* (6.11-18) is a recapitulation which 'sharpens and sums up the main points of the case'.[70] Paul again denounces his opponents (6.12-13), boasts in the cross of Christ (6.14), relativizes the value of circumcision (6.15), places supreme value on the καινὴ κτίσις (6.15b), and pronounces a conditional blessing on all who

follow 'this rule' (6.16). 'The whole argument in the letter leads up to
this rule in v. 16. Paul shows in the *narratio* (1.12-2.14) that he has
consistently followed the rule, while the opponents followed either
another or no standard (cf., especially, 2.14). The *probatio* (3.1-4.31),
no less than the parenesis (5.1-6.10), has implicitly and explicitly
(5.6) made the point that Paul's rule is to be followed'.[71]

In the light of the evidence which we have considered, it is clear
that Paul's entire argument in Galatians is a closely knit, unified
whole without any dangling, unrelated addenda. Thus the *narratio*
should not be considered 'as ancilliary to the main purpose of the
letter'.[72] The *exhortatio* should not be bracketed off from the rest of
the letter as a semi-independent ethical treatise, as if Paul was here
warning against ethical problems unrelated to the real crisis in
Galatia.[73] The *probatio* (3.1-4.31) should not be viewed as 'an
extended theological digression which is unrelated to the situation in
Galatia'.[74] Any interpretation of Galatians which treats any one
section as independent from the rest of the argument has been
rendered suspect by Betz's rhetorical analysis which demonstrates
the unity of the argument. This unity has important implications for
our exegetical analysis of Paul's use of the Abraham story. The
function and purpose of each citation of the Abraham story must be
determined not merely by its relation to its immediate context but
also by its function in the argument as a whole.

A Defect: The Analysis of the Probatio
In his discussion of chapters 3-4, Betz confesses that 'admittedly, an
analysis of these chapters in terms of rhetoric is extremely difficult'.[75]
His claim that the 'apparent confusion' in this section actually
follows Quintilian's advice 'to diversify by a thousand figures'
appears to be a rather desperate attempt to keep Galatians within the
mold of classical forensic rhetoric.[76] Besides Paul's use of *interrogatio*
(3.1-5) and *exemplum* (3.6f), Betz is not able to find other significant
features which relate directly to classical forensic rhetoric.[77] Forensic
rhetoric must therefore be judged to be too narrow a category to
encompass adequately Paul's eclectic use of a wide variety of
rhetorical techniques.

Our interest is especially related to Gal. 3-4, and therefore it is
necessary to develop a supplement to Betz's rhetorical analysis of
that section which will enable us to give a more detailed description
of the rhetorical function of Paul's use of the Abraham story. In the

next chapter our description of Paul's use of the stylistic device called *chiasmus* and of various rhetorical techniques in Gal. 3-4 is an attempt to provide such a supplement.

CHAPTER 3

RHETORICAL ANALYSIS B: CHIASTIC STRUCTURES AND RHETORICAL TECHNIQUES

What we have argued in the previous chapter is that an analysis of the rhetorical genre and structure of the argument helps in understanding the basic rhetorical function of Paul's use of the Abraham story in Galatians. A more detailed analysis of Gal. 3 and 4, however, can be achieved by observing Paul's use of chiastic structures and of various rhetorical techniques. And these we desire to highlight in this chapter.

1. *Chiastic Structures in Galatians*

The literary device known as 'chiasmus' is a criss-cross pattern resembling the Greek letter X, and hence its name. For example:

The *first* shall be *last*

and the *last first*

$$\begin{array}{cc} A & B \\ & \times \\ B & A \end{array}$$

Words or concepts are stated in the order A, B, C, and then repeated in the reverse C, B, A. This stylistic device is common in classical Greek literature[1] and in the OT.[2] It is not, however, identified in the classical rhetorical handbooks.[3]

John Welch in *Chiasmus in Antiquity* attempts to establish objective criteria for chiastic analysis:

> It is reasonable to require significant repetitions to be readily apparent, and the overall system to be well-balanced. The second half of the system should tend to repeat the first half of the system in a recognizable inverted order, and the juxtaposition of the two central sections should be marked and higly accentuated. Longer passages are more defensibly chiastic where the same text also

contains a fair amount of short chiasmus and other forms of parallelism as well. Key words, echoes, and balancing should be distinct and should serve defined purposes within the structure.[4]

Yet Welch recognizes that

> the evidence of chiasmus is not entirely objective and quantifiable. Wherever synonyms, cognates, antitheticals, or logically proximate terms appear in a chiastic system, substantial subjective judgment is again involved in the process of deciding which terms in the first portion of the system match (if at all) with particular terms in the second portion of the system.[5]

N.W. Lund in *Chiasmus in the New Testament: A Study in Formgeschichte* illustrates many simple and complex chiastic structures in several of Paul's letters, but does not draw any examples from Galatians.[6] J. Jeremias, on the other hand, suggests that the entire letter to the Galatians is build on a chiastic pattern.[7] As Jeremias understands Paul in Galatians, 1.11-12 is a response to two accusations in which Paul claims that his gospel is not κατὰ ἄνθρωπον (1.11) nor is it παρὰ ἀνθρώπου (1.12). Jeremias then sees Paul expanding this response in a chiastic pattern, i.e. in reverse order: the gospel is not παρὰ ἀνθρώπου (1.13-2.21), nor is it κατὰ ἄνθρωπον (3.1-6.10). So Paul develops the theme of the divine origin of his gospel in his autobiography (1.13-2.21); then he demonstrates the scriptural nature of his gospel in his exposition of Scripture (3.1-6.10).

F. Mussner uses Jeremias' chiastic analysis as the basis for the structure of his commentary on Galatians: I. Das paulinische Evangelium nicht παρὰ ἀνθρώπου (1, 12—2, 21), II. Das paulinische Evangelium nicht κατὰ ἄνθρωπον, sondern κατὰ τὴν γραφήν (3, 1-6, 10).[8] Likewise, Jeremias' analysis is reflected in J.C. Beker's understanding of the letter. For, as Beker says, Paul's intention is

> to dismantle the opposition by arguing for the integrity of his apostolate and his gospel. Therefore, the relation of the apostle to the gospel constitutes the theme that dominates the literary structure of the letter. The theme, which is subsequently unfolded chiastically, is stated in Gal. 1.11-12: 'the gospel which is preached by me is not man's gospel (κατὰ ἄνθρωπον). For I did not receive it from man (παρὰ ἀνθρώπου), nor was I taught it, but it came through a revelation about Jesus Christ'. 1. '*The apostle*': Gal. 1.13-2.21. Paul's gospel does not derive 'from a human source' (παρὰ ἀνθρώπου); to the contrary, it is directly from God, and this

constitutes his apostleship. 2. '*The gospel*': Gal. 3.1–5.25. Paul's
gospel is not 'according to human standards' (κατὰ γραφήν, Gal.
3.1–4.31) and verified by the Spirit (Gal. 5.1–25).[9]

Nils Dahl, however, objects to Jeremias' analysis since it is not
clear where the treatment of one theme ends and that of the other
begins.[10] Indeed, as we noted in our analysis of the autobiography,[11]
1.13–2.14 is not only a defense of the divine origin of Paul's gospel but
also an introduction to the essential content and nature of the gospel.
Moreover, if we follow Welch's criteria for chiastic analysis, the
parallel between 1.13–2.21 and 3.1–6.10 is not a valid example of
chiasmus since it is not based on significant repetition or a well-
balanced system.[12]

The most comprehensive attempt to locate chiastic patterns in
Galatians is John Bligh's commentary on Galatians. Bligh's starting
point is the chiasm observed by J.B. Lightfoot in Gal. 4.4–5.[13]

A	The Son of God was born a man
B	He was born under the law
B	to redeem those under the law
A	that all men might become sons of God

This clue led Bligh to suspect that the whole of Galatians might be a
large chiasm centered upon the chiasm of 4.4–5. As a first step toward
outlining the chiastic nature of the entire letter, Bligh focused on
what he calls the central chiasm of 4.1–10.[14]

4.1a	A a minor is like a slave
4.1b	B though a lord
4.2	C subject to guardians
4.3	D so we are subject to elements
4.4a	E but God sent His Son
4.4b	F born of a woman
4.4c	G subject to the law
4.5a	G to redeem those under the law
4.5b	F that we might receive the adoption as sons
4.6	E God sent the Spirit of His Son
4.7	D you are no longer a slave
4.8	C not knowing God you were slaves
4.9a	B but now that you know God
4.9-10	A how can you turn back to slavery.

then Bligh observed that this chiasm is sandwiched between two
passages that correspond to each other:[15]

3.5-29   Arguments from Scripture
4.1-10   Central Chiasm
4.11-30   Arguments from Scripture.

By following this process of analysis, Bligh arrived at what he claims to be the structural pattern of the whole letter:[16]

A Prologue, 1.1–1.12
B Autobiographical section, 1.13–2.10
C Justification by faith, 2.11–3.4
D Arguments from Scripture, 3.5–3.29
E Central chiasm, 4.1–4.10
D Arguments from Scripture, 4.11–4.31
C Justification by faith, 5.1–5.10
B Moral section, 5.11–6.11
A Epilogue, 6.12–6.18.

This pattern is then outlined by three main divisions, each of which is chiastic in structure according to Bligh:

I 1.1–3.4 First main division
II 3.5–4.31 Second main division
III 5.1–6.18 Third main division

This process of chiastic analysis led Bligh to the conclusion that:

> The whole Epistle forms one great chiasm, which I propose to call 'the primary chiasm'. Within the primary chiasm there are three large 'secondary chiasms'; and each of the three secondary chiasms contains three 'tertiary chiasms'. The first tertiary chiasm overlaps with the second, and the eighth with the ninth. Each tertiary chiasm divides into two or more 'quartan chiasms', and within these there are several smaller chiasms which might be called 'quintan'.[17]

It is, of course, necessary for Bligh to revise the text of Galatians at a number of points so as to diagram more adequately these complex chiastic patterns in Galatians. In fact, Bligh suggests on the basis of the chiastic patterns he finds in Galatians that 'the archetype from which the whole manuscript tradition derives was neither St. Paul's autograph nor a transcript of it, but a copy reproduced from memory'; and so he argues that 'the whole manuscript tradition may contain some small omissions and corruptions which it is no longer possible to discern'.[18] Yet Bligh claims to be able to discern these omissions and corruptions by evaluating the extant text in the light of its chiastic patterns. Thus he omits 2.9-10, 5.3, 6.1; transfers 2.3 to follow 2.9; transfers 2.8 to follow 2.2; places 3.7 before 3.6, 3.14b before 3.14a, 4.10 before 4.9b, and 4.18 before 4.17.[19] With these changes and a number of others, well-balanced chiastic patterns emerge.

The frequency of Bligh's changes in the text has made it appear to many that the chiastic patterns which he 'finds' are actually imposed upon the text by his own Procrustean design. Confidence in his analysis is further shaken when we observe that many of his parallel terms are poorly matched. For example, it is difficult to see how the autobiographical section (1.13–2.10) is parallel to the moral section (5.11–6.11), as Bligh maintains. In addition, as Betz observes,

> the 'chiastic patterns' the author finds at every conceivable point in the letter have nothing to do with literary forms and composition as we know them from the study of literary documents from antiquity. As a result of Bligh's analysis, Paul's Galatians looks like a strange jigsaw puzzle of chiastic patterns; one which has no analogy anywhere in literature.[20]

Despite, however the exaggeration of Bligh's claim to find chiastic patterns everywhere, there are valid examples of chiastic patterns in Galatians, such as at 4.4–5 and 5.17. The larger pattern which Bligh finds in 4.1-10 also appears to be a fairly accurate representation of the pattern which Paul often used to express his thoughts. For as John Hurd observes, Paul was able 'to work his way to the center of an idea and then to unwind the sequence so as to end where he began'.[21]

With our purpose being to examine Paul's use of the Abraham story, it is helpful to take a closer look at Bligh's treatment of Gal. 3-4. According to Bligh, Gal. 2.14–5.13 is essentially Paul's speech to Peter at Antioch, which speech was revised by the addition of certain phrases and sections that would relate directly to the situation at Galatia.[22] The first chiastic pattern in this section actually begins at 2.11 and extends to 3.4.[23] The direct address to the Galatians in 3.1 is Paul's editorial adaptation of the Antioch discourse to this new epistolary context.[24] Thus Gal. 3.5-29 is diagrammed by Bligh as follows:[25]

A	Those who believe are sons of Abraham and heirs to his blessing. All nations are to share in this blessing, 3.5-9.
B	Those who trust in the law are under a curse, 3.10-12.
C	Christ has redeemed us from the curse of the law, so that all nations may receive the blessing of Abraham, 3.13-14a.
D	The promised Spirit is given through faith, 3.14b.

E	The covenant is not invalidated by the law, 3.15-16a.

E   The covenant is not invalidated by the law, 3.15-16a.
F-F1   The law was a temporary measure, 3.16b-20.
E1   The law was not opposed to the covenant, 3.21a.
D1   The promised blessing is not given through the law, 3.21b.
C1   The promised blessing is given to all through faith, 3.22.
B1   Those under the law are liberated through faith, 3.23-25.
A1   Those who believe in Christ are sons of Abraham, whatever their nationality of social status, or sex, 3.26-29.

As we have already observed, Bligh calls 4.1-10 the central chiasm of the letter. Bligh sees 4.8-10 as having been originally addressed to Gentile Christians at Antioch.[26] In that address to Peter, these verses were immediately followed by the allegory of Sarah and Hagar (4.21-30). Bligh believes that 4.11-20 could not have been part of the Antioch Discourse since it contains so many personal reminiscences of Paul's work at Galatia.[27] So he claims that it was skillfully inserted into the Galatian letter to form a chiasmus with 4.21-30.[28]

Bligh's analysis of 2.14-4.31, however, fails to take into consideration the epistolary features which unify the entire letter as a rebuke-request directed to the crisis at Galatia. Our epistolary analysis of 3.1-4.11 has highlighted the way in which Paul begins and ends this section with rebuking questions, with these questions forming an integral part of the rebuke section of the letter.[29] The results of our analysis have likewise called into question Bligh's attempt to interpret this entire section as Paul's speech at Antioch. Moreover, Bligh's chiastic treatment of 3.4-4.30 fails to convince since it requires the transposition of so many phrases.[30]

Nevertheless, having said all this, Bligh's chiastic understanding of 3.5-29 reflects, to some extent, certain features of the structure of this section. For when our epistolary analysis is combined with a close examination of the repetition of certain key terms and antithetical expressions,[31] it is possible to observe a chiastic pattern of thought which can be outlined in simplified form as follows:

  a rebuking questions (3.1-5)
  b bestowal of the Spirit (3.2, 5)
  c faith—sonship (3.6-9)
  d faith—law (3.10-14)
  e promise—law (3.15-18)
  e law—promise (3.19-22)
  d law—faith (3.23-25)
  c sonship—faith (3.26-29)
  b bestowal of the Spirit (4.1-7)
  a rebuking question (4.8-11)

And since, it seems, the Abraham argument is developed within this chiastic pattern, its function should be explained in terms of its relation to the rebuking questions which enclose it, the witness to the bestowal of the Spirit which introduces it, and the contrast between the promise and the law which is the central focus of this chiastic pattern.

2. *Rhetorical Techniques*

A recent approach in the application of rhetorical analysis to Paul's letters is the identification of rhetorical techniques employed by Paul in his argumentation.[32] The concern here is not with questions of rhetorical genre or comprehensive arrangement of materials which we covered in the last chapter, but with specific types of arguments such as the argument from authority, the argument by definition, the argument by dissociation, etc. A wide variety of rhetorical techniques is described by Chaim Perelman and L. Olbrecht-Tyteca in what George Kennedy claims is 'the most influential modern treatise on rhetoric', *The New Rhetoric: A Treatise on Argumentation*.[33] It is not anachronistic to use the categories of the new rhetoric to explicate Paul's rhetorical techniques in Galatians for (1) the new rhetoric is a description of general, common traits of argumentation derived from a close examination of both ancient and modern examples of argumentation.[34] (2) the new rhetoric is actually a revival and further development of the classical tradition;[35] and (3) the new rhetoric has been applied to biblical literature and appears to function well as a description of the structures and techniques of various biblical arguments.[36]

The following fifteen rhetorical techniques of argumentation in Galatians have been selected for discussion because they appear to be most intimately related to Paul's use of the Abraham story.

(1) *Argument from Authority*

Paul's initial emphasis on his apostleship in Gal. 1.1. establishes a certain *ethos* as a platform for his entire argument. Classical rhetoricians recognized that 'the orator persuades by moral character' (*ethos*),[37] but they required that '*ethos* should be accomplished through the speech and not be a matter of authority or the previous reputation of the orator'.[38] Perelman observes that many arguments are structured by the use of *ethos*, which he calls 'prestige arguments'. In his view, 'the prestige argument appears in its most characteristic form in the argument from authority, which uses the act or opinion of a person or group of persons as a means of proof in support of a thesis'.[39] Perelman also notes that 'as soon as there is a conflict between authorities, the problem of the basis of the authority is raised'.[40] Since *ethos*, the prestige argument, appears so prominently in the argumentation of Galatians, it is important to consider how Paul's argument is structured by it.

Paul's designation of himself as an apostle in 1.1 goes beyond his references to his apostolic status elsewhere in his writings, and suggests that apostolic authority will be an important feature in his argument. The double denial of any dependence on human agency or authority for the legitimacy of his apostleship and the claim to a divine commission serve to signal an emphasis which, when fully developed, will be a major structural element in his entire argument.

Yet 1.6-9 is not, as might have been expected, a direct development of Paul's claim to apostolic authority. Paul moves instead to an analysis of the problem at Galatia and a definition of the gospel which excludes any possible alternative versions. He then subordinates both himself and any angel from heaven to the one true gospel (1.8-9).[41] In this way Paul responds to an apparent challenge to his authority and establishes at the outset the one ultimate measure of genuine authority: adherence to the gospel which he preached. If any one preaches another gospel, he forfeits his claim to authority; he is under a curse.

After the *anathema* upon all who deviate from the final standard for authoritative preaching (1.8-9), Paul declares his own subordinate position as a Χριστοῦ δοῦλος (1.10), which, as he sees it, precludes any possibility that he is seeking the approval of men. His authority is not dependent upon man's approval but upon his faithful service to Christ, who has commissioned him to apostleship. For the authority of the *apostle* of Christ rests upon the fact that he is the *servant* of Christ.

The origin and nature of the gospel which Paul preaches (1.11, 12) is related to the fact that he is a servant of Christ. The οὐκ... οὐδε... οὐτέ... ἀλλά construction of vv. 11-12 corresponds to the οὐκ... οὐδέ... ἀλλά construction of v. 1 where he speaks of the nature of his apostleship. His denial of any human dependence and his claim to a divine commission in v. 1 is elaborated in vv. 11-12 in a denial of dependence on human tradition and the claim to divine revelation for his preaching. So Paul's authority is based on a gospel that was not received from men but came through a revelation of Jesus Christ.

This contrast between human tradition and divine revelation is developed in the autobiography (1.13–2.21). Here Paul presents his own great reversal from a zealous propagation of the traditions of Judaism (1.13-14) to a proclamation of the revelation of God's son (1.15-16). Although both parts of his life are viewed as being under the sovereignty of God, who set him apart from his mother's womb (1.15), it was the call of God by his grace and the revelation of his son which formed the basis for Paul's preaching of the gospel to the Gentiles (1.16).[42] In fact, both the traditions of Judaism and the traditions of the apostles at Jerusalem are excluded as the basis of his gospel-proclamation (1.16-24). 'The first part of Paul's report on his dealings with Jerusalem', as B. Holmberg points out, 'is dominated by what has been called 'alibi-reasoning' ('I was not there')'.[43] But although Paul was unknown by sight to the churches in Judea (2.22), he was well known for his preaching the gospel ('the faith' [2.23]). It was his reputation for preaching the faith which won him the approval of those who did not even know him. Thus a major motif in the autobiographical section is Paul's authority on the basis of his independence from human traditions and his preaching of the gospel as received by revelation.

Paul's account of the apostolic council at Jerusalem (2.1-10) begins with another reference, the third in Galatians, to his guidance by divine revelation (2.2).[44] Here Paul introduces a new accent in the account of his relation to the authority of the Jerusalem church. He has already stressed the independence of his apostolate. Here he acknowledges that he presented the gospel which he preached among the Gentiles to the οἱ δοκοῦντες for their approval.[45] His major emphasis here, however, is not on his need for approval, but on the approval and recognition which he received from the δοκοῦντες, the στῦλοι. Titus was not forced to be circumcised (2.3-5); nothing was added to Paul (2.6); the gospel (2.7) and the grace (2.8-9) given to Paul were recognized; and he was given the right hand of fellowship by the 'pillars' of the Jerusalem church. The position or rank of these 'pillars' does not matter to him (or to God! [2.6]). Adherence to the 'truth of the gospel' (2.5) is the only legitimate basis of authority in Paul's view. Thus there should not be, even for a moment, any submission to those who deviate from the truth of the gospel for they have lost the right to exercise authority (2.5).

It is on this basis that Paul opposed Peter at Antioch (2.11-14). Peter and those who joined him were influenced by 'some from James' and their 'fear of the circumcision group'. When, however, Paul saw that they were not walking according to the ultimate standard of authority, 'the truth of the gospel' (2.4), he rebuked them because they stood condemned (2.11).

Thus, although Paul recognizes the priority of the apostles in Jerusalem (1.17) and the benefit of their approval (2.1-10), he nevertheless establishes a higher authority to which the 'pillars', the false brethren, an angel from heaven, and even Paul himself are all to be subordinated: the authority of 'the truth of the gospel'. Whoever perverts the gospel is under a curse (1.8-9), must be resisted (2.5), and rebuked (2.11-14).[46]

This argument from authority establishing 'the truth of the gospel' as the touchstone of genuine authority is the preface to Paul's scriptural exposition of the nature of the gospel. Paul interprets the Abraham story in such a way as to undergird the gospel which he received and preaches, and so to provide a biblical basis for his authority. Only after his authority is firmly founded in his autobiographical account of loyalty to the gospel and in his exposition of the Abraham story does Paul make his appeal for the allegiance of the Galatian believers (4.12-20).[47] Even then, however, Paul first gives an allegorical interpretation of Scripture (4.21-31) before finally announcing in a clear, authoritative tone his decision regarding their case (5.2).

If Paul's appeal for his converts' allegiance (4.12) and his 'apostolic decree' (5.2) had followed directly after his description of the situation at Galatia (1.6-7), it would have been clear that Paul based his authority simply on his apostolic position (1.1). Such a basis, however, would have left him at a severe disadvantage with respect to those whose priority and popularity could not be challenged. Paul, therefore, responds to the conflict between authorities by arguing that the gospel is the only final standard of authority. In his autobiography and in his interpretation of the Abraham story, he seeks to demonstrate his faithfulness to this standard, in contrast to those who have deviated from it. His adherence to the 'truth of the gospel' in his life as well as in his preaching (2.19-20; 6.14-15)—even in the face of persecution (5.11; 6.17)—makes his authority invulnerable. So he has the authority to establish the canon for the Israel of God (6.16). And so his argument from the authority structures his entire argument.

(2) *Argument by Definition*

In his glossary of argumentative figures, W.J. Brandt points out that 'arguments habitually depend on definitions'.[48] And Paul's argument in Galatians is certainly no exception. His definitions of key terms play an important role in the structure of the argument. A definition is a proposed relationship between concepts; it is a way of classifying something so that it is associated with certain values and expressions and dissociated from other values and expressions. Whenever this proposed relationship is disputed, it is justified by some form of argumentation.[49]

The most important term defined in Galatians is 'the gospel'.[50] The definition of this term is elaborated in all the successive stages of the argument. When 'gospel' is first introduced as the focus of the problem at Galatia, the quality of uniqueness is attributed to it: there is only one gospel; there is no other gospel. This initial point in the process of defining the 'gospel' is supported by a series of antitheses which contrast the one true gospel with any perversion of it.[51] Paul further identifies this one and only gospel as the gospel which he had originally preached to the Galatians (1.8) and which they had originally received (1.9).[52]

This gospel is then characterized in general terms as to its nature (οὐκ ἔστιν κατὰ ἄνθρωπον) and its origin (οὐδὲ γὰρ ἐγὼ παρὰ ἀνθρώπου παρέλαβον αὐτὸ οὔτε ἐδιδάχθην, ἀλλὰ δι᾽ ἀποκαλύψεως Ἰησοῦ Χριστοῦ [1.11, 12]). The origin of the gospel is the revelation of Jesus Christ (1.12), the revelation of God's son in Paul (1.16). But this record of revelation is also a statement about the content and nature of the gospel. For it seems best to understand the genitive in the construction δι᾽ ἀποκαλύψεως Ἰησοῦ Χριστοῦ (1.12) to be an objective genitive since it is God who reveals his son (ἀποκαλύψαι τὸν υἱὸν αὐτοῦ ἐν ἐμοί [1.15-16]) in order that Paul might preach him (ἵνα εὐαγγελίζομαι αὐτόν [1.16]).[53] This use of αὐτόν as the accusative object of the verb εὐαγγελίζομαι indicates the Christocentric nature of Paul's gospel. In 1.23 the accusative object of εὐαγγελίζομαι is τὴν πίστιν, which means that the 'gospel' is equivalent to 'the faith'.[54]

Paul also defines his gospel in terms of his mission to the Gentiles: ἵνα εὐαγγελίζομαι αὐτόν ἐν τοῖς ἔθνεσιν (1.16), τὸ εὐαγγέλιον ὃ κηρύσσω ἐν τοῖς ἔθνεσιν (2.2), and ἐνήργησεν καὶ ἐμοῦ εἰς τὰ ἔθνη (2.8). This intimate association of his Gentile mission with his understanding of the gospel is emphasized in the statement that he was entrusted with τὸ εὐαγγέλιον τῆς ἀκροβυστίας (2.7). Paul concedes that there is also a gospel τῆς περιτομῆς (2.7b). But these cannot be interpreted as two different gospels since Paul emphatically insists that there is only one gospel (1.7-9). Thus the distinction between the gospel of Peter and that of Paul relates primarily to the persons addressed.[55]

In both the record of the conference in Jerusalem (2.1-10) and the account of the conflict with Peter in Antioch (2.11-14), Paul appeals to the 'truth of the gospel' as his basis for resisting any attempt to compel the Gentile convers to judaize: Titus was not circumcised 'that the truth of the gospel might be preserved' (2.5); Peter was rebuked because contrary to the truth of the gospel he tried to 'compel the Gentiles to live like Jews' (2.14). Thus Paul defines the 'truth of the gospel' in a way that relates directly to the freedom (2.4) of Gentile believers from the obligations of the Jewish law.

In the next occurrence of the term 'gospel', Paul uses the verb form to link the gospel with the promise given to Abraham: προϊδοῦσα δὲ ἡ γραφὴ ὅτι ἐκ πίστεως δικαιοῖ τὰ ἔθνη ὁ θεός προευηγγελίσατο τῷ Ἀβραὰμ ὅτι ἐνευλογηθήσονται ἐν σοὶ πάντα τὰ ἔθνη (3.8). After making this identification of the gospel with the promise, Paul drops the term 'gospel' and develops a definition of the promise (3.14, 16, 17, 18, 19, 21, 22, 29; 4.23, 28). Since, however, the gospel is identified with the promise, the process of defining the promise becomes in actuality a continuation of the definition of the gospel. For just as the gospel is related to benefits for the Gentiles, so the promise is related to blessing for the Gentiles as well (3.8, 14, 29; 4.28).

Thus Paul's definition of the 'gospel' bears a major share of the weight in the structure of his argument. In our exegetical study of Gal. 3-4 we will pay special attention to the ways in which Paul uses the Abraham story to undergird and defend this definition. We will also observe the rhetorical function of his definition of other key terms such as πίστις, οἱ ἐκ πίστεως, νόμος, and οἱ ἔργων νόμου.

(3) *Argument by Dissociation of Ideas*
Closely related to the argumentative use of definition is the argumentative technique of 'the dissociation of ideas'.[56] Definition is the classification of something so that it is associated with certain values and expressions and dissociated from other values and expressions. When the process of dissociation is developed by a series

of antithetical pairs, the argumentative technique of the dissociation of ideas forms the structure of the argument. W.J. Brandt labels this technique a *'structural distributio'*. He explains that 'in arguments one sometimes finds antitheses used over and over again to remind the reader of some fundamental *distributio* set up earlier'. He defines *distributio* as a 'division of a concept or action and an apportioning of its parts'.[57] Perelman clarifies the nature of this division of concepts by a review of the fundamental dissociation of 'appearance' and 'reality' in the history of philosophical argumentation.[58] The dissociation of ideas functions argumentatively not only by dividing the concept (not that, but this) but also by apportioning the divided parts (this belongs to us; that belongs to them). It is, in fact, this apportioning that gives the *distributio* its argumentative force.[59]

That Paul's argument in Galatians is structured by the dissociation of ideas is evident from the development of his antithetical pairs: curse/blessing, works/faith, flesh/spirit, law/Christ, law/Spirit, slavery/freedom, bondwoman/freewoman, son of bondwoman/son of freewoman, present Jerusalem/heavenly Jerusalem, convenant from Sinai/covenant of promise. These antithetical pairs elaborate the basic distinction between the 'other' gospel and the one and only gospel. Paul states this distinction in terms of 'appearance' and 'reality': in reality there is only one gospel (1.7); the 'other' gospel is from those who wish μεταστρέψαι τὸ εὐαγγέλιον τοῦ Χριστοῦ (1.7). This fundamental division between the real and the apparent, the true and the false gospels, provides the basic framework for Paul's argument. For Paul not only distinguishes between the gospel of Christ and the 'other' gospel, he also apportions the elements of his gospel (the blessing, faith in Jesus Christ, the Spirit, the promise, freedom) to 'us', Paul and the Galatian believers, whereas he apportions the elements of the other gospel (the curse, the works of the law, flesh, and slavery) to 'them', the errorists at Galatia.

Paul's interpretation of the Abraham story plays a leading part in this process of distinguishing and apportioning. Certain texts are used to clarify the antithetical pairs (see the exegetical analysis of Gal. 3.6-18). The allegorical treatment of the Hagar and Sarah story (4.21-31) is a continuation of this process through the voice of the law itself (τὸν νόμον οὐκ ἀκούετε; [4.21]). The allegorical definitions of Hagar, Mount Sinai, and the present Jersalem dissociate Paul's presentation of the biblical story from contemporary interpretations of it.[60] Thus the Abraham story functions as the foundational underpinning for the structural *distributio*, the dissociation of ideas.

(4) *Argument by the Severance of the Group and its Members*
Paul's dissociation of ideas in his argumentation also involves the
dissociation of the group and its members by the use of the rhetorical
technique of severance. Argumentation concerning a group and its
members often reasons from the individual–group connection to an
evaluation of the individual member or the group.[61] On the one
hand, membership in a given group can raise the presumption that
certain qualities will be found in its individual members. On the
other hand, the value of an individual member reflects on the
group.[62] When, however, the fault in an individual compromises the
reputation of the whole group, the technique of severance may be
employed to dissociate that member from the group. In this case, an
argument is structured to demonstrate the incompatibility between
adherence to certain theses and membership in the particular group.
This argument seeks the exclusion of the person who no longer
shares the opinions of the group.[63]

Paul's argument in Galatians is structured to persuade the
Galatian churches to expel the errorists. The command for their
exclusion is taken from the Abraham story: ἔκβαλε τὴν παιδίσκην
καὶ τὸν υἱὸν αὐτῆς (4.30).

It is important to note the clear distinction that Paul makes
between the Galatians themselves and the intruders. Brinsmead
tends to loose sight of this distinction. He assumes that 'the
Galatians are in an important sense the offending party, and the
whole letter is written because of their espousal of an offending
theology... There is no division into heresies of the intruders and
heresies of the Galatians'.[64] This assumption allows him to treat all
of Paul's words to the Galatians as responses to the intruders, and so
he proceeds to infer the nature of the opponents' theology from the
response of Paul to the Galatians. But, in fact, the argument of the
entire letter elaborates the distinction which exists between the
Galatians and the troublemakers.

While the Galatians are in the process of deserting (note the
present tense of μετατίθεσθε [1.6]) because of having been bewitched
(3.1) and hindered (5.7), they are, nevertheless, not the ones causing
trouble or seeking to distort the gospel (1.7). They are not the leaven
in the lump (5.9) or the sons of the bondwoman (4.30). Paul is
confident that his converts will agree with him (5.10a). But the
opponents, who are the offending party, will bear their judgment
(5.10b). And this distinction between the Galatians ('you') and the
opponents ('they') is an important feature in the structure of the

argument. It is clearly presented in 1.7, 3.1, 4.17; 4.29-30; 5.9-10, 12; 6.12-13. The Galatians are, indeed, rebuked—but only in order that they might exercise their proper role as the true sons of Abraham and of the freewoman, and so expel the sons of the bondwoman.

In persuading the Galatians to take this action. Paul uses a series of epithets to characterize the intruders. The role of epithets in argumentation is to present the viewpoint chosen by the speaker in the presentation of his data.[65] Data are not presented for argumentative purposes without attributing an interpretation and meaning to them. So Paul colors the facts about the intruders by using such epithets as will emphasize their most reprehensible qualities.

G.B. Caird poses an appropriate question in asking: 'When Paul in his letters refers to his opponents, are these passages descriptive or evaluative, i.e., do they provide an adequate basis for the reconstruction of the views he is attacking, or do they merely or mainly depict his reaction to these views?'[66] The argumentative function of epithets in Galatians implies that this question should be answered by emphasizing that Paul's references to his opponents are primarily evaluative rather than descriptive. Paul's argumentation is designed to hammer a wedge between the Galatians and errorists so as to split them apart. The errorists are troublemakers and perverters of the gospel (1.7); they are, therefore, under a curse (1.8-9); they are guilty of witchcraft (3.1); they do not seek the Galatian believers for good (4.17); they are children of Hagar, the bondwoman (4.29); they have obstructed the race (5.7); they are leaven in the lump (5.9); they are troublemakers who will bear their own judgment (5.19); they only seek to circumcise the Galatian believers so that they can boast in their flesh and avoid persecution for the cross of Christ (6.12); they do not keep the law themselves (6.13).

Thus Paul takes the role of prophet and judge: he places the errorists under the curse and calls on the Galatian believers to recognize their rights as inheritors of the blessing. And he uses the Abraham story—both the exposition of the blessing of Abraham and the curse of the law in 3.6-14 and the allegorical treatment of the distinction between Hagar and Sarah amd their sons in 4.21-31—to validate this severance of the intruders from the Galatian Christians.

(5) Argument Concerning the Difference of Degree and Order
The transformation of difference of degree into difference of order accentuates that which separates the terms of one order from the

terms of another order. Such arguments point to phenomema which mark or cause the break between the two orders.[67]

Paul's arguments for the difference of order between the law and the promise, in contradistinction to the intruders who saw no difference, emphasize the temporary, mediated, negative purpose of the law in contrast to the permanent, revelatory, life-giving nature of the promise. The coming of Christ in the fullness of time is set forth as the sign and cause of the break between the order of law and the order of promise (3.19–4.7).

(6) *Argument for Presenting Theses as Incompatible*

The purpose of presenting two theses as incompatible is 'to point out the existence of circumstances which make unavoidable a choice between the two propositions'.[68] The trouble-makers in Galatia attempted to demonstrate that the Galatian Christian needs to follow the Mosaic law in order to inherit the blessings promised to Abraham.[69] In response Paul draws attention to the incompatibility between the way of gift and the way of payment (3.18). This fundamental incompatibility is presented in order to force the Galatians to make a choice between the gospel as preached by Paul and that taught by the intruders.

(7) *Argument by Enthymeme*

Aristotle stated that 'all orators produce belief by employing as proofs either examples or enthymemes and nothing else'.[70] An example is a form of induction; it attempts to persuade by appealing to the more specific. An enthmeme is called by Aristotle a 'rhetorical syllogism'. W.J. Brandt defines an enthymem as a 'syllogism with a premise omitted'.[71] Often an enthymeme constitutes the major argument. In such a case, Brandt calls it a 'structural enthymeme'.

> The writer arguing an enthymeme has a departure point, an implied major premise, functioning as a point of agreement. In their presumed assent to the major premise, the writer and the reader are one, the enthmeme functions to lead the reader from that point of agreement to a further, and perhaps novel, conviction by revealing conclusions implicit, but by no means self-evident, in the major premise when it is applied to particular cases.[72]

An enthymeme in argumentation may run from premise to conclusion or from conclusion to premise. Different terms signal the presence of enthymemes:[73]

Premise to conclusion	Conclusion to premise
therefore	since
hence	for
thus	because
which shows that	for the reason that

Paul's use of γάρ[74] and ὅτι[75] often signals the presence of enthymemes in his argumentation. As is common in argumentation, the major premises in Paul's deductive proofs (enthymemes) are not usually expressed explicitly, but simply taken for granted.[76] Likewise, just as syllogistic reasoning often moves from a conclusion to the premise for that conclusion, so Paul frequently presents his conclusion first as a thesis and then moves to his premise.

His thesis that the gospel which he preached to the Galatians is the ultimate standard by which to measure any 'other' gospel (1.6-9) is deduced from the minor premise that his gospel was received by divine revelation (1.11-12). The implicit major premise is that all messages received by revelation from God have ultimate authority. This is a structural enthymeme since it shapes the entire argument of Galatians. The autobiography (1.13-2.21) develops the minor premise by providing evidence that Paul's gospel was received not from human tradition but by divine revelation. The argument from the Abraham story (3.6ff) further develops its divine source and nature, and so the authority of his message. From the same premises, Paul deduces that the gospel of the intruders is under a curse since it contradicts the ultimate standard set by his message (1.8, 9).

In addition to this basic structural enthymeme, there are other enthymemes in Paul's argumentation which will be discussed in our exegetical analysis of the Abraham story.

(8) Argument by Example
Argument by example is the opposite of argument by enthmeme in that it attempts to persuade by appealing to the more specific rather than the more general. Perelman explains that 'argumentation by example—by the very fact that one has resorted to it—implies disagreement over the particular rule the example is invoked to establish'.[77] An example may also function as an illustration 'to strengthen adherence to a known and accepted rule by providing particular instances which clarify the general statement'.[78] And an example may serve as a model (or anti-model) which is presented to incite the audience to imitate behavior inspired by it.[79]

These different functions for the argument by example can be seen in Paul's two uses of the Abraham story. Abraham's faith confirms the rule that righteousness comes by faith and not by the works of the law. Since this 'rule of faith' has already been established by the Galatians' own experience of God supplying the Spirit and working miracles among them by the 'hearing of faith' (3.5), the Abraham account is used, first of all, as an historical illustration in order to secure adherence to this rule. In 3.6, καθώς links the experience of the Galatians and the example of Abraham, and so presents double confirmation for the rule of faith.

The Abraham story, however, not only serves to secure adherence to a general rule, it also provides a model to imitate. The appeal to imitate the faith of Abraham is implicit in the conclusion that οἱ ἐκ πίστεως, οὗτοι υἱοί εἰσιν Ἀβραάμ (3.7). In the development of this theme of the children and heirs of Abraham who are rebuked for not exhibiting the faith of Abraham, Paul juxtaposes an appeal to imitate him (γίνεσθε ὡς ἐγώ [4.12]) and a portrayal of the Galatians as his own children (τέκνα μου [4.19]). Paul, in fact, positions himself alongside of Abraham as a model to be emulated. Thus the model loyalty of Paul to the truth of the gospel, as has been portrayed in the autobiography, is paralleled to the model faith of Abraham, as explicated in the exposition of the Abraham story. For as Abraham exemplified the truth of the gospel, so did Paul. And so the argument of Galatians is structured to set forth these parallel models.

This parallel between Abraham and Paul is continued both in the allegory of Hagar and Sarah of 4.21-31 and in Paul's remarks of 5.10-12. The command given to 'cast out the bondwoman and her son' is cited as a guideline for the Galatian believers. Further, it is exemplified by Paul's own 'cutting remarks' about judgment (5.10) and the mutilation (5.12) of the troublemakers. Thus the presentation of Abraham and himself as models is developed by Paul to persuade the Galatian believers to imitate the attitudes and actions of these models toward the troublemakers.

(9) The Means-End Argument
Argumentation is often structured to enhance the value of something by demonstrating that it is the means to an end of exalted value. Conversely, something may be devalued by showing that it is the means to a debased end.[80]

Paul builds his argument to show the supreme value of his gospel in contrast to the message of the Judaizers. To do this he links his gospel to the promise given to Abraham (3.8), which is then demonstrated to be the means to the highly valued end of the blessing for the Gentiles (3.9, 14). So Abraham is presented not only as the example-model of faith, but also as the recipient of the promise, the beginning of salvation-history.

The contrast between the promise and the law is designed to prove that the law cannot be a means for life or righteousness (3.21), that anyone who tries to use the law as a means to righteousness is under a curse (3.10), and that the law is the means to the curse and imprisonment under sin (3.22-23). Nevertheless, the law does not annul or thwart the purpose of the promise (3.17-21), even though the inheritance comes not by the law but by the promise (3.18). The cross of Christ and the response of faith, on the other hand, are presented as the means of obtaining the blessing (3.6-14). Thus the means-end argument is an important rhetorical technique in Paul's exposition of the Abraham story.

(10) *The Argument of Direction*

The thesis of an opponent may be resisted in argumentation by attempting to show that the step advocated will lead to a 'slippery slope', which will allow no stopping and which will end in total capitulation.[81] Paul employs this argument when he opposes the acceptance of the requirement of circumcision on the grounds that it will lead to the keeping of the whole law, losing Christ, and falling from grace (5.2-4).

(11) *Argument by Sacrifice*

In argumentation by sacrifice, sacrifice is presented as evidence of the value of the thing for which the sacrifice is made.[82] Paul frequently points to the sacrifice of the cross as highlighting the value of the freedom in Christ for which the sacrifice of the cross had been made and which the troublemakers were attempting to destroy (1.4; 2.4; 2.20, 21; 3.1, 13-14; 4.4; 5.1).

What Perelman calls the 'pathos of useless sacrifice'[83] is also an important feature of the argument by sacrifice as used by Paul. The totally unacceptable proposition that Χριστὸς δωρεὰν ἀπέθανεν (2.21) is the basis of Paul's argument against the law.[84] Paul's interpretation of the Abraham story includes this argument by sacrifice especially in 3.13-14, where Paul states that the promised blessing of Abraham is obtained for the Gentiles by the sacrifice of Christ becoming a curse.

(12) *Argument by Transitivity*

Perelman defines transitivity as 'a formal property of certain relations which makes it possible to infer that because a relation holds between *a* and *b* and between *b* and *c*, it therefore holds between *a* and *c*.[85] The argument in Gal. 3 that Christ became a curse for us and that we inherit the blessing in him can be understood in terms of the argument by transitivity.[86]

(13) *Argument Concerning the Inclusion of the Part in the Whole*

This common rhetorical technique is based on the principle that 'what is true of the whole is true of the part'.[87] In the development of his dominant theme in Galatians of the inclusion of the Gentiles in Christ, Paul utilizes the argument concerning the inclusion of the part in the whole to demonstrate that what is true of Christ is true of Gentile believers, for they are in Christ by faith. Paul's statements regarding the 'seed of Abraham' (3.16) and the heirs of Abraham (3.29) are a formulation of this argument. For since Christ is the heir of the promise of Abraham, the Galatian believers are heirs of the Abrahamic promise because they are in Christ.

(14) *Argument by Repetition and Amplification*

Argumentation is designed to draw attention to certain theses. The speaker increases their 'presence' in the mind of his hearers by repetition and amplification.[88] Likewise in the structure of Paul's Galatian argument, repetition of key words is an important element. The focus of each section can be largely determined by simply counting what word is repeated most often. In 3.6-14, πίστις or πιστεύειν is used eight times. Επαγγελία is used in 3.14 and repeated seven times in 3.15-22. Πίστις does not appear in this section until 3.22; it is then repeated five times in 3.23-29. Thus the repetition and amplification of key terms in 3.6-29 clearly indicates the movement and structure of the Abraham argument.[89] And the repetition of ἐλευθερία (5.1, 13), ἐλεύθερα (4.22, 23, 26, 30, 31), and ἐλευθερόω (5.1) serves to establish the focus of the Hagar–Sarah allegory.

(15) *Argument by Personification*

An abstract concept or value can be given a sense of concreteness and presence by using the argumentative technique of personification.

When negative or positive personal traits are attributed to a concept, it becomes a distinct entity which evokes a specific personal response.[90] So Paul's personification of the law as a jailer and a paedagogos (3.22-24) is an example of this technique.

PART II

EXEGESIS AND FUNCTION OF THE ABRAHAM STORY

CHAPTER 4

THE ABRAHAM ARGUMENT OF GAL. 3.1-29:
PAUL'S BIBLICAL REBUKE

Our analysis of the function of the Abraham argument in Gal. 3 attempts to integrate and apply the results of our epistolary and rhetorical analyses. First, however, in order to gain a clear picture of the Abraham argument, we must observe the relation of this argument to (1) the rebuke section of the letter (1.1–4.11) and (2) the *propositio* (2.15-21). Then we will be in a position to carry out a detailed analysis of Gal. 3.1-29.

1. *The Rebuke Section* (1.1–4.11)

The Abraham argument in Gal. 3 is subordinate to the framework provided by Paul's expressions of rebuke.[1] In the initial rebuke, Paul accuses his readers of desertion to perverted gospel (μετατίθεσθε ἀπὸ τοῦ καλέσαντος ὑμᾶς ἐν χάριτι Χριστοῦ εἰς ἕτερον εὐαγγέλιον, 1.6).[2] He places anyone who distorts the gospel of Christ under a curse (1.7-9). The restatement of this rebuke in 4.9 charges the readers with a return to paganism (πῶς ἐπιστρέφετε πάλιν ἐπὶ τὰ ἀσθενῆ καὶ πτωχὰ στοιχεῖα οἷς πάλιν ἄνωθεν δουλεύειν θέλετε;).[3] The argument is prefaced by a series of rebuking questions in 3.1-5 which imply that the Galatian Christians were exchanging their experience of the Spirit for dependence on the flesh (3.3). Each of these expressions of rebuke depicts the Galatians' change of direction as a complete reversal of their conversion experience and posits an absolute dichotomy between Paul's message and the message of the intruders.

As we observe in our consideration of the opponents' theology,[4] it is likely that they presented circumcision and the observance of the Mosaic law as necessary requirements for inclusion in the covenant people of God and for progress toward perfection. They probably persuaded the Galatian believers to accept their 'gospel' on the basis that the Abraham story itself demanded circumcision and obedience to the law. Our review of the history of the interpretation of the Abraham story in Jewish literature brings to light many strands of tradition which synthesized the Abraham story with the demand for a meticulous observance of the Mosaic law.[5] Thus it seems probable that the opponents used these traditions to support their case. And as a result of their propaganda, it appears that the Galatians came to view their change as progress, not desertion, and the intruders' message as a completion, not a contradiction of Paul's message.

It was necessary, therefore, for Paul to support his rebukes of his converts for their change of mind, which was a complete reversal, by reinterpreting the Abraham story in a way that hammered a wedge between his gospel and the other gospel. Selected features of the Abraham tradition were formulated to legitimate the anathemas and antitheses contained in his rebukes. In his use of the Abraham story, the dissociation of ideas such as faith/works of the law, faith/law, and promise/law created a sharp contrast between his message and the message of the opponents, and, as we shall see below, caused him to present a different Abraham from that of the common portrayals in the contemporary Jewish literature.

Paul's rebukes in 1.6 and 3.1-5 are followed by disclosure statements in 1.11, 13 and 3.7.[6] 1.11-12 is a programmatic statement introducing the nature (οὐκ ἔστιν κατὰ ἄνθρωπον) and origin (οὐδὲ γὰρ ἐγὼ παρὰ ἀνθρώπου παρέλαβον αὐτὸ οὔτε ἐδιδάχθην ἀλλὰ δι' ἀποκαλύψεως Ἰησοῦ Χριστοῦ) of Paul's gospel as the central themes of the rebuke section; 1.13 starts Paul's autobiography; and 3.7 launches the Abraham argument. It is important to note that the thesis statement of 1.11-12 is elaborated by the autobiographical section and the Abraham argument in roughly parallel fashion.

The autobiographical statements comprise primarily an argument by definition—viz., the definition of the gospel.[7] The Abraham argument continues this definition in terms of the promise. In Paul's autobiography, the definition of the gospel emphasizes (1) the revelatory origin of the gospel (1.12, 16, 2.2), (2) the Christological center of the gospel (1.12, 15-16), and (3) the mission to the Gentiles (1.16; 2.2; 2.7-8). The autobiographical section also stresses (4) that the 'truth of the gospel' (2.5, 14) demands the freedom of the Gentiles from any attempt to force them to judaize (2.3-6, 11-14).

In the Abraham argument, the same features of the gospel are disclosed: (1) the scriptural citations confirm the revelatory origin of Paul's gospel; (2) the message of Christ crucified is central (3.1, 13); (3) the gospel announced to Abraham promises blessing for the Gentiles (3.8, 14); and (4) this gospel excludes 'works of the law' as the basis for the inclusion of Gentiles in the Abrahamic sonship.

These parallels between Paul's autobiography and his Abraham argument point to the objectives of the argument: *First*, Paul uses the Abraham story to authenticate the validity and authority of the revelation to him. The authority of Paul's position and message had been undermined by the intruders. Paul's argument from authority is buttressed by several converging lines of evidence: the divine origin of his apostleship (1.1); the revelatory origin of his gospel (1.12, 16); denial of dependence on the Jerusalem leaders (1.16-24); and yet their approval of his message (2.6-9). The bedrock foundation for all these arguments from authority is the extensive argument from the Abraham story in chs. 3-4. For just as the Abraham story was frequently used and expanded to support diverse positions in the Jewish literature of the Second Temple Period, so it is adapted by Paul here to undergird his gospel.

Second, Paul interprets the Abraham story to show its consistency with his gospel.[8] Paul's exposition of the Abraham story is Christocentric: (1) the door for Gentiles to receive the blessing of Abraham has been opened by Christ in his death (3.13, 14); and (2) the seed of Abraham is Christ (3.16).

Third, Paul develops the Abraham argument to defend his mission to the Gentiles. The inclusion of the Gentiles in the sonship and blessing of Abraham is the major theme of Gal. 3.[9]

Fourth, the Abraham story is used to destroy the opponents' biblical basis for compelling the Gentiles to judaize. In contrast to the use of Abraham in much of contemporary Jewish literature, Paul dissociates the Abrahamic promise and its blessing from the law and works of the law. This dissociation is designed to explode any attempt to use Abraham as an example for circumcision and law-observance.

2. The Propositio (2.15-21)

Our rhetorical analysis has highlighted both the *function* and the *form* of Gal. 2.15-21.[10] As for the former, these verses have a dual function, being both a summary of the preceding narrative section and an introduction to the following argument.[11] As a summary they are directly linked to Paul's rebuking speech to Peter at Antioch by the continuation in verse 15 of the same contrast between Jew and Gentile as in verse 14. The reason given for Paul's rebuke is that the withdrawal of Peter and other Jewish Christians from table-fellowship with the Gentiles was an act of 'hypocrisy' (v. 13), for 'they did not walk a straight path (οὐκ ὀρθοποδοῦσιν)[12] with regard to the truth of the gospel' (v. 14). The violation of the truth of the gospel did not come by Peter living ἐθνικῶς καὶ οὐχὶ Ἰουδαϊκῶς, but by his withdrawal from Gentile Christians on the basis of Jewish laws of ritual purity. This separation implied that Gentile Christians were required to adhere to Jewish practices as a basis for table-fellowship with Jewish Christians. In this way, Peter was guilty of transgressing the truth of the gospel by compelling Gentiles to judaize (ἰουδαΐζειν, v. 14c).[13]

The specific issue at stake is the Gentile question: Is it necessary for Gentiles to adopt Jewish customs in order to be included in table-fellowship with Jewish Christians?[14] Behind this question, however, stands the more fundamental issue: Is the truth of the gospel or is the law the basis for determining the question of fellowship between Jewish and Gentile Christians?[15] Verses 15-21 are addressed to this fundamental issue raised by the hypocrisy of Peter at Antioch. These verses are also addressed to the Galatian believers, since this issue of compelling Gentiles to live like Jews is precisely the central issue in the Galatian crisis.

The *propositio* introduces the key terms of the argument, which are then developed in the following chapters: δικαιόω (2.16, 17; cf. 3.8, 11), δικαιοσύνη (2.21; cf. 3.6, 21), ἔργα νόμου (2.16; cf. 3.2, 5, 10), διὰ νόμου (2.19, 21; cf. 3.11, 21), πίστις Ἰησοῦ Χριστοῦ (2.16; cf. 3.2, 5, 7, 8, 9, 11, 12, 14, 22, 23, 24, 25, 26), πιστεύω (2.16; cf. 3.6, 22), Χριστῷ συνεσταύρωμαι, Χριστὸς ἀπέθανεν (2.19, 21; cf. 3.1, 13), and ζῶ (2.20; cf. 3.11, 12, 21). Although these terms are elaborated and nuanced in the ensuing argument, their primary definitions must be established on the basis of their use in this summary of Paul's dispute with Peter regarding the fellowship of Jews and Gentiles in the Church.

As for the form of the *propositio*, we have spoken of that as being
(a) the point of agreement (2.15-16), (b) the point of disagreement
(2.17-18), and (c) the thesis to be developed (2.19-21).[16] Here we
would elaborate as follows:

(a) *The point of agreement* (2.15-16)
Paul presents the substance of verse 16 as a matter commonly
accepted, not as an issue of dispute. The formula εἰδότες ὅτι (or
οἴδαμεν) is frequently used by Paul to introduce a dogmatic
proposition which is known and accepted.[17] The repetition of the
emphatic use of the pronouns—ἡμεῖς (v. 15), καὶ ἡμεῖς (v. 16) and
καὶ αὐτοί (v. 17)—indicates that these verses primarily express the
position of *Jewish* Christians (ἡμεῖς φύσει ᾿Ιουδαῖοι, v. 15).[18] Paul is
here developing the same *a fortiori* argument which he began in verse
15:[19] If Peter, being a Jew, lived as a Gentile and not as a Jew, how
could he require Gentiles to live as Jews (v. 14)? If we who by birth
are Jews and not sinners of the Gentiles (v. 15) confess (εἰδότες) that
we believe in Christ Jesus in order to be justified by faith in Christ
and not by the works of the law (v. 16), then we must also recognize
that Gentiles can only be justfied by faith in Christ, and not by the
works of the law. This last apodosis is not expressly stated, but it is
implied and is more fully developed in chapter 3.

Although the meaning of δικαιόω has long been the subject of
controversy,[20] it may be fairly stated that the forensic sense of this
term in Paul's letters is generally recognized.[21] As a legal metaphor
δικαιόω speaks of God's judgment in favor of someone. Dunn also
points to the covenantal nature of the term: 'God's justification is
God's recognition of Israel as his people, his verdict in favor of Israel
on grounds of his covenant with Israel'.[22] The convenantal aspect of
the judicial pronouncement is the key to understanding its meaning
in Gal. 2.16. Paul's use of δικαιόω in this context is connected with
the Jewish consciousness of covenant status expressed in verse 15:
Jews are included within God's covenant people by birth; but
Gentiles are 'sinners' (ἁμαρτωλοί) because they are outside the
covenant.[23] This Jew–Gentile contrast is intimately linked with the
threefold use of the term δικαιόω in verse 16 by the emphatic καὶ
ἡμεῖς. Paul's point is that the judicial pronouncement of God that
declares someone to be within the covenant people is not based on
Jew–Gentile distinctions. The covenant is no longer conceived in
nationalistic terms. Even though as Jews they claimed a privileged
status, now as Jewish Christians they know that only those who

believe in Jesus Christ are declared by God to belong to the covenant family.[24] The main emphasis of the argument here is that faith in Christ excludes Jewishness as the determining criterion for covenantal status.

This interpretation of δικαιόω is related to the understanding of the phrase ἐξ ἔργων νόμου in 2.16 in terms of 'Jewishness'. The meaning of τὰ ἔργα νόμου in Galatians has usually been defined either as a straightforward reference to actions performed in obedience to the Mosaic law[25] or as a negative reference to legalism— the prideful attempt to establish one's own righteousness through obedience to the law.[26] The first definition draws some support from 3.10 where Paul expands the meaning of τὰ ἔργα νόμου to include 'all the works written in the book of the law'. The second points to 6.13 where Paul impugns the motives of those who desire the Gentile believers to be circumcised ἵνα ἐν τῇ ὑμετέρᾳ σαρκὶ καυχήσωνται. But both these definitions obscure the specific reference of Paul's use of τὰ ἔργα νόμου in 2.16.

In the context of Paul's record of the disputes at Jerusalem (2.3-6) and Antioch (2.11-14), the phrase 'works of the law' refers to circumcision and the Jewish laws of ritual purity. Observance of these laws served as the essential marks of Jewishness.[27] As Dunn observes, 'they functioned as badges of covenantal membership. A member of the covenant people was, by definition, one who observed these practices in particular'.[28] Thus when Paul excludes the possibility of being justified by the works of the law, as he does three times in 2.16, he is not, at this point at least, abrogating the observance of the Mosaic law in general or attacking a prideful attitude. What he is denying is that God's recognition of covenant status for Gentiles depends in any way on observing these distinctively Jewish practices. Paul is appealing to the confession of Jewish Christians themselves that believing in Christ Jesus, not living Ἰουδαϊκῶς (v. 14), is the basis for being justified. It is participation in the death and resurrection of Christ (vv. 19-20), not identification with the Jewish people, that is the basis of membership in the covenant people of God. Hence, faith in Jesus as Messiah is the badge of covenant membership—which badge excludes the marks of Jewish identity as signs of covenant membership.

Recently there have been a number of defenses of the interpretation of the genitive Ἰησοῦ Χριστοῦ as subjective genitive in the phrases διὰ πίστεως Ἰησοῦ Χριστοῦ (Gal. 2.16a) and ἐκ πίστεως Χριστοῦ (2.16c).[29] According to this view, the phrase refers to the faith or faithfulness of Christ. This interpretation accords well with Paul's emphasis elsewhere on the obedience of Christ, with the fact that πίστις is undoubtedly used by Paul in some cases to refer to the faithfulness of God, and with the Hebrew idea of faithfulness often latent in the Septuagintal use of πίστις.[30] Moreover, it can be claimed that this sense of πίστις removes the redundancy between the use of the verb πιστεύω and the noun πίστις in 2.16 and 3.22.[31] But such an interpretation does not fit the specific argument that Paul is developing in 2.15-16. For the main clause of 2.16—καὶ ἡμεῖς εἰς Χριστὸν Ἰησοῦν ἐπιστευσαυεν—expresses in personal terms the experience of Jewish Christians (καὶ ἡμεῖς, cf., ἡμεῖς φύσει Ἰουδαῖοι, v. 15). Thus faith *in* Christ is the focal point of this main clause and, hence, of the entire sentence. The dependent clauses express the reasons and purposes for faith in Christ.

The fact that Christ is the object of the verb πιστεύω in the main clause probably indicates that Christ should be taken as the object of the noun πίστις in the clauses which precede and follow the main clause.[32] The first clause states in general terms the theological conviction that 'man' is not justified by the works of the law but through faith in Jesus Christ. This principle is paralleled by the purpose clause which says the same thing in personal terms (ἵνα δικαιωθῶμεν ἐκ πίστεως Χριστοῦ). In the final clause, Paul paraphrases Ps. 143.2 to show the universal scope (πᾶσα σάρξ) of the same principle.[33] Thus the triple repetition of the key terms δικαιόω, πίστις, πιστεύω, ἔργα νόμου is not simply a redundancy; it serves the purpose of universalizing the personal experience of Jewish Christians. The purpose of this generalization is to show that since Jewish Christians put their faith in Christ on the basis of the conviction that faith in Christ, and not the work of the law (Jewishness), is the basis of justification for 'any man' and 'all flesh', then Jewishness (circumcision, purity laws, etc.) should not be required for the inclusion of Gentiles in the covenant people of God.

The point of agreement is confirmed by the experience of the Gentile believers at Galatia (3.1-5). For just as Jewish Christians had come to know that they were justified by faith in Christ, and not by any Jewish privileges or practices, so Gentile believers experienced the Spirit, the sign of covenant blessing (v. 14), by their faith response to the message of Christ crucified, not by the acceptance of circumcision, Jewish purity laws, or Sabbath observance (4.10). The exclusion of the works of the law as a basis for justification is developed more fully in 3.10-12, 19-25. There the definition of the phrase is expanded to include all the works commanded by the Mosaic law (3.10).

The point of agreement is elaborated more fully in the Abraham argument: Abraham's faith is the original and, therefore, fundamental mark of covenant membership (3.6-7); the original covenant with Abraham included the promise of blessing for the nations (3.8-9); the way of blessing for the Gentiles is opened by the cross of Christ (3.13-14); all those in Christ, who is the seed of Abraham (3.16), inherit the promise to Abraham (3.29); the precedence of the Abrahamic covenant over the Mosaic law means that the Mosaic law cannot nullify or redefine the terms of the Abrahamic covenant (3.15-18).

(b) *The point of disagreement* (2.17-18)

Paul's statement of disagreement contains the charge leveled against his position (2.17) and his refutation of that charge (2.18). Many view v. 17 as Paul's reconstruction of the argument of his opponents.[34] In the context of his reply to Peter it relates directly to the situation at Antioch. But as an introduction to chapter 3, it also reflects the viewpoint of his opponents at Galatia.

The argument of the opponents evidently consisted of two premises and a conclusion: (1) you are seeking to be justified in Christ; (2) you are found to be sinners; (3) therefore, Christ is a servant of sin. The first premise was certainly accepted by Paul. For as Paul says in v. 16, being justified in Christ is the substance of the common confession of all Christians, whether Jewish or Gentile.

The major question in the interpretation of the second premise is the sense of the word 'sinners' (ἁμαρτωλοί).[35] Does this term refer to the pre-conversion status or the post-conversion status of Jewish Christians? The first option appears to follow the logic of verses 15-16—that Jewish Christians before their conversion recognized that they, too, like Gentiles, were sinners, and hence could only attain justification through faith in Christ, not by the works of the law.[36] This interpretation, however, fails to provide an adequate basis for the accusation that Christ promotes sin (Χριστὸς ἁμαρτίας διάκονος). The acknowledgement of one's sinful position and dependence on God's grace for justification in Christ does not require the conclusion that Christ promotes sin, since justification of sinners by grace through faith could conceivably have been followed by a strict observance of the law. Within Judaism, the recognition of sin and free remission of sin through the sacrificial system did not imply that the sacrificial system promoted sin, since observance of the law was the expected response to the grace of atonement.[37]

This first interpretation of ἁμαρτωλοί also fails to fit well with the incident at Antioch.[38] The criticism of Paul, Peter, and the other Jewish Christians was not because of their conviction as to their status as sinners, but because of their practice of living like Gentiles. While undoubtedly theological conviction can be seen to underlie ethical practice, the focus of the opponents' criticism was the Jewish Christians' neglect of Jewish purity laws and, thus, their removal of the distinction between Jew and Gentile.[39]

The second interpretation of ἁμαρτωλοί is a better reflection of the situation at Antioch. Paul, and for a time Peter, had been viewed as 'sinners' because they were eating with Gentiles, and hence disregarding certain statutes of the law. Such behavior put them on the same level as Gentiles, those outside the covenant.[40] This interpretation also makes better sense of the accusation that Christ promotes sin. The fact that they were seeking to be justified in Christ and at the same time breaking laws by living ἐθνικῶς raised the question as to whether Christ is not actually an agent of sin. If identification with Christ promoted unlawful identification with Gentiles, then, it seems to have been argued, Christ promotes sin.

Paul frames this argument of the opponents in the form of a conditional question and counters it with an indignant μὴ γένοιτο.[41] There is considerable debate among scholars whether Paul's μὴ γένοιτο is a negation of the truth of one or both of the premises,[42] or only a negation of the conclusion invalidly derived from premises accepted as true.[43] The confusion exists partly because of the differences of perspective expressed, first in the opponents' argument and then in Paul's rejection of their conclusion.[44] The perspective of the opponents is the perspective of the law—viz., that by the standard of the law, eating a meal with Gentiles shows Jewish Christians to be sinners. The perspective of Paul was the 'truth of the gospel'—viz., that by the standard of the gospel, table-fellowship of Jewish Christians with Gentile believers was not sinful. On the contrary, withdrawal from table-fellowship was hypocrisy; it was a violation of the truth of the gospel. Thus the conclusion of the opponents (that Christ is the agent of sin) is wrong, because what they judge to be sinful (eating with Gentiles) is not really sinful.[45]

Paul's restatement of the charge against his position reflects not only the crisis at Antioch but also the Galatian crisis. For just as the failure of Jewish Christians at Antioch to observe the Jewish food laws caused them to be demoted to the same category as Gentiles, ἁμαρτωλοί,[46] so the failure of Gentile Christians at Galatia to observe circumcision kept them, it was argued, from being promoted to the category of the sons of Abraham. Did this common failure of Jewish Christians and Gentile Christians to keep the law mean that Christ is a minister of sin or that the law is opposed to the promises of God (2.17; 3.21)? Paul rejects both charges—μὴ γένοιτο. He begins his countercharge in 2.18, but the entire Abraham argument of chapter 3 is constructed to answer this accusation.

The introduction of Paul's countercharge in v. 18 with γάρ indicates that Paul is offering an explanation for his rejection of the opponents' charge.[47] Many scholars interpret Paul's argument to be against the rebuilding of the law on the grounds that rebuilding the law will prove him to be a transgressor for breaking the law.[48] In other words, the transgression of breaking the law is admitted, if the law is reestablished. So the transgression of verse 18 is equivalent to the sin of verse 17. However, the contrast between παραβάτης and ἁμαρτωλοί suggests that Paul views the rebuilding of the law rather than the breaking of it as the real transgression.[49] By his conduct, Paul declared that laws which create distinctions between Jewish and Gentile Christians are invalid. While he admits that breaking them would cause him to be classified with the ἁμαρτωλοί (v. 17) from the perspective of the law, he goes on to insist that any submission to those commands of the law which he had broken would in fact constitute transgression (v. 18) from the perspective of the gospel.

The implication of this assertion in the present context is that Peter's reversion to observance of the Jewish food laws was the real transgression.[50] According to verse 14a, the real transgression of Peter was that he did not live consistently according to the truth of the gospel. The gospel had destroyed all essential distinctions between Jews and Gentiles, and hence rendered all laws which upheld those distinctions no longer operative. Whoever observed all the Jewish law—and so maintained such Jew–Gentile distinctions— denied the truth of the gospel. Whoever lived according to the truth of the gospel that denied such Jew–Gentile distinctions, would inevitably violate the standards of the law that required these distinctions. Duncan makes this point in his comment on 2.18:[51]

> If it is regarded as 'sin' for a Jewish-Christian to eat with a Gentile,
> it is sin only in the sense of a technical breach of a regulation; but if
> a Christian allows such a regulation to stand between him and

eating with a brother-in-Christ, then he is breaking God's law in a much more heinous sese, for he is doing violence to the will of God as clearly revealed in Christ.

This same sense of παραβάτης can be observed in Rom. 2.25, 27 where those who have the written code and circumcision are still accounted guilty as being transgressors of the law.

By his use of the Abraham argument Paul demonstrates that denial of the truth of the gospel by rebuilding these Jew–Gentile distinctions is a denial of the promise of blessing for the Gentiles (3.8). The conclusion of chapter 3 indicates that Paul's primary purpose for the Abraham argument is to prove that the Jew–Gentile distinctions have been removed in Christ (3.28)—or, as stated in the *propositio*, that they must not be rebuilt (2.18).

(c) *The thesis statement* (2.19-21)

Before taking up the Abraham story, however, Paul first sets forth in 2.19-21 his own personal confession of faith as a paradigm for all believers.[52] This paradigmatic statement serves as an explanation of the denial in v. 17 that Christ is the servant of sin and of the assertion in v. 18 that rebuilding the legal distinction between Jew and Gentile is transgression. In v. 19 Paul declares that he has experienced death to the law by the intrumentality of the law (διὰ νόμου). Διὰ νόμου has traditionally been interpreted in terms of Paul's introspective, subjective experience with the law. As Burton puts it, 'the law . . . by his experience under it taught him his own inability to meet its spiritual requirements and its own inability to make him righteous, and thus led him finally to abandon it and to seek salvation in Christ'.[53] Although such a view may be deduced from Paul's discussions of the law elsewhere, the immediate context does not suggest that this kind of introspective experience was the means of Paul's death to the law. Rather, in context, Paul declares that his death was accomplished by identification with the cross of Christ— Χριστῷ συνεσταύρωμαι.[54] The interpretation of διὰ νόμου in light of the statement Χριστῷ συνεσταύρωμαι makes it clear that death to the law through the law is accomplished by identification with the death of Christ. According to the amplification of the meaning of Christ's death in 3.13, the law pronounced a curse on Christ as he hung on the cross. In this sense, Christ died διὰ νόμου. By bearing the curse for his people, Christ redeemed them from its penalty. Being crucified with Christ, the believer also dies because of the curse of the law on one who hangs on the cross—and so, in this sense, he also dies διὰ νόμου.[55] Now that Christ and the believer have died under the curse of the law, they are no longer under the curse and are, therefore, free from the condemning power of the law.

The perfect tense of συνεσταύρωμαι points to a permanent condition of the Christian in relation to the law—viz., he remains dead and fully punished. Since the law can no longer condemn the Christians, it can no longer be used to classify Jewish Christians who eat with Gentiles as sinners. If a Christian attempts to rebuild the separation between Jews and Gentiles on the basis of the law (v. 18), he denies the essence of the truth of the gospel—viz., Χριστῷ συνεσταύρωμαι. It is the message of Christ crucified (3.1) that should have fortified the Galatian believers to resist any attempt to make them judaize.

Death to the law is not moral license, but the means for achieving the highest goal—ἵνα θεῷ ζήσω (2.19). This ζωή θεῷ is empowered by Christ; it is lived by faith in Christ; it is motivated by the sacrificial love of the Son of God (2.20). Only by participation in the death (Χριστῷ συνεσταύρωμαι) and resurrection (ζῇ δὲ ἐν ἐμοὶ Χριστός) of Christ can one achieve the goal of living for God.[56] Participation in the death and resurrection of Christ does not nullify the grace of God (v. 21a). On the contrary, it is the attempt to attain righteousness διὰ νόμου that negates the value of Christ's death (v. 21b). The possibility of righteousness διὰ νόμου (v. 21) is excluded by the experience of the Christian who διὰ νόμου died to the law by participation in the crucifixion of Christ in order that he might live to God (v. 19). It is the reality of the Christian's experience as to the efficacy of Christ's death that cancels the option of righteousness by the law.[57] The occurence of διὰ νόμου in v. 19 and v. 21 brings life (ἵνα θεῷ ζήσω) (v. 19) and righteousness (δικαιοσύνη) (v. 21) into close association. This same association of life and righteousness is found in 3.21: εἰ γὰρ ἐδόθη νόμος ὁ δυνάμενος ζῳοποιῆσαι, ὄντως ἐκ νόμου ἂν ἦν ἡ δικαιοσύνη. In succinct form, Paul has set forth in 2.19-21 his thesis that the gospel, not the law, is the source of life and righteousness. The law has been excluded as the source of life and righteousness because to use it in this way negates the value of Christ's death and separates Jews and Gentiles.[58] So Paul uses the Abraham story to prove that the truth of the gospel is that Christ's death is the source of life and righteousness (3.13) and that Jews and Gentiles are one in Christ (3.28-29).

3. Analysis of Paul's Abraham Argument (3.1-29)

As we observed earlier in considering the chiastic structures of Galatians,[59] the development of the major themes in Gal. 3.1–4.11 can be viewed as a conceptual chiasm:

- a rebuking questions (3.1-5)
- b bestowal of the Spirit (3.1, 5)
- c faith—sonship (3.6-9)
- d faith—law (3.10-14)
- e promise—law (3.15-18)
- e law—promise (3.19-22)
- d law—faith (3.23-25)
- c sonship—faith (3.26-29)
- b bestowal of the Spirit (4.1-7)
- a rebuking question (4.8-11)

This chiastic structure will provide the framework for our analysis of the Abraham argument in Gal. 3.1-29.

(a) *Rebuking Questions and* (b) *the Bestowal of the Spirit* (3.1-5)

The Abraham argument is introduced by five barbed questions which rebuke the Galatians for their foolishness.[60] They have failed to understand the significance of the message of Christ crucified (3.1); they have not realized the implications of their experience of the Spirit (3.2-5). The Galatian believers were essentially guilty of the same offense as Peter—viz., they had denied the truth of the gospel by their foolish behavior.[61] In light of Christ's death and the experience of the Spirit they should have known better than to succumb to the bewitching influence of the intruders.[62] Paul formulates his questions as sharp antitheses which are designed to break this bewitching spell by showing the contradiction between the Galatians' interest in the works of the law (vv. 2, 5) and the flesh (v. 3), on the one hand, and , on the other ἡ ἀκοὴ πίστεως and their experience of the Spirit. Their past (vv. 2, 3) and present (v. 5) experience of the Spirit is a well-known, indisputable fact. So Paul argues from their experience to prove the validity of his dissociation of ἡ ἀκοὴ πίστεως (vv. 2, 5) from τὰ ἔργα νόμου and the dissociation of 'beginning in the spirit' from 'finishing in the flesh'. This argument by dissociation forces the readers to choose between mutually exclusive alternatives. They are not permitted to accept the both-and synthesis of the intruders. It is an either-or choice.

The nature of the alternatives has been disputed. We have already considered various interpretations of the phrase 'works of the law' and suggested it has specific reference to regulations of the Jewish community which maintain their distinctive, national identity.[63] In other words, Paul is reminding his converts that they did not have to become Jewish proselytes in order to receive the Spirit in the first place (3.2) or to continue to experience the supply of the Spirit and miracles in their lives (3.5). The meaning of the phrase 'works of the law' is clarified by the use of σάρξ in 3.3. R. Jewett has cogently argued that 'works of the law' (3.2, 5) and 'flesh' (3.3) should be taken as synonymous in light of 6.13 (θέλουσιν ὑμᾶς περιτέμνεσθαι ἵνα ἐν τῇ ὑμετέρᾳ σαρκὶ καυχήσωνται) where flesh refers to circumcised flesh.[64] Therefore, 'works of the law' refers principally, though not exclusively, to circumcision and other marks of Jewish identity.

The exact meaning of ἡ ἀκοή is difficult to determine. The basic options have been outlined by Hays:[65]

If ἀκοή means 'hearing':

   a) (πίστις = 'believing') 'by hearing with faith'[66]
   b) (πίστις = 'the faith') 'by hearing "the faith"'
      = 'by hearing the gospel'.[67]

If ἀκοή means 'message, proclamation':

   c) (πίστις = 'believing') 'from the message that enables faith'[68]
   d) (πίστις = 'the faith') 'from the message of "the faith"'
      = 'from the gospel-message'.[69]

Hays chooses the fourth option, principally because he supposes that 'Paul's primary intention is not at all to juxtapose one type of human activity ('works') to another ('believing–hearing') but rather to juxtapose human activity to God's activity, as revealed in the 'proclamation'. The antithesis would then lie between human 'works' and God's ἀκοή (message) which comes *extra nos*'.[70] Such an interpretation fits Hays' thesis that the gospel story provides the substructure for the entire chapter. But his interpretation of ἐξ ἀκοῆς πίστεως fails to observe the specific reference of Paul's argument.

There is no evidence that Paul is arguing generally against 'human activity'. What he argues against is a very specific type of human activity summarized in the question addressed to Peter in 2.14. Paul is fighting against any attempt to make his converts turn to judaizing. When this specific reference is kept in mind, it is not difficult to see the antithesis of 3.2, 5 as being a juxtaposition of one type of human activity (works of the law) to that of another (hearing-believing). And if this is so, then the parallelism between these two alternatives serves as evidence for understanding 'faith' in the subjective sense of 'believing'.[71]

Furthermore, the use of the verb πιστεύω in 3.6 is confirmation that Paul is referring to a response of faith. The comparative conjunction καθώς sets up a correspondence between the faith response of the Galatians and Abraham's faith response. Hays, following Gaston, argues that 'the primary point of the comparison must be God's working in both cases, rather than the faith of Abraham and the Galatians'.[72] But since the inference which Paul draws in 3.7 from his quotation of Gen. 15.6 focuses on πίστις, we must conclude that πίστις is the point of the comparison and must be interpreted in light of Gen. 15.6. And if this be so, then it refers to the human activity of believing. It is more likely, therefore, that the phrase ἐξ ἀκοῆς πίστεως denotes this response ('by hearing with faith') than it does the message which evoked the response ('from the message that enables faith').

The dissociation of 'beginning in the spirit' and 'finishing in the flesh' sets up the antithesis between spirit and flesh which recurs in 4.29; 5.16-23; and 6.8. In 4.23, 29, the son 'born according to the flesh' is clearly a reference to the Jew who holds to the Sinai convenant (4.24) and to the present Jerusalem (4.25) as the bases of his identity. This is the same one who desires to boast in circumcised flesh—i.e., in the proselytization of Gentile believers at Galatia (6.13). Jewett observes that 'the opposition between flesh and spirit is thus not rooted in Hellenistic dualism inherent in the terms themselves but rather in the historical conflict between those depending upon their circumcision in the flesh and those depending on Christ'.[73] Jewett then generalizes: 'man's alternative is between trusting in that which his own flesh can accomplish and in trusting in Christ'.[74] While Jewett's observation captures the specific meaning of the contrast between flesh and spirit in its context, his generalization tends to move us too far away from the issues at stake at Galatia. Paul's specific point is that the Galatians' alternative is between (1) living by the Spirit which they received when they believed the message of Christ crucified, and (2) seeking perfection by circumcision (and other rites such as food laws and Sabbath observance), which would identify them as proselyte Jews. By means of the antitheses in his questions, Paul attempts to make the Galatians realize that it is

112   *Abraham in Galatians*

foolish to judaize since that has obviously not played a part in their experience of the Spirit. He wants them to be compelled by the facts of their own experience to answer his last question ἐξ ἀκοῆς πίστεως.[75]

(c) Gentiles are Identified as Sons of Abraham by their Faith (3.6-9)

Paul's quotation of Gen. 15.6 in 3.6 is directly linked to the expected answer in verse 5—viz., ἐξ ἀκοῆς πίστεως.[76] The Galatians' expected answer is confirmed by the authority of Scripture. The conjunction καθώς may be an abbreviated form of the introductory formula καθὼς γέγραπται, which Paul uses elsewhere.[77] What stands written in Scripture is set forth as the final arbiter in the dispute. Paul assumes that the Galatians also accepted the normative value of Scripture. As Mussner remarks, 'Paulus ist φύσει Ἰουδαῖος und rabbinisch geschult. Und so kennt er die gottliche Autoritat der Schrift und ihre umfassende und normative Geltung'.[78]

The argument from authority is not only an argument from the authority of Scripture; it is also an argument from the model of Abraham's faith. The words καθὼς Ἀβραάμ which introduce the text of Scripture draw attention to Abraham. It is assumed that if the experience of the Galatians corresponds to the experience of the Patriarch, then their experience conforms to the will of God. Bonnard notes that 'la figure scripturaire d'Abraham servira donc à révéler aux Galates la volonté actuelle de Dieu pour eux: il ne s'agira pas d'imiter Abraham, mais de se laisser instruire par lui des intentions permanentes de Dieu à l'égard de son peuple'.[79] The pattern established by Abraham's relationship with God is employed by Paul, just as it is so often used in Jewish literature, as a standard for the behavior and as a basis for the identity of God's people.[80]

Verses 6 and 7 taken together form an argument by enthymeme. The conclusion (ἄρα) in v. 7 is derived from the implicit premise that as God dealt with Abraham, so he will deal with all men.[81] The explicit premise states that 'Abraham believed God and it was reckoned to him for righteousness' (v. 6). Paul expects the Galatians to draw the logical conclusion that οἱ ἐκ πίστεως, οὗτοι υἱοί εἰσιν Ἀβραάμ.

Mussner notes that this is not the conclusion which we might have expected: 'Paulus formuliert diesen Schluss nicht so, wie zunächst zu erwarten wäre: "Erkennt also, dass der Mensch aus Glauben gerechtfertigt wird und nicht aus Gesetzeswerken"'.[82] Yet this unexpected conclusion alerts us to the central issue in the dispute; it signals that the reason why Paul's conclusion refers to Abrahamic sonship rather than to righteousness is that Abraham sonship was the disputed issue at Galatia.[83] As we observed in dealing with the opponents' use of Abraham, the circumcision campaign was probably supported by a reference to God's original command to Abraham to receive circumcision with all his household as a sign of the covenant in the flesh (Gen. 17).[84] Along with the command came the warning that the one who was not circumcised would be cut off from God's people for he had broken the covenant. No doubt the record of Abraham's faithful obedience to this command of God—as well as to the entire Mosaic law—was enjoined on Galatian Christians as the standard for inclusion in Abrahamic sonship. Perhaps Gen. 15.6 was used by the opponents to support their crusade. If so, it would have been interpreted in line with the usual contemporary Jewish interpretation of the verse, which understood the faith of Abraham as equivalent to his righteous behavior—viz., his acceptance of circumcision, his observance of Mosaic law, and his faithful obedience when tested.[85] This interpretation involved taking ἐλογίσθη αὐτῷ εἰς δικαιοσύνην to mean that 'his faith is naturally reckoned as righteousness, for this is what it really is, viz., obedience to God's will'.[86] And so on this basis, the uncircumcised Galatian believers were excluded from the Abrahamic covenant.

Paul uses Gen. 15.6 to redefine the basis of Abrahamic sonship. In his interpretation, the verse proves that the sign of the covenant—the true sign of Abrahamic sonship—is faith, not circumcision.[87] The key word that Paul picks out of his quotation is ἐπίστευσεν. The noun πίστις in verse 7 is directly linked to the verb form in verse 6, and so has the same meaning. This bond of meaning between the verb and the noun undermines the attempts of Howard, Gaston, and Hays to interpret the noun πίστις throughout this chapter as a reference to the faith, faithfulness, or faith-act of Christ. For the words καθώς (v. 6) and ἄρα (v. 7) link the noun πίστις in v. 5 to the verb πιστεύω in v. 6 and the noun πίστις in v. 7 in an unbreakable chain.[88] And this connection makes it clear that οἱ ἐκ πίστεως (v. 7) include the Galatian Christians who, like Abraham, believe, and therefore are the sons of Abraham. Thus the word 'son' is used in the Semitic sense to connote spiritual kinship.[89]

Paul's use of Gen. 15.6 in this way to redefine the sign of the covenant as faith involves a redefinition of the term faith. The meaning of οἱ ἐκ πίστεως is determined by the first occurrence of ἐκ πίστεως where the object of faith is emphasized by a threefold repetition:

διὰ πίστεως Ἰησοῦ Χριστοῦ	(2.16a)
εἰς Χριστὸν ἐπιστεύσαμεν	(2.16b)
ἐκ πίστεως Χριστοῦ	(2.16c)

Faith is primarily defined as 'faith in Christ'. That is why Paul can speak of the time 'before faith came' (3.23a), the time when faith was revealed (3.23b) and the time when faith came (3.25). Paul reads Gen. 15.6 through the lens of his experience of faith in Christ.[90] There is no attempt here to spell out the relation of Abraham's faith to the Christian's faith in Christ. That relation is worked out in Rom. 4 where Paul argues that Abraham's trust in the ability of God to keep his promise by giving life to the dead is similar to the Christian's belief in him who raised Jesus from the dead. In Gal. 3, however, Paul simply makes the point that it is faith in Christ that marks the Galatians as the sons of Abraham, who also believed.

Paul's definition of faith in this passage does not entail a dissociation of faith from works in general, as is so often claimed. Paul clearly states in 5.6 that πίστις δι' ἀγάπης ἐνεργουμένη. Rather, faith is dissociated from a certain type of works, namely, circumcision and such other works as were used as means of gaining or maintaining Jewish identity.[91] For Paul, faith in Christ is the means of identification with the covenant people of God; faith in Christ is the sign of the covenant. The restrictive sense of οὗτοι in verse 7 implies an exclusion of all who are not οἱ ἐκ πίστεως from the covenant people.[92] And in 3.10 Paul develops the severance of ὅσοι ἐξ ἔργων from the covenant blessing.

Paul's definition of faith implies that he did not understand ἐλογίσθη αὐτῷ εἰς δικαιοσύνην as his opponents probably did, to mean that Abraham's faith was reckoned to be equivalent to Abraham's righteous behavior—defined in terms of distinctively Jewish customs (nationalistic righteousness).[93] The meaning of righteousness for Paul is clarified by the close connection of this passage with v. 5. As Bruce points out:

> The connexion implied in καθώς would be lost unless there were the closest possible link between receiving the Spirit and being justified. True, Abraham, could not be said to have received the Spirit through faith, for he lived in the age of promise, not of

fulfilment ... The Galatians, who lived in the age of fulfilment, had received the Spirit as well as a righteous standing before God—alike by faith.[94]

The correspondence of God's activity among the Galatians—supplying the Spirit and working miracles (v. 5)—with the reckoning of righteousness (v. 6) shows that righteousness is more than a forensic concept connoting judicial acquittal.[95] Righteousness also connotes the gracious activity of God among his people, those whom he has aquitted and brought within covenant relationship. Paul's point here is that the experience of the Spirit in the lives of Gentiles who were outside the sphere of Jewish law demonstrates that it was their faith and not their observance of the law which brought about their status and their experience of God's activity among them as the covenant people of God—just as it was Abraham's faith which was the basis for his status and his experience of God's miraculous activity within the covenant.[96]

Paul moves his argument forward in midrashic fashion by qualifying the interpretation of his first text with a second quotation.[97] The purpose of this second quotation is to amplify the definition of the phrase οἱ ἐκ πίστεως. That this is the aim of the quotation can be seen by looking ahead to the inference which Paul draws from it: ὥστε οἱ ἐκ πίστεως. . . (v. 9). The conclusion from Gen. 15.6 that οἱ ἐκ πίστεως are sons of Abraham (v. 7) apparently did not go far enough for Paul. He desires to support this conclusion with additional scriptural authority. He is concerned to prove that the principle of righteousness by faith attested for Abraham in Gen. 15.6 is explicitly extended by Scripture itself to the Gentiles, i.e., that God's covenant with Abraham includes blessing for the Gentiles.[98] The text which Paul quotes is an amalgamation of Gen. 12.3 and Gen. 18.18.[99] The phrase πάντα τὰ ἔθνη from Gen. 18.18 is inserted in place of the phrase πᾶσαι αἱ φυλαί. This change highlights Paul's concern to quote an explicit scriptural reference to the Gentiles. His primary purpose is to demonstrate that Scripture witnesses to the inclusion of the Gentiles in the blessing promised to Abraham.

The opponents may have interpreted this promise of blessing for Gentiles in Abraham (ἐν σοί) to mean that Gentiles will be incorporated among the descendants of Abraham by circumcision and the observance of the Mosaic law, and so receive the blessing.[100] Paul, however, interprets the promise as a prophecy (προϊδοῦσα ἡ γραφή) of the present experience of Gentile believers.[101] Scripture foresaw what the Galatians have experienced. And so Paul takes the pains to show that their experience of the Spirit by faith in Christ is parallel to Abraham's experience of being accounted righteous by faith (vv. 5-6). In v. 14 he makes it clear that their experience of the Spirit equals the experience of the promised blessing of Abraham. Because[102] the Scripture foresaw that it would be by faith that God would justify the Gentiles, it preached the gospel—i.e., Paul's gospel to the Gentiles (1.16; 2.8-9)—beforehand to Abraham.

Viewed from the perspective of present fulfillment,[103] this scriptural promise legitimated Paul's argument for the inclusion of the Gentiles in the full blessing of Abraham. It put matters not on the basis of proselytization, i.e., circumcision and the observance of the Mosaic law, but on the basis of faith in Christ. Thus Paul draws the conclusion: ὥστε οἱ ἐκ πίστεως εὐλογοῦνται σὺν τῷ πιστῷ Ἀβραάμ.

The noun πίστεως and the adjective πιστῷ are linked in the progression of the argument to the verb ἐπίστευσεν in Gen. 15.6 and should therefore be translated 'those who believe' and 'believing'.[104] The attempt by Hays, Gaston, and Howard to interpret ἐκ πίστεως and οἱ ἐκ πίστεως as references to the faithfulness of God or the faith of Christ fails to take into account this close connection between these nouns and the verb in Gen. 15.6. It is true, as Hays points out, that the Gentiles are not blessed simply because they believe as Abraham believed. The blessing to the Gentiles comes because of the promise made to Abraham.[105] But Hays seems to miss the flow of the argument when he makes an absolute dichotomy in saying, 'The Gentiles are blessed not on the analogy of Abraham, but 'in' him'.[106] Paul's argument cannot be so easily reduced to one category. Verses 5-7 argue on the basis of the analogy of Abraham's faith. That is the point of the comparative conjunction καθώς. Verses 8-9 build on that argument and carry it forward by pointing to the promise of blessing in Abraham.[107] The analogy of faith is the basis of solidarity with Abraham. The solidarity with Abraham is the basis of sharing in the blessing promised to Abraham.[108] The Gentiles who are blessed with Abraham are those who, like him, believe.

(d) *The Severance of* ὅσοι ἐξ ἔργων νόμου *from* οἱ ἐκ πίστεως (3.10-14)
Having included Gentile believers within the circle of Abrahamic blessing, Paul now develops an argument by severance to exclude ὅσοι ἐξ ἔργων νόμου from that circle. This radical severance of these two groups intensifies his rebukes for foolishness. Galatian believers

had been lured into thinking that they could only be included fully in the promised blessing of Abraham by keeping the law of Moses. Thus οἱ ἐκ πίστεως became merged with οἱ ἐξ ἔργων νόμου. Paul, however, utterly rejects this synthesis; 'those of faith' are already within the circle of the Abrahamic blessing (v. 9), while 'those of the works of the law' are under a curse (v. 10). The scriptural authority for the severance of these two groups of people is derived from two sets of antithetical texts: the first contrasting the promise of blessing for Gentiles in Abraham (Gen. 12.3; 18.18) with the pronouncement of a curse upon all those who do not keep all the law of Moses (Deut. 27.26); the second setting the principle that the righteous shall live by faith (Hab. 2.4) in opposition to the principle that the one who does these things (the commands of the law of Moses) shall live in them (Lev. 18.5).

The interpretation of Paul's use of these texts is the subject of extensive controversy. The basic problem in the interpretation of his use of Deut. 27.26 is the difficulty of relating this text to the opening statement that 'whoever is of the works of the law is under a curse'. The text seems to state the opposite: 'Cursed is everyone who does not abide by all the things written in the book of the law, and do them'. How can Paul support his statement that those who are of the works of the law are under a curse with a text that says that those who do not keep the law are under a curse? Most interpreters resolve this contradiction by assuming that Paul left his minor premise unstated.[109] This premise states that no one has in fact fulfilled all the law. The argument is an enthymeme: the explicit major premise is the biblical text (all who do not keep all that is written in the book of the law are under a curse); the implicit minor premise is the universal lack of fulfillment of all the law; the conclusion is the opening phrase of the verse (whoever is of the works of the law is under a curse).

McGonigal,[110] following D. Fuller, his mentor,[111] rejects this interpretation because it takes the phrase 'works of law' as a reference to what the Mosaic law actually demands and, therefore, the Mosaic law is set over against faith. According to McGonigal, 'this interpretation is impossible, for, as we have already seen, the phrase "works of law" does not refer to what the Mosaic law commands, but rather to the distortion of that law which makes it a means of self-glorification through religious actions'. Thus the phrase 'works of the law' is interpreted as a reference to prideful legalism.

Cosgrove uses this same definition in his reconstruction of the argument of 3.10-12:[112]

10a	All legalists are under a curse
10b	Because Deut. 27.26 (the Mosaic law itself) lays a curse on such attempted bribery of God (=legalism).
11a	Moreover, that no one is justified before God by legalism is evident,
11b	because Hab. 2.4 says, 'He who through faith is righteous shall live',
12a	and legalism is not from faith
12b	but rather legalism is 'he who does them shall live by them' way of salvation (as you legalists are always saying).

This reconstruction of the argument, however, which is based upon the definition of 'works of the law' as being actions directly opposed to the revelatory Mosaic law, ignores Paul's clear definition of 'the works of the law' seen in his use of an equivalent phrase in quoting Deut. 27.26—viz., πᾶσιν τοῖς γεγραμμένοις ἐν τῷ βιβλίῳ τοῦ νόμου τοῦ ποιῆσαι αὐτά (3.10b). For as Robertson points out, 'works of the law' and 'doing' the written requirements of the Mosaic Law are, in this verse, essentially identical.[113]

Another reconstruction is developed by Bultmann and Schlier who argue that the curse is 'because man's effort to achieve his salvation by keeping the law only leads him into sin, indeed this effort itself in the end is already sin. ... sin is man's self-powered striving to undergird his own existence in forgetfulness of his creaturely existence'.[114] Schlier explains that 'der Fluch haftet ... an dem ποιεῖν selbst, sofern es sich auf die ἔργα νόμου bezieht'.[115] Yet in opposition to this interpretation, it must be pointed out that the curse is incurred for *not* doing the law rather than for *doing* it.[116]

Sanders argues that Paul's use of Deut. 27.26 does not imply any implicit premise about a failure to fulfil the law.[117] As Sanders sees it, Paul chose this text only because it connects 'law' with 'curse'. The text is used as something of a negative proof for the positive statement in 3.8, which statement alleges that Gentiles will be blessed in Abraham. The word 'blessed' naturally suggests its antithesis, 'cursed'. Paul states in 3.10a that those who are of the works of the law are under a curse. But he then moves on in vv. 11 and 12 to argue that righteousness is not by the law because it is by faith, and so the law is not of faith. According to Sanders, Paul's argument against the law, therefore, is not based on the premise that the law cannot be fulfilled; it is based on the dogmatic conclusion that righteousness cannot be by the law because it is by faith in Christ. Thus Sanders asserts that Paul's rejection of 'the works of the law' is simply the consequence of his conviction that righteousness is found in Christ. Furthermore, Sanders claims that Paul's concept of righteousness is not the Jewish concept of maintaining one's status in the covenant. 'Righteousness by faith' language in Paul is transfer terminology which describes 'a transfer to the body of the saved'. And since Christ effects this transfer, the law cannot be the means of transfer.[118]

Sanders' interpretation is significant in that it builds upon the primary emphasis in Paul's argument against the law: the implications of the gospel message (2.19-20, 21; 3.1, 13). There remains, however, grounds for claiming, against Sanders, that 3.10 contains an additional, albeit minor, argument against the law.[119] D. Moo points out that the quotation of Deut. 27.26 in 3.10 is intended to explain why (γάρ) a curse comes upon all those who are of the works of the law. Moreover, the text clearly attributes the curse to 'not remaining in *all* the things written in the book of the law'. In other words, as Moo observes, 'the curse is specifically expalined to be the result of *failure to do the law*. Thus, although Paul does not state in so many words that no one does the law, his assertion that 'all who' (ὅσοι) rely on 'works of the law' for justification are cursed makes sense only if, in fact, 'all' fail to do the law'.[120]

Failure to keep the law is explicitly attributed to the οἱ περιτεμνό-μενοι in 6.13.[121] In the context of the Galatian dispute, the appellation ὅσοι ἐξ ἔργων νόμου refers primarily to those who were persuading the Galatian believers to enter their circle by keeping the law. Paul points out that the people of this circle were not keeping the law themselves. It may be that 3.10 has in mind such occasions of law-breaking.[122] Paul seems especially concerned to prove to the Galatians that the very ones who were inviting them to join the group of law-keepers were under a curse since they themselves were law-breakers. His argument appears to include *a fortiori* reasoning: if the law-keepers themselves are under a curse since even they have not kept *all* the law, then the risk of incurring a curse is even greater for Gentile believers who accept only certain items of the law in order to identify with Israel. An acceptance of such items—such as circumcision—obligates them to keep the whole law (5.3). And if 'those of the works of the law' cannot keep the whole law (6.13, cf. 2.14), then surely the Galatian believers will not be able to do so either. Hence, they will surely be under a more severe curse.

The reality of this curse is intended to dissuade Galatian believers from seeking to belong to 'those of the works of the law' and so placing themselves under the curse.[123] Paul's argument is designed to demonstrate the foolishness of seeking membership among ὅσοι ἐξ ἔργων νόμου. So Paul attempts to accomplish a complete severance of the ὅσοι ἐξ ἔργων νόμου from the οἱ ἐκ πίστεως.

In verses 11-12 the argument by severance is restated in a way that parallels the severance in verses 8-10. The thesis statement of v. 11a is parallel to the thesis statement of v. 8a, though expressing its opposite:

v. 8a: ἐκ πίστεως δικαιοῖ τὰ ἔθνη ὁ θεός
v. 11a: ἐν νόμῳ οὐδεὶς δικαιοῦται παρὰ τῷ θεῷ δῆλον

The citation in 11b is similar to the inference drawn in v. 9 that is based upon the citation in v. 8b.

v. 9   οἱ ἐκ πίστεως εὐλογοῦνται.
v. 11b ὁ δίκαιος ἐκ πίστεως ζήσεται.

The thesis statement of 12a is a corollary of the thesis statement of 10a:

v. 10a   ὅσοι γὰρ ἐξ ἔργων νόμου εἰσίν, ὑπὸ κατάραν εἰσίν
v. 12a   ὁ δὲ νόμος οὐκ ἔστιν ἐκ πίστεως

The citation in 12b is parallel to the citation in 10b and states its converse:

v. 10b   ἐπικατάρατος πᾶς ὃς οὐκ ἐμμένει πᾶσιν τοῖς γεγραμμένοις
                  ἐν τῷ βιβλίῳ τοῦ νόμου τοῦ ποιῆσαι αὐτά.
v. 12b   ὁ ποιήσας αὐτὰ ζήσεται ἐν αὐτοῖς

The contrast between 'the righteous one by faith' (v. 11) and 'the one who does them' (v. 12) adds to the contrast already established between 'the blessed' (vv. 8-9) and 'the cursed' (v. 10). And this additional contrast is constructed to dissociate righteousness (v. 11a) and faith (v. 12a) from the law.

The proposition that 'by the law nobody is justified before God' is an echo of the confession of Jewish Christians in 2.16.[124] The use of ἐν νόμῳ (3.11a) rather than ἐξ ἔργων νόμου (2.16; 3.2, 5, 10) is a reflection of LXX language in v. 10 (ἐμμένει ...) and v. 12 (ἐν αὐτοῖς). The ἐν is not instrumental; it expresses the primary orientation of life, the sphere of existence. This statement of v. 11a is not based upon the assumption of universal failure to keep the law; rather it is proved by the 'obvious' fact (δῆλου ὅτι)[125] presented in the paraphrase of Hab. 2.4 that ὁ δίκαιος ἐκ πίστεως ζήσεται.[126] Paul uses the Hab. 2.4 text as a mirror of Christian experience—his own (cf. 2.16-21) and the Galatians' (cf. 3.1-8). All three terms in the citation have already been defined in light of Christian experience. Ἐκ πίστεως is shorthand for ἐκ πίστεως Χριστοῦ, 'by faith in Christ' (2.16).[127] The phrase ὁ δίκαιος ἐκ πίστεως repeats the thesis that both Jewish Christian (2.16) and Gentile Christians (3.8a) are justified by faith in Christ.[128] The close connection between δικαιοσύνη and ζωή (2.19-21; cf. 3.21) is given biblical confirmation by the insistence that spiritual life depends upon righteousness gained through faith (cf. 2.19-20; 6.8).[129] Thus it is Christian experience backed by biblical authority which excludes the possibility that anybody can be justified before God by law (v. 11a). Hence, righteousness is dissociated from law.

In v. 12a faith is dissociated from the law: 'the law is not of faith'. This dissociation is explained by Lev. 18.5 which offers life on the basis of doing the works of the law. The law is not of faith because it demands doing the works of the law as the way to life, whereas it has just been demonstrated (v. 11) that righteousness by faith is the way to life.[130] The offer of Lev. 18.5, therefore, is demonstrated to be purely hypothetical. The clear implication of 3.21 is that the law is not able to make alive. The law demands perfect obedience (v. 10) and offers life on the basis of this perfect obedience (v. 12), but in itself the law is incapable of engendering life or righteousness before God (3.21).[131]

Paul is not making an abstract contrast here between 'believing' and 'doing'.[132] His rebuke, rather, is aimed at the folly of depending on the works of the law as a means of participating in the life and blessing of the covenant people of God.[133]

The place of the Christological statement of 3.13-14 in Paul's argument has been variously interpreted.[134] Sanders says that 'Gal. 3.13 is not the keystone of the argument, but has a subsidiary place in explaining how the curse (3.10) is removed'.[135] Beker sees 3.13-14 as simply one of at least three different soteriologies presented by Paul in Gal. 3 which cannot be harmonized or arranged hierarchically.[136] On the other hand, H. Kuhn claims that 3.13 provides 'den exegetischen Schlussel' for the entire argument.[137] And Hays argues that the Christological statement of 3.1, 13-14, 22, 26-28, and 4.3-6 provide the 'narrative substructure' for Gal. 3-4.[138] For our purposes, it is important to see how this statement functions in the rebuke section of Galatians, and so clarify its role in the Abraham argument.

The central place of Paul's statement in vv. 13-14 is appreciated when it is viewed as an amplification of his rebuke in vv. 1-2. The Galatian believers, who were so foolish as to turn from the message of Christ crucified (v. 1) and the reception of the Spirit (v. 2) to the works of the law, are confronted again with the cross of Christ (v. 13) as the means to the reception of the Spirit (v. 14b). The sudden juxtaposition of Χριστός (v. 13) and νόμος (vv. 10-12) dramatically emphasizes the dissociation of these two alternatives:[139] to live ἐν νόμῳ (v. 11; or ἐν αὐτοῖς, v. 12) leaves one under the curse of the law and shuts the door to justification before God; to live ἐν Χριστῷ Ἰησοῦ (v. 14a) frees one from the curse of the law and opens the door to the blessing of Abraham—i.e., the reception of the Spirit (v. 14b), by means of Christ becoming a curse on the cross. Thus Paul has attempted to expose fully the foolishness of the Galatians by sharpening the argument by dissociation and developing the argument by sacrifice. From Paul's perspective, these arguments reveal how absurd it is for Galatian believers to attempt to gain by means of the works of the law the benefits already secured for them through the sacrificial work of Christ. As Paul declared in his *propositio* (2.21), the attempt to gain these benefits by the works of the law implies that the death of Christ has no value.

The argument by severance is also taken a step further by the description of Christ's redemptive work and its results in vv. 13-14. The cross of Christ effectively places those in Christ (v. 14) within the circle of the Abrahamic blessing and the sphere of the Spirit. By implication, those who are 'of the works of the law' are excluded from the blessing enjoyed by the covenant people of God, the sons of Abraham. It is important, however, to observe that the law itself has not been discredited,[140] overruled,[141] or simply annulled,[142] as some have supposed. The law still has the power to condemn those 'who are of the works of the law' (v. 10) and not 'in Christ' (v. 14). But, as the redemptive statement of v. 13 makes clear, because Christ liberated all of 'us' from the curse of the law, the law no longer has the power to condemn 'us'.

The pronoun ἡμῶν (v. 13) is regarded by some as an exclusive reference to Jewish Christians;[143] by others as an inclusive reference to Jewish and Gentile Christians.[144] This debate needs to be evaluated in light of Paul's development of the argument by severance. The aim of his argument is to demonstrate that the cross of Christ accomplishes a complete severance of οἱ ἐκ πίστεως from ὅσοι εἰσι ἐξ ἔργων νόμου. In contrast, the pronoun ἡμῶν most certainly refers to οἱ ἐκ πίστεως, which expression must certainly include both Jewish and Gentile Christians. The use of the pronoun is not well explained as an attempt to emphasize a distinction between Jewish and Gentile Christians. Such a view runs counter to the aim of the argument by severance. Its occurrence is more adequately explained on the basis that ὑπὲρ ἡμῶν was a common catechetical and liturgical formula in early Christian statements about the death of Jesus.[145]

Moreover, the teleological structure of the statement in vv. 13-14 tells against the restriction of ἡμῶν to Jewish Christians alone. The two climactic ἵνα clauses in v. 14 specify the recipients of the benefits of Christ's redemptive work: they are (1) the Gentiles (εἰς τὰ ἔθνη, v. 14a) and (2) 'we [who] receive (λάβωμεν) the promise of the Spirit through faith' (v. 14b). The initial position of the phrase εἰς τὰ ἔθνη highlights Paul's emphasis on the inclusion of Gentile believers *qua* Gentiles within the Abrahamic blessing as a result of Christ's redemption from the curse of the law.[146] And certainly λάβωμεν refers to all Christians, including the Galatian believers who received the Spirit (τὸ πνεῦμα ἐλάβετε) by faith (3.2).

Paul, of course, does not explain in Galatians how Gentiles incurred the curse of the law from which Christ redeems them.[147] His objective in this letter is to argue that since the severance of οἱ ἐκ πίστεως from ὅσοι ἐξ ἔργων νόμου has been accomplished by the redemptive work of Christ, it is ludicrous for Gentile Christians to think of becoming part of ὅσοι ἐκ ἔργων νόμου.

At this point it is helpful to consider what Paul says about how the cross of Christ accomplished the severance of 'those of faith' from 'those who are under the curse of the law'. The logic of Paul's presentation has been explained in terms of substitution, interchange, exchange and/or narrative logic.

(i) The use of ὑπέρ in v. 13 is taken by many as a reference to Christ taking the place of his people and bearing their curse.[148] Since ὑπέρ can sometimes bear this substitutionary sense,[149] and since the substitutionary idea can be seen in 1.4 (cf. 2 Cor. 5.21), it would be imprudent to dismiss the presence of this idea here.[150] It is, however, important to note with Fitzmyer that the curse in 3.13 has a different cause from that of 3.10.[151] For according to 3.13, Christ became a curse not because he sinned—or because he took the curse of those who did—but because of the verdict of the law against anyone who hangs on a tree. Here the cross is presented as the cause of the curse upon Christ. Moreover, to see only a narrow concept of substitution here may engender the false impression, as Byrne warns, that Paul portrays Christ as bearing all the curse so that we can escape scot-free.[152] Such an impression is contradicted by Paul's emphasis on the believer's death *with* Christ (2.19; 5.24; 6.14). Thus the believer is free not because he escapes death but because he participates in the death of Christ.

(ii) M. Hooker explains what was accomplished by the cross in terms of 'interchange'.[153] She emphasizes incarnation as the means by which Christ entered into our experience under the curse of the law and the resurrection as the means by which we enter into his experience by sharing in his resurrection.[154] It must be observed, however, that although incarnation and resurrection are factors at other points in Paul's Galatian letter, they are not in view here in 3.13-14.

(iii) The analysis of vv. 13-14 by Hays clarifies the 'narrative substructure' undergirding Paul's formulation. Hays develops the diagram of the 'actantial model' which presents the relation among the 'actants' (agents and objects) within the narrative sequence:[155]

Sender ————————→ Object ———————————→ Receiver

Helper ——————————→ Subject◄——————— Opponent

The actantial roles are described by Hays as follows:[156]

(a)   The Sender is the figure who establishes the mandate in the contract syntagm.

(b)   The Subject is the figure who receives the mandate.

(c)   The Object is the thing or quality which the Sender went to communicate to someone.

(d)   The Receiver is the figure to whom the Sender wants to communicate the Object.

(e)   The Opponent is the figure or force that seeks to prevent the Subject from carrying out the mandate.

(f)   The Helper is the figure or force that aids the Subject in carrying out the mandate.

Hays fills in this actantial model with the contents of 3.13-14:[157]

```
          ( freedom              )    ──────► "us" (Jews)
God ────► { blessing of Abraham  }    ──────► Gentiles
          ( Spirit               )    ──────► "us" (Jews and Gentiles)

pistis ────► Christ ◄──────────────────── curse of the law
```

So Hays explains the accomplishment of the cross in terms of 'narrative logic': 'In 3.13 Christ acts as a representative figure, taking the curse upon himself in order to set his people free from it. . . . The logic of such a transaction must be a narrative logic: it depends upon the 'pattern of exchange'.[158]

This analysis of the narrative substructure in Gal. 3 supports our view that the story of the cross is central in Paul's response to the Galatian crisis. But although Hays' analysis illumines the narrative substructure of Paul's argument, it does not sufficiently examine the rhetorical superstructure. Paul reasons from the structure of the gospel story. And his line of reasoning needs to be examined in terms of rhetorical structures and techniques.

I propose that an important contribution can be made to this discussion regarding the logic of the transaction described in vv. 13-14 by analyzing Paul's statement in terms of the argument by transitivity. As we observed in our discussion of rhetorical techniques, 'transitivity is a formal property of certain relations which makes it possible to infer that because a relation holds between a and b and between b and c, it therefore holds between a and c'.[159] The relation of believers (a) to Christ (b) is the focal point of the coordinate prepositional phrases at the end of the two purpose clauses in v. 14: ἐν Χριστῷ Ἰησοῦ . . . διὰ τῆς πίστεως.[160] The expression ἐν Χριστῷ Ἰησοῦ signifies the relation of identification with Christ, which identification operates as the primary premise for the entire argument (cf. 3.27-28).[161] The article τῆς before πίστεως is resumptive, pointing the reader back to the role of faith in 2.16, 20; 3.2, 5, 6, 9, 11.[162] Thus this reference to faith in 3.14b is a further development of Paul's argument by repetition that it is 'through faith' that union with Christ is effected, which faith transfers one from the realm of curse to the realm of blessing.

The believers' relation to Christ is developed in two directions in the argument by transitivity in vv. 13-14. First, the believer is viewed as identified with Christ the crucified. Paul highlights this aspect of Christ's relation with 'us' by the use of the rabbinic practice of *gezerah shawah*, quoting Deut. 21.23 (ἐπικατάρατος πᾶς), which links this passage with his quotation of Deut. 27.26 in v. 10 (ἐπικατάρατος πᾶς).[163] His use of ἐπικατάρατος instead of κεκατηραμένος (LXX) in quoting Deut. 21.23[164] serves to signal Christ's relation with all who were cursed by the law. Although there is a different cause for the curse in v. 10 than in v. 13, Paul's point seems to be that by virtue of his death on the cross Christ became cursed—in line with the verdict of Deut. 21.23—and so entered into relation with all those cursed by the law. Thus the link between Deut. 21.23 and 27.26 is established: Christ entered into the condition of being under a curse (v. 13, quoting Deut. 21.23); Christ entered into the condition of all of 'us' who are under the curse (v. 10, quoting Deut. 27.26). Christ's relation with all who are under the curse of the law (v. 13) opened the way for the relation of all believers with him in his death to the claims of the law (cf. 2.19). As Byrne says, 'Christ has redeemed us from the curse of the Law in that he has provided the opportunity of dying proleptically with him and so of being free from it from now on'.[165]

A second way in which Paul develops the argument by transitivity is in terms of the believers' relation with Christ, the seed of Abraham. The expression ἐν Χριστῷ Ἰησοῦ (v. 14a) echoes the phrase ἐν σοί in the preannouncement of the gospel to Abraham in v. 8. At the same time it presupposes the proposition in v. 16 that Christ is the seed of Abraham, the heir of the promises made to Abraham.[166] The transitivity of the relation here involves the inference that because a relation holds between the believer and Christ and between Christ and the seed of Abraham (v. 16), it therefore holds between the believer and the seed of Abraham: believers are recipients of the promise by virtue of being 'in Christ' (v. 14a) 'through faith' (v. 14b). This inference is spelled out in v. 29.[167]

This analysis of the argument by transitivity presents the believer's identification with Christ, the crucified one, as the basis for redemption from the curse of the law. It also sets forth the believer's identification with Christ, the seed of Abraham, as the basis for the reception of the blessing of Abraham (i.e., the Spirit). That 3.13-14 is not just a subsidiary point in Paul's argument but rather the key to the entire argument is confirmed by the emphasis in the salutation (1.4), by the thesis statement (2.19-20), by Paul's sharp rebuke (3.1-2), by his ethical appeal (5.24), and by his final recapitulation (6.14) that it is only through identification with Christ in his death on the cross that freedom from all the claims of the law and participation in the promised blessings can be acquired.

In light of the Galatian believers' own experience of receiving the Spirit by faith in Christ crucified (3.1-2), Paul defines the content of the promise as the Spirit.[168] In introducing the term 'promise' Paul launches the next stage of his argument, which develops the dissociation of 'promise' (3.14, 16, 17, 18 [2x], 21, 22, 29) from 'law' (3.17, 18, 19, 21 [3x], 23, 24).

(e) The Dissociation of the Promise and the Law (3.15-18)

Gal. 3.15-18 is an expansion of the rebuke in 3.3: 'Are you so foolish? Having begun in the spirit are you now seeking perfection in the flesh?' The Galatians had been mesmerized by the argument that they must move on from the elementary things of their new-found faith in Christ and their experience of the Spirit to an observance of the Mosaic law.[169] Behind this argument was the traditional Jewish understanding of the Abrahamic covenant in terms of the Mosaic law.[170] Indeed, the term covenant became synonymous with law.[171] The argument was also evidently based on the conviction that only the true seed of Abraham, i.e., Jewish people who observed the law, were heirs of the blessings promised in the Abrahamic covenant. The Galatians were being urged to believe that in order to progress in their experience of these blessings they had to enter the covenant people by means of circumcision and keeping the Mosaic law.

In Gal. 3.15-18 Paul develops a definition of the covenant which refutes the nomistic and nationalistic theology of the intruders. The nomistic understanding of the Abrahamic covenant is exploded by the dissociation of the covenant and the law. Paul uses an argument by example[172] to accomplish this dissociation. Although it is difficult to determine whether he has in mind Greek,[173] Roman,[174] or Jewish[175] jurisprudence, the central point of Paul's example is clear: 'As a valid will cannot be contested or altered by additions, so the promise of God which is His original 'testament' cannot be invalidated by the law which came later'.[176] Paul is not reducing the Abrahamic covenant to the concept of a human testament.[177] He is interested only in one point of comparison between the testament and the covenant—viz., the irrevocable nature of both. The nature of this comparison between a human testament and the divine covenant implies an *a fortiori* argument: if in human affairs one cannot alter a testament which has been ratified, then it is inconceivable that the

Abrahamic covenant—which was previously ratified by God—can in any way be modified by the Mosaic law.

In this argument, Paul equates the promise and the covenant and splits apart the covenant promise from the law. True, Paul does not continue to use the term 'covenant' in his argument. Nonetheless, his use of 'promise' as an equivalent term for 'covenant' in v. 17 and his frequent repetition of 'promise' in the argument indicate that he is determined to capture the concept of the covenant for his own use against the troublemakers.[178] Some scholars have argued that the infrequent use of διαθήκη and the lack of emphasis on Exodus motifs indicate that covenantal categories are not central in Paul's thought.[179] But the fact that Paul rarely uses διαθήκη does not necessarily mean that the covenant concept has a subordinate place in his theology. Sanders himself argues that the covenant idea was foundational in rabbinic theology even though the term *berith* was rarely used.[180] Probably the reason why Paul did not use διαθήκη after 3.17 was precisely because it has been almost inseparably linked in Jewish tradition with the Mosaic law, circumcision, and the election of the Jewish nation. So Paul drops the term to avoid confusing his understanding of the covenant with this Jewish nomistic, nationalistic understanding. But he maintains the concept of the covenant in this argument for his Gentile mission by defining the Abrahamic covenant in terms of a promise of blessing for Gentiles.[181]

Paul achieves the dissociation of the promise from the law by using his perspective of salvation history against his opponents. Whereas they probably argued that Galatian believers needed to move beyond their claim to be the sons of Abraham to an acceptance of the Mosaic law, Paul argues that because the law came 430 years after the promise it could not annul or be attached to the promise as a condition of inheriting the promised blessings. In Paul's view, those who seek the inheritance through the law have failed to recognize the precedence of the promise in salvation history. They are left with only the law; they are excluded from the covenant; they have lost the inheritance.

The redefinition of κληρονομία is an essential part of Paul's argument. The troublemakers' definition is reflected in the protasis of v. 18: ἐκ νόμου ἡ κληρονομία.[182] Keeping the law was considered to be a necessary condition for claiming the inheritance. Against this position, Paul defines the inheritance as ἐξ ἐπαγγελίας. The precedence of the promise in salvation history, as Paul sees it, has already established the basis for this dissociation of ἐκ νόμου ἡ κληρονομία from ἐξ ἐπαγγελίας [ἡ κληρονομία]. So Paul adds to this argument by drawing attention to the gift character of the promised inheritance.[183] Paul points out the incompatability between receiving the inheritance as a gift on the basis of a promise and receiving it as a payment for keeping the law. This technique of presenting the compatability of two mutually exclusive principles[184] is used by Paul as a way to drive home his rebuke for the foolish error of viewing something as a payment which had already been received as a gift.

The content of the gift is the sum total of the blessings surveyed in this chapter: sonship, Spirit, righteousness, life, and redemption. Such a redefinition of the inheritance in terms of the eschatological blessings is paralleled in intertestamental Jewish texts which understand the promise of the land in an eschatological sense as the blessing of God awaiting the people of God in the eschaton.[185]

The nationalistic view of the covenant is refuted by Paul's parenthetical definition of the key term σπέρμα in the Abrahamic covenant. Although his definition flies in the face of a contemporary Jewish nationalistic interpretation of this term, it reflects Jewish practices of exegesis.[186] The goal of Paul's interpretation of the generic singular is to remove the necessity of entering the Jewish nation in order to participate in the blessing of Abraham. The messianic definition of σπέρμα removes Jewish national boundaries as the limits of the inheritance of the Abrahamic blessing.[187] The link Paul makes between Abraham and Christ bypasses the Mosaic law and the Jewish nation as channels for the reception of the promises to Abraham, with the result that Christ alone is the channel of the promised blessing.[188]

Bjerklund notes that the argument of 3.15-18 reaches the same conclusion as that of 3.6-14: 'das Erbe, oder wie wir auch sagen können, den Geist empfängt man nicht durch das Gesetz, sondern weil Gott es verheissen hat'.[189] This convergence of arguments from Scripture and from human example is designed to reinforce the rebuke for foolishness which sets the tone for this entire section of the letter.[190]

(e') *The Difference of Order between the Promise and the Law* (3.19-22)

The two rhetorical questions in 3.19-21 disclose Paul's own sense of what might very well be evoked by his argument. The fact that Paul thinks that his readers might be led to question whether he has

denied any purpose to the law (Τί οὖν ὁ νόμος;) and might interpret
the law as opposed to the promise (ὁ οὖν νόμος κατὰ τῶν
ἐπαγγελιῶν;) suggests that he views the dissociation of the promise
from the law as the major feature of his argument. In this section the
relation of the promise and the law is more fully defined by three
arguments concerning the difference of order between them.[191] This
difference is demonstrated by a description of the negative purpose of
the law, by setting out a temporal framework for the law, and by
reference to the mediated origin of the law.

The negative purpose of the law is described by two complementary
phrases:

   i.   τῶν παραβάσεων χάριν προσετέθη (v. 19).
  ii.   συνέκλεισεν ἡ γραφὴ τὰ πάντα ὑπὸ ἁμαρτίαν (v. 22).

Our understanding of the first phrase is enhanced by interpreting
it in light of the second.[192] For the imprisonment of all under sin (ὑπὸ
ἁμαρτίαν) is accomplished by the addition of the law, which adds the
dimension of conscious transgression (παράβασις) against the
revealed will of God.[193] In this sense, the addition of the law
increases sin, and thereby imprisons all under sin. So the χάριν of
v. 19 signifies purpose rather than cause.[194]

The negative, condemning purpose of the law is emphasized by the
repetition of the ὑπό phrases: 'Scripture imprisons all *under* sin'.
This image of imprisonment *under* sin is developed in the next
section by the metaphors of being confined *under* the law (v. 23) and
disciplined *under* the pedagogue (vv. 24-25). Since the reference to
'Scripture' in v. 22 apparently recalls the quotation of Deut. 27.26 in
3.10, these ὑπό phrases are an amplification of the condition depicted
as being *under* a curse in 3.10.[195] This ὑπό condition is further
dramatized by the ὑπό phrases in 4.2-5:

    '*under* guardians and trustees' (4.2)
    '*under* the elements of the world' (4.3)
    '*under* law' (4.4, 5)

The sevenfold repetion of the ὑπό phrases serves to increase the
feeling of the oppressive presence of the law.[196] Thus the door to any
attempt to use the law as a means to any positive goal is effectively
slammed shut.

A positive role for the law is explicitly denied by the unfulfilled
conditional sentence of v. 21. Since righteousness cannot be gained
by the law (as shown by the unreality of the apodosis), it is clear that
the law has not been given with the power to make alive (as the

unreality of the protasis implies). This line of reasoning moves from the absence of the effect (righteousness) to the absence of the cause (the power to make alive).[197] The connection between righteousness and ζῳοποιῆσαι implies that ζῳοποιῆσαι is to be taken in a soteriological sense as a reference to the eschatological ζωή.[198] Since the law cannot produce life, it is unable to produce righteousness; it leads only to imprisonment under sin, condemnation under the curse, and death.

This negative purpose of the law was established, Paul says, 'in order that the promise might be given by faith in Jesus Christ to those who believe' (3.22). The ἵνα clause relates the purpose of the law to the promise. For the law contributes in a negative way to the bestowal of the promise by removing every other basis for participating in the benefits of the promise except faith in Jesus Christ. The accomplishment of the law is that it reduces *all*—both Jews and Gentiles—to only one way of escape from the prison of sin, to only one way of obtaining the benefits of the promise: faith in Christ.

The emphasis on *all* in v. 22 undercuts the troublemakers' insistence that Israel's possession of the law set her apart from Gentile sinners and gave her exclusive claim on the Abrahamic promise.[199] Paul's emphasis in speaking of the negative purpose of the law is that the law reduces Jews to the same status as Gentiles— *all* are locked up under sin.[200] Therefore, identification with the Jewish people by circumcision and acceptance of the Mosaic law does not remove one from the circle of sinners and bring one into the sphere of righteousness, blessing, inheritance, and life. Rather, it leaves one imprisoned under sin. The common imprisonment of both Jews and Gentiles under sin is presented as preparing the way for the inclusion of *all* believers—both Jews and Gentiles—in the circle of blessing, which is the sphere of those who are sons of God on the basis of being in Christ by faith (v. 26).

Paul's second argument with regard to the difference in order between the promise and the law involves his setting out a temporal framework for the law: 'added. . . until the seed should come to whom the promise was made'(v. 19). This temporal limitation for the function of the law is a primary feature in the next section (vv. 23-25):

πρὸ τοῦ δὲ ἐλθεῖν τὴν πίστιν (v. 23a);
εἰς τὴν μέλλουσαν πίστιν ἀποκαλυφθῆναι (v. 23b).
εἰς Χριστόν (v. 24);
ἐλθούσης δὲ τῆς πίστεως (v. 25).

Four additional temporal boundary signs for the law are posted in
4.1-4:

ἐφ' ὅσον χρόνον ὁ κληρονόμος ἐστιν (4.1);
ἄχρι τῆς προθεσμίας τοῦ πατρός (4.2);
ὅτε ἦμεν νήπιοι (4.3);
ὅτε δὲ ἦλθεν τὸ πλήρωμα τοῦ χρόνου (4.4).

The function of the Mosaic law as a jailer, pedagogue, guardian, or
trustee of the people of God is limited to a specific era of salvation
history—which era ended when Christ, the fulfillment of the promise
and the object of faith, came. To live now under the reign of the law is
to turn back the clock of history and to live as if Christ had not
come.[201] Thus the desire of the Galatians to come under the law is
not progress; it is retrogression.

The third way in which Paul speaks of the law in separating it
from the promise is by referring to its mediated origin in 3.19b-20.
These verses are notoriously enigmatic.[202] Nevertheless, it is helpful
in our interpretation of these verse to set them in the context of the
argument of this section. As we have seen, Paul's definition of the
law's negative purpose and his emphasis on its temporality have
served to separate the law qualitatively from the promise. It is
reasonable, therefore, to assume that his comments about the double
mediation of the law through angels and Moses also serves to show
that the law is different in order from the promise. On the one hand,
the promise was given directly by God to Abraham and is fulfilled in
Christ, the seed of Abraham. On the other, the law was given
through angels by the hand of Moses.[203] Since the law is distanced
from God by numerous intermediaries, it cannot offer direct access
to God.[204] But by faith the Galatian converts have already entered
into the experience of the Spirit (3.1-5), which is the fulfillment of
the promise (3.14).

This contrast between mediated and direct experience is designed
to put the law on a level different from the promise.[205] The same
contrast is developed in 4.1-11 where the experience of the Spirit
crying in our hearts 'Abba, Father' is contrasted to being under
guardians, stewards, the elements of the world, and the law. In 4.8-10
the direct experience of knowing God and being known by him is
contrasted to the attempt of the Galatian believers to observe ritual
days, months, years, and seasons. Evidently, Paul's converts were
being persuaded that if they would observe the rituals of the Jewish

people, they would experience new dimensions of spiritual life and blessing—that if they would become members of the people of God (i.e., Jews), they would be guaranteed an intimacy with God. Paul, however, warns them that nothing could be further from the truth. The circumstances in the giving of the law show that it had a mediated origin. Thus the law does not provide direct access to God. Only the fulfillment of the promise in the bestowal of the Spirit to those in Christ does (3.1-5, 14; 4.6-8).

Paul's affirmation that 'God is one' (3.20) may also imply a contrast between the universality of God and the particularity of the law.[206] The universality of God is expressed in the promise for πάντα τὰ ἔθνη (3.8). The particular focus of the law is specified by its mediation through Moses to the Jewish people for a historical period. The position of the troublemakers in Galatia, that one had to become a Jew in order to be rightly related to God, limited the sphere of God's blessing to the Jewish nation. But the unity of God implied that God is the God of the Gentiles as well as the God of the Jews (cf. Rom. 3.29-30). Furthermore, the fact that Gentiles received the promise of the Spirit by faith without becoming Jews was viewed by Paul as a witness to the universality of God.

Paul's devaluation of the law to a different, inferior order from the promise on the ground of its negative purpose, temporary function, and mediated origin leaves the Galatian converts without any sound reason for turning to the law.

(d') *The Time of Faith distinguished from the Time of Law* (3.23-25)
In this section Paul turns from the dissociation of promise and law (3.15-22) to a renewed disscussion of the contrast between faith and law (3.23-25; cf. 3.10-14).[207] He expands and dramatizes his dissociative definitions of faith and law by employing the rhetorical technique of personification:[208] 'the faith' being personified as a co-liberator with Christ, with the law personified as a jailer and a pedagogue. By dividing the biblical time line between the reign of law and the coming of faith, Paul is able to separate these two hypostasized forces to different time periods. The double inclusio which frames the sentence in vv. 23-25 effectively draws our attention to this conflict between faith and law.[209]

a πρὸ τοῦ δὲ ἐλθεῖν πίστιν
b ὑπὸ νόμον ἐφρουρούμεθα
a ἐλθούσης δὲ τῆς πίστεως
b οὐκέτι ὑπὸ παιδαγωγόν ἐσμεν

The personification of 'the faith'[210] as a co-liberator is brought about by parallelling the coming of Christ (the Seed, v. 19b) and the coming of faith (vv. 23a, 25a). His use of the verb ἀποκαλυφθῆναι with πίστις also signals this identification, since ἀποκαλύπτειν is used in 1.12 and 1.16 to refer to the revelation of Jesus Christ. Moreover, the temporal sense of εἰς Χριστόν in v. 24 relates the event of Christ's coming to the coming of faith.[211]

The personification of faith in these verses is the occasion of some debate. Betz, for example, argues that 'faith' here 'describes the occurrence of a historical phenomenon, not the act of believing of an individual'.[212] This dichotomy between historical and personal has been pushed to the extreme by Lietzmann and Mundle, who claimed that 'the faith' refers to Christianity or to Christian doctrine.[213] Taking a different course, Hays' position is that πίστις refers primarily to the faithfulness of Jesus Christ.[214] He builds his thesis on an analysis of the narrative structure of this section and points to the similarities in the narrative patterns of 3.23-29 and 4.3-7. In both of these passages the story line moves from (1) the imprisonment or slave-like condition of God's people, to (2) their deliverance by the coming of the faith or of God's son, to (3) their new status as sons and heirs. And from this similarity of story line, Hays argues that πίστις must be seen as a reference to the faithfulness revealed in Christ Jesus.[215] Diverse though they are, all of these interpretations understand the coming of faith in terms of salvation history, rather than as a reference to the personal experience of believers.

Against such interpretations, a number of commentators stress that Paul still retains in his use of 'the faith' here a personal dimension of trust in Christ. Mussner, in reaction to Lietzmann's abstraction, draws attention to both the historical and personal qualities inherent in the term:

> mit τὴν πίστιν wird das vorhergehende ἐκ πίστεως ('Ιησοῦ Χριστοῦ) anaphorisch wiederaufgenommen (genau wie nachher im V. 25), d.h., 'der' nun gekommene Glaube ist jener heilbringende Glaube an Jesus Christus, der den Gläubigen den Verheissungssegen bringt. Einen abstrakten geschichtslosen Glauben kennt Paulus nicht![216]

Oepke also notes that 'πίστις als Heilsprinzip objektiviert, aber noch fides *qua creditur*'.[217] This combination of the historical and personal dimensions of πίστις can be understood when we observe, as Dahl reminds us, that Paul is interpreting Scripture in light of the 'events of the recent past and present—the coming of Jesus, his death and resurrection, the mission to the Gentiles and the outpouring of the Holy Spirit'.[218] In this light, 'Paul as an apostle identifies the faith which is proclaimed in Scripture with faith in the crucified Messiah, Jesus Christ'.[219]

The exegetical observations which we have made in this chapter confirm this perspective. We noted that Paul compared the personal experience of the Galatians' faith in Christ with the faith of Abraham, and, on the basis of that comparison, concluded that they were sons of Abraham.[220] Paul's emphasis is on the experience of Jewish and Gentile Christians whose faith in the coming of Christ radically altered their relation to the law. Since 'Christ's coming actualizes faith'[221] which releases believers from the oppressive yoke of the law, Paul can speak of the coincidence of the coming of faith and the coming of Christ. The faith that came was not an abstract principle or impersonal, historical phenomenon; it was a personal response of faith to the coming of Christ. Thus, the coming of faith 'may be understood', as Bruce remarks, 'both on the plane of salvation—history and in the personal experience of believers'.[222] The relation of this faith to Abraham's faith is explained by Oepke:

> Der Glaube ist als endgultiger Heilsweg in Gottes Rat von Ewigkeit her vorgesehen, wurde aber erst, als die gesetzte Frist verstrichen war (s.z. 4,4), als solcher geoffenbart. Gemeint ist dabei immer der Glaube an Christus. Im Glauben Abrahams ist dieser Glaube nur erst vorgebildet.[223]

The personification of the law is expressed by two perjorative epithets:[224] a jailer (v. 23) and a pedagogue (v. 24-25). The verb φρουρέω (v. 23) carries the idea of holding in custody or confining.[225] Combined with the verb συγκλείω it points to the imprisoning power of the law. The conjuction ὥστε at the beginning of v. 24 indicates that the image of the παιδαγωγός is meant to be taken as an extension of the legal imagery of v. 23. It is, therefore, clear that Paul is not ascribing a positive, educative role to the law in his use of παιδαγωγός. Rather, the role of the παιδαγωγός is that of a disciplinarian.[226] Like a jailer, the law imprisoned under sin (vv. 22-23); like a παιδαγωγός, the law condemned and disciplined (vv. 24-25). For Paul, however, this oppressive power of the law was not meant to be permanent. It had a temporary role which was concluded by the coming of Christ (εἰς Χριστόν) and the coming of faith (εἰς τὴν μέλλουσαν πίστιν ἀποκαλυφθῆναι).[227] The personification of the law graphically portrays the options facing the Galatian coverts: either they can succumb to the imprisoning power of the law, which has been relegated to the past by the coming of Christ, or they can live by the liberating power of faith in Christ, which sets them free from the tyranny of the law. There is no middle ground.

(c') *The inclusion of Gentiles in Christ, the seed of Abraham* (3.23-29)

The main point of Gal. 3.26-29 has to do with the inclusion of Gentiles in Christ, the seed of Abraham. The abrupt shift to the second person plural highlights the fact that Paul is stressing the place of Gentile believers.[228] Paul's argument for the inclusion of Gentiles presupposes that what is true of the whole is true of the part:[229] Christ is the whole; the Galatian believers are the parts in him. Their inclusion in Christ is reiterated in each verse:

ἐν Χριστῷ˙ Ἰησοῦ[230]	(v. 26)
εἰς Χριστόν	(v. 27a)
Χριστὸν ἐνεδύσασθε	(v. 27b)
εἷς ἐστε ἐν Χριστῷ Ἰησοῦ	(v. 28)
ὑμεῖς Χριστοῦ	(v. 29)

The conjuction γάρ in vv. 27 and 28b and the conditional sentence of v. 29 indicate that being in Christ is the ground of the Gentiles' inclusion on an equal basis in the people of God, and so they are designated here by the term 'sons of God' (v. 26) and 'seed of Abraham' (v. 29).[231] Since Christ (the whole) is the Son of God (2.20) and the seed of Abraham to whom the promises were spoken (3.16), believers (the parts) included in him are also sons of God, the seed of Abraham, and heirs according to the promise. Israel is redefined here to be equivalent to those who belong to Christ. Existence in Christ is defined as existence in the reconstituted Israel; Christ is the realm of promised blessing and inheritance.[232]

The reality of the inclusion of Gentiles in Christ is represented in v. 27 by two metaphors: baptism and 'putting on'. Paul's words here seem designed to remind the Galatian Christians of their baptism. In fact, four lines of evidence support the view that vv. 27-28 include a portion of a baptismal liturgy.[223] (i) These two verses could be omitted without breaking the flow of the passage.[234] One could, in fact, move from the affirmation of sonship in Christ (v. 26) to the conclusion that all those who belong to Christ are the seed of Abraham, heirs according to the promise (v. 29), without noticing the omission of vv. 27-28. 'Sons of God' and 'seed of Abraham' are used as parallel, equivalent titles for Israel; and sonship directly implies heirship.[235] Thus vv. 27-28 may be viewed as material which Paul inserted in his argument to substantiate his point. (ii) The parallelism between v. 26 and the last phrase of v. 28 may be viewed as evidence that v. 26 was sparked by—or, at least, reminded Paul of—a similar phrase in baptismal confession. If this be so, then the γάρ in v. 29 introduces the baptismal confession as confirmation of Paul's bold statement that *all* (πάντες) Galatian believers are sons of God (v. 26), *for*, as the baptismal confession affirms, they are *all* (πάντες) one in Christ (v. 28).[236] (iii) The supposition that vv. 27-28 are a quotation from a liturgical piece helps to explain why v. 28 includes references to slave-free and male-female categories, when, in fact, neither of these has direct relevance to the argument of Galatians.[237] (iv) The verbal similarity of Gal. 3.27-28 to 1 Cor. 12.13 and Col. 3.11 may be taken as evidence that Paul was drawing on a fairly standardized traditional formula.[238] In sum, these four considerations tend to support Betz's thesis that 'Paul has lifted Gal. 3.26-28, in part or as a whole, from a pre-Pauline liturgical context'.[239]

But however we judge the provenance of vv. 26-28 (or vv. 27-28), the important point to note is that the metaphor of baptism was used by Paul to draw the Galatian Christians back to their initiation into Christ and the Christian community. It was surely Paul's intention to reawaken their memory of their baptism in order to renew their sense of belonging to Christ—and hence to renew their sense of belonging to the convenant people of God. In light of his emphasis on faith in the context,[240] it is inconceivable that Paul is presenting the ritual of baptism itself as the means of entry into Christ.[241] As Byrne says, 'Paul speaks in terms of baptism here because it represents the objective social expression of the internal decision of faith. As something which all the Galatians have received on some known public occasion, it can be pointed to as the incontrovertible foundation of the new status which all share'.[242]

The metaphor of 'putting on Christ' (Χριστὸν ἐνεδύσασθε) may have been drawn from the act of re-robing in the ceremony of baptism. This metaphor also pictures the reality of complete identification with Christ. The argumentative force of these two metaphors,[243] baptism and 'putting on', is registered in v. 28. Identification by race, class, or sex no longer has any significance because of complete identification with Christ. The relation of this argument of inclusion in Christ to the entire Abraham argument is immediately apparent. The equal status of all believers as sons of God and the seed of Abraham, which status is based upon their equality in Christ, renders any attempt to gain superior status by circumcision or law-observance of no value whatsoever. Furthermore, the conjuction (γάρ) in v. 26 implies that the inclusion of Gentile believers within Israel (as redefined by Paul) is the reason why 'we' are no longer under the pedagogical rule of the law (v. 25).[244] Since full status in the covenant people of God is granted and maintained simply by inclusion in Christ by faith, there is no longer any need for the law as the means to secure or maintain that status. Paul reasons from the inclusion of Gentile believers in Christ, as symbolized by the ceremony of baptism,[245] to the liberation of all believers from the tyranny of the law.

In his conclusion that Galatian believers are the 'sons of God', the 'seed of Abraham' and the 'heirs', Paul has moved in his conceptual chiasm back to a restatement of his thesis that they are the 'sons of Abraham' (v. 7).[246] Paul's use of these terms as synonymous titles for Israel, the covenant people of God, at both the beginning and the end of his Abraham argument indicates that the inclusion of Gentile believers in the people of God on the basis of their inclusion in Christ is the premise of his entire argument.[247] It is the conceptual framework for understanding the inclusive language of v. 8 (ἐνευλογη-θήσονται ἐν σοὶ πάντα τὰ ἔθνη) and v. 14 (ἵνα εἰς τὰ ἔθνη ἡ εὐλογία τοῦ Ἀβραάμ γένεται ἐν Χριστῷ Ἰησοῦ). And it is the presupposition behind the redefinition of the seed of Abraham as a reference to Christ (v. 16).

The argument based on the inclusion of the part in the whole—i.e., of Gentile Christians in Christ, the seed of Abraham—is developed to substantiate the rebuke for foolishness. This rebuke is given force by demonstrating that any attempt by Galatian Christians to gain status or receive blessing by the works of the Mosaic law is absurd, since they have already been included within the realm of full inheritance in which there is no racial or national hierarchy. If Paul is quoting from a baptismal liturgy, as seems likely, he would be vividly reminding his converts of their beginning, as referred to in

3.3. The foolishness of the Galatians, therefore, is revealed as either ignorance or neglect of their baptismal confession. Had they realized that their baptism already symbolized full inclusion in the seed of Abraham, and hence their position as heirs of the promise to Abraham, they would never have been influenced by the troublemakers' claim that circumcision and law-observance were necessary. The rebuke for their change of direction in 3.3 is to be understood in the light of 3.26-29 as a rebuke for deserting their own baptismal vows. The rebuke for that change of direction is repeated in 4.8-11 where the Galatian believers are reproached for becoming enslaved to the law (4.10) when they were in fact free sons (4.6-7).

CHAPTER 5

THE HAGAR-SARAH ALLEGORY OF GAL. 4.21-31:
PAUL'S BIBLICAL APPEAL

1. *The Traditional Perspective*

The Hagar–Sarah allegory of Gal. 4.21-31 has been traditionally viewed as a sub-section of Paul's argument that begins at 3.1, with 3.1-4.31 therefore seen as one continuous section. The basis for this view is the continuity of subject matter in 3.1-4.31. For these two chapters have throughout similar themes: the Abraham story, questions regarding sonship and heirship, and contrasts of promise and law, flesh and spirit, and freedom and slavery. Moreover, the development of these themes in both chapters is based on an exposition of OT texts that are related to the Abraham story.

Representatives of the Traditional View
Burton lists 4.21-31 as point ten in a series of arguments in the 'refutatory' portion of Galatians (3.1-4.31) and calls it a 'supplementary argument'.[1] He suggest that 'before leaving the subject of the seed of Abraham it occurs to the apostle, apparently as an afterthought, that he might make his thought clearer and more persuasive by an allegorical interpretation of the story of Abraham and his two sons'.[2]

Betz labels 4.21-31 as the sixth and final argument in the *probatio* section (3.1-4.31).[3] He explains that the allegory was a rhetorical device which enabled Paul to return to the *interogatio* method used in 3.1-5.[4] In that paragraph Paul's questions had compelled the Galatians to admit that the evidence of their experience of the Spirit supported his case and thus demonstrated that they were ἀνόητοι. But Paul, as Betz views matters, does not leave the Galatians at the level of fools. By introducing the allegory with a question (Λέγετέ μοι, οἱ ὑπὸ νόμον θέλοντες εἶναι, τὸν νόμου οὐκ ἀκούετε;), he gives them an opportunity to clear themselves of the accusation of foolishness. 'Through the allegory 4.21-31 he then lets the Galatians find the truth for themselves'. Thus Betz finds 4.21-31 to be the fitting rhetorical conclusion to the *probatio* (3.1-4.31).[5] Betz's rhetorical analysis forms the basis for F. Vouga's study of 'La construction de l'historie en Galates 3-4'.[6] Vouga recognizes that these two chapters contain various genres: 'ils se réfèrent à l'évidence (3.1-5), à l'Ecriture' (3.6-14), 'à l'usage juridique' (3.15-18), 'à la tradition tradition chrétienne' (4.1-11), 'au *topos* de l'amitié' (4.12-20) and 'à l'allégorie scripturaire' (4.21-31).[7] Yet despite the diversity of these genres Vouga maintains the traditional perspective that these two chapters are an unbroken chain of proofs:

> Ils constituent en fait un ensemble de preuver par l'histoire qui se développe en 7 points: A. 3.1-5: preuve par l'histoire spirituelle des Galates; B. 3.6-14: preuve par l'histoire de la bénédiction d'Abraham; C. 3.15-18: preuve par l'histoire des promesses; D. 3.19-29: preuve par la place de la Loi dans l'histoire de la promesse; E. 4.1-11: preuve par l'histoire de la libération; F. 4.12-20: preuve par l'histoire des relations des Galates avec l'apôtre; G. 4.21-31: preuve par l'histoire des deux fils d'Abraham. Certains font référence à l'histoire personnelle des destinaires (A. 3.1-5; F. 4.12-20), d'autres à l'histoire de la promesse (B. 3.6-14; C. 3.15-18; G. 4.21-31) alors que D (3.19-29) et E (4.1-11) argumentent à partir de la tradition chrétienne et jouent sur les deux régistres.[8]

According to Vouga's analysis, Gal. 4.21-31 functions as a repetition of the Abraham argument already developed in chapter 3.[9]

Even Bligh's ingenious attempt to find chiastic structures in the letter does not deviate significantly from this traditional perspective.[10] Thus 4.21-30 is seen as a chiasmus within a larger chisamus—'Sara and Hagar: Paul and His Opponents' (4.11-30)—which is part of an even larger chiasmus—viz., 'Argumentative Sections of the Epistle' (3.5-4.30).[11] According to Bligh, the entire chiasm 3.5-4.30 is the substance of Paul's speech to Peter in the confrontation at Antioch described in 2.11-14.[12] Of course, Bligh has to admit that certain elements addressed directly to the Galatians (3.1; 4.12-20) were inserted into this Antioch speech when the letter was composed.[13] But Bligh views the allegory itself as the climax of the Antioch speech. So he writes:

> In the discourse at Antioch, this passage [4.21-31] was the final demonstration from Scripture that the law of Moses has no place in

the Gentile churches and must be excluded from them. Christians must no longer look to the law-observing church of Jerusalem as their mother-church.[14]

As we noted earlier, Bligh's analysis has been subjected to a detailed examination by Barrett, who finds Bligh's claim that 4.11-30 is a balanced chiasmus to be entirely unconvincing.[15] In response to Bligh's assertion that 4.21-30 was composed first as the final climax to Paul's speech in Antioch, and that 4.11-20 was 'skillfully added to form with it the symmetrical pattern of 4.11-30',[16] Barrett asks, 'is it really conceivable either that Paul composed these two apparently spontaneous outbursts (that to the Galatians and that at Antioch) with such refined literary polish, or that by a piece of good fortune they happened to fit together into chiastic form?'[17] Barrett shows that under close scrutiny, the chiastic structure which Bligh purports to find is a 'clumsy, unbalanced, unconvincing chiasmus'.[18]

Having set aside Bligh's approach as unsatisfactory, Barrett develops his own explanation for the place of 4.21-31 in Paul's argument. Barrett seeks to demonstrate that Paul was forced to reinterpret the Hagar–Sarah story because of its prominent place in his opponents' circumcision campaign.[19] His insights regarding the opponents' use of Abraham are positively assessed in our consideration of the opponents' theology[20] and are integrated into our analysis of the allegory. It should be noted here, however, that these insights do not effect Barrett's acceptance of the traditional view which sees 3.1–4.31 as one continuous section.

Reservations Regarding the Traditional View

Despite this consensus as to 3.1–4.31 being an unbroken train of argumentation, some reservations can be detected among scholars. Burton's statement that 4.21-31 appears to be an 'afterthought'[21] and Oepke's opinion that 'er ist dem Apostel wohl erst nachträglich eingefallen'[22] suggest that there may be reasons to question the traditional view on the unity of 3.1–4.31.

The unity of 3.1–4.11 as a section on its own makes it difficult to see how 4.21-31 is related structurally to that section. Recent studies have demonstrated the coherence of 3.1–4.11 on the basis of both its rhetorical structure[23] and its narrative sub-structure.[24] And this emphasis on the structural unity of 3.1–4.11 serves to sharpen the question of how to integrate 4.21-31 into that section. The fact that Hays treats only 'the narrative substructure of 3.1–4.11' and ignores

4.21-31 indicates the degree to which this latter section is viewed as an awkward, easily detachable appendage.[25]

A second reason to question attempts to unite 4.21-31 with 3.1-4.11 has to do with the intervening section 4.12-20, which is viewed by most as an interruption in the flow of argumentation. Beker claims that 'it is difficult to find any natural and obvious breaks in the argument from Gal. 2.11 until 5.26'; yet he concedes that 'Galatians 4.12-20, with its direct personal appeal to the Galatians, seems the most obvious interruption'.[26] Most commentators recognize the 'direct appeal' nature of 4.12-20 and so treat it as a kind of parenthetical aside or a lighter argument introduced as a change of pace.[27] J. White simply removes 4.12-20 from his outline of this section—with the unfulfilled promise that he will treat it at a later time.[28] If 3.1-4.11 and 4.21-31, then, serve the same function and belong to the same section of the letter, it is difficult to know what to do with the intervening section 4.12-20, which appears to serve a different function as a 'direct personal appeal'.

A third reason to question the validity of the traditional view is the difference between the two types of scripture exposition in 3.1-4.11 and 4.21-31. As our analysis of Paul's exegetical methods indicates, there is an atomistic, midrashic approach to Scripture in 3.6-29 and a typological-allegorical approach in 4.21-31.[29] And this shift of hermeneutical procedure in 4.21-31 should be taken, I suggest, as a clue that a change of direction has occurred in Paul's letter.

Fourth, the emphasis on freedom in this section provides a reason to link it more closely with the opening of the paraenetic section in 5.1-13 than with the argument from Scripture in 3.1-4.11. For although the language of freedom is related to the discussion of imprisonment under law and redemption from law in 3.19-4.11, the repetitive use of ἐλευθερία vocabulary in 4.22, 23, 26, 30, and 31 establishes a strong verbal bond with the introduction to the paraenetic section of 5.1-13.[30]

For these reasons, the place of 4.21-31 in the structure and argument of Paul's Galatian letter needs to be reassessed. Our epistolary and rhetorical analyses of the letter led us to conclude that at 4.12 Paul turns from rebuke and begins his request[31]—or, in rhetorical terms, he shifts from forensic to deliberative rhetoric.[32] Understood in this context 4.21-31, I propose, should be seen as an appeal to the Galatians through the words of Torah to carry out certain instructions and to adhere to a specific course of action. The function of the paragraph is not primarily to continue the rebuke of the Galatians for past foolishness and desertion under the influence of the troublemakers, but to request them in biblical words to expel those troublemakers and to adhere to the gospel of freedom. Set, then, in this new perspective, the main features of the Hagar-Sarah allegory stand out in clear relief. It is this new view of the function of the Hagar-Sarah allegory, as illumined by epistolary and rhetorical analyses, that must now be more closely examined, giving particular attention to such matters as the imperatival focus of the paragraph, the allegorical definition of key terms, and the conceptual framework for ethics presented.

2. *A New Perspective: Paul's Biblical Appeal*

The Imperatival Focus

If 4.21-31 is a part of the request section of the Galatians, we should expect that its primary point will be in line with the first explicit request of the letter at 4.12. So the quotation of Gen. 21.10 in 4.30 needs to be examined to see if, in fact, its request relates in some more or less direct manner to the initial request of 4.12.

Barrett insists that the imperative of 4.30 'is not (*pace* Bligh) a call to the Gentile Christians in the church of Antioch to rise up and expel their Jewish Christian brethren; it is rather the command of God to his (angelic) agents, and expresses what the fate of each party is to be'.[33] If Barrett's interpretation of the imperative is correct, then the function of the allegory does not differ substantially from the exposition of the Abraham story in 3.1-4.11. In both cases the biblical data is used to demonstrate the radical difference between the position of the troublemakers and Paul's position, and thus to substantiate Paul's rebuke for their foolish synthesis of the two positions.

In contrast to Barrett, however, A.T. Lincoln claims that 'the OT quotation in 4.30 is in fact the punchline of Paul's polemical midrash'.[34] According to Lincoln, 'Paul sees the first part of the quotation as constituting a call for decisive resistance on the part of the Galatian believers'.[35] And a number of lines of evidence support Lincoln's interpretation, which evidence need be laid out briefly here.

First, the initial request of 4.12, 'Become as I am!', really amounts to a call for decisive resistance against the troublemakers. Paul developed his autobiography to illustrate how that at Jerusalem (2.3-5) and at Antioch (2.11-14) he had decisively resisted pressures from Jewish Christians similar to those faced by the Galatian churhes. His own stand against those 'Ishmaels' is now supported by the command of Scripture (Gen. 21.10 in Gal. 4.30), which command Paul requests his converts to follow as well.[36]

Second, in 5.1 Paul paraphrases the 'call for decisive resistance' expressed by the command of Gen. 21.10 in his own words: 'Stand fast, therefore, and do not submit again to the yoke of slavery'.[37]

Third, in 4.17 Paul describes the troublemakers' circumcision campaign as an attempt to exclude the Galatians (ἐκκλεῖσαι ὑμᾶς θέλουσιν) from the enjoyment of their full inheritance in the Abrahamic covenant, apart from the observance of the Mosaic law. Now he commands them to turn the tables on those troublemakers. For since the Galatian Gentile Christians are the true heirs of the promise, they must exclude the troublemakers (ἔκβαλε τὴν παιδίσκην καὶ τὸν υἱὸν αὐτῆς).[38]

Fourth, the question with which Paul introduces the Hagar–Sarah story prepares the way for a discussion of an imperative. To those who want to be under the law, Paul asks them if they have heard what the law says (4.21). Such a question sets up a call for an imperative. The way to be under the law is to follow the commands of the law.[39] So to those who want to be under the law, Paul gives a specific command to follow.

Fifth, the epigrammatic statement in 5.9 that a little leaven leavens the whole lump may be read in the light of 1 Cor. 5.6 ('Purge out the old leaven!') as an indirect appeal to expel the troublemakers.[40] And Paul's own 'cutting remarks' about his race (5.12)[41] may be seen as a bit of shock treatment intended to help the Galatian believers to view the troublemakers as simply mutilators of the flesh, and so to exclude them on that basis. After all, the Torah clearly commanded that a mutilated person be excluded from the Jewish congregation (see Deut. 23.1).[42]

Sixth, the request in Gal. 4.30 for this severe action to be taken is consonant with the pronouncement of anathema in 1.8-9 upon anyone—even an angel, or Paul himself—who would preach a gospel contrary to the one originally given by Paul to the Galatians.[43]

Thus, it appears, the focal point in the Hagar–Sarah allegory is the imperative to expel the bondwoman and her son. Paul's use of the biblical story is intended to support his appeal for the Galatian believers to expel the troublemakers from their churches.

Allegorical Definitions

In his application of the imperative in the Hagar-Sarah story to the Galatian churches, Paul constructs a series of allegorical definitions. Contemporary Jewish exegesis of the Hagar-Sarah story supported the position of the troublemakers.[44] So Paul finds it necessary to redefine the terms of the story so that he can draw out its real meaning as he sees it, as opposed to the customary Jewish understanding. Paul claims that the true meaning of the terms can only be understood when it is realized that the Hagar-Sarah story is an allegory (ἅτινά ἐστιν ἀλληγορούμενα [4.24]).

In our study of rhetorical techniques we observed that when a technical definition is opposed to a customary definition in argumentation, the technical definition is sometimes justified by an appeal to scientific or popular etymology.[45] And this is what is true of Paul's argumentation here. The definitions which he develops to reverse the customary interpretation of the story are derived from an allegorical method of exegesis which resorts to the etymology of Hagar's name and word-associations between names.[46] It is important, therefore, to review briefly the allegorical definitions which Paul constructs in his attempt to validate his use of the imperative.

The basic purpose of Paul's allegorical definitions is to establish the identification of the troublemakers with Hagar and Ishmael (4.24b-25) and the identification of the Galatian believers with Sarah and Isaac (4.26.28). The identification of Hagar and Ishmael with the troublemakers is developed in four steps.

1. αὗται γάρ εἰσιν δύο διαθῆκαι, μία μὲν ἀπὸ ὄρους Σινᾶ εἰς δουλείαν γεννῶσα, ἥτις ἐστίν Ἁγάρ.
2. τὸ δὲ Ἁγὰρ Σινᾶ ὄρος ἐστὶν ἐν τῇ Ἀραβίᾳ.
3. συστοιχεῖ δὲ τῇ νῦν Ἰερουσαλήμ.
4. δουλεύει γὰρ μετὰ τῶν τέκνων αὐτῆς

The first step identified Hagar with the Sinaitic covenant and the children of Hagar with the children of that Sinaitic covenant.[47] The logic of this correlation is based on the implicit premise that the children of a slave woman are slaves. Therefore, if Hagar represents the covenant from Mount Sinai, then the children of that covenant are destined to be slaves—since the children of Hagar, the slavewoman, were destined to be slaves. Paul has, of course, already sought to demonstrate through such a line of reasoning in chapter 3 that those who adhere to the Sinaitic covenant are imprisoned and enslaved by it (3.19–4.10). His allegorical interpretation here, however, is not intended primarily as an additional proof of the same point. It is rather presented as a first step towards identifying the troublemakers with Hagar's children so that he can apply the imperative of Gen. 21.10 to the crisis in Galatia.

The second step strengthens the Hagar–Sinaitic covenant comparison. Such a comparison contradicts the customary understanding that the Sinaitic covenant was given to the descendants of Isaac and so was unrelated to Hagar and her descendants.[48] Paul seeks, however, to establish the Hagar–Sinaitic covenant equation on the basis of a Hagar– Mount Sinai equation. This equation appears to rest on two points: the etymological meaning of Hagar's name and the geographical location of Mount Sinai. The use of the neuter article τό with the female name Ἁγάρ indicates that Paul's concern is the name itself.[49] In a way which is now the cause for interminable debate, Paul considers the name 'Hagar' to be a reference to Mount Sinai.[50] Paul also appears to defend his Hagar–Mount Sinai equation by his reference to the geographical location of Mount Sinai ἐν τῇ Ἀραβίᾳ. Thus Hagar represents Mount Sinai because Mount Sinai is in Arabia, which is the land of the descendants of Hagar and Ishmael.[51]

The third step in Paul's identification of the children of Hagar as the troublemakers in Galatia is his assertion that Mount Sinai corresponds to the present Jerusalem. This addition of Jerusalem to the allegorical equation only makes sense on the supposition that the troublemakers themselves were closely identified with the Jerusalem church. It is likely, therefore, that Jerusalem is mentioned in Paul's allegory in order to increase the number of points of contact between his Jerusalem orientated opponents and the descendants of Hagar. A.T. Lincoln suggests that 'Paul's reference to Jerusalem and his emphatic formulation in the next verse—'But the Jerusalem above is free, she is our mother'—was provoked by the fact that one of the slogans of the Judaizers was Ἰερουσαλὴμ ἥτις ἐστιν μήτηρ ἡμῶν'.[52]

Paul supports his Mount Sinai–Jerusalem equation by his forth step which draws attention to a common characteristic of slavery which he attributes both to the children of the Sinaitic covenant and to the children of Jerusalem—viz., the proud repository of the traditions of the Sinaitic covenant. Since the Sinaitic covenant was received at Mount Sinai and revered at Jerusalem, and since the Sinaitic covenant enslaved all who received and revered it,[53] it

followed in Paul's thought that Mount Sinai and Jerusalem could be
equated on the basis of this common characteristic of slavery.
Furthermore, since the demands of the Sinaitic covenant were being
stressed by the troublemakers and since they emphasized the
authority of the Jerusalem church, it also follows that they are
themselves in slavery and can therefore appropriately be identified as
the children of Hagar, the slavewoman.

Admittedly, this attempt to follow Paul's process of allegorical
definition assumes a number of debatable points. But whatever
rationale Paul used for his equations of Hagar with Mount Sinai and
the present Jerusalem, the goal of all these equations is the
imperative of v. 30. In other words, Paul's allegorical interpretation
is not, as many have taken it, a broadside against all Jews or Judaism
in general.[54] Its aim is the identification of the troublemakers in
Galatia with Ishmael, and hence the implementation of their
expulsion in obedience to the demand of the law to ἔκβαλε τὴν
παιδίσκην καὶ τὸν υἱὸν αὐτῆς.

The identification of the Galatian believers with the children of
Sarah begins with a contrast between the present Jerusalem, whose
children are in slavery, and the Jerusalem above, which is free.
Gaston, noting the νῦν and ἄνω are not really opposites, suggests
that 'Paul's logic seems to make sense only if the two references are
somehow related, the one explaining the other'.[55] A.T. Lincoln, on
the other hand, shows how the mixed nature of the antithesis
between the two Jerusalems carries well Paul's emphasis on realized
eschatology:

> The emphasis on realized eschatology comes in a setting where
> Paul has to stress in the face of Judaizing opposition that his
> readers' salvation is already complete. By faith the Galatians are
> already members of the heavenly Jerusalem. The enticement of the
> fuller gospel held out to them by those purporting to represent
> Jerusalem could add nothing to such a status. It could only detract,
> for if they succumbed they would thereby become enslaved to the
> law so characteristic of the earthly Jerusalem. The heavenly
> Jerusalem by contrast stands for the new order of salvation bound
> up with the new age which is accessible now to faith.[56]

The *present* Jerusalem is considered to be part of 'the present evil
age' (1.4). The double use of the present tense (ἐστιν)—'the
Jerusalem above *is* free, she *is* our mother'—indicates that the
apocalyptic image of the eschatological heavenly Jerusalem[57] is

considered by Paul to be a reality now being experienced by the Galatian believers.

From this identification of his converts as the children of the Jerusalem above, Paul moves on toward his goal of identifying them as the children of Sarah. Isaiah 54.1, a prophecy of the future prosperity of Jerusalem, is applied by Paul to the Jerusalem above, the mother of the Galatian believers. In light of the tendency of the early church to interpret Isaiah 40–66 Christologically,[58] it is not surprising that Paul appropriates this prophecy for the Galatian church.[59] The quotation is, in fact, easily associated with Sarah, since both Sarah and Jerusalem were barren women.[60] Moreover, the children borne by these barren women were not the result of natural processes (κατὰ σάρκα) but were the result of the activity of God (κατὰ πνεῦμα). This similarity, of course, provides another link with the Galatian believers, who came to birth κατὰ πνεῦμα and were now being called upon by the troublemakers in Galatia to live their lives κατὰ σάρκα. Yet a further link between Gentile believers, the children of Sarah, and the Jerusalem above is the fact that the prophecy of the multiplication of the children of Sarah and Jerusalem was understood by Paul to refer to the ingathering of the Gentiles.[61]

Thus Paul's allegorical definitions, as based on these word associations and conceptual links, lead to the assertion of 4.28: ὑμεῖς δὲ, ἀδελφοί, κατὰ Ἰσαὰκ ἐπαγγελίας τέκνα ἐστέ. The equation in 4.29 of Ishmael's persecution of Isaac and the opponents' persecution of Galatian Christians is the final step in the identification of the children of Hagar and Sarah. This identification is constructed by Paul to justify his use of the biblical command to expel the bondwoman and her son, which he interprets as a command to Gentile, Galatian Christians to expel the Jewish-Christian trouble-makers.

Conceptual Framework for Ethics

While the Hagar–Sarah allegory serves primarily as the basis for Paul's biblical appeal to resist the influence of the intruders, it also as a consequence, serves as the foundation for the ethical instructions of the rest of the letter.

The ethical instructions given in 5.13–6.10[62] have often been viewed as directed toward a problem or 'front' different from the problem addressed in 3.1–5.12.[63] The problem which Paul faces in chs. 3 and 4 is obviously some form of nomism; the problem under discussion in 5.13–6.10 is presumed to be a form of libertinism, since Paul warns his readers in 5.13 μόνον μὴ τὴν ἐλευθερίαν εἰς ἀφορμὴν τῇ σαρκί, describes the opposition of the flesh to the spirit, and lists the works of the flesh (5.19-21). Do these verses (5.13–6.10) indicate that Paul's opponents were, after all, not nomists, but libertines?[64] Or are they Paul's answer to a set of opponents (libertines) different from those (nomists) he addressed in the previous section?[65] Or is 5.13–6.10 Paul's defense against misinterpretations of and accusations against his law-free gospel?[66] Or does this section indicate that while the intruders were nomists, the resident problem in the Galatian churches was a struggle with the flesh, libertinism?[67]

None of these common explanations of Paul's apparent change of direction in 5.13ff adequately accounts for the relation of the Hagar-Sarah allegory to the ethical section.[68] If, however, as I have proposed, epistolary analysis indicates that 4.12–6.10 is the request section of the letter and that the allegory states in biblical terms what is then applied in paraenetical terms, then the close relation between the allegory and the ethical section needs to be more closely examined.

The way in which 4.21-31 provides a foundational framework for the ethical section can be seen by observing Paul's use of the ἐλευθερία—δουλεία and πνεῦμα—σάρξ antitheses. The fact that Paul introduces the story without reference to the names, Hagar and Sarah, but rather with their epithets, slave woman and free woman, points to his emphasis on the slavery–freedom antithesis in 4.21-31.[69] The repetition of this antithesis underscores its importance:[70]

v. 22: ἕνα ἐκ τῆς παιδίσκης   ἕνα ἐκ τῆς ἐλευθέρας
v. 23: ὁ μὲν ἐκ τῆς παιδίσκης   ὁ δὲ ἐκ τς ἐλευθέρας
v. 24: εἰς δουλείαν γεννῶσα
v. 25: δουλεύει γὰρ μετὰ τῶν τέκνων αὐτῆς,
v. 26: ἡ δὲ ἄνω Ἰερουσαλὴμ ἐλευθέρα ἐστιν.
v. 30a: ἔκβαλε τὴν παιδίσκην καὶ τὸν υἱὸν αὐτῆς
v. 30b: οὐ γὰρ μὴ κληρονομήσει ὁ υἱὸς τῆς παιδίσκης μετὰ τοῦ υἱοῦ τῆς ἐλευθέρας
v. 31: διό, ἀδελφοί οὐκ ἐσμέν παιδίσκης τέκνα ἀλλὰ τῆς ἐλευθέρας.

In Paul's quotation of Gen. 21.10 he makes the contrast between slavery and freedom explicit by substituting the phrase μετὰ υἱοῦ τῆς ἐλευθέρας for μετὰ τοῦ υἱοῦ μου Ἰσαάκ.[71] The conclusion of 4.31 is a restatement of the slavery–freedom antithesis so that it cannot be missed. The association of Hagar, the slave woman, with the Sinaitic covenant indicates that slavery is considered to be adherence to the Mosaic law. Freedom, on the other hand, is associated with the promise.

Gal. 5.1 repeats the slavery–freedom antithesis: τῇ ἐλευθερίᾳ ἡμᾶς Χριστὸς ἠλευθέρωσεν. στήκετε οὖν καὶ μὴ πάλιν ζυγῷ δουλείας ἐνέχεσθε. Gal. 5.2-4 clearly indicates that the yoke of slavery referred to here is the law. The stress in this verse is on the imperative στήκετε—the command to preserve and protect freedom in Christ from the danger of falling back into slavery to the law. The word πάλιν indicates that Paul is making an equation between the condition of Gentiles before their faith in Christ and the condition of Jews under the law without Christ.[72]

After the emphatic declaration in 5.2-12 that faith and Christ, on the one hand, and circumcision and law, on the other hand, are exclusive alternatives, Paul's imperatative of 5.13 echoes the command of 5.1. In both 5.1 and 5.13 there is first an indicative statement regarding freedom in Christ, which is then followed by an imperative and a warning. In 5.1 Paul commands the Galatians to stand fast; in 5.13 he exhorts them to serve one another in love. The warning of 5.1 is against a return to slavery; in 5.13 it is against giving opportunity to the flesh.

The fact that in 5.13 Paul warns that the flesh is the danger to freedom in Christ, instead of slavery to the Law, has led many to suppose that Paul begins to attack libertinism and lawlessness in 5.13.[73] The description of the warfare between the flesh and the spirit in the verses which follow is understood to confirm this supposition. But it should be noted that the Hagar–Sarah allegory has already established that freedom is threatened by both the Sinaitic covenant and the flesh. In other words, Paul uses the allegory to identify slavery with both the Sinaitic covenant and the flesh. Those who are according to the flesh, like Ishmael, are identified with those who are proponents of the Sinaitic covenant. And in light of the freedom-slavery antithesis in the allegory, it would appear that the imperatives in 5.1 and 5.13 are aimed against the same threat to freedom in Christ: the threat of nomism which boasts in the flesh.

The fact that this same threat is addressed in the conclusion of the letter at 6.12-13 confirms this interpretation. Paul has not changed fronts to fight against libertinism in 5.13-6.10. His attack against the works of the flesh is a continuation of his attack against the works of the law. The intruders campaign for circumcision and the law evidently led to social disorder and a lack of love in the Galatian community. In Paul's list of the works of the flesh these social sins receive the major emphasis.[74] Thus Howard is right to conclude that

Paul's ethical section is neither an attack on the libertinism of non-Jewish opponents nor a defense of his gospel in the face of charges of libertinism. His thought is far removed from either of these. Rather his language suggests that the thrust of his argument is the theological claim that to be under the law is to be under sin. His words are directed specifically to a judaizing situation which would force the Galatians to complete their salvation by moving from the Spirit to the flesh.[75]

This interpretation of the ethical section is supported by observing Paul's use of the flesh–spirit antithesis in the allegory and the ethical section. The warfare between the flesh and the spirit described in 5.13-24 is already portrayed in the allegory: ὁ κατὰ σάρκα γεννηθεὶς ἐδίωκεν τὸν κατὰ πνεῦμα (4.29). R. Jewett argues that

there are good reasons to insist that the character of 'flesh' is formally the same in both passages. In both, it stands in opposition to Christ and his realm. In both passages it is the flesh which takes the offensive against the spirit and in both it reduces man to slavery. Furthermore, the nature of the flesh is formally similar in both passages; it is at once a cosmic sphere and a realm of human capability or action. And one wonders if it has not been the failure to grasp this last mentioned point which is partially responsible for disguising the close parallelism between these two passages. In Gal. 4.21-31, 'he who is born according to the flesh' refers to the concrete person of Ishmael (v. 23) as well as to the present believers in the law (v. 29). But the term reaches beyond concrete personal reality to the sphere of the old covenant which was enacted in history (vv. 24ff.), a sphere which dominated those who belonged to it until Paul's day. Thus Paul can say that all who presently belonged to this sphere were slaves just as Hagar was. Σάρξ is both personal and extra-personal in its scope. The same could be said for σάρξ in Gal. 5.13ff. On the one had man's concrete bodily flesh constitutes the source of sensual desires, and on the other hand it acts independent of man to oppose the spirit.[76]

And yet despite these remarkable similarities between the use of 'flesh' in the allegory and in the ethical section, Jewett maintains that 'there seems to be considerable disparity between the situation of trusting circumcised flesh which is dealt with in Gal. 4.21ff. and the situation of sensual libertinism which is dealt with in Gal. 5.13ff'.[77]

It is instructive to note, however, that in the ethical section, Paul's description of the opposition of the flesh and the Spirit is developed as a way of explaining the Christian's relationship to the law. The law is still the central factor in Paul's thinking (5.14, 18, 23, 6.2). In light of 5.18, it is still his concern to show how to live so as not to be under the law. His statement that the one who is led by the Spirit is not under the law implies that a life under the law is a life subject to the desires of the flesh. The works of the flesh, then, are to be seen as the result of living under the law rather than under the guidance of the Spirit. The result of living under the guidance of the Spirit is the fruit of the Spirit, against which there is no law (5.23). For love fulfills the law (5.14). It is the Spirit, not the Law, which has the power to liberate one from the desires of the flesh. 'Clearly the law dominates this section of Paul's letter. The law is still the problem', as D. Fletcher points out.[78] It is the attempt of the troublemakers to apply the law that they may boast in the circumcised flesh of the Galatians (6.13) which evokes the strong imperative of 4.30, 5.1, and 5.13. These imperatives are best understood as a unified series of appeals.

Thus the biblical appeal (4.21-31) sets the stage for the authoritative appeal (5.1-12) and the ethical appeal (5.13-6.10). The description in 5.13ff of the opposition of the flesh against the spirit and of freedom from slavery under the law is built upon the foundation established by Paul's construction of those antitheses in the Hagar–Sarah allegory.

3. *Conclusion*

We have observed that the traditional view of 4.21-31 as simply a supplement to Paul's argument beginning at 3.1 is unsatisfactory for a number of reasons. The new perspective gained by our epistolary and rhetorical analyses enables us to see that the Hagar–Sarah allegory was carefully crafted by Paul to add biblical weight to his request that the Galatians protect their freedom in Christ by expelling the troublemakers. The terminology developed in the allegory lays the foundation for viewing Gal. 5 as a unified appeal to preserve this freedom against the threat of nomism.

CONCLUSIONS AND IMPLICATIONS

The aim of this work has been to describe the function of Paul's use of the Abraham story in the light of our epistolary and rhetorical analyses. The details of that description have been provided above and cannot be recounted here. It will, however, be helpful to draw together the main lines of our research in a summary statement and then suggest a few major implications for Pauline theology which arise out of our study.

Summary Statement

The Function of the Abraham Argument (3.6-29)

Our epistolary analysis of Galatians leads to the conclusion that Paul used a rebuke-request form common in Hellenistic letters. The recognition of this form enables us to see that the autobiographical section (1.13-2.14) and the Abraham argument (3.6-29) are subordinate to Paul's expressions of rebuke and function as substantiation of that rebuke for desertion to another gospel (1.6-7; 3.1-5; 4.9-11). Our consideration of the opponents' use of the Abraham tradition[1] and our study of the portraits of Abraham in Jewish literature[2] indicate that the historical context for Paul's development of his Abraham argument was the intrusion into the Galatian churches of a theology which used the Abraham story to support the demand for circumcision and the observance of the Mosaic law. In order to demonstrate how foolish it was to succumb to the influence of this 'bewitching' theology, Paul reinterpreted the Abraham story in a way that dissociated his gospel from the 'other gospel'.

Although Paul's interpretation of the Abraham story reflects some Jewish exegetical principles,[3] our understanding of the Abraham argument is primarily guided by an analysis of its rhetorical features. The Abraham argument is to be classified within the genre of forensic rhetoric since it serves to provide evidence for Paul's self-defense and accusations: in the autobiography Paul defends his loyalty to the gospel revealed to him; in the Abraham argument Paul presents the biblical basis of his gospel.

The *proposito* (2.15-21) functions rhetorically as the introduction to the Abraham argument. The key terms disclosed in the *propositio* are defined in the Abraham argument. The point of agreement (justification is by faith in Christ, not by the works of the law), the point of disagreement (Jew/Gentile distinctions cannot be rebuilt), and the major thesis (participation in the death of Christ exlcudes the possibility of life or righteousness through the law) as set forth in the *propositio* are defended in the Abraham argument.

Our analysis of chiastic structures within Galatians shows that the Abraham argument is enclosed within rebuking questions (3.1-5; 4.8-11) and descriptions of the bestowal of the Spirit (3.1, 5; 4.4-7). The hinge of the central chisamus is the dissociation of the Abrahamic promise from the Mosaic law (3.15-3.22).

Our examination of the various rhetorical techniques employed by Paul in the development of his Abraham argument reveals that Paul's basic objective is to redefine the key terms of the Abraham story in such a way that Gentile believers are identified as the sons of Abraham and separated from the advocates of the law (οἱ ἐξ ἔργων νόμου). This severance of the advocates of the law from the Galatian churches depends on the dissociation of the Abrahamic covenant and the Mosaic law. Paul devalues the role of the law by showing that it belongs to a different, inferior order from that of the Abrahamic promise by virtue of its negative purpose, its temporary function, and its mediated origin. The Galatian converts are left without any sound reason for turning from the gospel (=Abrahamic covenantal promise) to the Mosaic law. Thus Paul shows that his rebuke of his Galatian converts for their foolishness is well-founded.

The Function of the Hagar–Sarah Allegory (4.21-31)
Our epistolary analysis highlights the fact that the Hagar–Sarah allegory is in the request section of the letter which begins at 4.12. Our rhetorical analysis sugests that Paul's use of the Hagar–Sarah allegory should be classified within the genre of deliberative rhetoric rather than forensic rhetoric, since his primary aim is no longer to accuse or defend but to persuade the Galatian believers to adopt a certain course of action.

The salient point of the allegory is the imperative of 4.30 which applies to the Galatian situation the biblical command to cast out the slave woman and her son. To those who want to be under the law (4.21), Paul provides a command to follow (4.30) which directs the Galatian churches to cast out the troublemakers. Since Gentile believers were identified with the children of Hagar by the opponents' use of this biblical text, it was necessary for Paul to redefine the terms of the story to suit his purpose.

Our analysis of the rhetorical technique of dissociative definitions clarifies the way in which Paul developed allegorical definitions to oppose the customary definitions of the Gen. 21 story. Although the etymological rationale for these allegorical definitions is now somewhat obscure and the occasion of much debate, the theological framework for them is clearly provided by the Abraham argument in the previous section of the letter. The dissociation of the Abrahamic covenant of promise from the Mosaic covenant of law (ch. 3) enables Paul to proceed with his allegorical dissociative definitions of the two women, the two sons, the two covenants, and the two Jerusalems.

The new perspective gained from our epistolary analysis helps us to see that the imperative of 4.30 is one link in a continuous chain of imperatives which begins at 4.12 and extends through the ethical section. Paul's personal appeal to the Galatian Christians to become like him in his loyalty to the gospel of freedom in Christ (4.12) is supported by the biblical imperative of 4.30, which Paul presents as a divine sanction for the expulsion of the promoters of the spurious gospel of bondage to the law. This biblical appeal is restated in Paul's own authoritative appeal to stand firm in the freedom procured by Christ (5.1); it is then applied in his ethical appeal (5.13) to use this freedom in a way that does not lead to bondage under either the flesh or the law.

The close link between these imperatives in the request section of the letter points to the unity of that section. In light of this analysis, the ethical appeal (5.13) has the same purpose as the personal appeal (4.12), the biblical appeal (4.30) and the authoritative appeal (5.1): all four of these imperatives request the Galatian churches to protect and defend the freedom gained by faith in Christ.

Implications for Pauline Theology

Although this study is primarily a description of the structure of Galatians and of Paul's use of Abraham in the light of epistolary and

rhetorical analyses, there are some significant implications for
Pauline theology which emerge. It is, of course, not possible to enter
into a full discussion of these issues here. It is, however, important to
conserve the results of our work by sketching out some of the
theological insights which can be derived from our analyses.

Inclusion of the Gentiles and Justification by Faith
In current discussion the purpose of the Abraham argument in
Galatians is viewed as either (1) a scriptural argument for the
doctrine of justification by faith apart from the works of the law—a
soteriological purpose,[4] or (2) a scriptural defense of the identity of
the Gentile church as the sons of Abraham—an ecclesiological
purpose,[5] or (3) a scriptural basis for Paul's mission to preach the
gospel to the Gentiles—a missiological purpose.[6] Yet rather than
reducing Paul's argument to any one of these purposes, it is possible
to correlate these three purposes on the basis of our analyses.

    These three purposes for the Abraham argument can be viewed as
three concentric circles. The inner circle is the immediate context of
the Abraham story in Gal. 3.6-16. The citations in 3.6 (Gen. 15.6)
and 3.8 (Gen. 12.3; Gen. 18.18) either contain or are explained by
'justification by faith' language. Furthermore, these citations are
related to the contrast between faith and the works of the law (2.16;
3.2, 5) and to a chain of seven OT quotations (3.6-16) which
undergirds the dissociation of faith from the law. This context
indicates that one purpose for Paul's use of the Abraham story is to
show that justification is by faith in Christ apart from the works of
the Mosaic law.

    The middle circle is the context of the entire section of the letter
which contains the Abraham argument (3.1-4.11). The theme of this
section is the Gentiles' experience of the Spirit and their inclusion as
true sons of Abraham, and so heirs of the promise. The opening verse
of Paul's exposition on Gen. 15.6 ('so you see that it is men of faith
who are the sons of Abraham', 3.7) and the closing verse of his
exposition ('if you are Christ's then you are Abraham's offspring,
heirs according to the promise', 3.29) demonstrate that one of the
purposes of the Abraham argument is to identify Gentile believers as
the people of God, the true sons of Abraham.

    The outer circle is the context of the letter itself and Paul's
expressed purpose for writing to the Galatians. An examination of
the introduction and conclusion of the letter indicates that Paul's

purpose in writing was to defend his mission to Gentiles, which he had received by a special revelation from Christ, against those who would pervert his gospel by compelling the Gentiles to receive circumcision, and hence, the whole law. His use of Gen. 12.3 to qualify and apply his quotation of Gen. 15.6 is evidence that a dominant interest of Paul was the blessing promised for all the Gentiles. When it is observed that this promised blessing is further interpreted as the gift of the Spirit to uncircumcised Gentiles in 3.14, it then is reasonable to conclude that the Abraham argument serves Paul's purpose of defending his mission to the Gentiles.

With evidence to indicate that in Galatians the Abraham story serves all three purposes, it becomes inappropriate to force an either/ or choice and argue that Paul's use of this story serves only one purpose. But if the Abraham story serves all three purposes, how do these purposes relate to each other?

When seen in the context of the development of Paul's thought in Galatians, it seems plausible to argue along the following lines with regard to the relation between these purposes.

1. The overall purpose of the letter is to defend Paul's mission to the Gentiles. To achieve this purpose Paul rebukes his Gentile converts for departing from the gospel preached beforehand to Abraham and commands them to expel those who have perverted this gospel. Thus the Abraham story serves this overall purpose.

2. The defense of Paul's mission, however, is supported by an extended argument for the inclusion of uncircumcised Gentiles as sons of Abraham.

3. Furthermore, the argument for the inclusion of uncircumcised Gentiles is supported by an argument for justification by faith in Christ apart from the works of the law.

It is possible to view these three purposes for the Abraham argument as a series of steps in the development of Paul's theology. (1) The historical beginning point in Paul's line of theological reasoning is his unique call by the crucified and risen Messiah to preach the gospel to the Gentiles. (2) In Paul's mind, this mission implies and demands the inclusion of the Gentiles as sons of Abraham without compelling them to become Jews, i.e., to accept circumcision and the Mosaic law. His mission was to publicly portray Jesus as crucified (3.1, 13) so 'that in Christ Jesus the blessing of Abraham might come upon the Gentiles' (3.14). (3) The inclusion of uncircumcised Gentiles in the blessing of Abraham by faith in Christ led Paul to the doctrine of justification by faith in Christ apart from the works of the law. Since the blessing of God, the gift of the Spirit, was actually received by the Gentiles through faith in the proclamation of the cross of Christ, all other means of receiving the blessing of Abraham are excluded. Thus obedience to the Mosaic law cannot be the way to life and righteousness.

These three steps appear to provide a basic, rudimentary outline for the development of Paul's thought. At least it seems clear that Paul's starting point was the revelation from the risen Christ of his Gentile mission. It is important to remember, however, that the historical point of beginning for a line of argument is not the same as the logical basis for that argument. Neither is the primary psychological motivation for an argument the same as the logical basis for that argument. It may well be that Paul's defense of his call and mission in Gal. 1-2 reveals the historical starting point for his theology. Or, though it is more difficult to prove, a case can be made for the thesis that 'Paul's major theological concern' (i.e., his primary psychological motivation) was 'the justification of the legitimacy of his apostleship to and gospel for the Gentiles'.[7] But neither the historical starting point for his argument nor the motivation for that argument provide the logical grounds on which his argument is built or from which it proceeds.

Viewed from the perspective of *logical* progression, the Abraham story serves the purpose of defending a doctrine of justification by faith in Christ apart from the works of the law. This doctrine is the logical basis for the inclusion of the Gentiles. Since one is justified by faith apart from works of the law, the uncircumcised Gentiles can be included as recipients of the promise by faith in Christ. And this doctrine is, in turn, the logical basis for the Gentile mission of Paul. For since Gentiles are included by faith apart from the works of the law, Paul's mission to and gospel for the Gentiles is valid.

The Galatian Church and the Israel of God

Paul concludes his letter with a benediction: καὶ ὅσοι τῷ κανόνι τούτῳ στοιχήσουσιν, εἰρήνη ἐπ᾽ αὐτοὺς καὶ ἔλεος καὶ ἐπὶ τὸν Ἰσραὴλ τοῦ Θεοῦ (6.16). The relation between those who are loyal to Paul's rule and the 'Israel of God' has been the subject of extended scholarly discussion.[8] The grammatical arguments are not conclusive: the third καὶ of the sentence may be taken as either epexegetic[9] or ascensive.[10] Thus it is grammatically possible to read Paul's benediction either as making an equation between the Galatian church and the Israel of God or as distinguishing between the Galatian church and the Israel of God. Those who argue for the latter position interpret 'Israel of God' as a reference to Jewish Christians,[11] to Jewish Christians who agree with the rule of 6.15,[12] to the nation Israel,[13] to pious Israel within the Jewish nation,[14] or to those within Israel who will receive the good news of Christ, the mercy of God.[15]

Without engaging in an extended discussion of this issue, our analysis of Galatians suggests that Paul has equated Galatian believers and the Israel of God. Paul uses the Abraham argument and the Hagar–Sarah allegory to identify the Galatian believers as being the sons of Abraham, the seed of Abraham, the heirs of the covenantal promises to Abraham, the recipients of the blessing of Abraham, and the children of Sarah, the free woman, through promise according to the spirit. Furthermore, the Abraham argument is constructed to accomplish the severance of those who are according to the flesh amd of the works of the law from the Galatian believers, who are the sons of Abraham and the children of Sarah. It would be contrary to the structure and direction of Paul's entire argument to interpret this final statement of the letter in terms of a distinction between Galatian believers and the true people of God, the 'Israel of God'.[16] Admittedly, Paul does not use this expression of his converts or of the church elsewhere. And, certainly, he makes distinctions between Gentile believers and Israel in his other letters.[17] But an analysis of Galatians supports the view that—at least in this case—Paul has taken over the name of Israel for Gentile believers in Christ and the Galatian church.

Paul's Critique of Judaism
Paul's letter to the Galatians has often been read as a wholesale attack on Judaism for its legalism.[18] Our analysis, however, has shown that Paul's rebuke is aimed at Galatian Christians who were departing from the true gospel and at Jewish Chrstians who were perverting that gospel. There is no basis for broadening the scope of this attack to include all of Judaism.

Furthermore, it is not accurate to say that Paul accuses Jewish Christians of legalism. He says in 2.15-16 that the common confession of Jewish Christians is that justification is by faith in Jesus Christ, not by the works of the law. In other words, Paul does not say that Jewish Christians have a legalistic attitude toward their own salvation. The problem is not really legalism. It is nationalism—viz., the demand that all Gentile Christians must become part of the Jewish nation before they can enjoy the full blessing of God. The particular works of the law being called for are badges of membership in the Jewish nation. Paul's response to this problem is that Galatian believers have already experienced the full blessing of Abraham since they have received the Spirit by faith in Christ. So they already belong to the people of God. Furthermore, as Paul argues from the Abraham story, the original badge of membership in the family of Abraham was exhibited by Abraham himself in his response of faith, for Abraham believed God (Gal. 3.6).

The Covenantal Pattern
Our analysis of Paul's use of the Abraham story in Gal. 3–4 points to a convenantal pattern in Paul's thought.[19] The Abrahamic covenant is interpreted in the light of the Christ event as the OT basis of Christian faith. It is true that διαθήκη itself is not prominent in Paul's argument. The term is found in 3.15 where it serves as part of an example from a human will or testament which cannot be changed or annulled once it has been ratified. In 3.17, however, it is used to refer to the διαθήκην προκεκυρωμένημ ὑπὸ τοῦ Θεοῦ, the covenant which God ratified with Abraham 430 years before the law. Here ἐπαλλελία is used as a synonym for διαθήκη, and the frequent repetition of ἐπαγγελία in the unfolding of the Abraham argument suggests something of the significance of the covenantal promise to Abraham in Paul's thought. The term promise was probably used instead of covenant in order to facilitate the dissociation of the Abrahamic covenant from the Mosaic law. Covenant and Torah had become synonymous terms in Jewish literature. So, it seems, Paul drops the term covenant, but retains the concept of the Abrahamic covenant as the central focus of his Abraham argument by his constant reference to the Abrahamic promise.

Morna Hooker has set forth the basic structure of the covenantal pattern as being 'divine initiative > human response > obedience or adherence to the divine will > future judgment'.[20] This pattern not only represents the structure of the OT covenants, it can also be seen in Paul's use of the Abrahamic promise in his letter to the Galatians.[21] Paul emphasizes the *divine initiative* in his preface, which announces as the essence of the gospel that Christ has rescued us from the present evil age (1.4). Through God's initiative both the Galatians (1.6; cf. 5.8, 13) and Paul (1.15) were called into relationship with God by grace. The appropriate *human response* to God's grace expressed in Christ is faith in Christ. This was the response of Abraham, and it is the response of the sons of Abraham (3.6-7). But Paul also expects that the response of faith will be accompanied by *obedience or adherence to the divine will*. Obedience is not measured by keeping the law of Moses but by an active response to the gospel of Christ. So Paul rebukes those at Antioch for not living according to the truth of the gospel (2.14); so he asks his Galatian converts as to who hindered them from obeying the truth (5.7); and so he declares that 'faith works through love' (5.6). In closing the Galatian letter, Paul sets out his understanding of the gospel as the standard (κανών) to which Galatian churches must adhere (6.15-16). And he warns that *future judgment* awaits the troublemakers (5.10)—those who practise the works of the flesh (5.21) and those who sow to the flesh (6.7-8).

Paul's argument has all the principal elements of the covenantal pattern. He uses the Abraham story to present the Galatians' covenantal privileges and covenantal obligations. Their fundamental privilege is that they are heirs of the Abrahamic promise—that promise which has already been at least partially fulfilled in their experience of the Spirit and which came through faith in Christ who became a curse for them on the cross (3.13-14). This privilege forms the basis of their fundamental obligation; for since they live by the Spirit, they are also to walk according to the Spirit (5.25).

So Paul uses the Abraham story as the biblical foundation for both the indicative and the imperative of Christian life.

APPENDICES:

CONTEXTUAL AND HISTORICAL STUDIES

APPENDIX 1

THE OPPONENTS' USE OF THE ABRAHAM TRADITION

1. Methodological Considerations

Since Paul wrote to his Galatian converts in order to rebuke them for shifting their allegiance to the perverse gospel of certain 'trouble-makers',[1] an identification of these agitators and their theology is a necessary prerequisite for an accurate appraisal of Paul's rebuke. Unfortunately, however, extensive discussion of the identity and theology of the intruders has only generated a wide diversity of conflicting theories.[2] The intruders have been identified as Jewish Christians, Gentile Christians, non-Christian Jews, residents of Galatia, resident of Judea, Judaizers, syncretistic Jewish Christians, Gnostic Jewish Christians, mystic-apocalyptic, ascetic, non-conformist, Jewish Christians akin to Essene propagandists, judaizing and libertine pneumatics, envoys of the Jerusalem apostles, and/or competitors of the Jerusalem apostles.

Before we can make any progress in identifying Paul's opponents at Galatia, we must first establish certain fundamental principles of a sound methodology.[3] Here we would outline five:

(1) A first principle of such a sound methodology is certainly the recognition that the letter itself is the primary source of evidence.[4] Attempts to interpret Galatians in the light of the current religious situation in Asia Minor illuminate interesting features of Hellenistic mystery religions and Judaism in that area.[5] But it remains difficult to relate this data to the issues encountered by the Galatian churches. Likewise, endeavors to explain the heresy at Galatia in terms of data found in Paul's other letters (such as 1 Corinthians and Colossians) must always be tempered by the realization that the differences between these letters and Galatians presuppose significant differences between their respective situations.[6] Historical and

literary parallels, of course, can serve by way of corroborative evidence to the picture derived from the letter itself. But such data must be handled with care. For, as Brinsmead warns, 'we may crush a fragile piece of evidence for earliest Christianity if we too quickly interpret Galatians out of systems reconstructed from external materials'.[7]

(2) A second principle of a reliable methodology is the use of the genre and structure of the entire letter as a guide in the identification of the opponents. Tyson and Brinsmead have both, each in his own way, emphasized the need for this principle, as opposed to the rather common practice of using only certain texts or even just one portion of the letter.[8] However, Tyson's understanding of Galatians as a 'defensive letter' and Brinsmead's thesis that Galatians is a 'apologetic letter' need to be modified in light of the evidence which we brought forward that Galatians is a 'rebuke–request' letter.

Tyson's procedure is to list the main points of Paul's defense and then reverse them to identify the charges made against Paul by the opponents. So he summarizes Paul's defense as follows:[9]

1. My apostleship is not from human agency.
2. My contact with the στῦλοι has been infrequent, and I am not subordinate to them; I have clashed with them on some occasions but they have recognized my apostleship.
3. The στῦλοι have agreed not to require circumcision for Gentile Christians.
4. I do not now preach circumcision.
5. Sonship to Abraham is not a matter of physical descent.
6. Circumcision is not necessary to Christianity.

Tyson then works out the opponents' theology as a reversal of Paul's defensive statement:[10]

1. Paul's apostleship is human.
2. Paul has had frequent contact with the στῦλοι: he is their subordinate; he tries to please them.
3. The στῦλοι require circumcision.
4. Paul preaches circumcision.
5. Physical descent from Abraham is required for justification.
6. Circumcision is necessary to Christianity.

This group of charges, according to Tyson, comes from a consistent 'Judaizing' point of view which does not see itself as opposed to Paul.

Furthermore, the opponents were Jewish-Christians native to Galatia.[11]

Tyson's method, of course, is not totally without merit. Yet Brinsmead rightly points out that 'Tyson is incorrect in concluding that Galatians is only defensive. It is also offensive, but even further, it is dialogical'.[12] Brinsmead's own effort to identify the opponents' theology, however, neglects to include an explanation of the criteria by which he decides which of Paul's terms sometimes reflect, sometimes contradict, and sometimes redefine the traditions of the opponents.[13] As a result, Brinsmead's 'dialogical' analysis all too often appears to be based on his own arbitrary speculations, which seem to be more influenced by obscure literary parallels than the data of the text itself.[14]

If, however, we take Galatians as a rebuke–request letter and assume that Paul adequately understood his opponents,[15] then we can accept his statement of the cause for the rebuke as the starting point in our identification of the opponents. It is unlikely that Paul would have negated the persuasiveness of his argument by deliberately fabricating the central facts in the case, which his addresses knew first-hand. On the other hand, it is quite apparent that Paul colors the facts about the intruders by assigning motives and epithets to them which they would surely not have been willing to accept.[16]

(3) A third principle important for our methodology derives also from our epistolary and rhetorical analyses. For since Paul substantiated his rebuke first by developing his autobiography and then giving an exposition of the Abraham story, it must be taken as fairly certain that the major themes of these sections relate, at least in some manner, to the central tenets of the opponents' propaganda. The repetition and amplification of key terms, as we have seen, is a reliable way to trace Paul's development of these main themes.[17] And while caution, of course, must be exercised in relating these major themes to the theology of the opponents, still this is a safer procedure than relying primarily on such ambiguous texts as 5.3 and 6.13 or on such obscure terms as στοιχεῖα for the reconstruction of the opponents' theology.

(4) Careful analysis of Paul's process of redefining key terms is also important in determining the opponents' position.[18] Such 'mirror-reading' is admittedly hazardous. But if we limit ourselves strictly to terms that have been clearly redefined by Paul,[19] we may legitimately suppose that in redefining he is correcting the opponents' definitions.

(5) Finally, close attention to Paul's dissociation of ideas will reveal the synthesis of those ideas which the opponents had attempted to sell to the Galatian churches. As we noted on our survey of rhetorical techniques, dissociation of ideas is used in argumentation to dispute an unacceptable synthesis of those ideas.[20] These five methodological considerations should protect us, at least to some extent, from some of the common pitfalls in the identification of Paul's opponents. More importantly, they give direction to our discussion of one central aspect of their theology.

2. Circumcision and the Abrahamic Covenant

The one undisputed fact in Paul's description of the opponents' campaign at Galatia is their promotion of circumcision: οὗτοι ἀναγκάζουσιν ὑμᾶς περιτέμνεσθαι (5.12 cf., 5.2-12; 2.3-5). Since Gentiles in the Greco-Roman world would not normally have accepted circumcision,[21] it must be asked how the opponents were able to 'bewitch' the Galatian believers into accepting it.

Some scholars have viewed Paul's references to angels (1.8; 3.19), στοιχεῖα (4.3, 9), and the observance of ἡμέρας... μῆνας καὶ καιροὺς καὶ ἐνιαυτούς (4.10) as evidence that the opponents' rationale for circumcision contained elements either of Gnosticism[22] or of the Hellenistic Mystery Religions.[23] This perspective draws upon a wealth of material to show that Gnostic ideas[24] and Hellenistic categories[25] penetrated the religious practice of first century Judaism and Christianity. But it is difficult to show that either Gnosticism[26] or the Mystery Religions[27] advocated circumcision as a *necessary* requirement for spiritual progress. Furthermore, Paul's references to the role of angels in mediating the law (3.19) and to the observance of festivals (4.10) do not necessarily reflect Gnostic or pagan, syncretistic elements. Similar references to angels[28] and the observance of festivals[29] are found in various strands of Jewish literature. And Paul's use of the term στοιχεῖα may simply reflect Paul's attempt to discredit nomism by associating it with slavery to στιοχεῖα. In any case, this term is so notoriously difficult to interpret that it can hardly be used as a clear indication of any aspect of the opponents' theology.[30]

We should first of all attempt to discover the opponents' rationale for circumcision by an analysis of the major themes of Paul's argument against it. One of the most prominent features of Paul's argument in ch. 3 and 4 is the frequency of the name of Abraham (3.6, 7, 8, 9, 14, 16, 18, 29; 4.22). This extended treatment of Abraham is apparently developed by Paul in order to break the spell which the opponents had put upon his converts.[31] Thus it seems reasonable to suppose that the opponents had somehow linked their promotion of circumcision to the Abraham story.[32]

This supposition is confirmed when it is observed how closely circumcision and the Abrahamic covenant are linked in all strands of Jewish literature.[33] The Torah establishes circumcision as the sign of the Abrahamic covenant. Without this sign of circumcision it is impossible to maintain the covenant relationship: 'So shall my covenant be in your flesh an everlasting covenant. Any uncircumcised male who is not circumcised in the flesh of his foreskin shall be cut off from his people; he has broken my covenant' (Gen. 17.10-14). This connection between circumcision and the Abrahamic covenant is made so often in Jewish literature[34] that it becomes difficult to imagine how the opponents could have promoted circumcision without referring to Abraham.

Another useful piece of evidence is provided by Paul's vehement denial that he still preaches circumcision (5.11). Borgen infers from Gal. 5.11 (εἰ περιτομὴν ἔτι κηρύσσω...) that the opponents supported their circumcision campaign by their claim that 'Paul still preaches circumcision'.[35] Of course, Paul's reference to his missionary activity at Galatia (ἃ προλέγω ὑμῖν καθὼς προεῖπον, 5.21) indicates that his message included preaching against the works of the flesh (5.13, 16, 18, 19-21, 24). As Borgen sees it, the opponents defined Paul's preaching against fleshly passions and desires in terms of ethical circumcision.[36] So they presented their demand for bodily circumcision as the logical and necessary completion of Paul's demand for ethical circumcision.[37]

Borgen provides sufficient evidence to show that the ethical interpretation of circumcision as the removal of evil passions and desires was common at that time.[38] His theory appears to receive additional support from the suggestion of some scholars that Gal. 3.3 (ἐναρξάμενοι πνεύματι νῦν σαρκὶ ἐπιτελεῖσθε;) implies that the opponents were presenting bodily circumcision as the means of perfecting or completing what the Galatian believers had begun in their response to Paul's message.[39] However, Borgen's theory fails to explain what rationale the opponents might have given for their claim that physical circumcision was still necessary for the attainment of perfection.[40]

The opponents' rationale seems to be revealed by the way in which Paul inserts Gen. 15.6 as his answer to the series of questions in Gal. 3.1-5.[41] For Abraham is suddenly introduced as the proof that the Spirit (3.2, 5), perfection (3.3), miracles (3.5), and righteousness (3.6) come by way of faith, not by the works of the law (3.2, 5) or by the flesh (3.3).[42] Since Paul develops this argument to free his converts from the bewitching influence of the opponents, it may be inferred that they used Abraham as their proof that perfection was attained by circumcision. That message was an important part of the Abraham tradition beginning with Gen. 17 where the command to be perfect is followed by the instruction on circumcision.[43]

In light of the evidence that (1) the circumcision campaign is countered in Galatians by the extended treatment of Abraham, (2) circumcision is viewed in all Jewish literature as the necessary requirement for participation in the privileges of the Abrahamic covenant, and (3) circumcision is interpreted in Jewish literature as the means by which Abraham attained perfection, it is highly probable that the opponents' rationale for the necessity of physical circumcision was based on an appeal to the Abraham story. Such an appeal appears to have been enough to persuade the Galatian believers that they had to be circumcised in order to maintain their inheritance in the Abrahamic blessings of life and righteousness.[44]

If it is reasonable to suppose that the opponents referred to the Abraham story as the basis for their circumcision campaign, we may then ask what else they might have said about Abraham. What other Abraham traditions did they use in their propaganda? Here, again, the first step in our investigation must be a careful consideration of Paul's method of argumentation. Since in his argument Paul develops an antithetical, discontinous relationship between the Abrahamic promise and the Mosaic law (3.15-18) and between the faith of Abraham and the works of the Mosaic law (3.1-14)[45] it seems plausible to suppose that he is attempting to negate their synthesis of the Abrahamic promise and Mosaic law.[46] This supposition is substantiated by the evidence that one of the most prominent characteristics of Abraham in the Jewish literature of that period was his perfect obedience to the Mosaic law.[47] It is improbable that the agitators at Galatia mentioned Abraham without referring to his adherence to the Mosaic law. And the way in which Paul develops his allegory of Abraham's two sons immediately after his comment that the Galatians desired to be under the law (4.21), suggests that Paul is arguing against a theology which equated Abrahamic sonship with being under the law.[48]

Some scholars, however, have observed that Paul's solemn reminder in Gal. 5.3 (μαρτύρομαι δὲ πάλιν παντὶ ἀνθρώπῳ περιτεμνομένῳ ὅτι ὀφειλέτης ἐστὶν ὅλον τὸν νόμον ποιῆσαι) possibly indicates that the opponents were selective in their application of the Mosaic law.[49] For such a solemn pronouncement would hardly have been necessary if the opponents were emphasizing the same point. Apparently, it was this selectivity on the part of the opponents in their application of the law which called forth Paul's criticism in Gal. 6.13a.[50] It is unlikely that the opponents would have denied, *in principle*, Paul's point that the acceptance of circumcision includes the obligation to keep the whole law.[51] Yet it appears from the evidence in Paul's letter that they only required, *in practice*, the acceptance of circumcision and observance of certain Jewish festivals (4.19),[52] since these were the two minimum requirements for claiming the title and benefits of Abraham's children.[53]

Another emphasis in Paul's use of the Abraham story is his redefinition of the 'seed of Abraham'. The unusual way in which Paul uses this term in order to make it refer to Christ (3.16) and all those who belong to Christ (3.29) suggests that he is probably combatting the agitators' use of the traditional, strictly nationalistic definition of the term.[54]

Brinsmead hypothesizes that the opponents made use of the 'apologetic' picture of Abraham portrayed in the Hellenistic Jewish literature as 'the father of philosophy, astronomy, and culture'.[55] According to Brinsmead, this hypothesis explains why the Gentiles were so impressed by the opponents' use of Abraham that they wished to be circumcised. It is difficult, however, to maintain from the evidence in Paul's letter that he was confronting this 'apologetic' picture of Abraham in the Galatian situation.[56]

In conclusion, we may say that a fairly solid case has been made that the agitators themselves appealed to the Abraham story in their campaign to persuade the Galatian believers to be circumcised. In their use of the Abraham tradition, it is likely that they (1) argued that physical circumcision was the means to perfection, (2) fused together the Abrahamic covenant and the Mosaic law, and (3) emphasized the nationalistic sense of σπέρμα τοῦ Ἀβραάμ. According

to their promotional material, Abraham himself was the example
that validated circumcision and obedience to the Mosaic law.
Without circumcision and obedience to the Mosaic law it was
impossible to participate in the covenantal blessings promised to
Abraham. The Gentiles were bewitched by this propaganda which
emphasized the authoritative, scriptural basis for circumcision and
the Abrahamic blessings to be gained by it.

3. *Conclusions*

Admittedly, this investigation of the opponents' theology has been
limited to suit our own purposes. Nevertheless, we have found
sufficient evidence to confirm the traditional opinion that the
opponents were Jewish-Christians whose primary concerns were
nationalistic and nomistic: they saw membership in the Jewish
nation as the only means of blessing,[57] and they saw the acceptance
of circumcision and the Mosaic law as the only means of membership
in the Israel of God. It is also likely that Paul's polemic against the
'present Jerusalem' in the Hagar–Sarah allegory points to Jerusalem
as the home base for these opponents.[58] It was probably their appeal
to the superior authority of the στύλοι in Jerusalem which evoked
Paul's development of the autobiographical section.

This reconstruction is certainly not novel, but it reveals some of
the weaknesses of several recent hypotheses and brings into focus the
central issue of the Galatian crisis. The opponents were successfully
persuading the Galatians that it was necessary for them to become
proselyte Jews by means of circumcision and submission to the yoke
of the Mosaic law. Since the Abrahamic tradition defined in the light
of the Mosaic covenant was the theological basis of the opponents'
theology, Paul's primary aim was to redefine the Abrahamic
covenant in the light of Christ to demonstrate that faith in Christ is
the only basis for the inclusion of Gentile believers in that
covenant.

APPENDIX 2

ABRAHAM IN JEWISH LITERATURE

The study of the various portraits of Abraham in different strands of Jewish literature serves to highlight certain distinctive features of Paul's portrayal of Abraham in Gal. 3 and 4.[1] In our study of these portraits we will concentrate on those features which relate directly to the emphases of Paul in his reinterpretation of the traditions about Abraham—viz., the righteousness of Abraham, the faith of Abraham, the promised blessing for the seed of Abraham and for the Gentiles, and the relation of Abraham to the Mosaic Law.[2]

Two basic approaches have been taken by scholars in studying Abraham in Jewish literature *vis-à-vis* Paul's portrayal of Abraham.[3] The first sees Abraham in Jewish writings as the quintessence of *legalism*, the paradigm of self-righteousness which Paul deliberately contradicts. This 'These des Apostels-Gegen These des Rabbinismus' perspective is expressly stated in Strack-Billerbeck's survey of Jewish literature[4] and has surfaced in most commentaries on Galatians.[5] And it is this understanding that is vigorously attacked by E.P. Sanders.[6] The second approach is best epitomized by Sanders who argues that first century Judaism was not legalistic, but rather should be characterized by the expression '*covenantal nomism*',[7] and that therefore Paul did not develop his understanding of justification by faith in reaction to some supposedly legalistic system of works righteousness in Judaism. In Sanders' words, 'covenantal nomism is the view that one's place in God's plan is established on the basis of the covenant and that the covenant requires as the proper response of man his obedience to its commandments, while providing means of atonement for transgressions'.[8] Sanders is not willing to allow that covenantal nomism is another view (even though dominant) which may be placed alongside the traditional view that Judaism was a legalistic religion of works-righteousness. He has argued that 'that view is completely wrong: it proceeds from theological presuppositions and is supported by systematically misunderstanding and misconstruing passages in Rabbinic literature'.[9]

Although Sanders does not provide a comprehensive survey of traditions about Abraham,[10] his understanding of Judaism as covenantal nomism leads to a new perspective on the portrayal of Abraham in Jewish literature.[11] For rather than focusing solely on Abraham's righteous deeds, this theme needs to be viewed in the context of the overarching emphasis on God's covenant with Abraham. From the perspective of Sanders' thesis, therefore, Abraham's righteous deeds are not to be seen in Judaism as the basis of his salvation. Rather, they are to be viewed as Abraham's appropriate response to God's action in choosing and establishing the covenant with him.

Abraham's righteous deeds were, indeed, reckoned to be the basis of Abraham's righteousness. But righteousness in Judaism is a term that refers to the 'maintenance of status among the group of the elect' within the covenant relationship initiated by God.[12] Thus the view in Jewish literature that Abraham was rewarded for his righteous deeds and declared righteous on the basis of them does not imply, in Sanders' opinion, that Judaism is legalistic, since salvation (or, to use Sanders' term, 'getting in') depends on the grace of God as expressed in the covenant.[13]

Furthermore, Sanders seeks to demonstrate that the merits of Abraham were not seen in Judaism as a 'treasury' which could be used to offset the demerits of future generations.[14] His righteous deeds were considered beneficial to his descendants 'for they cause God to remember the covenant, to do good deeds for Israel, and to suspend punishment for transgression'.[15] It is the covenant which God made with Abraham which is the basis for Israel's relationship with the blessing from God.

This new approach to the Jewish understanding of Abraham *vis-à-vis* that of Paul's calls upon us here to re-evaluate the sources. So in our survey of the various Abraham traditions in Jewish literature, we will attempt to determine whether these traditions represent legalism or covenantal nomism. The comparison with Paul's portrait of Abraham is observed in the course of our analysis of Gal. 3 and 4.[16] However, before turning to the Jewish sources, a comment on our methodology in the use of these sources is required.

The problems of method in the study of Jewish literature have been widely recognized and debated.[17] As early as 1921, G.F. Moore admonished 'Christian writers on Judaism' that 'the critical ordering and evaluation of the Jewish sources is an indispensible prerequisite for any comparative study of Judaism and Christianity'.[18] The homogenization of references in all the different types of literature without regard to the diversity of theological perspectives and historical settings undermines the accuracy of the interpretation.[19] Admittedly, our brief review here of the traditions of Abraham in Jewish literature cannot hope to take into account all of the issues having to do with the state of the texts, dating of the texts, accuracy of attributions, or determining the historical setting and philosophical outlook of respective texts. Nonetheless, our study will attempt to follow Sandmel's advice 'to keep the different conceptions of Abraham separate from each other'.[20] So we propose to survey the subject according to the usual, broad divisions of Jewish literature: OT, Apocrypha-Pseudepigrapha, DSS, Philo, Josephus, Rabbinic.[21]

1. *The Old Testament*

The righteous conduct of Abraham is highlighted in Gen. 22.15-18 where his obedience in the test of sacrificing Isaac is posited as the basis for God's reconfirmation of his oath to bless Abraham, multiply his seed, and bless all the nations through his seed.[22] The complete scope of Abraham's obedience is described when this promise is repeated to Isaac in Gen. 26.3-5: 'because Abraham obeyed my voice and kept my charge, my commandments, my statutes, and my laws'. Abraham's obedience is also implied in the narrative by his response to the call of God (12.4) and his willingness to be circumcised (17.23).

The dominant emphasis in the OT stories of Abraham, however, is that of promise. As Westermann points out, 'the promise motif is associated with the Abraham cycle in a different and more emphatic way than with the other narrative cycles of patriarchal history'.[23] The narrative begins with God's call, election, and promise of blessing. The tension between the covenantal promises and obstacles to the fulfillment of these promises provides the basic framework for the entire narrative.[24] In context, Gen. 15.6 presents Abraham's faith as trust in God's promise to multiply him as the stars of heaven (15.5).[25] And it is this trust in the promise of God that is declared to be the basis for righteousness being reckoned to him.[26]

Most of the references to Abraham in the OT outside of Genesis are reminders of God's covenantal promises to Abraham.[27] The story of God's deliverance of the people from Egypt is introduced by the statement, 'God remembered his covenant with Abraham, with Isaac, and with Jacob' (Exod. 2.24). The biblical writers often repeat the promise that God gave the land to Abraham, to Isaac, and to Jacob (Exod. 6.8; 33.1; Num. 32.11; Deut. 1.8; 6.10; 9.5; 29.13; 30.20; 34.4). When God proposed to destroy Israel for her idolatry, Moses dissuaded God by reminding him of his promise to Abraham (Exod. 32.13). Likewise, the promise of national restoration is based upon the Abrahamic covenant (Lev. 26.42, 45).

The Deuteronomist stresses that God's election and redemption of Israel is not because of the great size of Israel or her righteousness, but because of the oath which he swore to their fathers, Abraham, Isaac, and Jacob (Deut. 7.8; 9.5). The Psalmist, after describing the exodus and the provisions for Israel in the wilderness, points to the cause for such blessing: 'He is mindful of his covenant forever . . . the covenant which he made with Abraham' (Ps. 105.8-9). In the covenant renewal ceremony depicted in Josh. 24, the election of Abraham (24.3) is the basis for the charge to the people: 'Therefore, fear the Lord, and serve him in sincerity and in faithfulness' (24.14); to which the people respond, 'the Lord our God we will serve, and his voice we will obey' (24.24). So too, the Abrahamic covenant was the basis for faith in the dark days of Israel's history (2 Chron. 20.7, 20; cf. 2 Kgs 13.23). The prayer of confession in the covenant renewal ceremony recounted in Neh. 9 begins with explicit references to the Genesis narrative:

> Thou art the Lord, the God who didst choose Abram and bring him forth out of Ur of the Chaldeans and give him the name Abraham; and thou didst find his heart faithful before thee, and didst make with him the covenant to give to his descendants the land of the Canaanite, the Hittite, the Amorite, the Perizzite, the Jebusite, and the Girgashite; and thou hast fulfilled thy promise, for thou art righteous (9.7-8).

Here an emphasis on God's election of Abraham and his covenant with him is combined with a reflection on Abraham's own response to the convenantal promises. And this reflection on Abraham's response appears to be an allusion to Gen. 15.6.

The references to Abraham in the prophetic writings focus on the identity of the people of Israel as the descendants of Abraham. Isaiah

29.22, 41.8, 51.2,[28] Jer. 33.26, and Mic. 7.20 are statements of reassurance to Israel based upon God's election of the seed of Abraham. On the other hand, Ezek. 33.24 is a warning against any presumptuous claim to the Abrahamic promise.

Our review of the OT references to Abraham indicates that the dominant feature in all of them is God's covenant with Abraham. The primary emphasis is not on Abraham's faith or obedience; it is on God's purpose in the election of Abraham and God's promises made to him.[29] The story of Abraham is recalled as the basis of the Jews' identity: they are the chosen seed of Abraham, the receipients of the blessings promised to Abraham. The faith-obedience of Abraham, as a matter of fact, is a minor theme in the Genesis narrative, and it is only mentioned in Neh. 9.7-8 outside of the Genesis account. God's promises to Abraham were used by the biblical authors (1) to motivate the seed of Abraham to obey the God of Abraham, and (2) to reassure the seed of Abraham that they would benefit from those promises.

2. *Apocrypha-Pseudepigrapha*

The Wisdom of Jesus the Son of Sirach (or *Ecclesiasticus*)
Ben Sirach, a professional scribe in the pre-Maccabean era (c. 195–175 B.C.E.), collected teachings on wisdom and Torah into a book similar in genre and contents to the canonical book of Proverbs.[30] His emphasis is on the practical wisdom of Torah observance. His starting point is the deuteronomic identification of covenant and Torah: Israel is God's chosen people; they have been given the covenant, which sets before them the commandments of Torah; obedience to the Torah is a necessary part of the covenantal status as God's chosen people.[31] Thus Sirach relates the covenant directly to the Torah (17.12; 24.23; 28.7; 44.20).

In this context, Ben Sirach recites the deeds of the heroes from Israel's past:[32]

> Let me now hymn the praises of men of piety;
>> Of our fathers in their generations (44.1). Their memory abideth
> for ever,
> And their righteousness shall not be forgotten (44.13).

After the record of the deeds of Enoch (44.16) and Noah (44.17-18), Abraham is presented:

a Abraham, the father of a multitude of nations,
b Tarnished not his glory;
c Who kept the commandment of the Most High,
d And entered into covenant with Him:
e In his flesh He engraved him an ordinance,
f And in trial he was found faithful.
g Therefore with an oath He promised him
h To bless the nations in his seed,
i To multiply him as the dust of the earth,
j And to exalt his seed as the stars;
k To cause them to inherit from sea to sea,
l And from the River to the ends of the earth (44.19-21).

This account of Abraham is obviously a pastiche of biblical allusions. It is noteworthy that Abraham's obedience to the Law (c) is mentioned before the reference to the covenant (d). This is a reversal of the biblical order (Gen. 12; 22; 26).[33] The identification of circumcision and the covenant (e) echoes Gen. 17.9-14.[34] The citation of Abraham's faithfulness in trial (f) appears to be a combination of Gen. 15.6a ('Abraham believed') and Gen. 22.1 ('God tested Abraham. . . ').[35] This combination redefines Abraham's faith as being obedience to God's command to sacrifice Isaac.[36] The result of Abraham's obedience to the Torah (c), his circumcision (e), and his faithfulness in the trial of binding Isaac (f) is the Lord's promise (g) to bless the nations through his seed (h), to multiply his posterity (i), and to guarantee the inheritance of the land (k-1).[37]

The Book of Jubilees
Jubilees is a midrashic elaboration of Genesis 1–Exodus 12, which Moses supposedly received from the angels on Mount Sinai (1.27, 29; 2.1). The author's pietism is seen most clearly in his pervasive emphasis on the absolute supremacy of the Mosaic law.[38] His expansion of the biblical Abraham story highlights this emphasis. For Abraham kept the Levitical law by observing the feast of first fruits (15.1, 2) and the feast of booths (16.20). And it was while Abraham was celebrating the feast of first-fruits that the Lord appeared to him, giving him an extended address on the great importance and absolute necessity of circumcision (15.9-34); and it was while Abraham celebrated the feast of booths that he rejoiced over the fact that God created and chose him, 'for He knew and perceived that from him would arise the plant of righteousness for eternal generations' (16.26, cf., 11.15-16; 12.19).

In Jubilees' elaboration of Gen. 22 we have the story of the evil prince, Mastema, who prompted God to test Abraham's faithfulness by commanding him to sacrifice Isaac (17.16). The author then provides a record of Abraham's faithfulness to God in previous testings:

> And the Lord knew that Abraham was faithful in all his afflictions; for he had tried him through his country and with famine, and had tried him with the wealth of kings, and had tried him again through his wife, when she was torn (from him), and with circumcision; and had tried him through Ishmael and Hagar, his maidservants, when he sent them away. And in everything wherein he had tried him he was found faithful, and his soul was not impatient, and he was slow to act; for he was faithful and a lover of the Lord (17.17-18).

After the record of the trial of Sarah's death the author notes:

> This is the tenth trial wherewith Abraham was tried, and he was found faithful, patient (19.8).

Likewise, the account of Abraham's last words to Isaac include a detailed summary of the sacrifical laws (22.1-20). And in ch. 23 the life of Abraham is summarized in these words:

> Abraham was perfect in all his deeds with the Lord, and well-pleasing in righteousness all the days of his life (23.10).

Thus Abraham is set forth in Jubilees as the model, despite numerous trials, of strict adherence to the Mosaic law—especially the laws of ritual observance. This portrayal of Abraham reflects the author's concern to maintain his people's national identity and ritual purity in the face of the pressures of Hellenism.[39]

1 Maccabees
1 Maccabees is an historical account of how the family of Mattathias rescued Israel from the attempt of Antiochus Epiphanes to force a complete Hellenization of Palestine. It was probably written sometime between 135 and 65 B.C.E.[40]

In the opening part of his final speech (2.50-52), Mattathias exhorts his sons:

> And now my children, be zealous for the Law, and give your lives for the covenant of your fathers. And call to mind the deeds of the father which they did in their generations; that you may receive great glory and an everlasting name. Was not Abraham found

faithful in the temptation, and it was reckoned unto him for righteousness?

The speech goes on the enumerate the exemplary deeds of the famous ancestors of Israel. Then in closing, it again stresses the supreme importance of the Law:

> And you, my children, be strong and show yourselves men on behalf of the Law; for therein shall ye obtain glory. . . take unto you all those who observe the Law, and avenge the wrong of your people. Render a recompense to the Gentiles, and take heed to the commandments of the Law (2.64, 67-68).

The function of the Abraham story in 1 Maccabees is clearly to inspire zealous obedience to the Law in the midst of persecution. The parallelism of 'be zealous for the law' and 'give your life for the covenant of your fathers' indicates that covenant and law were viewed as one entity. The author, in fact, has combined Gen. 22 ('in temptation') and Gen. 15.6 in much the same way as did Ben Sirach. But he has completed the quote from Gen. 15.6 ('Abraham was found faithful. . . and it was reckoned to him for righteousness'). In so doing, he has redefined the meaning of 'righteousness'.[41] For in contrast to the reckoning of righteousness on the basis of trust in God's promise (as in Gen. 15.6), righteousness here means obedience to God's command in the face of severe testing—or, more precisely, obedience to the Law in the midst of Hellenistic persecution.

The Book of Judith

Judith is a fictional account of how a heroine, Judith, rescued Israel from the armies of Nebuchadnezzar by slaying his commander-in-chief, Holofernes. It was evidently written to encourage Israel at a time of adversity,[42] and to show how deliverance comes through trust in God and strict observance of the Law. Although Judith, the widow of Manasses, was no match for the powerful armies of the enemy, she was victorious because of her prayers of faith and her conscientiousness in keeping the Law.

When Judith heard that the people of Israel had decided to surrender to the enemy, she inspired the rulers of the people to resist the enemy by recalling the trials of the fathers of Israel:

> Let us give thanks to the Lord our God, which trieth us, even as he did our fathers also. Remember all the things which he did to Abraham (8.25-26).

And as in Sirach, Jubilees, and 1 Maccabees, the faithfulness of Abraham in his trials is the prominent feature in this use of the Abraham story.

The Psalms of Solomon[43]
The eighteen psalms of the Psalms of Solomon express a radical distinction between the righteous, i.e., 'the Lord's pious ones', and sinners:

> And sinners shall perish for ever in the day of the Lord's judgment,
> When God visits the earth with His judgment. But they that fear
> the Lord shall find mercy therein, And shall live by the compassion
> of their God; But sinners shall perish foreword (15.13-15).

The pious of the Lord 'walk in the righteousness of His commandments, in the law which He commanded us that we might live' (14.2). The necessity of keeping the law is emphasized by equating it with the covenant: 'the law of the eternal covenant' (10.5). At the same time, however, the psalmist recognizes that the righteous are not sinless. Yet because of the covenant relationship, 'the Lord spares His pious ones, and blots our their errors by His chastening' (13.10).

It is from this theological perspective that reference is made to Abraham:

> Thou blessest the righteous, and dost not reprove them for the sins
> that they have committed; And Thy goodness is upon them that
> sin, when they repent. And, now, Thou are our God, and we the
> people whom Thou hast loved: Behold and show pity, O God of
> Israel, for we are Thine;
>   And remove not Thy mercy from us, lest they assail us. For
> Thou didst choose the seed of Abraham before all the nations, And
> didst set Thy name upon us, O Lord, And Thou wilt not reject us
> for ever. Thou madest a covenant with our fathers concerning us;
> And we hope in Thee, when our soul turns unto Thee. The mercy
> of the Lord be upon the house of Israel for ever (9.15-19).

Here the Abraham tradition functions as the basis for the identity of Israel: God chose the seed of Abraham before all the nations. So the covenant with Abraham is recalled as the source of hope for the Hasidim, for God remembers his covenant with the fathers and shows mercy to Israel.

The Testament of Levi[44]

The Testament of Levi is supposed to be the deathbed speech of the patriarch, Levi, to his sons. The importance of keeping the Law is stressed in relating how the details of the Law of the priesthood and of sacrifices were taught by Abraham to Isaac who in turn taught his son, Jacob, and his grandson, Levi (T. Levi 9.1-14; cf., *T. Benj.* 10.4). Abraham is also cited as the only source of hope for Israel at some future time of great judgment:

> And if you were not to receive mercy through Abraham, Isaac, and Jacob, our fathers, not one of our seed should be left upon the earth (15.4).

Thus in this document Abraham has a dual role, being both the model of Torah observance and the source of blessing for his posterity.

The Testament of Abraham[45]

Abraham is often referred to as 'righteous' and 'the most righteous one' by the author of the Testament of Abraham. His righteousness and intercession actually restores some who were less righteous back to life or enabled them to enter paradise (T. Abr. 18). His righteousness also caused the angel of death to approach him in a beautiful form (T. Abr. 16). And when Abraham asked the angel of death if he comes to all men in such a beautiful form, the response is:

> And Death said, 'No, my lord Abraham, your righteous deeds and the boundless sea of your hospitality and the greatness of your love of God have become a crown upon my head. I come to the righteous in beauty and in great gentleness and pleasant speech, but to the wicked I come in great rotteness and fierceness (T. Abr. 17).

The Assumption of Moses[46]

The first reference to Abraham in the Assumption of Moses, a midrash on Deut. 31.34, is found in a prayer of Israel at a time of tribulation:

> God of Abraham, God of Isaac, and God of Jacob, remember Thy covenant which Thou didst make with them, and the oath which Thou didst swear unto them by Thyself, that their seed should never fail from the land which Thou hast given them (3.8-10).

The following verses record the prayer of Daniel in exile:

> Lord of all, King on the lofty throne, who rules the world, and didst
> will that this people should be thine elect people, then thou didst
> will that thou should be called their God according to the covenant
> which thou didst make with their fathers (4.2).

The author then reassures his readers that such prayers, which recall
the covenant, will be answered:

> Then God will remember them on account of the covenant which
> he made with their fathers, and He will manifest His compassion in
> those times also (4.5).

Biblical Antiquities
Pseudo-Philo's *Biblical Antiquities* is a commentary on biblical
history from Adam to Saul.[47] Abraham is portrayed as a model of
holiness: he courageously refuses to participate in the building of the
tower of Babel (6.3); when the fire of judgment destroys 83,500
people, Abraham escapes without any sign of hurt in the burning
(6.17); he is raised above the heavens and shown the stars (18.5);
even the angels are jealous of Abraham (32.1). Abraham's faith is
defined as faithfulness to God for 'Abraham believed in me and was
not led astray with them'.

In the *Biblical Antiquities* there is also a clear statement about
God's election of and covenant with Abraham:

> And before them all I will choose my children Abraham, and I will
> bring him our of the land, and I will lead him into a land. . . There I
> will make my covenant with him, and his seed will I bless, and I
> will be called his God forever (7.4)

So the righteous life of Abraham and God's gracious covenant with
him are inextricably joined in this Jewish commentary on the biblical
story.[48]

The Apocalypse of Abraham
Apocalypse of Abraham is an apocalyptic response to the destruction
of the Temple in 70 C.E.[49] The author accuses the people of Israel of
turning to 'devilish idolatry' (ch. 26), which was what led to
punishment at the hands of the Gentiles. The foolishness of idolatry
is delineated in the first half of the book wherein Abraham's

coversion from idolatry is described (chs. 1-8). God's choice of Abraham and his command to him to leave Chaldea are presented as the result of Abraham's long search for God and his rejection of his father's practice of idolatry.

The second half of the book is a description of Abraham's ascent into heaven where he is given visions of God, the cosmos, and the future. A key theme throughout this latter section is the sharp distinction made between the descendants of Abraham and the Gentiles. For Abraham's visions of the cosmos and the future are divided into a left side and a right side: the left side is occupied by the Gentiles; the right side belongs to Israel, God's chosen people (chap. 22). Although God allows the Gentiles to destroy Jerusalem and the Temple as a result of Israel's sin (ch. 27), the final outcome of history will be the judgment of the Gentiles at the hand of Abraham's descendants (ch. 29).

Thus the Apocalypse of Abraham indicts the people of Israel for their sin, holding up Abraham's rejection of idolatry as their model. It also, however, reassures the people by repeatedly reminding them that as the descendants of Abraham they are guaranteed ultimate victory over the Gentiles because of God's promise to Abraham.

4 Ezra[50]

In the midst of the lament in 4 Ezra over the sin of Israel, the author rehearses the history of mankind and of Israel:

> When they practiced ungodliness before you, you chose for yourself one from among them whose name was Abraham; him you loved, and unto him only you revealed the end of times secretly by night; and with him you made an everlasting covenant and promised never to forsake his seed (3.13-15).

This brief history continues with the account of the giving of the Law to Jacob's seed (3.18-19). At this point, however, the author breaks into his narrative with a cry of despair:

> And yet you did not take away from them the evil heart, that your Law might bring forth fruit in them. For the first Adam, clothing himself with the evil heart, transgressed and was overcome; and likewise also all who were born of him. Thus the infirmity became inveterate; the Law indeed was in the heart of the people, but in conjunction with the evil germ; so what was good departed, and the evil remained (3.20-22).

Thus God's covenant with Abraham does not appear to offer the author of 4 Ezra any ultimate hope, since the sinfulness of the descendants of Abraham has brought about their destruction.[51]

2 Baruch

The author of 2 Baruch also refects on the cause and meaning of the destruction of the temple in 70 C.E.[52] But he is more optimistic than the author of 4 Ezra. In contrast to the black waters which represent the consequences of the Fall, Abraham is the source of bright waters; he is the source of hope in the midst of the darkest times. The hope of the author of 2 Baruch is based, in fact, on Abraham's righteous character and on the promise given to him:

> And after these waters thou didst see bright waters: this is the fount of Abraham, also his generations and advent of his son, and his son's son, and of those like them. Because at that time the unwritten law was named among them, and the works of the commandments were then fulfilled, and belief in the coming judgment was then generated, and hope of the world that was to be renewed was then built up, and the promise of the life that should come hereafter was implanted (57.1-3).

Summary

This collection of portraits of Abraham from the literature of the Apocrypha and Pseudepigrapha illustrates the significance of Abraham in Jewish history during the Second Temple Period. The bibilical statement as to Abraham's obedience is in this literature greatly expanded. In most of these texts Abraham is exalted as the perfect model of Torah observance (Sir. 44.19; *Jub.* 15.1, 2; 16.20, 26; 17.17-18; 23.10; 1 Macc. 2.50-52; *T. Levi* 9.1-14; *T. Benj.* 10.4; *T. Abr.* 17; *2 Baruch* 57.1-3). His faithfulness at times of testing (Sir. 44.19; *Jub.* 17.17-18; 19.8; 1 Macc. 2.52; Jdt. 8.25), his circumcision (Sir. 44.20; 1 Macc. 2.52), his rejection of idolatry (Jub. 12.1-14; *Apoc. Abr.* 1-8), and his hospitality (*T. Abr.* 17) all receive special attention and elaboration as marks of his perfect righteousness. And Abraham's righteousness is viewed as a cause for blessing to Abraham and his descendants (Sir. 44.21; *T. Abr.* 17, 18).

In this literature Abraham's righteousness is always depicted within the context of God's election and covenant. Some texts mention Abraham only to provide the covenantal basis for the identity and blessing of his descendants (Ps. Sol. 9.15-19; Assum.

Mos. 3.8-10; 4.5; 4 Ezra 3.13-15). In the face of national testing, Israel, in fact, has always based her hope on the covenant that God made with Abraham, which includes blessing on his descendants.

This covenantal framework that undergirds the apocryphal and pseudepigraphal literature confirms Sanders' thesis that Judaism was basically a religion of covenantal nomism rather than legalism. However, it is important, as well, to note that there are various nuanced versions of covenantal nomism in these somewhat diverse portraits of Abraham. At one end of the spectrum, God's gracious election of Abraham and his unconditional promises are the focus of attention. At the other end of the spectrum, it is nomistic behavior. While the idea of the covenant has not been totally eclipsed, it often becomes redefined. In these 'nomistic portraits' of Abraham, covenant becomes identified with the law—with the result that the election of God is viewed as God's response to Abraham's righteous character and law observance.

In this literature 'seed of Abraham' is synonymous with 'Jew'. Only in Sirach 44.21 is any hope extended to the Gentiles on the basis of the Abrahamic covenant. The Testaments of the 12 Patriarchs, of course, express a universalist hope for the nations (*T. Levi* 2.11; 4.4; 18.9; *T. Ash* 7.3; *T. Benj.* 9.2; 10.5, 8-10; *T. Dan.* 6.7; *T. Naph.* 8.3, 6). But this hope is not directly related to the Abrahamic covenant—and it may, in certain instances, reflect Christian interpolations. All the other so-called apocryphal and pseudepigraphical writings offer only a sharp contrast between the blessings promised to the descendants of Abraham and the fate of the Gentiles.

3. The Dead Sea Scrolls[53]

In the Damascus Rule the instruction given to all who enter the Covenant includes a reference to the example of Abraham:

> Abraham did not walk in it [evil], and he was accounted friend of God because he kept the commandments of God and did not choose his own will. And he handed them down to Isaac and Jacob, who kept them and were recorded as friends of God and party to the Covenant for ever (CD 3.2-4).

Abraham is also mentioned as an example of one who fulfills God's commands without delay:

> God made a Covenant with you and all Israel; therefore a man
> shall bind himself by oath to return to the Law of Moses, for in it
> all things are strictly defined... And on the day that a man swears
> to return to the Law of Moses, the Angel of Persecution shall cease
> to follow him provided that he fulfills his word: for this reason
> Abraham circumcised himself on the day that he knew (CD 16.1,
> 5-6).

This requirement of strict and immediate adherence to the Law of
Moses is set within the context of God's election and the covenant.
Vermes summarizes the importance of these concepts in the DSS as
follows:

> For the sectary, election was not an accident of birth, an inherited
> privilege. Every individual, even those born into the Community,
> was required to take the oath of the Covenant of his own free will
> because he had, as a person, been chosen by God from all eternity
> to become one of His elect.[54]

The Covenant was called the 'Covenant of Abraham' (CD 12.11).
Only the members of the sect were true members of the Covenant of
God. Admission was granted only to those born in Israel (1QS 6.13;
4QFlor. 1.4) who returned to the Law of Moses to submit to all of its
requirements as interpreted by the Community.

As the true heirs to the Abrahamic covenant, the members of the
community applied the promises of the covenant directly to
themselves. Thus in their interpretation of Genesis, the promise of
the land is related to the members of the Community, the true
descendants of Abraham, by the repetition of the phrase, 'to you and
your descendants after you' (1QapGen. 21.8-14).[55]

The portrait of Abraham in the DSS expresses, in itself, the very
essence of covenantal nomist: Abraham is the recipient of the
covenant and he is the perfect example of Torah observance. The
members of the covenant community respond to the gracious
promises of the covenant of Abraham by vowing to keep the whole
law of Moses.

4. *Philo*

Philo of Alexandria presents us with a double-image portrait of
Abraham: a literal and an allegorical Abraham. The literal Abraham
reflects, with elaboration, the general lines of the biblical narrative.

He is the historical figure who abandoned pagan astrology in
Chaldea, migrated to Palestine, sought true wisdom, and ultimately
achieved perfection in his piety toward God and in his practice of the
cardinal virtues. The allegorical Abraham is the same historical
figure viewed from the perspective of the inner journey of the soul.
He abandoned pantheistic materialism, achieved the freedom of his
soul from the slavery of bodily passions and senses, and finally
attained the perfect vision of the intelligble realm and the one true
God.[56] As Sandmel points out, 'the Abraham explicit literally or
implicit allegorically throughout Philo's writings is thoroughly
hellenized'.[57] For Philo's primary goal was to prove that all the best
elements of Greek philosophy are embodied in Abraham.[58]

A major feature in Philo's portrayal of Abraham is the patriarch's
relation to the divine law. The conclusion of *De Abrahamo* accents
this feature:

> To these praises of the Sage, so many and so great, Moses adds this
> crowning saying 'that this man did divine law and the divine
> commands'. He did them, not taught by written words, but
> unwritten nature (ἀγράφῳ τῇ φύσει) gave him the zeal to follow
> where wholesome and untainted impulse led him. And when they
> have God's promises before them what should men do but trust in
> them most firmly? Such was the life of the first, the founder of the
> nation, one who obeyed the law, some will say, but rather, as our
> discourse has shown, himself a law and an unwritten statute νόμος
> αὐτὸς ὢν καὶ θεσμὸς ἄγραφος) (*Abr* 275-276).

Philo's point here is to establish the priority of the law, and so he lays
stress on Abraham's observance of the Mosaic law. The Mosaic law
νόμος) was a later copy of the archetypal, unwritten law of nature
(φύσις). The priority involved is both a temporal priority and a
qualitative priority. This echo of the Platonic distinction between the
unwritten, nature law (φύσις) and the written, historical law (νόμος)
pervades all of Philo's works.[59] So when Philo explains why Moses
extolled Abraham and the other patriarchs, he is, in fact, setting forth
the purposes of his own work:[60]

> First he wished to show that the enacted ordinances are not
> inconsistent with nature; and secondly, that those who wish to live
> in accordance with the laws as they stand have no difficult task,
> seeing that the first generations, before any at all of the particular
> statutes was set in writing, followed the unwritten law with perfect
> ease, so that one might properly say that the enacted laws are

nothing else than memorials of the life of the ancients, preserving
to a later generation their actual words and deeds (*Abr* 5).

Philo is saying something quite different from the authors of
Sirach, Jubilees, and 1 Maccabees. Since these authors were
convinced that there was nothing higher than the law of Moses, they
raised Abraham up to that absolute norm by portraying him as a
meticulous observer of all the details of the Mosaic law. The rabbis,
as we shall see, even make Abraham a halakic observer of the oral
law of Moses. Philo, on the other hand, views the law of nature
which was expressed in the life of Abraham as the higher law, with
the law of Moses being only a copy.[61]

Likewise, when Philo speaks of circumcision, he does not
emphasize that it is the sign of the Abrahamic covenant, the mark of
identity for the Jewish people. Nor does he portray Abraham's
acceptance of it as obedience to the Mosaic law. Instead, he develops
a spiritual meaning for circumcision:[62]

> When the mind is circumcised and contains only necessary and
> useful things, and when at the same time there is cut off whatever
> causes pride to increase, then with it are circumcised the eyes also,
> as though they could not otherwise see (*QuGen*. III, 47).

Since, according to Philo, the foreskin symbolizes 'those sense-
pleasures and impulses' (*QuGen*. III, 52), he is prepared to agree with
those who want to abandon physical circumcision. For, as he sees
it,

> circumcision does indeed portray the excision of pleasure and all
> passions, and the putting away of the impious conceit, under which
> the mind supposed that it was capable of begetting by its own
> power (*Abr* 92).

Yet Philo, interestingly, says that this is not a sufficient basis for
neglecting physical circumcision.[63] His defence of physical circumcision, however, seems to have been seriously undermined by his
adoption of hellenistic categories to stress the spiritual meaning.[64]

Philo also interprets Abraham's faith along the lines of Greek
philosophy, for faith means to turn from the delusions of our senses
to a clear vision of the one Cause above all. Or, as he says in *De
Abrahamo*:

> Faith in God, then, is the one sure and infallible good, consolation
> of life, fulfillment of bright hopes... all-round betterment of the

soul which is firmly stayed on Him who is the cause of all things
and can do all things yet only wills the best. For, just as those who
walk on a slippery road are tripped up and fall, while others on a
dry highway tread without stumbling, so those who set the soul
travelling along the path of the bodily and the external are but
learning it to fall, so slippery and utterly insecure are all such
things; while those who press onward to God along the doctrines of
virtue walk straight upon a path which is safe and unshaken, so
that we may say with all truth that belief in the former things is
disbelief in God, and disbelief in them belief in God (*Abr* 268-
269).

So Abraham for Philo is the perfect example of faith, because his
mind

> did not remain for ever deceived nor stand rooted in the realm of
> sense, nor suppose that the visible world was the Almighty and
> Primal God, but using its reason sped upwards and turned its gaze
> upon the intelligent order which is superior to the visible and upon
> Him who is maker and ruler of both alike (*Abr* 88).

Sandmel observes that Philo's allocation of faith to the intelligible
realm and his denial that faith pertains to perceptible things
illustrates his great indebtedness to hellenistic categories and modes
of expression.[65]

Philo's interest in the promises made to Abraham is not so much
because of their value to Abraham's descendants as the basis for
God's blessing to Israel, but primarily because they were the basis for
Abraham's faith in God. And it is this faith that is the mark of
Israel's identity.[66] Thus although Philo accepts obedience to the law
of God as the inevitable expression of true faith, he understood
Abraham's faith primarily as Abraham's attitude toward the
promises of God.[67] So Gen. 15.6a frequently appears in Philo's
writings as a prooftext to highlight Abraham's response to the
promises (*Migr* 44 (Gen. 12.1); *Heres* 90, 94, 101 (Gen. 15.6-8); *Mut*
177 (Gen. 15.4; 17.17); *Mut* 186 (Gen. 17.17); *Quod Immut* 4 (Gen.
22.9); *Leg All* III 228 (Num. 12.7); *Abr* 262; *Virt* 216; *Praem* 27).
Gen. 15.6 also functions as Philo's proof that Abraham's faith was
perfect even when it might appear that he faltered (e.g. *Mut* 177
(Gen. 15.8).[68]

5. *Josephus*

The apologetic goals of Josephus are quite obvious in his introduction
of Abraham:

> He was a man of ready intelligence on all matters, persuasive with
> his hearers, and not mistaken in his inferences. Hence he began to
> have more lofty conceptions of virtue than the rest of mankind, and
> determined to reform and change the ideas universally current
> concerning God. He was thus the first boldly to declare that God,
> the creator of the inverse, is one... This he inferred from the
> changes to which land and sea are subject, from the course of sun
> and moon, and from all the celestial phenomena... (*Ant.* I. 154–
> 156).

Josephus' account of Abraham's visit to Egypt further embellishes
the reputation of Abraham as a wise philosopher-scientist:

> Abraham consorted with the most learned of the Egyptians, hence
> his virtue and reputation became still more conspicuous... thus
> gaining their admiration at these meetings as a man of extreme
> sagacity, gifted not only with high intelligence but with power to
> covince his hearers on any subject which he undertook to teach, he
> introduced them to arithmetic and transmitted to them the laws of
> astronomy (I. 165-168).

In addition to his 'apologetic' presentation of Abraham, Josephus
also includes a reference to Abraham's perfect obedience to the will
of God when he is commanded to sacrifice Isaac:

> Abraham, deeming that nothing would justify disobedience to God
> and that in everything he must submit to His will, since all that
> befell His favored ones was ordained by His providence... (I.
> 225).

So Abraham is recorded as explaining his obedience to Isaac as a
response to God's grace:

> It is to God I yield thee, to God who now claims from us this
> homage in return for the gracious favor He has shown me (I.
> 229).

Josephus explains that the reason God commanded Abraham to
make this sacrifice was,

> to test his soul and see whether even such orders would find him
> obedient. Now that He knew the ardour and depth of his piety. He

took pleasure in what He had given him and would never fail to regard with tenderest care both him and his race (I. 233-234).

According to Josephus, therefore, Abraham's obedience in the binding of Isaac should be viewed as a basis for God's blessings to the descendants of Abraham.

Josephus' final eulogy of Abraham declares that he was 'a man in every virtue supreme, who received from God the due honour for his zeal in His service' (I. 256). Abraham's virtue earned him God's approval and promise of reward:

> God commended his virtue and said, 'Nay, thou shalt not lose the rewards that are your due for such good deeds' (I. 183).

Abraham's descendants also recognized their dependence on the righteousness of Abraham, for in speaking later of Nehemiah, Josephus writes:

> Nehemiah delcares, 'Fellow Jews, you know that God cherishes the memory of our fathers, Abraham, Isaac, and Jacob, and because of their righteousness does not give up his providential care for us' (XI. 169).

In sum, the Abraham of Josephus is credited with virtues which would make him attractive in the Hellenistic world. The essential Jewish elements of the covenant and the relation of Abraham to the Mosaic law, however, are not featured in Josephus' account.[69]

6. Rabbinic References to Abraham[70]

The rabbinic portraits of Abraham enlarge on one prominent characteristic of the earlier portraits—viz., the righteousness of Abraham in terms of his observance of the Mosaic Law.[71] *Mishnah Kiddushin* concludes with this statement:

> And we find that Abraham our father had performed the whole law before it was given, for it was written, 'Because that Abraham obeyed my voice and kept my charge, my commandments, my statutes, and my laws' (*m. Kidd.* 4.14).

Even the most minute details of the oral law were viewed as having been kept by Abraham: 'our father knew even of *'erub tabshilin*' (*Gen. Rab.* 95.3; cf., *b. Yoma* 28b; *Gen. Rab.* 2.10). Furthermore, Abraham is reported to have claimed that all of the blessings which he enjoyed were the result of his obedience to the Torah: 'Thus said Abraham: 'All that has come to me is only because I engaged in Torah and good deeds" (*Gen. Rab.* 56.11).

Abraham's moral perfection was also directly connected with his circumcision:

> Great is circumcision, for despite all the religious duties which Abraham our father fulfilled, he was not called perfect until he was circumcised (*m. Ned.* 3.11; *Gen. Rab.* 46.1).

The sacredness of circumcision, the sign of the Abrahamic covenant, is indicated by the following prohibition:

> If a man profaned the sacred things. . . and makes void the covenant of Abraham our father. . . he has no share in the world to come (*m. Abot* 3.12; cf. *b. Sanh.* 99a; *b. Yoma* 85b).[72]

The portrayal of the righteousness of Abraham also draws upon the trial traditions:

> With ten temptations was Abraham our father tempted and he stood steadfast in them all to show how great was the love of Abraham our father (*m. Abot* 5.2, 3; cf. *Pirqe R. El.* 26; *'Abot R. Nat.* 33; *Gen. Rab.* 55.2; *Lev. Rab.* 3.11; 11.7).

The hospitality of Abraham is highlighted in some texts as the basis for Abraham's righteousness (*Gen. Rab.* 56:5; 49.4). In this context, some attention is given to Abraham's missionary efforts. For as a host he made converts (*Gen. Rab.* 39.14) and taught his guests the blessing (*Gen. Rab.* 43.7). Indeed, it is even said that he was circumcised late in life so that circumcision would not be objectionable to proselytes (*Gen. Rab.* 46.2).

As a result of his obedience to the Torah, his circumcision, his hospitality, and his many other righteous deeds, Abraham is frequently referred to as the 'righteous man' by the rabbis. In fact many scripture texts which refer to righteousness and the righteous one are applied to Abraham—e.g., '"he that sows righteousness" (Prov. 14.8) alludes to Abraham' (*Gen. Rab.* 44.2); '"thou hast loved righteousness" (Ps. 45.8) is applied to Abraham' (*Gen. Rab.* 49.10); '"the Lord tries the righteous" (Ps. 11.5) refers to Abraham' (*Gen. Rab.* 55.2).

God's election and covenant are sometimes explained as the consequence of Abraham's righteousness. In a Genesis midrash, the comparison of Noah ('Noah walked with God') and of Abraham

('Walk before me') makes God appear to be indebted to Abraham:

> R. Nehemiah said: He [Noah] might be compared to a king's friend
> who was plunging about in the dark alleys, and when the king
> looked out and saw him sinking in the mud, he said to him, 'Instead
> of plunging about in dark alleys, come and walk with me'. But
> Abraham's case is rather to be compared to that of a king who was
> sinking in dark alleys, and when his friend saw him he shone a light
> for him through the window. Said he to him, 'Instead of lighting
> me through the window, come show a light before me'. Even so did
> the Holy One, blessed by He, say to Abraham: 'Instead of showing
> a light for me from Mesopotamia and its environs, come and show
> one before me in Eretz Israel' (*Gen. Rab.* 30.10).

In other passages, however, the obedience of Abraham is interpreted
not as a cause of God's blessing but as a response to the gracious
blessing of the Holy One. In a discussion of the name 'Mamre', one
Rabbi is cited as arguing that mamre refers to the person who
rebuked (*himrah*) Abraham and convinced him to be circumcised by
reminding him of all that the Holy One had already done for him
(*Gen. Rab.* 42.8; cf., 2.3; 44.4).

The benefits acquired through the righteousness of Abraham are
spoken of as being immense, both for himself and for his posterity.
Abraham himself was rewarded for each footstep (*Gen. Rab.* 39),
with his greatest rewards awaiting him in the world to come (*Gen.
Rab.* 44.4). And his descendants, no matter how poor, were to be
granted special status because they were the seed of Abraham (*m. B.
Kam.* 8.6; *m. B. Mes.* 7.1). Each of Abraham's righteous deeds was
rewarded by some miracle for his descendants. Because he bowed to
the three visitors, kings bowed to them (*t. Sotah* 4). Because he
cleaved the wood for the sacrifice of Isaac, the Red Sea was cleaved
for them (*Gen. Rab.* 55.8). Because Abraham defeated the kings at
night, God defeated the Egyptians on Passover night (*Gen. Rab.*
43.3).

The faith of Abraham is also viewed as the basis for the blessing of
his descendants. because of his faith, God split the Red Sea (*Mekilta,
Beshalah* 3); the children are to be called sons of believers because
scripture says: 'and he believed in the Lord' (*Gen. Rab.* 30.12). A
significant reference to the benefit of the faith of Abraham is found in
a commentary on the Song of Moses (Exod. 15):

> Through whose merit does Israel recite the Song? through the
> merit of Abraham, because he believed in the Holy One, blessed be

He, as it says, 'And he believed in the Lord' (Gen. 15.6). This was the faith which Israel had inherited and concerning which it is written, 'But the righteous shall live by his faith' (Hab. 2.4) (*Ex, Rab.* 23.5).

The blessing for the nations through Abraham, however, consists in relief available to them if they turn to Israel for advice:

> 'and in thee shall all the families of the earth be blessed'. Now if that is meant in respect of wealth, they are surely wealthier than we! But it was meant in respect of counsel: when they get into trouble they ask our advice, and we give it to them (*Gen. Rab.* 39.12).

The true seed of Abraham are the descendants of Jacob (Gen. Rab. 53.12). There was disagreement among the Rabbis regarding the right of proselytes to be called 'sons of Abraham'. In the Mishnah (*m. Bikk.* 1.4), proselytes are denied the right to use the formula given in presenting first fruits (Deut. 26.3) because they could not speak of 'our father'. R. Judah the Prince, however, defended the right of a proselyte to be called a son of Abraham:

> R. Judah said that he *can*, as it says of Abraham, 'a father of many nations I have made thee' (Gen. 17.5); that is, 'Hitherto thou was a father only in Aram, but henceforth thou shalt be a father for all nations'. R. Joshua b. Levi said: 'the rule is according to R. Judah'. A case came before R. Abbahu, and he decided it according to R. Judah (*y. Bikk.* 1.4).

Bamberger insists that the view of R. Judah prevailed among the Tannaim.[73] Other texts support this conclusion:

> 'The father of all proselytes was Abraham'. Therefore when a proselyte is named, he is called N., son of our father Abraham (*Tanh.B.* 32a; see also *Pesiq. R.* 108a).

Yet proselytes were distinguished from native-born Israelites by being not included among the elect of Israel. The Rabbis explained that Abraham and his seed were chosen, but others, such as Jethro and Rahab, were brought near to God even though he did not choose them:

> Happy is he whom the Holy One, blessed be He, has chosen even though He has not brought him near to Himself, and happy is the man whom He has brought near even though He has not chosen him (*Num. Rab.* 3.2).

E.P. Sanders notes this difference, as follows:

> The native-born Israelite to be sure accepts the covenant with the impetus given by the understanding that, he, his forebearers and his descendants were especially called and set aside by God. Native-born Israelites are generally considered by the Rabbis to be 'in' unless they give evidence of being apostate (they 'break off the yoke', etc.). The proselyte, on the other hand, must bear the burden of proof to show that he accepts the covenant and intends to keep the commandments.[74]

Yet Sanders contends that this difference does not put the native-born Israelite and the proselyte on a different basis for salvation: 'the formal relationship of *accepting* and *keeping* is the same'.[75] It is, however, doubtful that Sanders' contention can be fully maintained. For whereas the Jew is born into the covenant relationship and accepts what is already his, the proselyte must prove by circumcision and willingness to keep the law that he accepts the covenant. And this difference seems to have led some Rabbis to treat proselytes in a legalistic manner, while, at the same time, viewing their own realtionship with God in terms of covenantal nomism.

The portrait of Abraham in rabbinic literature must be place in the context of covenantal nomism. But the Rabbis so shaded the portrait of the patriarch that the rewards of Abraham's nomistic behavior became highlighted, with the result that the salvific character of the covenant became nearly lost in the shadows. For when the covenant is mentioned in the rabbinic materials, it is interpreted in exclusive, nationalistic terms.

Sandmel's summary of rabbinic conceptions of Abraham points to the most prominent features of their portrait:

> The rabbinic literature reads back into the career of the patriarch its own interests and concerns. Abraham observes the written Torah and the Oral Torah. He sits in an Academy learning *halakot*. He gives tithes; he prays. He travels to the site of the Temple; he teaches the Grace after meal.
> ... Abraham is depicted in such terms that were one to be a perfect imitator of Abraham, he would thereby be conforming to the highest rabbinic standards and be an executor of rabbinic laws. To the rabbis, one might say, Abraham is a rabbi.[76]

7. *Conclusion*

The presence of both God's convenantal-promises and Abraham's righteous behavior in the various portraits of Abraham is sufficient basis for concluding that in Jewish literature Abraham is portrayed in the context of covenantal nomism. But the ways in which these two themes are variously treated in the different strands of Jewish literature suggest that covenantal nomism was variously understood within Second Temple Judaism. Some texts (especially OT, and, in different ways, the Psalms of Solomon and Philo) emphasize the priority of the covenant with Abraham over the Mosaic Law and interpret Abraham's faith primarily in terms of a response to the covenantal promises. Other texts (especially Sirach, Jubilees, I Maccabees, and the rabbinic writings) interpret the Abrahamic covenant in terms of the Mosaic Law and view faith as a response of obedience to that Law.

Paul's use of the Abraham story is more closely aligned to the first emphasis. However, his Christocentric reinterpretation of the Abrahamic covenant, his inclusion of Gentile believers within that covenant, his separation of the Mosaic law and exclusion of non-Christian Jewish lawkeepers from that covenant, and his understanding of faith as exclusively faith in Christ serve to highlight the fact that his portrait of Abraham must be seen in an entirely different category.

APPENDIX 3

PAUL AND JEWISH EXEGESIS

A common approach to the interpretation of Gal. 3 and 4 is by way of examining Paul's argument from Scripture in light of the then current Jewish exegetical procedures. The widespread consensus among scholars that Paul 'employed standard tecniques of Scriptural exegesis, occasionally even using some of the rules of rabbinic hermeneutics' appears to confirm the validity of this approach.[1] And if, as E.E. Ellis contends, 'Gal. 3 is largely a Midrash on the Abrahamic history',[2] then Paul's use of that history should be clarified by a comparison with the characteristics of midrash.

One major difficulty, however, which this approach faces is the definition of midrash. At the level of etymology, 'midrash' is a transliteration of מדרש, the Hebrew participle which means 'interpretation'.[3] Attempts by specialists in the field to develop more technical definitions have generated much debate, but little consensus.[4] A.G. Wright laments:

> The word midrash at present is an equivocal term and is being used to describe a mass of disparate material. Indeed, if some of the definitions are correct, large amounts, if not the whole of the Bible, would have to be called midrash. Hence, the word as used currently in biblical studies is approaching the point where it is no longer really meaningful.[5]

One of the basic reasons for this confusion is that Jewish hermeneutics have been described from the different perspectives of literary genre, hermeneutical axioms, and exegetical methods.[6] Thus, Wright derives his definition of midrash in terms of literary genre from a study of the characteristics of rabbinic literature. He specifies three types of midrashic literature: exegetical (brief comments on the text), homiletical (more extended discussion of texts), and narrative ('rewritten Bible').[7] D. Moo defines midrash in terms of the hermeneutical axioms of rabbinic Judaism. These axioms include the authority and relevancy of Scripture, a non-eschatological perception, and the twin occupations of affirming Israel's identity and directing Israel's conduct—with material appearing in two forms, *haggadah* and *halakah*, and stemming from two *Sitze im Leben*, the synagogue and the school.[8] Longenecker's treatment of midrash is essentially a description of the exegetical methods of the rabbis in light of the seven heremeneutical rules of Hillel, the thirteen rules of Ishmael, and the thirty-two rules of Eliezer.[9] Without attempting to resolve the debate regarding the definition of midrash, we will consider how each of these three perspectives on midrash applies to Paul's use of the Abraham story in Gal. 3. Then we will examine the typological-allegorical use of the Hagar–Sarah story in Gal. 4.

1. *Midrashic Exegesis in Gal. 3*

Literature Features

Bonsirven has highlighted the similarity between Paul's introductory citation formulas and rabbinic practice.[10] Thus, if the use of καθώς in 3.6 is an abbreviated form of καθώς γέγραπται, it reflects rabbinic style.[11] So, too, as often occurs in rabbinic literature, Scripture is personalized and speaks in 3.8: προϊδοῦσα δὲ ἡ γραφὴ προευηγγελίσατο.[12] Likewise, γέγραπται γὰρ ὅτι (3.10) and ὅτι γέγραπται (3.13) are similar to rabbinic introductory formulas.[13] And the introductory formula of 3.16 (οὐ λέγει. . .ἀλλά) bears resemblance to expressions in rabbinic texts.[14] On the level of introductory formulas, therefore, the exposition of Scripture in Gal. 3 is similar to rabbinic midrash.

There are, however, a number of distinctive literary features of rabbinic midrash which are not found in Gal. 3.[15] There are, for example, no explicit quotations from other interpreters of Scripture with the names of those interpreters attached. The exposition of Scripture in Gal. 3 is not a collection of independent units of interpretation, nor is there more than one comment of interpretation per unit of Scriptural text. So when an example of rabbinic midrash is set alongside Gal. 3.1-18, the differences appear to place the two passages in somewhat different literary genres.

Hermeneutical Axioms

Paul certainly shares the common theological presuppositions of all Jewish interpreters that Scripture is authoritative and relevant for the community.[16] He also uses it as the basis for affirming the identity of the community as the elect people of God.[17] His attitude toward the Torah, however, precludes the possibility of developing a rabbinic type of *halakah*.[18] Furthermore, Paul's eschatological orientation put him closer to the hermeneutical axioms of Qumran *pesher* exegesis.[19] Most importantly, Paul's use of the OT was determined by the new revelatory foundation, God's revelation in Christ.[20] This theological perspective is the fundamental difference between him and both the rabbis and Qumran sectarians.

Thus on the level of literary features and hermeneutical axioms, Gal. 3.1-18 does not appear to merit the designation rabbinic midrash.

Exegetical Methods
Usually when the term midrash is applied to Gal. 3 it denotes rabbinic exegetical methods.[21] Although a full discussion of the hermeneutical systems of Hillel and the Tannaim is beyond the limits of our study,[22] it is important to note the basic features of the rabbinic method of interpretation.

Hermeneutical rules to guide the practice of exegesis were gradually developed.[23] The codification of the seven fundamental rules of rabbinic exegesis is attributed by the Talmud to Hillel (c. 60 B.C.E.-20 C.E.).[24] J. Bowker provides a summary of the meaning of these rules:[25]

1. *Qal wahomer*: what applies in a less important case will certainly apply in a more important case.
2. *Gezerah shawah*: verbal analogy from one verse to another; where the words are applied to two separate cases it follows that the same considerations apply to both.
3. *Binyan ab mikathub 'ehad* building up a family from a single text; when the same phrase is found in a number of passages, then a consideration found in one of them applies to all of them.
4. *Binyan ab mishene kethubim*: building up a family from two texts; a principle is established by relating two texts together; the principle can then be applied to other passages.[26]
5. *Kelal upherat*: the general and the particular; a general principle may be restricted by a particularisation of it in another verse; or conversely, a particular rule may be extended into a general principle.

6. *Kayoze bo bemaqom 'aher*: as is found in another place; a difficulty in one text may be solved by comparing it with another which has points of general (though not necessarily verbal) similarity.

7. *Dahar halamed me 'inyano* a meaning established by its context.

The primary purpose of these seven hermeneutical rules (*middoth*) was to describe how to make deductions from the text in order to contemporize the revelation of God for the needs of the community.[27] In other words, midrash started with the text of Scripture—usually a short phrase or just a single word—and extended the meaning of that text by means of the hermeneutical rules. This process of interpretation is succinctly described by Moore as,

> an atomistic exegesis, which interprets sentences, clauses, phrases, and even single words, independently of the context or the historical situation, as divine oracles; combines them with other similarly detached utterances; and makes large use of analogy of expressions, often by purely verbal association.[28]

Daube[29] and Lieberman[30] have stressed the influence of Hellenistic rhetoric in the formulation of the *middoth* of Hillel. Lieberman claims:

> Although we possess no evidence that the Rabbis borrowed their rules of interpretation from the Greeks, the situation is quite different when we deal with the formulation, terms, categories and systematization of these rules. The latter were mainly created by the Greeks, and Jews most probably did not hesitate to take them over and adapt them to their own rules and norms.[31]

Daube says that 'just as the Romans succeeded in latinizing the rhetorical notions they used, so the 'classical' Tannaitic Rabbis succeeded in hebraizing them'.[32] In light of the parallels which Daube and Lieberman have drawn between the *middoth* of Hillel and Hellenistic rhetoric, P. Alexander advices caution in any attempt to demonstrate that Paul engaged in rabbinic midrash or that he was a Hillelite.[33] For some of the parallels between Hillel and Paul may simply indicate that both were independently influenced by Greek sources.[34] Or, as Alexander says, 'the rules in question may be 'natural' to human discourse or argument, or typical in general of early rhetoric'.[35] So with this caveat in mind, we turn to a somewhat cursory survey of Gal. 3 in terms of Paul's exegetical methods *vis-à-vis* those of rabbinic midrash.

In the comparative study of the exegetical methods used by Paul in Gal. 3 and the rabbis in their midrashim, ten parallels have been adduced.

(1) *The Formation of a Chain of Quotations*: In Rabbinic midrash, one Scripture text is normally united with several others on the same theme.[36] Paul's combination of seven explicit OT quotations in the short span of eleven verses (Gal. 3.6-16) resembles this practice.[37]

(2) *The Repetition of Key Words*: As often found in rabbinic middrash,[38] the chain of quotations in Gal. 3.6-16 has been welded together by the repetition of Paul's key-words: πίστις (οἱ ἐκ πίστεως), δικαιόω (δικαιοσύνη), ἔθνη, εὐλογία, νόμος (οἱ ἐξ ἔργων νόμου), κατάρα (ἐπικατάρατος). And the quotations have evidently been chosen because they contain and define these *Stichwörter*.[39]

(3) *The Explanation of Scripture by Scripture*: Behind the rabbinic practice of combining quotations on a similar theme is the fundamental methodological principle that Scripture is to be interpreted by Scripture.[40] The way in which Paul uses the quotation of Gen. 12.3/ 18.18 (Gal. 3.8) to interpret and apply his use of Gen. 15.6 (Gal. 3.6) is an illustration of the same principle at work.[41]

(4) *Merged or Amalgamated Quotations*: Although merged quotations are found in rabbinic midrash,[42] such a practice is more characteristic of the Qumran pesher treatment of the text.[43] In Gal. 3.8, Paul merges Gen. 12.3 and Gen. 18.18 in order to include the key-word ἔθνη.[44]

(5) *Formulation of Theological Thesis*: The rabbis would normally begin a midrash with a quotation which highlighted a proposition to be demonstrated in the ensuing commentary.[45] The citation of Gen. 15.6 (Gal. 3.6) stands as a foundational thesis for the interpretation which follows. Also Paul may be using his understanding of Hab. 2.4 as the theological thesis which undergirds his use of πίστις and οἱ ἐκ πίστεως.[46]

(6) *Implications from the Text*: In midrash the meaning of the text is extended to meet the needs of the community.[47] The use γινώσκετε ἄρα ὅτι (3.7), ὥστε (3.9), and ἵνα. . .ἵνα (3.14) all signal that Paul is drawing out the implications of his texts to meet the needs of the Galatian church.[48]

(7) *Interpretation by Analogy*: Hillel's second and sixth rules state that one text may be interpreted by another which has points of verbal (rule 2) or general (rule 6) similarity.[49] So when Paul introduces the Abrahamic promise in 3.8 by quoting Gen. 12.3/

18.18, his focus is on the nations and Abraham as the beneficiaries of the promise (3.9). In 3.16, however, one word from a generally similar text (τῷ σπέρματί σου, Gen. 13.15/17.8/24.7) enables him to shift the focus to Christ as the sole recipient of the promise.[50]

(8) *Resolution of Contradiction*: H. Schoeps outlines Paul's use of Hab. 2.4 (Gal. 3.11) and Lev. 18.5 (Gal. 3.12) to show how Paul used the method later codified as the thirteenth *middah* or R. Ishmael: 'If two verses are contradictory, one should find a third verse in order to overcome the contradiction'.[51] Paul sets up the antithesis of a prophetic text ('The righteous shall live by faith') and a Torah text ('He who does them shall live by them') to make the point that life by faith is opposed to life by doing the Law. Paul then resolves the contradiction by his reference to ἡ εὐλογία τοῦ Ἀβραάμ (3.14), which recapitulates his quote of Gen. 15.6 (3.6).

N. Dahl accepts Schoeps' suggestion that Paul presents Hab. 2.4 and Lev. 18.5 as contradictory, and then resolves this contradiction by the use of R. Ishmael's hermeneutical rule.[52] But Dahl interprets R. Ishmael's thirteenth *middah* differently from Schoeps:

> The basic rule is that two scriptural passages contradicting one another should be upheld with the help of a distinction in the interpretation of the two contexts.
>
> ... Thus the task which confronted an exegete when he encountered an apparent contradiction in Scripture was not to find a third passage which would resolve this conflict. It was necessary first to establish which text contained the valid halakah, the correct statement, or fundamental teaching. Then it was requisite to find a satisfactory explanation of the conflicting text to maintain its validity. This is clear from the typical rabbinic formulation of the problem: 'One scriptural passage says. . ., but another passage says, ... How are both these passages to be upheld?'[53]

This interpretation of the rabbinic method for resolving contradictory texts is then used by Dahl as a guide for unravelling the structure of Paul's argument in the rest of Gal. 3. For according to Dahl, vv. 13-18 establish that Hab. 2.4 is the text which contains the fundamental teaching; vv. 19-25 explain how to interpret the contradictory text (Lev. 18.5).[54]

Dahl maintains that v. 14a (ἵνα εἰς τὰ ἔθνη ἡ εὐλογία τοῦ Ἀβραάμ γένηται ἐν Χριστῷ Ἰησοῦ) presents a paraphrase of God's oath to Abraham in Gen. 22.18 ('In your offspirng shall all the people of the earth be blessed'). Paul's insertion of the words 'in Christ

Jesus' in place of 'in your offspring' anticipates the messianic interpretation of Abraham's offspring which he develops in 3.16. So the redemption from the curse of the law by the death of Christ (v. 13) has opened the way for the fulfillment of God's promise to Abraham. And the fact that the Gentiles have received the Spirit by faith (vv. 14b, cf. 3.2, 5) demonstrates that the fulfillment has indeed taken place—i.e., *by faith*. Thus the validity of Hab. 2.4 is substantiated.[55]

In vv. 15-18 Paul shows that the validity of the promise is not negated by the law, since—as an illustration from civil law regarding a man's will highlights—the Abrahamic covenant cannot be annulled or added to once it has been ratified. Therefore, the law, which came 430 years after the ratification of the Abrahamic covenant, does not make that promise void. As Dahl says, 'Paul is asserting that promise—and therefore also the words "by faith"—have an unconditional validity which the Law does not abrogate'.[56]

Paul returns to the problem of the contradictory text when he asks: Τί οὖν ὁ νόμος: (v. 19). Paul answers the question by describing the temporary, subordinate function of the law. So the law is not against the promises of God (v. 21). Rather, the law contributes to the realization of the promises (vv. 22-25).

Dahl notes that it is Paul's definition of faith in terms of faith in the crucified Messiah, Jesus Christ, which caused him to see a contrast between Hab. 2.4 and Lev. 18.5. His dissociation of faith and works of the law, of course, deviated from the rabbinic view. Nevertheless, as Dahl concludes, 'in no other place is his style of argumentation more similar to that of the rabbis than in Galatians 3'.[57]

Although Schoeps and Dahl have not been able to demonstrate an exact correspondence between the rabbinic rule for handling contradictory texts and Paul's treatment of Hab. 2.4 and Lev. 18.5,[58] they have both pointed to a significant feature in the structure of Paul's argument. For the juxtaposition of these two texts supports Paul's antithetical contrast between faith and law.[59]

(9) *Atomistic Exegesis—the Generic Singular*: It has often been observed how closely Paul's distinction between the plural (τοῖς σπέρμασιν) and the singular (τῷ σπέρματι) in 3.16 agrees with the attention given to grammatical forms by the rabbis.[60] The generic singular 'seed' was usually interpreted in the Targumim and Talmud as a collective, referring to the sons of Israel.[61] But 'seed' was also

understood by the rabbis to be a specific singular, referring to an individual, e.g. Isaac, Solomon, or Seth.[62] Debate among scholars will undoubtedly continue, but perhaps the best way to understand Paul's interpretation of 'seed' in 3.16 is to view it here as an instance of his use of the rabbinic method of occasionally treating the generic singular as a specific singular.[63] By this method, he is able to counteract the common nationalistic interpretation which treated 'seed' as a collective singular, meaning Jews or the Jewish nation.[64] However, once he has restricted the reference of 'seed' to Christ, the true descendant of Abraham, he is then able to move on in his argument to the use of the collective sense and refer to those who belong to Christ (ὑμεῖς Χριστοῦ) as the 'seed' of Abraham.[65] Thus, the term 'seed' has been redefined and circumscribed in a way that contrasts with rabbinic theology, but corresponds with rabbinic methodology.[66]

(10) *Interpretation Established by Context*: The seventh rule of Hillel, that meaning may be determined by context, is illustrated in Gal. 3.17 where Paul establishes the precedence of the Abrahamic promise over the Mosaic law by pointing to the scriptural context: the law was given 430 years after the promise.[67] This distinction between the time of the confirmation of the promise to Abraham and that of the giving of the law stands in stark contrast to the rabbinic claim that Abraham knew and kept even the minutest details of the Mosaic law.[68]

The temporal distinction Paul makes here is in agreement with the chronological calculations of the rabbis.[69] In Gen. 15.13 the covenant 'between the pieces' includes a prophecy that 'your descendants will be sojourners in a land that is not theirs, and will be slaves there, and they will be oppressed for 400 years'. Exod. 12.40, however, states that the people of Israel dwelt in Egypt for 430 years. The rabbis resolved this discrepancy by explaining that the 430 years were reckoned from the covenant of Gen. 15 to the exodus, and that the 400 years were reckoned from the birth of Isaac.[70] Paul, it seems evident, has in mind the confirmation of the covenant described in Gen. 15,[71] and so he specified the time span between promise and law as 430 years, even though the passage he is working from (Gen. 15.13) explicitly says 400 years. It seems fair, therefore, to say that such precision probably reflects Paul's awareness of the rabbinic explanation.

Conclusions

The question of Paul's use of rabbinic methods of interpretation is difficult to determine. There are certainly many elements of rabbinic methodology which are not reflected in Pauline exegesis.[72] Some of the similarities do not necessarily demonstrate dependence; they may simply reflect procedures common to all writers,[73] and are, therefore, not any more rabbinic than the use of papyrus. Evidence, however, has been provided to suggest that rabbinic exegetical methods were employed by Paul in his Abraham argument in Gal. 3. Yet there remains sufficient ambiguity in the explication of Paul's use of these methods to warrant our attempt to apply other analyses in clarification of Paul's use of the Abraham story. For while insights derived from parallels between Pauline and rabbinic exegetical methods illuminate some features of hermeneutics, my thesis is that epistolary and rhetorical analyses are required—not simply as a supplement but as an essential basis—for understanding the function and structure of Paul's Abraham argument.

2. *Typological–Allegorical Exegesis in Gal. 4.21-31*

In dealing with the Hagar-Sarah relationship of 4.21-31, Paul states his exegetical method in v. 24: ἅτινα ἐστιν ἀλληγορούμενα. Ἀλληγορεῖν can mean to speak allegorically or to explain allegorically.[74] The former meaning best fits this context for in verse 30 Paul challenges his readers to listen to the law and asks them τί λέγει ἡ γραφή; according to Paul, the Hagar-Sarah story speaks allegorically to the specific issues in the Galatian churches.[75]

But Paul's use of ἀλληγορούμενα, however, does not automatically decide the question as to the exact nature of his exegetical method. The Antiochene fathers John Chrysostom and Theodore of Mopsuestia insisted that Paul incorrectly described as allegory what is in fact a type.[76] And many later commentators have taken the same view. Thus O. Michel says that in Gal. 4.24 'Paulus denkt mehr typologisch als allegorisch im eigentlichen Sinne'.[77] A.T. Hanson concurs that 'the "allegory" is really an elaborate piece of typology'.[78] On the other hand, Schoeps claims that it is 'allegorical rather than typological'.[79] And Longenecker concurs, maintaining that 'Gal. 4.21-31 is a highly allegorical representation of Old Testament history'[80] and that it 'may well represent an extreme form of Palestinian allegorical interpretation'.[81] A.T. Lincoln represents a mediating position in arguing that 'though the basic framework of Paul's treatment of the OT in Gal. 4.21ff is typological, in his attempt to make its application specific he uses what we would now call allegory'.[82]

Although the distinction between allegory and typology has been blurred and disputed in recent scholarship,[83] R.P.C. Hanson proves a sound definition of these terms which can serve as the basis of our discussion:

> Typology is the interpretating of an event belonging to the present or recent past as the fulfilment of a similar situation recorded or prophesied in Scripture. Allegory is the interpretation of an object or person or a number of objects or persons as in reality meaning some object or person or a later time, with no attempt made to trace a relationship of 'similar situation' between them.[84]

Typological Features in Gal. 4.21-31

Paul interprets Gen. 21 within the salvation-historical framework already established in Gal. 3. Within this framework Paul sees a real correspondence between the historical situation of the two sons of Abraham and the two sorts of descendants of Abraham in his own day, those born according to the flesh and those born according to the Spirit.[85] This correspondence is emphasized by the grammatical construction of 4.29 (ὥσπερ τότε . . . καὶ νῦν).[86] Then, as now, the son according to the flesh persecuted the son according to the promise. So since the Galatian believers were the persecuted and not the persecutors, they were obviously the sons of the free woman through the promise.[87] They were experiencing the fulfilment of a similar situation in the life of Isaac recorded in Gen. 21.

Paul bases his interpretation of the passage on the real correspondence between the historical event in the life of Isaac (the type) and the fulfilment of that even in salvation-history in the life of the Galatian church (the antitype).[88] On this basis, Paul rephrases the words of Sarah in Gen. 21.10 as a divine command: ἀλλὰ τί λέγει ἡ γραφή; ἔκβαλε τὴν παιδίσκην καὶ τὸν υἱὸν αὐτῆς. οὐ γὰρ μὴ κληρονομήσει ὁ υἱὸς τῆς παιδίσκης μετὰ τοῦ υἱοῦ τῆς ἐλευθέρας. And Gal. 4.31 is the natural conclusion which Paul draws from this interpretation:διό, ἀδελφοί, οὐκ ἐσμὲν παιδίσκης τέκνα ἀλλὰ τῆς ἐλευθέρας.

So it appears that Lincoln is right when he says that 'if Paul's interpretation of the OT had simply included vv. 22, 23, 28-30, then there would be no difficulty whatsoever in recognizing the passage as typology'.[89] The difficulty, however, comes when we attempt to describe Paul's method of interpretation in vv. 24-27. For the correspondence between Hagar and Mt. Sinai and the present Jerusalem is not an historical correspondence. Although some scholars attempt to explain the connection on the basis of various rabbinical practices of exegesis, it is still important to recognize that Paul has resorted to a form of Jewish allegorical interpretation at this point in the development of his argument.

Jewish Allegorical Interpretation
The Jewish practice of allegorical interpretation was most prominently practised by Philo of Alexandria.[90] We have already noted Philo's allegorical interpretation of the Abraham story.[91] In his interpretation of the Hagar–Sarah story, Sarah represents virtue and true wisdom, whereas Hagar represents general education. So Philo uses the allegory to contrast the superior value of true wisdom, which is found in the sacred scriptures, to general education which prepares one for secular work. In that allegory, Isaac is the true philosopher trained in holy scriptures; Ishmael is the sophist, unable to perceive eternal ideals.[92]

On his allegorical approach, Philo saw the OT as primarily a book of symbols which have hidden meanings beyond the literal, historical sense. His allegorical interpretation of these symbols was guided not by the constraints of the text but by his desire to demonstrate that the Jewish Scriptures contained the essence of Greek philosophy.[93]

Philo was not the only, or even the first, Jewish proponent of allegorical exegesis.[94] The Alexandrian Aristobulus (middle of 2nd century B.C.E.) used an allegorical approach in his interpretation of the law of Moses.[95] And the Letter of Aristeas contains an example of interpreting the ritual prescriptions of Mosaic law in an allegorical fashion.[96]

The practice of allegorical exposition was also to be found in scribal circles in Palestine.[97] David Daube argues, as we noted earlier, that Palestinian exegesis was influenced by Alexandrian procedures by way of Hillel, whose teachers were reputed to be Alexandrians.[98] Büchsel notes:

> For the Palestinians, too, it is in keeping with the dignity of Scripture that it has many meanings. 'As the hammer causes many sparks to fly, so the word of Scripture has a manifold sense'. In

view of all this, it seems overwhelmingly probable that the allegorical exposition of Scripture came to the Palestinians from the Alexandrians, so that in the last analysis it derives from the Greek influence in its Palestinian form.[99]

And there are several examples of allegorical exegesis in our extant rabbinic literature, which serve to highlight the fact that the rabbis were not adverse to employing this method.

There are also a number of examples of allegorical exegesis in the Qumran documents,[100] one of which is especially illuminating for our purpose of understanding Paul's exegetical practice in Gal. 4. For in the Damascus Rule the text of Num. 21.18 ('the well which the princes dug, which the nobles of the people delved with the stave') is followed by the interpretation:

> The Well is the Law, and those who dug it were the converts of Israel who went out of the land of Judah to sojourn in the land of Damascus. God called them all princes because they sought Him, and their renown was disputed by no man. The Stave is the Interpreter of the Law of whom Isaiah said, He makes a tool for His work (Isa. 54.16); and the nobles of the people are those who come to dig the Well with the staves with which the Stave ordained that they should walk in all the age of wickedness—and without them they shall find nothing—until he comes who shall teach righteousness at the end of days.[101]

There is no historical correspondence between the Stave and the Interpreter of the Law, or between the process of digging a well with staves and the study of the Law with the methods ordained by the Interpreter of the Law. This allegorization of the text is worked out from an eschatological perspective of 'the end of days' which enables the writer to see a hidden meaning in the text. Thus the words of the text are treated as symbols which gain their meaning from the experiences of the Qumran community.[102]

Paul's Allegorical Interpretation

In Paul's interpretation of Gen. 21, the two parallel columns of people and places[103] gain their meaning from the experiences of the Christian community at Galatia. Paul, of course, is not using the text as did Philo to expound neo-Platonic philosophical principles. Nevertheless, he is giving a meaning to the various terms of the text in an allegorical fashion.

Paul's allegorical treatment is apparently motivated by the

exigencies of the crisis at Galatia, Paul was confronted with the historical fact that Isaac's descendants are Jews and Ishmael's descendants are Gentiles.[104] Furthermore, he was probably faced with a situation where his opponents were already using the Gen. 21 story in support of their own case that Jews, the descendants of Sarah, were the only legitimate heirs of the promise, and Gentiles, the descendants of Hagar, were excluded from the promise.[105] In response to such circumstances, Paul was forced to argue *ad hominem*.[106] To do so, he had to reverse the common, literal interpretation of Gen. 21 by allegorizing the text.

The theological framework for Paul's allegorical interpretation stems from the Abraham argument of Gal. 3. For in that argument Gentile converts were identified as true sons and heirs of Abraham in the same sense as Isaac on the basis of the promise given to Abraham and their experience of the Spirit. The Abraham argument also set out a contrast between the Abrahamic covenant as the means of life and righteousness and the Sinaitic covenant as the means of slavery. Thus when the Genesis account is read as allegory, it is not surprising that Sarah and her counterpart, the Jerusalem above, the true mother Zion,[107] should be identified as the mother of the Galatian believers in Christ. And it follows naturally enough that Sarah can also be equated with the covenant of promise, which promise included Abrahamic blessings for Gentiles as the seed of Abraham. All of these equations are reasonable inferences from the Abraham argument.

Conversely, a natural consequence of Paul's definition of these terms in the allegorical equation is that Hagar becomes a symbol of the covenant from Mount Sinai. At this point in his argument, however, Paul's definition of terms in the allegorical equation becomes difficult to follow. Perhaps it was his own recognition of this difficulty which caused him to preface his treatment of Hagar with the explanation, ἅτινά ἐστιν ἀλληγορούμενα. The link between Hagar and the covenant from Mount Sinai and the present Jerusalem is certainly enigmatic, and, upon any interpretation, extremely difficult to explain. All that can be confidently affirmed is that Paul was allegorizing the text in line with his theological perspective.

The perplexing statement of 4.25a, τὸ δὲ ᾿Αγὰρ Σινὰ ὄρος ἐστιν ἐν τῇ ᾿Αραβίᾳ. συστοιχεῖ δὲ τῇ νῦν ᾿Ιερουσαλήμ,[108] has been explained by Barrett as an instance of rabbinic *kenin homer*, where a significant word is ingeniously reinterpreted.[109] According to Barrett, Paul gives the name Hagar a fresh reinterpretation so that the woman Hagar is identified with Mount Sinai where the law was given.[110] Barrett, however, does not explain what etymological argument Paul might have had in mind to support this identification.[111]

It is this identification of Hagar with Mt. Sinai which has caused the most difficulty in the interpretation of the verse. It has been suggested that Paul used a cabbalistic method of *gematria* to equate the numerical value of the words Ἀγὰρ Σινᾶ and the words νῦν Ἰερουσαλήμ,[112] or that he was equating the name Hagar with the Arabic word for rock (*hadjar*) which was associated with Sinai,[113] or that he was refering to *el Hegra*, a location 200 miles north of Midian.[114] The identification of Hagar with Mt. Sinai has also been explained simply on the basis of the geographical reference ἐν τῇ Ἀραβία which locates Mount Sinai outside the land of promise in a land of peoples known as the Arabians, the sons of Hagar.[115] All of these solutions to Paul's Hagar–Sinai and Sinai–present Jerusalem equations, however, are problematic. The major difficulty with them is their apparent lack of validity in the face of the fundamental Jewish conviction that the Mosaic law had been given to the descendants of Isaac at Mount Sinai and had nothing to do with Hagar.[116]

The most satisfactory explanation of Paul's allegorical equations is simply stated in v. 25b; δουλεύει γὰρ μετὰ τῶν τέκνων αὐτῆς. In Paul's allegorization of the text, slavery is the common feature that links Hagar, the covenant given at Mount Sinai, and the present Jerusalem.[117] Paul has already attributed this feature of slavery to the Mosaic law (3.22-24; 4.1-10) and to a certain faction at Jerusalem (2.4). His allegorization, therefore, is not to be read as a wholesale attack on Judaism as such, but as a counterattack upon that Jewish-Christian faction within the church at Jerusalem which tried to rob Gentile believers of their freedom by requiring them to be circumcised (2.3-6) and which was now attempting to do the same thing at Galatia. It was this actual experience of 'troublemakers' in the church that gave rise to Paul's allegorical treatment of the text and is the key to its interpretation.

Conclusion

Our examination of Paul's hermeneutical approach to the Hagar-Sarah story confirms the position that his basic typological interpretation is supplemented by an allegorical treatment in order to relate the people in the story to the specific issues in the Galatian church, and so to counteract the troublemakers' use of the same text.

This explanation of Paul's typological-allegorical method, however, still leaves the basic question regarding the function of the allegory in the context of the letter unresolved. It is this question that we address in our exegesis of Gal. 4.21-31 in light of our epistolary and rhetorical analyses.

NOTES

Notes to Introduction

1. Thomas Dozemann, '*Sperma Abraam* in John 8 and Related Literature: Cosmology and Judgment', *CBQ* 42 (1980), pp. 345-58; Lloyd Gaston, 'Abraham and the Righteousness of God', *Horizons in Biblical Theology* 2 (1980), pp. 36-68; D.H. King, 'Paul and the Tannaim: A Study in Galatians', *WTJ* 45 (1983), pp. 340-70; Halver Moxnes, *Theology in Conflict: Studies in Paul's Understanding of God in Romans* (NovTSup, 53; Leiden: Brill, 1980); Terrance McGonigal, '"Abraham Believed God": Genesis 15.6 and its Use in the New Testament' (Ph.D. Dissertation, Fuller Theological Seminary, 1981); Manfred Oemig, 'Ist Genesis 15,6 ein Beleg für die Anrechnung des Glaubens zur Gerechtigkeit?' *ZAW* 95 (1983), pp. 182-97; O.P. Robertson, 'Genesis 15.6: New Covenant Expositions of an Old Covenant Text', *WTJ* 42 (1980), pp. 259-89; E.P. Sanders, *Paul, the Law, and the Jewish People* (Philadelphia: Fortress, 1983); Hans Schmid, 'Gerechtigkeit und Glaube: Genesis 15.6 und sein biblisch-theologischer Kontext', *EvT* 40 (1980), pp. 396-420; Donald D. Sutherland, 'Genesis 15.6: A Study in ancient Jewish and Christian Interpretation' (Ph.D. Dissertation, Southern Baptist Theological Seminary, 1982). Interest continues unabated. See especially J.S. Siker, 'Disinheriting the Jews: The use of Abraham in Early Christian Controversy with Judaism from Paul through Justin Martyr' (Ph.D. Dissertation, Princeton Theological Seminary, 1988).

2. Since an understanding of these issues is necessary for an accurate exegesis of Galatians, a summary of the relevant data is presented in three appendices: Appendix 1: The Opponents' Use of the Abraham Tradition; Appendix 2: Abraham in Jewish Literature; Appendix 3: Paul and Jewish Exegesis.

3. T. McGonigal, '"Abraham Believed God"', p. 328.

4. George Howard, *Paul: Crisis in Galatia* (SNTSMS, 35; Cambridge: Cambridge University Press, 1979), p. 57.

5. L. Gaston, 'Abraham and the Righteousness of God', *Horizons in Biblical Theology* 2 (1980), p. 53.

6. See Robert W. Funk, *Language, Hermeneutic and Word of God* (New York: Harper & Row, 1966), p. 251.

218   *Abraham in Galatians*

7. John L. White, *The Form and Function of the body of the Greek Letter:
A Study of the Letter-Body in the Non-Literary Papyri and in Paul the
Apostle* (SBLDS, 2; Missoula: Scholars Press, 1972).
8. See below, p. 224 n. 80.
9. Nils A. Dahl, 'Paul's Letter to The Galatians: Epistolary Genre,
Content, and Structure' (an unpublished seminar paper for the SBL Paul
Seminar, 1973).
10. Hans Dieter Betz, *Galatians: A Commentary on Paul's Letter to the
Churches in Galatia* (Hermeneia; Philadelphia: Fortress, 1979). His work is
foundational for the research of other scholars such as B.H. Brinsmead,
Galatians—Dialogical Response to Opponents (SBLDS, 65; Chico: Scholars
Press, 1982), pp. 42-87; Gerd Luedemann, *Paul, Apostle to the Gentiles:
Studies in Chronology* (trans. F.S. Jones; Philadelphia: Fortress, 1984),
pp. 46-80; F. Vouga, 'La construction de l'histoire en Galates 3-4', *ZNW* 75
(1984), pp. 259-69; *idem*, 'Zur rhetorischen Gattung des Galaterbriefs',
ZNW 79 (1988), pp. 291-92; Robert G. Hall, 'The Rhetorical Outline of
Galatians: A Reconsideration', *JBL* 106 (1987), pp. 277-87; J. Smit, 'The
Letter of Paul to the Galatians: A Deliberative Speech', *NTS* 35 (1989),
pp. 1-26; James Hester, 'The Rhetorical Structure of Galatians 1.11-2.14',
JBL 103 (1984), pp. 223-33.
11. Betz, *Galatians*, p. 129.
12. John Bligh, *Galatians in Greek: A Structural Analysis of St. Paul's
Epistle to the Galatians with Notes on the Greek* (Detroit: University of
Detroit Press, 1966); *idem*, Galatians: *A Discussion of St. Paul's Epistle*
(Householder Commentaries 1; London: St. Paul's Publications, 1969). See
below p. 76.
13. Wilhelm Wuellner, 'Paul's Rhetoric of Argumentation in Romans',
CBQ 38 (1976), pp. 330-51.
14. Folker Siegert, 'Argumentation bei Paulus: Gezeigt an Röm 9-11'
(Ph.D. Dissertation, Evangelisch-Theologischen Fakultät an der Eberhard-
Karl-Universität zu Tübingen, 1983).
15. Chaim Perelman and L. Olbrechts-Tyteca, *The New Rhetoric: A
Treatise on Argumentation* (trans. J. Wilkinson and P. Weaver; Notre Dame:
University of Notre Dame Press, 1969).
16. The limits of this study preclude a full evaluation and application of
other methods of analysis such as discourse analysis of the letter's
grammatical structure (see Joseph Grimes, 'Signals of Discourse Structure',
SBLASP 8 [1975], I, pp. 151-65), analysis of the diatribe style of argumentation
(see Stanley K. Stowers, *The Diatribe and Paul's Letter to the Romans*
([SBLDS 57; Chico: Scholars Press, 1981]), and a structuralist approach to
the narrative structures in the letter (see Richard B. Hays, *The Faith of Jesus
Christ: An Investigation of the Narrative Substructure of Galatians 3.1–4.11*
[SBLDS 56; Chico: Scholars Press, 1983]; Daniel Patte, *Paul's Faith and the
Power of the Gospel: A Structural Introduction to the Pauline Letters*

Notes to Chapter 1

[Philadelphia: Fortress, 1983]; Dan O. Via, Jr., 'A Structural Approach to Paul's Old Testament Hermeneutics', *Int* 28 [1974], pp. 201-20; John H. Pilch, 'Paul's Usage and Understanding of *Apokalypsis* in Galatians 1-2: A Structural Investigation' [Ph. D. Dissertation, Marquette University, 1972]; Bernard C. Letegan, 'Structural Analysis as a Basis for Further Exegetical Procedures', *SBLASP*, pp. 341-60).

Notes to Chapter 1

1. W.G. Doty, 'The Concept of Genre in Literary Analysis', *SBLASP* 2 (1972), p. 439: 'It may be necessary to keep characteristic motifs in view, but identifications of subject matter are of dubious value, since related subjects may be expressed in several genres'.

2. Adolph Deissmann, *Light from the Ancient Near East* (trans. L. Strachan; Grand Rapids: Baker, 1978; reprint of Hodder & Stoughton edn p. 234). For a critical analysis of Deissmann's classification of Paul's letters, see W.G. Doty, 'Classification of Epistolary Literature', *CBQ* 31 (1969), pp. 183-99. Doty explains Deissmann's letter/epistle distinction on the basis of the theological and scholarly positions against which Deissmann directed his writings. Deissmann was reacting to (1) the interpretation of Paul as 'a system-proud dogmatician' (p. 185), (2) the criticism of Paul as a poor or decadent classicist (p. 187), and (3) 'the mechanically conceived doctrine of inspiration as applied to the NT' (p. 188). Doty concludes that Deissmann's letter/epistle distinction 'was formed due to sensitivities other than merely the deriving of a critical tool' (p. 189), and that the absolute letter/epistle distinction should be dropped and replaced with a much more elaborate multiple classification scheme (p. 198).

3. A. Deissmann, *Light from the Ancient Near East*, p. 237

4. J. Sykutris, 'Epistolographie' in *Real-Encyclopädie der classischen Altertumswissenschaft* (eds. A. Pauly, G. Wissowa, *et al.*; Stuttgart: Metzlersche, 1931) Supplement 5, pp. 218-19.

5. Paul Wendland, *Die urchristlichen Literaturformen*, in *Handbuch zum Neuen Testament* (eds. W. Bauer, M. Dibelius, *et al.*; Tübingen: J.C.B. Mohr, 1912) Erster Band: Dritter Teil, p. 344; cf. Otto Roller, *Das Formular der paulinischen Briefe: Ein Beitrag zur Lehre vom antiken Briefe* (Stuttgart: Kohlhammer, 1933), p. 32, who also draws special attention to the important conclusion 'dass alle paulinischen Briefe... wirkliche Briefe sind'. W. Doty, 'Classification of Epistolary Literature', p. 192, says that 'the most positive contribution of Deissmann's work in this area was to direct attention to each letter *on its own*, with rigorous attention to the specific situation and relationship attaining between writer and addressee/s'.

6. Demetrius, *On Style* (trans. W. Rhys Roberts; LCL; London: Heinemann, 1927), p. 445; W. Rhys Roberts (p. 270) identifies the author of

On Style as Demetrius of Tarsus (first century AD); cf. A.J. Malherbe, 'Ancient Epistolary Theorists', *Ohio Journal of Religious Studies* 5 (1977), p. 5: 'the exact date of this treatise is still in dispute, suggestions for it ranging from the third century BC to the first century AD. The sources of the treatise, however, do appear to go back perhaps to the second century, and at the latest, to the first century BC'.

7. See W. Doty, *Letters in Primitive Christianity* (Guides to Biblical Scholarship: New Testament Series; Philadelphia: Fortress Press, 1973), pp. 6-8, for a discussion of 'non-real' letters.

8. Against B. Brinsmead, *Galatians–Dialogical Response to Opponents*, SBLDS 65 (Chico: Scholars Press, 1982), pp. 37-40, who dismisses Hellenistic papyrus letters as an appropriate genre for Paul's letters and turns instead to classical, rhetorical literature. See my evaluation below, pp. 25-27.

9. Stykutris, 'Epistolographie', p. 187.

10. Doty, 'The Classification of Epistolary Literature', pp. 196-97.

11. *Ibid.*, p. 198.

12. Stykutris, 'Epistolographie', p. 218.

13. Wendland, *Die urchristlichen Literaturformen*, p. 345

14. For example, Plato, *Letter 7*, which is cited by Betz and Brinsmead as a literary precedent for Galatians. See below, p. 26.

15. Evidence for this is to be found in a series of dissertations directed by Robert Funk: John L. White, *The Greek Letter*; idem, *The Form and Structure of the Official Petition: A Study in Greek Epistolography* (SBLDS, 5; Missoula: SBL, 1972); Chan-Hie Kim, *The Form and Structure of the Familiar Greek Letter of Recommendation* (SBLDS, 4; Missoula: SBL, 1972).

16. Deissmann, *Light from the Ancient Near East*, p. 237.

17. J. White, *The Greek Letter*, p. 3; against Brinsmead, *Galatians*, p. 40. Brinsmead claims that White contradicts himself by agreeing with Deissmann that 'the common letter tradition is the primary *Gattung* to which the Pauline letter belongs' and then later saying that Deissmann was wrong in 'his proposal that the common letter tradition was the literary genre to which the Pauline letter belongs' (Brinsmead, p. 224 n. 49; see White, *The Greek Letter*, p. 68). White, however, does not say that Deissmann's proposal was wrong, just that it was 'an over-simplification'. The need to correct this over-simplification (see my comments below) does not negate the validity of the general classification of Paul's letters within the Hellenistic common letter tradition.

18. Brinsmead, *Galatians*, p. 39.

19. *Ibid.*

20. *Ibid.*, p. 224 n. 44.

21. See Malherbe, 'Ancient Epistolary Theorists', pp. 8-11; cf. W. Doty, *Letters*, p. 10; J. White and K. Kensinger, 'Categories of Greek Papyrus Letters', *SBLASP* 10 (1976), pp. 79-91; Chin-Hie Kim, *The Form and*

Function of The Familiar Greek Letter of Recommendation; *idem*, 'The Papyrus Invitation', *JBL* 94 (1975), pp. 391-402; T. Mullins, 'Petition as a Literary Form', *NovT* 5 (1962), pp. 46-54.

22. I am idebted here to Nils A. Dahl, 'Paul's Letter to the Galatians: Epistolary Genre, Content, and Structure', an unpublished paper for the SBL Paul Seminar, 1973. Although I have independently developed an argument for the rebuke-request structure of Galatians, I acknowledge that Dahl's observations first sparked my thinking in this direction.

23. Cf. Robert Funk, *Language, Hermeneutic and Word of God* (New York: Harper and Row, 1966), pp. 254-63.

24. White, *The Greek Letter*, p. 3.

25. Betz, 'The Literary Composition and Function of Paul's Letter to the Galatians', *NTS* 21 (1975), p. 354; *Galatians*, p. 14; Brinsmead, *Galatians*, p. 42. Betz also says that Galatians should be classified as an example of the 'magical letter' genre and the 'heavenly letter' genre. However, Betz's use of these terms is not so much an attempt to describe the epistolary genre of Galatians as an effort to provide an analogy to clarify his suggestion that Paul expected his letter to the Galatians to bring immediate curses or blessings upon them depending upon their response.

The concept of the 'heavenly letter' is very broad. R. Stube, *Der Himmelsbrief: Ein Beitrag zur allgemeinen Religionsgeschichte* (Tübingen: J.C.B. Mohr, 1918), refers to ancient Egyptian letters for the dead (pp. 28, 30), OT passages such as Ex. 20.2; 34.1; Is. 6; Jer. 1; Ez. 3.13 (pp. 33-34), the Koran (p. 39), and the Book of Mormon (p. 41) as examples of 'heavenly letters'. He comments, 'Die Idee göttlicher Briefe können wir in A.T. wie im spätern Judentum direkt erweisen. Ausdrücklich vom Schreiben Gottes wird beim Sinaigesetz gesprochen' (p. 33). Thus it is clear that the 'magical-heavenly letter' is not a very helpful guide for defining what type of Hellenistic letter Galatians is or describing the epistolary structure of Galatians.

Papyri Graecae Magicae: Die griechischen Zauberpapyri (eds., K. Preisendanz and A. Henrichs; Stuttgart: Teubner, 1973), cited by Betz, gives examples of 'magical' letters. But these must be classified differently as to epistolary genre than Galatians in light of their different epistolary structure and content. See J. Sykutris, 'Epistolographie', p. 206: 'Gewöhnlich zerfallen solche Briefe in drei Teile: eine Einleitung über die Fundumstände des Briefes und ihre Entzifferung, sittlich-religiöse Verheissungen und Strafandrohungen, magische Schutzmittel gegen allerlei Gefahr'. Wayne Meeks, in his 'Review of H.D. Betz, *Galatians*', *JBL* 100 (1981), p. 306, asks, 'will anyone who has actually read the Zauberpapyri to which Betz refers and then reads Galatians, really imagine that he is reading the same kind of literature?'

26. Betz, *Galatians*, p. 15.

27. *Ibid.*

28. Plato, *Letter 7* (LCL; *Plato*, vol. 7, trans. R.G. Bury; London: Heinemann, 1967), p. 474.

29. Isocrates, *Antidosis* (LCL; *Isocrates*, vol. 2; London: Heinemann, 1968), p. 189.

30. Cf. Andrew Momigliano, *The Development of Greek Biography* (Cambridge, Mass.: Harvard University Press, 1971), p. 59.

31. Isocartes, *Antidosis*, p. 191.

32. Demosthenes, *De Corona* (LCL; *Demosthenes*, vol. 2, trans. C.A. Vance; London: Heinemann, 1963), pp. 14-15.

33. Cicero, *Brutus* (LCL; *Cicero*, vol. 5, trans. H.M. Hubbell; London: Heinemann, 1962), p. 5.

34. A, Momigliano, *The Development of Greek Biography*, p. 60.

35. David Aune, 'Review of H.D. Betz, *Galatians*', *RelSRev* 7 (1981), p. 324, notes that 'his [Betz's] interest in Momigliano's comments on the apologetic letter has tended to obscure the fact that Momligiano's central subject on pp. 57-62 is *autobiography*, not the apologetic letter (though the two can, of course, be combined)'. Wayne Meeks, 'Review of H.D. Betz, *Galatians*', p. 306, makes a valid criticism of Betz; 'He does not offer us a single instance of the apologetic letter with which we can compare Galatians. We are therefore asked to interpret Galatians as an example of a genre for which no other example can apparently be cited'.

36. For a discussion of the relation of oral speech forms to literary rhetoric and the relation of literary rhetoric to Galatians, see pp. 55-60.

37. Betz, *Galatians*, p. 15.

38. Brinsmead, *Galatians*, p. 37.

39. See especially the work of J. White, *The Greek Letter*; idem, 'Epistolary Formulas and Cliches in the Greek papyrus Letters', *SBLASP* 14 (1978), pp. 289-319; idem, 'Introductory Formulae in the Body of the Pauline Letters', *JBL* 90 (1971), pp. 91-97; idem, 'The Greek Documentary Letter Tradition, Third Century B.C.E. to Third Century C.E.', *Semeia* 22 (1981), pp. 89-106; T.Y. Mullins, 'Disclosure as a Literary Form in the New Testament', *NovT* 7 (1964), pp. 44-50; idem, 'Formulas in New Testament Epistles', *JBL* 91 (1972), pp. 380-90; idem, 'Petition as a Literary Form', *NovT* 5 (1962), pp. 46-54; idem, 'Visit Talk in the New Testament Letters', *CBQ* 35 (1973), pp. 350-58; W. Doty, *Letters in Primitive Christianity*; C. Bjerkelund, *Parakalô: Form, Funktion und Sinn der parakalô-Sätze in den paulinischen Briefen* (Bibliotheca Theologica Norvegica 1; Oslo; Universitets-forlaget, 1976). Older works include F. Exler, *The Form of the Ancient Greek letter. A Study in Greek Epistolography* (Washington, D.C.: Catholic University of America, 1923); H. Koskenniemi, *Studien zur Idee und Phraseologie des griechischen Briefes bis 400 n. Chr.* (Helsinki: Tiedakatemie, 1956); H.G, Meecham, *Light from Ancient Letters; Private Correspondence in the Non-Literary Papyri of Oxyrhynchus of the First Four Centuries and its Bearing on New Testament Language and Thought* (London: George Allen &

Unwin, 1923); O. Roller, *Das Formular der paulinischen Briefe* (BWANT, 4; Stuttgart: W. Kohlhammer Verlag, 1923).

40. For information on opening and closing formulas in Greek papyrus letters see O. Roller, *Das Formular der paulinischen Briefe*; White, 'Epistolary Formulas and Cliches in Greek Papyrus Letters', pp. 289-99.

41. For information on thanksgiving sections and prayer formulae in Greek papyri, see Paul Schubert, *Form and Function of the Pauline Thanksgivings*; T. Mullins, 'Formula in New Testament Epistles', p. 382; H. Koskenniemi, *Studien*, p. 139.

42. Cf. J. White, *The Greek Letter*, p. 40; *idem*, 'Introductory Formulae', pp. 95-96; Koskenniemi, *Studien*, p. 75.

43. See examples below, pp. 33-42.

44. Cf. White, *The Greek Letter*, p. 21.

45. *Ibid.*, p. 42. White calls this a 'compliance statement'.

46. *Ibid.*, pp. 11-15; 'Introductory Formulae', p. 93; *idem*, 'Epistolary Formulas', pp. 302-303; T. Mullins, 'Disclosure Formulae', pp. 46-49; J.T. Sanders, 'The Transition from Open Epistolary Thanksgiving to body in the Letter of the Pauline Corpus', *JBL* 81 (1962), p. 349.

47. Cf. J. White, *The Greek Letter*, pp. 34-38; *idem*, 'Introductory Formulae', p. 93; *idem*, 'Epistolary Formulas', pp. 301-302; T. Mullins, 'Petition', pp. 47-54.

48. Cf. J. White, *The Greek Letter*, p. 21, p. 83; *idem*, 'Introductory Formulas', p. 97. T. Mullins, 'Formulas', p. 386, however, objects, arguing that the formulaic use of a verb of hearing or learning lacks 'the structural rigidity necessary for a form'.

49. Cf. J. White, *The Greek Letter*, pp. 31-32.

50. *Ibid.*, pp. 49-51; *idem*, 'Epistolary Formulas', p. 307; Robert Funk, 'The Apostolic *Parousia*: Form and Significance', in *Christian History and Interpretation* (ed. W.R. Farmer, C.F.D. Moule, R.R. Niebuhr; Cambridge: Cambridge University Press, 1967), pp. 249-68.

51. Cf. J. White, *The Greek Letter*, pp. 24-25.

52. *Ibid.*, pp. 57-58.

53. *Ibid.*, pp. 16-18.

54. *Ibid.*, pp. 18-20.

55. *Ibid.*, p. 29: 'The vocative is employed intermittently, during the Roman period, as a means of making transitions in all three body sections'.

56. T. Mullins, 'Formulas', p. 387.

57. Cf. R. Funk, *Language, Hermeneutic and Word of God*, pp. 259, 256-57.

58. Cf. P. Schubert, *Form and Function of the Pauline Thanksgivings*, p. 35.

59. Cf. James M. Robinson, 'Die Hodajot-Formel in Gebet und Hymnus des Frühchristentums', in *Apophoreta: Festschrift für Ernst Haenchen* (ed.,

W. Eltester; Berlin: Töpelmann, 1964), pp. 194-235; J.T. Sanders, 'The Transition from Opening Epistolary Thanksgiving to Body in the Letters of the Pauline Corpus', *JBL* 81 (1962), pp. 358-62.

60. R. Funk, *Language, Hermeneutic and Word of God*, p. 270; see also W. Doty, *Letters in Primitive Christianity*, pp. 27-43.

61. *Ibid.*, p. 271.

62. J. White, *The Greek Letter*, pp. 62-66, distinguishes between major and minor transitional formulae in the papyrus letters.

63. P. Schubert, *Form and Function of the Pauline Thanksgivings*, p. 180.

64. R. Funk, *Language, Hermeneutic and Word of God*, p. 257.

65. Forty-three extant letters ranging from 252 BC to fourth century AD have it: P. Apoll. 6.2; 26.13; 29.7; 32.2; 63.23; 64.4; P. Herm. 11; P. Cairo Zen. 59060.10; B.G.U. 850.3; 1041.12; 984.19; 1079.2; P. Ryl. 235.6; 573.7; 693.2; P. Tebt. 27.34; P.S.I. 502.12; P. Cornell 52.5; P. Mich. 479.4; 500.3; 209.6; P. Lips. 107.2; S.B. 6222.4; 8244.3; 9106.2; 9654; P. Baden 35.6; P. Genev. 57.3; P. Princ. 98.16; P. Grenf. 77.8; 92.1; P. Harris 157.7; P. Lond. 1075; P. Merton 28.4; 80.3; P. Oxy. 113.20; 123.5; 1223.3; 1348; 2728.5; 2729.4; 3063.11; 2783.6.

66. T. Mullins, 'Formulas', p. 385.

67. See P. Oxy. 3063.11-16.

68. Mullins, 'Formulas', p. 387.

69. John Hurd, 'Concerning the Structure of 1 Thessalonians' (an unpublished paper for SBL Paul Seminar, 1972), p. 20. See 1 Thess. 2.13, 14; 4.1, 2; 4.13, 14; 5.1, 2; 5.12, 14.

70. Cf. Mullins, 'Petition', p. 47.

71. J. White and K. Kensinger, 'Categories', p. 85.

72. *Ibid.*, pp. 79, 90 n. 7; cf. P. Mich. III, 209; VIII, 479; 500 for references to previous correspondence or an expression of thanksgiving (introduced by εὐχαριστῶ, χάρις, ἐχάρην). See also B.G.U.I, 332, I, 423; IV, 1081; P. Mich. VIII, 475, 473, 474, 498.

73. C. Bjerkelund, *Parakalô*, p. 139.

74. *Ibid.*, p. 146.

75. *Ibid.*, p. 154.

76. *Ibid.*, p. 177.

77. *Ibid.*, p. 178.

78. Mullins, 'Petition', p. 48.

79. *Ibid.*, p. 50.

80. John White, in his analysis of the epistolary structure of Galatians, overlooks this rebuke-request structure. He says that 'the expression of astonishment in Gal. 1.6 (introduced by θαυμάζω), like that of the common Greek letter, is both an expression of dissatisfaction and an intimation that communication has broken down. It does not function however, as the background to a request for a letter. The object of Paul's dissatisfaction is not the Galatian's failure to write but their apparent rejection of the gospel'

('Introductory Formulae in the Body of the Pauline Letter', p. 96). True, the rebuke section does not function as the background to a request for a letter when the object of Paul's dissatisfaction is understood as the Galatians' failure to write. But the rebuke section does function as the background to his request for loyalty to the true gospel as preached and exemplified by Paul—for the object of Paul's rebuke is, as White himself says, the Galatians' 'apparent rejection of the gospel'. Θαυμάζω letters express rebuke for other reasons than the failure to write. See P. Baden 35; P. Merton 80; P. Oxy. 3063; P. Oxy. 1223.

John White's outline of Galatians, which is based upon his analysis of epistolary conventions, actually excludes a consideration of Gal. 4.12-20:

Letter Opening 1.1-5
Body-Opening Formulae 1.6-14
    1. The expression of astonishment 1.6
    2. Statement of compliance 1.6
    3. Disclosure formula 1.11
    4. The use of the verb ἀκούω 1.13
Body-Middle 1.15-4.31
Part I 1.15-2.21
Part II 3.1-4.11/4.21-31
Body-Closing 5.2-12
    1. The motivation for writing—
       responsibility formula 5.2
    2. The confidence formula 5.10
    3. The apostolic *parousia* formula 5.11-12
Paraenesis 5.13-6.10
Letter Conclusion 6.11-18.

The only explanation given for this exclusion of 4.12-20 is a footnote which states that 'Gal. 4.12-20 is provisionally excluded from the body-middle section because, for reasons to be adduced subsequently, it should be analyzed in connection with the body closing' (White, *The Greek Letter*, p. 90 n. 32). But the only mention of 4.12-20 which White makes subsequent to this statement is (in agreement with Funk's suggestion) that 4.12-20 and 6.11 are possible substitutes for the apostolic *parousia* (p. 109).

White then goes on to argue that 5.11-12 should be identified as the surrogate for Paul's apostolic *parousia*. His primary reason for this is that 5.11-12 is the proper point in the body for expecting the statement of apostolic *parousia* following the 'motivation for writing-responsibility formula' in 5.2 and the 'confidence formula' in 5.10 (pp. 109-11). This argument, however, demands too much of a rigid adherence to a set form on Paul's part. Paul's clearest reference to his desire for a visit is in 4.20. This statement of desire for an apostolic visit is combined with six other epistolary conventions (4.11, 12, 13, 15, 19, 21). Such a cluster of conventional expressions should not be excluded from a consideration of the epistolary structure of Galatians; it signals, in fact, a major turning point in the letter.

81. Imperatives dominate the tone and structure of the rest of the letter 4.27, 30; 5.1, 13, 14, 16; 6.1, 2, 5, 6, 7, 9, 10.

82. Μαρτυρῶ (4.15) and μαρτύρομαι (5.3) appear to be used as substitutes for the usual disclosure formulae here and in Rom. 10.2; Col. 4.13; Eph. 4.17.

83. R. Funk, *Language, Hermeneutic and Word of God*, pp. 266-70; *idem*, 'Apostolic *Parousia*', pp. 249-68; cf. Mullins, 'Visit Talk', pp. 350-58, who argues that 'visit talk' (apostolic *parousia*) is a common epistolary theme rather than a form or formula. Funk's detailed analysis, however, presents substantial evidence for it as having been a conventional, literary form.

84. R. Funk, 'Apostolic *Parousia*', p. 249.

85. *Ibid.*, p. 251.

86. *Ibid.*, pp. 266-67.

87. E.g., Rom. 15.14-33; Phil. 2.19-30; 1 Thess. 2.17-3.8; Phlm 22.

88. See J. White, *The Greek Letter*, p. 92 n. 34, on Paul's use of λέγω in Galatians. He describes the 'quasi-formulaic role' that λέγω performs in 3.15-4.31. The verb is used eight times (3.15, 16, 17; 4.1, 21, 30; 5.2, 16). In 3.16 and 4.30 it introduces an OT citation. In 3.17 and 4.1 it introduces an explanatory phrase. In 3.15, it provides a transition to an illustration. In 4.21 it is used as a question to introduce the allegory of Hagar and Sarah. And in 5.2 and 16 Paul uses λέγω to present his authoritative decision and ethical appeal. In this last instance, the verb functions almost as a substitute for a request verb.' See J. Sanders, 'The Transition from Opening Epistolary Thanksgiving to Body in the Letters of the Pauline Corpus', pp. 353-54. Cf. Rom. 9.1; 12.3; 15.8; 1 Cor. 1.12; 7.8, 12, 29, 35; 15.50, 51; 1 Thess. 4.15. Paul's use of this verb may also reflect his use of the diatribe style (R. Bultmann, *Der Stil der paulinischen Predigt*, 10, 13, 45; J. White, *The Greek Letter*, p. 92 n. 34).

89. See discussion below, pp. 193-94.

90. M.L. Stirewalt, 'Official Letter Writing and the Letter of Paul to the Churches of Galatia' (unpublished paper for SBL Paul Seminar), pp. 34-35.

91. Cf. Dahl, 'Paul's Letter to the Galatians', p. 91.

92. J. White, *The Greek Letter*, p. 102.

93. In this case, Paul does not include a 'responsibility formula'.

94. See below, pp. 150-54; against White who separates paraenesis from the 'body' of the letter.

95. J. White, *The Greek Letter*, pp. 104-105.

96. Cf. Dahl. 'Paul's Letter to the Galatians', p. 45.

97. Cf. Otto Merk, 'Der Beginn der Paraenes im Galaterbrief', *ZNW* 60 (1969), pp. 83-104. Merk lists the different starting points of the paraenesis suggested in the history of the debate as a) 4.12, b) 4.21, c) 5.1, d) 5.2, e) 5.7, f) 5.13. For a recent discussion and defense of 5.13 as the starting point, see D.K. Fletcher, 'The Singular Argument of Paul's Letter to the Galatians' (Ph.D. Dissertation, Princeton Theological Seminary, 1982), pp. 121-40. See

also John Barclay, *Obeying the Truth: A Study of Paul's Ethics in Galatians* (Edinburgh: T.&T. Clark, 1988), pp. 23-26.
    98. This definition of paraenesis is developed by D. Bradley, 'The Topos as a Form in the Pauline Paraenesis', *JBL* 72 (1953) p. 238. See Barclay, *Obeying*, pp. 147-55.
    99. As David Bradley claims, *ibid.*, p. 239,
    100. See below, pp. 150-54.
    101. See J. White, *The Greek Letter*, p. 96, on Paul's use of ἄρα οὖν to signal transitions.
    102. Cf. 1 Cor. 16.21; 2 Thess. 3.17.
    103. Gordon Bahr, 'The Subscriptions in the Pauline Letters', *JBL* 89 (1969), pp. 27-41.
    104. *Ibid.*, p. 35.
    105. *Ibid.*
    106. I am not answering the question as to whether Paul himself wriote the whole letter or only took up the pen at 6.11. My point is simply that 6.11-18 fulfills the function of the subscription as defined by Bahr.
    107. See below, pp. 65-66, 69-70.

Notes to Chapter 2

    1. Betz, *Galatians*, p. 24.
    2. Hübner, 'Der Galaterbrief und das Verhältnis von antiker Rhetorik und Epistolographie', *TLZ* 4 (1984), p. 245.
    3. Aristotle, *Rhetoric*, 1.2.1 (LCL, 22.15); cf. W.J. Brandt, *The Rhetoric of Argumentation* (New York: Bobbs-Merrill, 1970), p. 24; E Corbett, ed., *Rhetorical Analyses of Literary Works* (London: Oxford University Press, 1969), xiii.
    4. There has been mounting interest of late in the study of the rhetorical nature of Paul's letters. Besides H.D. Betz and B.H. Brinsmead, see H. Hübner, 'Der Galaterbrief und das Verhältnis von antiker Rhetorik und Epistolographie', pp. 242-250; J. Hester, 'The Rhetorical Structure of Galatians 1.11-2.14', *JBL* 103 (1984), pp. 223-33; G. Luedemann, *Paul, Apostle to the Gentiles: Studies in Chronology* (tr. F. Jones; Philadelphia: Fortress, 1984), pp. 46-81 (Luedemann adopts Betz's analysis of the rhetorical form of Galatians); G. Kennedy, *New Testament Interpretation through Rhetorical Criticism* (Chapel Hill: The University of North Carolina Press, 1984); M. Kessler, 'A Methodological Setting for Rhetorical Criticism', *Semitics* 4 (1974), pp. 23-36; *idem*, 'An Introduction to Rhetorical Criticism of the Bible', *Semitics* 7 (1980), pp. 1-27; W, Wuellner, 'Paul's Rhetoric of Argumentation in Romans', *CBQ* 38 (1976), pp. 330-51 ('. . . I propose to replace the traditional priority on propositional theology and the more recent priority on letters as literature with the new priority on letters as

argumentation' [p. 330]); F. Forrester, 'Rhetorical Structure and Design in Paul's Letter to Philemon', *HTR* 71 (1978), pp. 17-33; Robin Scroggs, 'Paul as Rhetorician: Two Homilies in Romans 1-11', in *Jews, Greeks, and Christians: FS W.D. Davies* (eds., Robert Hamerton-Kelly and Robin Scroggs; Leiden: Brill, 1976), pp. 271-298; Folker Siegert, 'Argumentation bei Paulus, gezeigt an Rom. 9-11' (PhD dissertation, Tübingen, 1983). For a recent bibliography see Duane F. Watson, 'The New Testament and Greco-Roman Rhetoric', *JETS* 31 (1988), pp. 465-72.

5. See Plato, *Gorgias*, especially 450, 457, 463, 471d; George Kennedy, *The Art of Persuasion in Greece* (Princeton: Princeton University Press, 1963), pp. 61-68; *Classical Rhetorical and Its Christian and Secular Tradition from Ancient to Modern Times* (Chapel Hill: The University of North Carolina Press, 1980), pp. 45-52; W. Jaeger, *Paideia: The Ideals of Greek Culture* (trans. G. Highet; 3 vols; Oxford: Blackwell, 1945), vol. III pp. 47-70, 182-196.

6. Cf. E. Corbett, *Classical Rhetoric for the Modern Student* (2nd edn New York: Oxford University Press, 1971), pp. 33-39; G. Kennedy, *The Art of Persuasion in Greece*, pp. 10-12.

7. G. Kennedy, *New Testament Interpretation*, p. 10: 'Even if he had not studied in a Greek school, there were many handbooks of rhetoric in common circulation which he could have seen. He and the evangelists as well would, indeed, have been hard put to escape an awareness of rhetoric as practised in the culture around them, for the rhetorical theory of the schools found its immediate application in almost every form of oral and written communication'. See also D. Clark, *Rhetoric in Greco-Roman Education* (New York: Columbia University Press, 1967), pp. 60-61; G. Kennedy, *The Art of Persuasion in Greece*, pp. 7-8.

8. M. Dibelius, *Paul* (ed. W.G. Kümmel; trans. F. Clark; London: Longmans, 1953), p. 31.

9. M. Hengel, *Judaism and Hellenism* (trans. John Bowden; 2 vols.; Philadelphia: Fortress Press, 1975), vol. I, pp. 81-83, 312.

10. E.A. Judge 'The Reaction against Classical Education in the New Testament', *The Journal of Christian Education* 77 (1983), p. 9.

11. D. Daube, 'Rabbinic Methods of Interpretation and Hellenistic Rhetoric', *HUCA* 22 (1949), pp. 239-64; see also D.M. Hay, 'What is Proof? Historical Verification in Philo, Josephus, and Quintilian', *SBLASP* 17.2 (1979), pp. 87-100; R.M. Grant, 'Hellenistic Elements in Galatians', *ATR* 34 (1952), pp. 223-26.

12. See below, pp. 61-65; cf. J.P. Sampley, '"Before God, I do not lie" (Gal. 1.20): Paul's Self-Defense in the Light of Roman Legal Praxis', *NTS* 23 (1977), p. 478: 'it is striking how much Paul's letter does what the handbooks recommend'.

13. Betz, *Galatians*, p. 1.

14. *Ibid.*, pp. 46, 114.

15. In terms of Kessler's introduction to rhetorical criticism, I am interested primarily in a synchronic rather than a diachronic method. See Martin Kessler, 'A Methodological Setting for Rhetorical Criticism', *Semitics* 4 (1974), p. 31.

16. G. Kennedy, *Classical Rhetoric*, p. 8.

17. Quintilian, 3.2.3; see also Aristotle, *Rhetoric*, 1.1.1.

18. E. Corbett, *Rhetorical Analyses of Literary Works*, p. xxvii: 'a good deal of the rhetorical criticism of literary works that has been done by modern critics is conducted according to the rationale and in the terminology of classical rhetoric'.

19. G. Kennedy, *New Testament Interpretation*, pp. 10-11.

20. Cf. the methodology outlined by G. Kennedy, *New Testament Interpretation*, pp. 33-38. The first two stages of his methodology are the determination of the rhetorical unit and the definition of the rhetorical situation. Galatians is the rhetorical unit. The rhetorical situation is discussed in the determination of the species and treated more fully in the chapter on the theology of Paul's opponents. See below, pp. 97-107.

21. See Aristotle, *Rhetoric*, 1.3.1-9 (LCL, 22.33-39); Kennedy, *The Art of Persuasion in Greece*, p. 87; *idem*, *Classical Rhetoric*, p. 72, 19.20; D. Clark, *Rhetoric in Greco-Roman Education*, pp. 70-71; W. Brandt, *The Rhetoric of Argumentation*, pp. 12-14.

22. Betz, *Galatians*, p. 24.

23. D. Aune, 'Review of H.D. Betz, *Galatians*', p. 325; F. Church claims that 'it is to deliberative rhetoric, as the genre that is least elaborate and most conducive to Paul's hortatory purpose, that one should look for patterns that may underlie his argumentation' ('Rhetorical Structure and Design in Paul's Letter to Philemon', p. 19); see also J. Smit, 'The Letter of Paul to the Galatians: a Deliberative Speech', *NTS* 35 (1989), pp. 1-26.

24. G. Kennedy, *New Testament Interpretation*, p. 145.

25. *Ibid.*

26. Betz, *Galatians*, p. 254.

27. Kennedy, *New Testament Interpretation*, p. 146; Quintilian 3.4.9.

28. *Ibid.*

29. *Ibid.*

30. *Ibid.*, pp. 146-47.

31. Brandt, *The Rhetoric of Argumentation*, pp. 13-14.

32. Cf. Luedemann, *Paul, Apostle to the Gentiles*, p. 52: 'he is not rejecting accusations of the opponents as is generally assumed. He is rather on the offensive in an ironical way. Paul takes up common charges against sophists and charlatans and, insofar as he rejects them for himself, holds them up as a mirror for his opponents'. But Luedemann does admit that 'the accusation "he persuades men and seeks to please them" is readily conceivable as coming from the lips of an opponent' (p. 50); cf. George Lyons, *Pauline Autobiography: Toward a New Understanding* (SBLDS 73; Atlanta: Scholars Press, 1985), pp. 75-176.

33. See J. Paul Sampley, '"Before God, I do not lie", (Gal. 1.20): Paul's Self-Defense in the Light of Roman Legal Praxis', p. 481: 'Paul ... in his letter to the Galatians, takes steps basic to the legal procedure of his time...'
34. Betz. *Galatians*, p. 24.
35. See N. Dahl, 'Paul's Letter to the Galatians', p. 82: 'Beginning with 4.12 Paul addresses the present state of affairs, attempting to shape the future of the Galatian churches. Reminders of past and rebuking questions are found also in 4.13-16 and 5.6, but they no longer function as framework for the whole movement of thought'.
36. Cf. Betz, *Galatians*, p. 24: 'The actual delivery of the speech includes a whole range of weapons relating to modulation of voice and to gestures, all of which a letter makes impossible. In his remarks Paul is fully aware of these disadvantages, as shown in 4.18-20'.
37. Betz, *Galatians*, p. 253.
38. See above, pp. 57-58.
39. Aristotle, *Rhetoric*, 1.3.5 (LCL, 22.35): 'The end of the deliberative speaker is the expedient or harmful; for he who exhorts (ὁ προτρέπων) recommends a course of action as better, and he who dissuades (ὁ ἀποτρέπων) advices against it as worse'. Dahl, 'Paul's Letter to the Galatians', p. 92, points out the 'apotreptic' and 'protreptic' elements in the letter from 4.21 onward: 'The uncompromising pronouncements in 5.2ff. form the climatic conclusion to the 'apotreptic' part of the letter. The positive, 'protreptic' part follows in the paraenetic section, i.e., from 5.13ff. onward'.
40. Aristotle, *Rhetoric*, 3.13.1-3.19.6; Cicero, *De inv.*, 1.14.19; *Rhet. ad Her.*, 1.3.4; George Kennedy, *The Art of Persuasion in Greece*, p. 11; E. Corbett, *Classical Rhetoric for the Modern Student*, pp. 299-38. This list of six parts is a compilation derived from the major classical handbooks. Some rhetoricians recognized only four parts (e.g., Aristotle); others added other sections and subsections (e.g., Cicero).
41. Betz, *Galatians*, pp. 16-23.
42. The references to Betz in this list of features indicate page numbers in his commentary, *Galatians*.
43. Betz, 'The Literary Composition and Function of Paul's Letter to the Galatians', p. 371.
44. *Ibid.*
45. The numbers in parentheses on these two pages refer to the numbers in the left hand column of the table of parallels.
46. See above, pp. 27-29.
47. See G. Kennedy, *Classical Rhetoric*, pp. 123-24.
48. Exod. 3-6; Isa. 6; Jer. 1.
49. False prophets: Jer. 6.13, 26.7, 8, 11, 16; 27.9; 28.1; 29.1, 8 (=LXX Jer. 6.13; 33.7, 8, 11, 16; 34.9; 35.1; 36.1, 8); hypocritical heart: LXX Job 36.13.

50. Josh. 24.2-3; Neh. 9.7-8; Isa. 51.2.

51. See below.

52. According to Betz, the *narratio* begins at 1.12. But this splits the unified construction of 1.11-12: οὐκ. . .οὐδε. . .οὐτε. . .ἀλλά, cf. 1.1. It seems best to recognize 1.11-12 as a part of the introduction which defines the basic issue and also provides a transition to the *narratio*. See above, p. 43; J. Hester, 'The Rhetorical Structure of Galatians 1.11-2.14', p. 225. 'The presence of γάρ in 1.11 and 12 would seem to argue for the unity of those verses in such a way as to disallow Betz's separation of them into two different components of the outline'. H. Hübner, 'Der Galaterbrief und das Verhältnis von antiker Rhetorik und Epistolographie', p. 249: 'Die *narratio* beginnt m. E. nicht mit 1, 12, sondern mit 1, 13'.

53. Gal. 4.12-20 records certain facts which relate directly to the history of the situation in Galatia: Paul's first evangelistic trip to the Galatians, their enthusiastic response, and their subsequent withdrawal from Paul under the influence of those who sought after them. *Contra* Betz, this section, rather than 1.13-2.14, fulfills the requirement for the first type of *narratio* as defined by Cicero, *De inv.* 1.19.27 (see above).

54. Quintilian describes two types of *narratio*: 'there are two forms of statement of facts in forensic speeches. The one expounding the facts of the case itself, the other setting forth facts which have a bearing on the case' (4.2.11). See also Quintilian 4.2.17; 7.1.12; H. Lausberg, *Handbuch der literarischen Rhetorik* (2 vols.; Munich: Hueber, 1960), I, pp. 165-67; cf. Brinsmead, *Galatians*, p. 50. Gal. 1.13-2.14 is an example of the second type of *narratio*.

55. εὐαγγέλιον and εὐαγγελίζομαι are the key terms of the *exordium* and the *narratio*. εὐαγγέλιον: 1.6, 7, 11; 2.2, 5, 7, 14. εὐαγγελίζομαι: 1.8 (twice), 9, 11, 16, 23; 4.13.

56. Quintilian refers to the argumentative force of the *narratio*: 'What difference is there between a *probatio* and a *narratio* save that the latter is a *probatio* put forward in continuous form, while a *probatio* is a verification of the facts as put forward in the *narratio*' (4.2.79). From this perspective, J.T. Sanders rightly emphasizes the argumentative force of Gal. 1-2 ('Paul's Autobiographical Statements in Galatians 1-2', *JBL* 85 (1966), p. 342).

57. Betz's conclusion appears to be valid: 'The literary analysis has shown that he defends primarily his gospel, that is, the 'gospel of uncircumcision'. This gospel is, of course, intimately connected with his own vocation and apostolic office so that his apostolic authority depends entirely upon the outcome of the defense of his gospel' (*Galatians*, p. 28). See the discussion below on 'Argument from Authority', pp. 79-82.

58. Betz, *Galatians*, pp. 62, 111-12: 'The term "compel" (ἀναγκάζω) must be seen in parallelism with 2.3, the demand to circumcise Titus, and the demand of the present agitators in Galatia to accept Torah and circumcision (6.13)'.

59. F.F. Bruce, *Galatians*, p. 136: 'He probably summarizes his rebuke to Peter and then develops its implications, thus passing smoothly from the personal occasion to the universal principle'.

60. See E.P. Sanders, *Paul and Palestinian Judaism*, p. 504.

61. Betz, *Galatians*, p. 119.

62. *Ibid.*, p. 124.

63. *Ibid.*, p. 125.

64. See above, pp. 63-64.

65. See below, p. 104.

66. See below, p. 106.

67. See below, pp. 107-108.

68. Betz, *Galatians*, p. 32.

69. *Ibid.*, p. 256.

70. *Ibid.*, p. 313.

71. *Ibid.*, p. 321.

72. Cf. H.W. Boers, 'Genesis 15.6 and the Discourse Structure of Galatians', p. 12.

73. See M. Dibelius, *From Tradition to Gospel* (trans. B. Woolf; London: Ivor Nicholson and Watson, 1934), pp. 238-39; 'The hortatory sections of the Pauline letters are clearly differentiated in material from what Paul otherwise wrote. In particular they lack an immediate relation with the circumstances of the letter' (p. 238). 'Thus, we see that the hortatory sections of the Pauline epistles have nothing to do with the theoretic foundation of the ethics of the Apostle, and very little with other ideas peculiar to him. Rather they belong to tradition' (p. 239). See also H. Boers, 'The Form-Critical Study of Paul's Letters: 1 Thessalonians as a Case Study', *NTS* 22 (1976), p. 153: 'In the case of Galatians the normal exhortation section (v. 13-vi. 10) is a mere appendage'. J.C. O'Neill, *The Recovery of Paul's Letter to the Galatians* (London: SPCK, 1972), p. 67, claims that 5.13-6.10 'has nothing in particular to do with the urgent problem Paul was trying to meet in his original letter'. For a recent treatment of the unity of Gal. 5-6 with the rest of the letter, see D.K. Fletcher, 'The Singular Argument of Paul's Letter to the Galatians' (PhD Diss., Princeton Theological Seminary, 1982), p. 271: 'The argument of the letter is best understood as a single argument against the law directed to a single audience'. See also John Barclay, *Obeying the Truth*, p. 216: 'Our conclusion is that his exhortation develops out of and concludes his earlier arguments'.

74. Cf. W. Marxsen, *Introduction to the New Testament* (trans. G. Buswell; Oxford: Blackwell, 1968), p. 58: 'It is very strange that we meet for the first time in this letter what was later called the Pauline doctrine of justification. . . the strange thing is that Paul develops his terminology in the face of a situation which he in fact misconceived'. So also W. Schmithals, *Paul and the Gnostics* (trans. John E. Steely; Nashville: Abingdon Press, 1972), p. 4: Schmithals maintains that all the sections in Gal. 3.1-5.12 in which the

Galatians situation is not directly addressed (3.6-14; 3.15-18; 3.19-4.7; 4.21-31) are simply current *topoi* of Paul's discussion with the Jews. 'None of these sections was conceived for the Galatian epistle'.

75. Betz, *Galatians*, p. 128.

76. So Aune, 'Review of H.D. Betz, *Galatians*', p. 325.

77. Brinsmead's discussion of this section (*Galatians*, pp. 82-83) depends upon an analysis of the literary device of *mot crotchet* as described by James Fischer in 'Pauline Literary Forms and Thought Patterns', *CBQ* 39 (1977), p. 216. See my description below of the rhetorical technique, 'Argument by Repetition', p. 92.

Notes to Chapter 3

1. G. Kennedy, *New Testament Interpretation through Rhetorical Criticism*, p. 28; J. Welch, ed., *Chiasmus in Antiquity: Structures, Analyses, Exegesis* (Hildesheim: Gerstenberg, 1981).

2. J. Welch, *Chiasmus in Antiquity*; I.M. Kikawada, 'The Shape of Genesis 11.1-9', in *Rhetorical Criticism: Essays in Honor of James Muilenberg*, eds., J. Jackson and M. Kessler (PTMS 1; Pittsburgh: The Pickwick Press, 1974), p. 23.

3. G. Kennedy, *New Testament Interpretation through Rhetorical Criticism*, p. 28.

4. Welch, *Chiasmus in Antiquity*, p. 13.

5. *Ibid.*

6. N.W. Lund, *Chiasmus in the New Testament: A Study in Formgeschichte* (Chapel Hill: University of North Carolina Press, 1942).

7. J. Jeremias, 'Chiasmus in den Paulusbriefen', *ZNW* 49 (1958), p. 153.

8. F. Mussner, *Galaterbrief*, pp. vii-viii, 77.

9. J. Beker, *Paul the Apostle*, pp. 44-45.

10. Dahl, 'Paul's Letter to the Galatians', pp. 76-77.

11. See above, pp. 46-47, 67-68.

12. Jeremias, 'Chiasmus in den Paulusbriefen', p. 153, also points to the chiastic structure of 5.17:

A   ἡ γὰρ σὰρξ ἐπιθυμεῖ
B   κατὰ τοῦ πνεύματος
B   τὸ δὲ πνεύματος
A   κατὰ τῆς σαρκός

Here as seems obvious, the objective criteria for chiastic analysis are met.

13. J. Bligh, *Galatians*, p. 37; cf. J. Lightfoot, *The Epistle of St. Paul to the Galatians* (Grand Rapids: Zondervan, 1969), p. 168.

14. Bligh, p. 38.

15. *Ibid.*, p. 39.

16. *Ibid.*

17. Bligh, *Galatians in Greek*, p. 2.

18. *Ibid.*

19. *Ibid.*, pp. 13. 58, 63, 19, 20, 36, 47, 42, see *idem, Galatians,* pp. 82, 124, 224-26, 236, 414-15, 426-27.

20. H. Betz, 'Book Review of John Bligh (*Galatians*)', *JBL* 89 (1970), pp. 126-27; see also critical reviews by C.F.D. Moule, *CQ* 2 (1970), pp. 343-44; C.K. Barrett, *Essays on Paul* (London: SPCK, 1982), pp. 155-58.

21. John Hurd, 'Concerning the Structure of 1 Thessalonians', p. 22.

22. Bligh, *Galatians*, pp. 235-36.

23. *Ibid.*, p. 174.

24. *Ibid.*, pp. 226-27.

25. *Ibid.*, p. 237.

26. *Ibid.*, p. 365.

27. *Ibid.*, p. 235.

28. *Ibid.*, p. 380.

29. See above, pp. 43-44.

30. See C.K. Barrett, *Essays on Paul*, pp. 157-58.

31. See below, p. 92.

32. W. Wuellner, 'Paul's Rhetoric of Argumentation in Romans'; Folker Siegert, 'Argumentation bei Paulus: Gezeigt an Röm. 9-11'.

33. Chaim Perelman and L. Olbrechts-Tyteca, *The New Rhetoric: A Treatise on Argumentation*, trans. J. Wilkinson and P. Weaver (Notre Dame: University of Notre Dame Press, 1969); Kennedy's statement in *New Testament Interpretation through Rhetorical Criticism*, p. 29.

34. Both of the works of E. Corbett, ed., *Rhetorical Analyses of Literary Works* (London: Oxford University Press, 1969) and Perelman and Olbrechts-Tyteca, *The New Rhetoric*, include a broad spectrum of ancient and modern literature from which the principles of new rhetoric are derived.

35. Perelman and Olbrechts-Tyteca, *The New Rhetoric*, p. 5: 'we hope that our attempts will contribute to the revival of an ancient and glorious tradition'.

36. F. Siegert, 'Argumentation bei Paulus', pp. 31-113, uses examples from the LXX to illustrate the applicability of each of Perelman's techniques of argumentation to biblical literature.

37. Aristotle, *Rhetoric*, 1.2.4.

38. Kennedy, *Classical Rhetoric*, p. 68.

39. *The New Rhetoric*, p. 305.

40. *Ibid.*, p. 309.

41. John H. Schütz, *Paul and the Anatomy of Apostolic Authority* (SNTSMS, 26; Cambridge University Press, 1975), p. 18.

42. Paul's account of his apostolic call may contain allusions to Peter's call; see J. Chapman, 'St Paul and the Revelation to St Peter, Matt. XVI,

p. 17', *Revue Benedictine* 29 (1912); J. Dupont, 'La Revelation du Fils de Dieu en faveur de Pierre (Mt. 16, 17) et de Paul (Ga. 1, 16)', *RSR* 52 (1964), pp. 411-20.

43. B. Holmberg, *Paul and Power: The Structure of Authority in the Primitive Church as Reflected in the Pauline Epistles* (ConBNT, 11; Lund: CWK Gleerup, 1978), p. 15.

44. See J. Pilch, 'Paul's Usage and Understanding of 'Apokalypsis' in Galatians 1-2: A Structural Investigation' (Ph.D. Dissertation, Marquette University, 1972), p. 191: 'He [Paul] undertakes a journey to Jerusalem because of divine prompting, or inspiration, or insight'. Cf. G. Howard, *Paul: Crisis in Galatia*, p. 38. Howard argues that the term 'revelation' in 2.2. refers to the same Damascus road vision indicated by the use of the term in 1.12 and 1.16.

45. B. Holmberg, *Paul and Power*, p. 22.

46. J. Schütz, *Paul and the Anatomy of Apostolic Authority*, p. 145.

47. Paul also uses the imagery of his parental role (4.19) as a basis for his authority.

48. Brandt, *The Rhetoric of Argumentation*, p. 132; Perelman and Olbrechts-Tyteca, *The New Rhetoric*, p. 210.

49. C. Perelman, *The Realm of Rhetoric*, trans. W. Kluback (Notre Dame: University of Notre Dame Press, 1982), p. 61; Brandt, *The Rhetoric of Argumentation*, p. 133.

50. See above, p. 231n. 55.

51. There is a ἕτερος gospel (another gospel of a different kind), but not an ἄλλος gospel (another gospel of the same kind [1.6, 7]). See below, pp. 84-85, on the argument by dissociation.

52. The core of the gospel which Paul preached is already presented in the prescript (1.1-5); see Brinsmead, *Galatians*, pp. 58ff.

53. See Betz, *Galatians*, p. 63.

54. J. Schütz, *Paul and the Anatomy of Apostolic Authority*, p. 38.

55. See E. Burton, *Galatians*, pp. 91-92.

56. Perelman and Olbrechts-Tyteca, *The New Rhetoric*, pp. 411-59.

57. Brandt, *The Rhetoric of Argumentation*, pp. 133-34.

58. Perelman, *The Realm of Rhetoric*, pp. 126-37; Perelman and Olbrechts-Tyreca, *The New Rhetoric*, pp. 436-51.

59. Brandt, *The Rhetoric of Argumentation*, p. 134.

60. See the discussion of 'dissociative definitions' in Perelman and Olbrechts-Tyteca, *The New Rhetoric*, pp. 44-50; see below, pp. 201-202.

61. Perelman and Olbrechts-Tyteca, *The New Rhetoric*, pp. 321-25.

62. *Ibid.*, p. 325.

63. *Ibid.*, pp. 324-25.

64. Brinsmead, *Galatians*, p. 69.

65. Perelman and Olbrechts-Tyteca, *The New Rhetoric*, p. 126.

66. G.B. Caird, *The Language and Imagery of the Bible* (Philadelphia: Westminster Press, 1980), p. 8.

236   *Abraham in Galatians*

67. Perelman and Olbrechts-Tyteca, *The New Rhetoric*, p. 345.
68. *Ibid.*, p. 201.
69. See below, pp. 172-73.
70. Aristotle, *Rhetoric*, 1.2.8.
71. Brandt, *The Rhetoric of Argumentation*, pp. 121, 128.
72. *Ibid.*, p. 61.
73. *Ibid.*, p. 37-38.
74. γάρ (34 times): 1.10, 11, 12, 13; 2.6, 8, 12, 18, 19, 21; 3.10 (twice), 18, 21, 26, 27, 28; 4.15, 22, 24, 25, 27, 30; 5.5, 6, 13, 14, 17 (twice); 6.3, 5, 7, 9, 13, 15, 17.
75. ὅτι (9 times in the causal sense): 2.11, 16; 3.11, 13; 4.6, 12, 20, 27; 6.8.
76. Cf. W. Viertel, 'The Hermeneutics of Paul as Reflected in Romans and Galatians' (PhD. Dissertation, Baylor University, 1976), misses the enthymemic nature of Paul's argumentation. He attempts to find explicit references to the major and minor premises and so rebuild Paul's logic according to formal syllogistic patterns. But as Aristotle observes, this is not the nature of deductive reasoning in rhetoric.
77. Perelman and Olbrecht-Tyteca, *The New Rhetoric*, p. 350.
78. *Ibid.*, p. 357.
79. *Ibid.*, pp. 362-69.
80. *Ibid.*, pp. 273-78.
81. Perelman, *The Realm of Rhetoric*, p. 88.
82. Perelman and Olbrecht-Tyteca, *The Realm of Rhetoric*, p. 248.
83. *Ibid.*, p. 251.
84. See Sanders, *Paul and Palestinian Judaism*, p. 482.
85. Perelman and Olbrecht-Tyteca, *The New Rhetoric*, p. 227.
86. See below, pp. 124-25.
87. Perelman and Olbrecht-Tyteca, *The New Rhetoric*, p. 231.
88. *Ibid.*, pp. 144, 174-75.
89. See below p. 109.
90. Perelman and Olbrecht-Tyteca, *The New Rhetoric*, p. 331.

Notes to Chapter 4

1. See above, 'Epistolary Analysis of Galatians', pp. 23-44; Dahl, 'Galatians', p. 82.
2. Μετατίθημι is a term for political desertion, which came to connote religious apostasy. See BAGD, 'μετατίθημι', pp. 513, 515; Maurer, 'μετατίθημι', *TDNT* 8, pp. 161-62; Betz, *Galatians*, p. 47 n. 41.
3. Ἐπιστρέφω is a term used by Paul to describe conversion (2 Cor. 3.16, 1 Thess. 1.9). The combination of πάλιν and ἐπιστρέφω indicates that, from Paul's perspective, his converts at Galatia were in the process of reversing their conversion.

4. See below, 'Appendix 1: The Opponents' use of Abraham', pp. 170-73.

5. See below, 'Appendix 2: Abraham in Jewish Literature', pp. 179-99.

6. See above, 'Epistolary Analysis', pp. 31-32.

7. Byrne, *'Sons of God'*, p. 142.

8. R. Hays, *The Faith of Jesus Christ*, p. 226: 'The Abraham story is for Paul taken up into the Christ story'.

9. See Howard, *Paul*, p. 57; Drane, *Paul*, pp. 24-38; Moxnes, *Theology*, pp. 208-209.

10. See above, 'Rhetorical Analysis', pp. 63-64, 68-69.

11. See above, 'Rhetorical Analysis', p. 68; Byrne, *'Sons of God'*, p. 143 ('The Antioch incident "overheard" in Galatia'); Burton, *Galatians*, p. 117; Lagrange, *Saint Paul, Epître aux Galates*, p. 45; Mussner, *Galaterbrief*, p. 135. Bligh, *Galatians*, p. 196, regards the rest of the letter to be Paul's response to Peter.

12. On the verb ὀρθοποδεῖν see Preisker, 'ὀρθοποδεῖν' *TDNT* 5, 451; Burton, *Galatians*, p. 110; Mussner, *Galaterbrief*, p. 144; Byrne, *'Sons of God'*, p. 143.

13. Cf. Dunn, 'The Incident at Antioch (Gal. 2. 11-18)', *JSNT* 18 (1983), pp. 3-57; P. Richardson, 'Pauline Inconsistency: I Corinthians 9.19-23 and Galatians 2.11-14', *NTS* 26 (1979-80), pp. 347-362; *idem, Israel in the Apostolic Church* (SNTSMS, 10; Cambridge: Cambridge University Press, 1969), pp. 93-97.

14. T. Wright, 'The Messiah and the People of God: A Study in Pauline Theology with Particular Reference to the Argument of the Epistle to the Romans' (D.Phil. Dissertation, Oxford, 1980), p. 98: 'the issue here is not "must one do good works in order to be served?", but "must one be a Jew in order to belong to God's people?"'

15. D. Fletcher, 'The Singular Argument of Paul's Letter to the Galatians' (Ph.D. Dissertation, Princeton Theological Seminary, 1982), p. 256.

16. See above, 'Rhetorical Analysis', p. 69.

17. Cf. Rom. 2.2; 3.19; 5.3; 6.9; 7.14; 8.22, 28; 1 Cor. 6.2, 3, 9; 8.4; 2 Cor. 1.7; 4.14; 5.1, 6; 1 Thess. 3.3; 5.2. See Mussner, *Gal.*, p. 168: 'Das Partizip εἰδότες meint also hier das "Glaubenswissen"'; J. Munck, *Paul and the Salvation of Mankind*, pp. 126-27; Byrne, *'Sons of God'*, p. 144; Betz, *Galatians*, p. 115-16; Brinsmead, *Galatians*, p. 70. Although δέ is omitted by P^{42} A D^2 M (Byzantine mss) and Syriac versions, it is fairly well attested (א B C D *al*). Dunn, 'The New Perspective on Paul', *BJRL* 65 (1983), p. 104 n. 25, argued that it was 'probably introduced by a scribe who misread the flow of Paul's thought and assumed that an adversative particle should be added'. But an adversative particle seems to fit the contrast between φύσει and εἰδότες. See Betz, *Galatians*, p. 115 n. 29.

18. Byrne, *'Sons of God'*, p. 144, emphasizes that ἡμεῖς. . .καὶ ἡμεῖς. . .καὶ αὐτοί provide the key to understanding this text; see also G. Klein,

'Individualgeschichte und Weltgeschichte bei Paulus: Eine Interpretation ihres Verhältnisses im Galaterbrief', *EvT* 24 (1964), pp. 126-65; for a critique of Klein's thesis that Paul completely secularized Jewish history, see W.G. Kümmel, 'Individualgeschichte' und "Weltgeschichte" im Gal. 2.15-21', in *Christ and the Spirit in the New Testament: Essays in Honour of C.F.D. Moule* (Cambridge: Cambridge University Press, 1973), pp. 157-73; and K. Berger, 'Abraham in den paulinischen Hauptbriefen', *MTZ* 17 (1966), pp. 48-49.

19.   Cf. Richardson, *Israel*, p. 95; Byrne, *'Sons of God'*, p. 143.

20.   See J. Ziesler, *The Meaning of Righteousness in Paul* (SNTSMS, 20; Cambridge: Cambridge University Press, 1972); P. Stuhlmacher, *Gerechtigkeit Gottes bei Paulus* (FRLANT, 87; Göttingen: Vandenhoeck & Ruprecht, 1965); K, Kertelge, *'Rechtfertigung' bei Paulus* (Münster: Aschendorf, 1967); idem, 'Zur Deutung des Rechtfertigungsbegriffs im Galaterbrief', *BZ* 12 (1968), pp. 211-22; M. Brauch, 'Perspectives on "God's Righteousness" in Recent German Discussion', in E.P. Sanders, *Paul*, pp. 523-43.

21.   Ziesler, *Righteousness*, p. 212, sees the verb as essentially relational or forensic and the noun and adjective as ethical, describing behavior within the relationship; also G. Schrenk, 'δικαιόω', *TDNT* 2. p. 215.

22.   Dunn, 'New Perspective', p. 105.

23.   Rengstorf, 'ἁμαρτωλός', *TDNT* 1, 324-25: 'Israel's consciousness of election and its conviction of being essentially different from the Gentiles reached its climax in the Rabbis. If the Jews are by nature holy, the Gentiles are by nature sinners. Thus it came about that the word ἁμαρτωλός became a technical term for the Gentile. The Gentile was ἁμαρτωλός in virtue of his not being a Jew and his failure to regulate his conduct according to the Torah'. See Jub. 23.23-24 ('In those days they shall cry aloud and call and pray that they may be saved from the hand of sinners, the Gentiles'.); 1 Macc. 1.34; 4 Ezra 3.30; Tobit 6.13; Clem *Hom* 11.16; *Wisd Sol* 13-15; *Letter Aristeas* 151-53; see Str-B 3.537.

24.   Wright, 'The Messiah and the People of God', p. 107; Dunn, 'New Perspective', p. 114.

25.   D. Moo, '"Law", "Works of the Law", and Legalism in Paul', *WTJ* 45 (1983), pp. 91-92; G. Bertram, 'ἔργον', *TDNT* II, p. 646.

26.   Burton, *Galatians*, p. 120; D. Fuller, *Gospel and Law: Contrast or Continuum?* (Grand Rapids: Eerdmans, 1980), pp. 88-105, 199-204; idem, 'Paul and "the works of the law"', *WTJ* 38 (1975), pp. 28-42; McGonigal, '"Abraham believed God"', p. 247: 'when Paul uses the phrase ἔργα νόμου in Galatians he has in mind the kind of legalism which appears to uphold the law, but actually runs counter to the law because the Judaizers are not relying upon God's grace but upon their ability to do meritorious deeds in order to obligate God to bless them'.

27.   Kertelge, 'Zur Deutung des Rechtfertigungsbegriffs im Galaterbrief', p. 215: 'Die ἔργα νόμου in v. 16 sind also der Ausdruck des jüdischen Selbstbewusstseins von v. 15'.

28. Dunn, 'New perspective', p. 108.

29. See especially R. Hays, *The Faith of Jesus Christ*, pp. 157-76; *idem*, 'Psalm 143 and the Logic of Romans 3', *JBL* (1980), p. 114 n. 32; G. Howard, *Paul*, pp. 46-65; *idem*, 'On the "Faith of Christ"', *HTR* 60 (1967), pp. 459-84; *idem*, 'The Faith of Christ', *ExpTim* 85 (1974), pp. 212-15; S. Williams, 'The Righteousness of God in Romans', *JBL* 99 (1980), pp. 272-77; L. Johnson, 'Rom. 3.21-26 and the "Faith of Jesus Christ"', *CBQ* 44 (1982), pp. 76-90; M. Hooker, 'Interchange and Suffering', in *Suffering and Martyrdom in the New Testament* (eds. W. Horbury and B. McNeil; Cambridge: Cambridge University Press, 1981), pp. 75-76. Earlier arguments for this interpretation were developed by J. Haussleiter, 'Der Glaube Jesus Christi und der christliche Glaube: ein Beitrag zur Erklärung des Römerbriefs', *NKZ* 2 (1891), pp. 109-45, 205-30; G. Herbert, '"Faithfulness" and "Faith"', *Theology* 58 (1955), pp. 373-79; H. Ljungman, *Pistis: A Study of its Pressuppositions and Its Meaning in Pauline Use* (Lund: Gleerup, 1964), pp. 38-40; T. Torrance, 'One Aspect of the Biblical Conception of Faith', *ExpTim* 68 (1957), pp. 111-14; R. Longenecker, *Paul, the Apostle of Liberty* (New York: Harper & Row, 1964), pp. 149-51; *idem*, 'The Obedience of Christ in the Theology of the Early Church', in *Reconciliation and Hope: FS L. Morris* (ed. R. Banks; Grand Rapids: Eerdmans, 1974), pp. 141-52; G. Taylor, 'The Function of πίστις Χριστοῦ in Galatians', *JBL* 85 (1966), pp. 58-76; E.R. Goodenough, 'Paul and the Hellenization of Christianity', in *Religions in Antiquity: Essays in Memory of E.R. Goodenough* (ed. J. Neusner; SHR 14; Leiden: Brill, 1968), pp. 45-46; D. Robinson, '"The Faith of Jesus Christ" in New Testament Debate', *Reformed Theological Review* 29 (1970), pp. 71-81.

30. Longenecker, *Paul*, pp. 149-50.

31. *Ibid.*, p. 150.

32. So Betz, *Galatians*, pp. 117-18; Bruce, *Galatians*, p. 139; Burton, *Galatians*, p. 121. In defense of the objective genitive, see Hultgren, 'The πίστις Χριστοῦ Formulations in Paul', *NovT* 22 (1980), pp. 248-63; J. Barr, *The Semantics of Biblical Language* (London: Oxford, 1961), pp. 202-203; Kertelge, '*Rechtfertigung*' *bei Paulus*, pp. 162-66; C.F.D. Moule, 'The Biblical Conception of Faith', *ExpTim* 68 (1957), p. 157; W. Schenk, 'Die Gerechtigkeit Gottes und der Glaube Christi', *TLZ* 97 (1972), pp. 161-74; P. Stuhlmacher, *Gottes Gerechtigkeit bei Paulus*, pp. 81-84; F. Neugebauer, *In Christus: Eine Untersuchung zum Paulinischen Glaubensverständnis* (Göttingen: Vandenhoeck & Ruprecht, 1961), pp. 150-56; Bultmann, 'πιστεύω', *TDNT* VI, p. 204.

33. Gal. 2.16d: ὅτι ἐξ ἔργων νόμου οὐ δικαιωθήσεται πᾶσα σάρξ.

Ps. 142.2 LXX: ὅτι οὐ δικαιωθήσεται ἐνώπιον σου πᾶς ζῶν

Ps. 143.2 MT: כי לא יצדק לפניך כל־חי The LXX is equivalent to the MT. Paul differs from the LXX in that he omits ἐνώπιον σου; he adds ἐξ ἔργων νόμου; and he changes πᾶς ζῶν to πᾶσα σάρξ. The omission of the phrase 'before you' does not change the meaning; it may have been regarded as a redundancy (so Betz, *Gal.*, p. 119). This phrase is retained in the allusion to the same passage in Rom. 3.20. The insertion of ἐξ ἔργων νόμου ties the allusion into the emphasis of his sentence and makes it prove his point. Dunn, 'New Perspective', p. 117, points out that with his use of σάρξ 'Paul has in view primarily and precisely those who think their acceptability to God and stand before God does depend on their physical descent from Abraham, their national identity'. This interpretation fits well with the concept of ὁ κατὰ σάρκα in 4.23, p. 29. But the use of πᾶσα in 2.16d and the parallel with ἄνθρωπος in 2.16a seems to indicate that Paul's primary intention here is to universalize rather than nationalize the reference. See also Schweizer, 'σάρξ', *TDNT* VII, p. 129; Jewett, *Paul's Anthropological Terms*, p. 98.

34. See Burton, *Galatians*, p. 125; Byrne, '*Sons of God*,', p. 145; Betz, *Galatians*, pp. 119-20.

35. For a review of the numerous interpretive problems in this verse, see J. Lambrecht, 'The Line of Thought in Gal. 2.14b-21', *NTS* 24 (1978), pp. 485-95; H. Feld, '"Christus Diener der Sünde": Zum Ausgang des Streites zwischen Petrus und Paulus', *TQ* 153 (1973), pp. 119-31.

36. This line of interpretation is developed by Byrne, '*Sons of God*', p. 145; Bruce, *Galatians*, p. 141; Lambrecht, 'Line of Thought', p. 491; Schlier, *Der Brief an die Galater*, pp. 95-96; Lightfoot, *Galatians*, pp. 116-17.

37. Note the recognition in the Qumran literature of sinfulness and the expression of dependence on the grace of atonement: 'I know that there is no righteousness in man and no perfection of way in a son of man; to God Most High belong all the works of righteousness' (1QH 4.30); 'I will call God my righteousness and the Most High the establisher of my goodness' (1QS 10.11).

38. Burton, *Galatians*, p. 121, makes this criticism.

39. Burton, *Galatians*, pp. 129-30; Feld, 'Christus Diener', pp. 129-30; R. Tannehill, *Dying and Rising with Christ: A Study in Pauline Theology* (BZNW 32; Berlin: Töpelmann, 1967), p. 56.

40. See above, p. 238 n. 23.

41. Paul's use of μή γένοιτο elsewhere shows that when μή γένοιτο stands alone (it is otherwise only in Gal. 6.14) it follows a rhetorical question; see Rom. 3.4, 6, 31; 6.2, 15; 7.7, 13; 9.14; 11.1, 11; 1 Cor. 6.15; Gal. 3.21. The sentence is a question whether we read αρα as an illative particle (ἄρα) in conformity with Paul's practice elsewhere (so Lambrecht, 'Line of thought', pp. 489-90; C.F.D. Moule, *An Idiom Book of New Testament Greek* [2nd edn; Cambridge: Cambridge University Press, 1963], p. 196; Bruce, *Galatians*, p. 141; Burton, *Galatians*, p. 126) or as an interrogative particle (ἆρα; so UBS 3rd edn; Nestle Aland, 26th edn).

42. Bultmann, 'Zur Auslegung von Galater 2, 15-18', in *Exegetica: Aufsätze zur Erforschung des Neuen Testaments* (ed. E. Dinkler; Tübingen:

J.C.B. Mohr, 1967), p. 396, regards the entire conditional sentence as an absurdity formulated by Paul in his argument against Peter; Betz, *Galatians*, p. 119, argues that Paul accepts the first premise as true and rejects the second as false.

43. So Lightfoot, *Galatians*, pp. 116-17; Burton, *Galatians*, p. 127; Byrne, '*Sons of God*', p. 145.

44. Fletcher, 'Singular Argument', p. 256.

45. *Ibid.*

46. See above, p. 238 n. 23.

47. *Pace* Lambrecht, 'Line of Thought', pp. 491-93, who argues that γάρ is not used in a causal sense but as an adversative equivalent to δέ.

48. Lightfoot, *Galatians*, p. 117; Mussner, *Galaterbrief*, p. 179; Betz, *Galatians*, p. 121; Bruce, *Galatians*, p. 142; Osiek, *Galatians*, p. 27.

49. Burton, *Galatians*, p. 131; Howard, *Paul*, p. 44; Cf. Schlier, *Der Brief an die Galater*, p. 60; Oepke, *Der Brief an die Galater*, p. 47.

50. Several commentators suggest that the use of the first person singular in this verse is a tactful reference to Peter's conduct in Antioch; so Burton, *Galatians*, p. 130; Schlier, *Der Brief an die Galater*, p. 60; Tannehill, *Dying and Rising*, p. 57; Oepke, *Der Brief an die Galater*, p. 177.

51. Duncan, *Galatians*, p. 69; see also D. Fletcher, 'Singular Argument', p. 261 ('The transgression is not of the law, but of the new status as a believer'); Ziesler, *Righteousness*, p. 173 ('The real sin is not infringing the law, but in disloyalty to Christ and to the new way of acceptability in and through him').

52. Betz, *Galatians*, p. 121 ('The prototypical example of what applies to all Pauline Christians'); Mussner, *Galaterbrief*, p. 178; Lambrecht, 'Line of thought', p. 493 n. 35; cf. E. von Dobschütz, 'Wir und Ich bei Paulus', *ZST* 10 (1933), pp. 251-77.

53. Burton, *Galatians*, p. 133; Bruce, *Galatians*, p. 143.

54. Tannehill, *Dying and Rising*, p. 59.

55. Bruce, *Galatians*, p. 143, discusses this interpretation as an option, but rejects it.

56. Schlier, *Der Brief an die Galater*, p. 99, and Brinsmead; *Galatians*, p. 73, claim that Paul is introducing the subject of baptism in Gal. 2.19-20. Betz, *Galatians*, p. 123, however, seems to be on safer ground: 'It is only in Romans 6 that Paul interprets the ritual of baptism in terms of death and resurrection together in Christ. That interpretation must be secondary and cannot be tied entirely to baptism in the way that Schlier does. In fact, it may be put the other way around; Gal. 2.19 may contain the theological principle by which Paul interprets the ritual of baptism in Romans 6'.

57. Sanders, *Paul, the Law, and the Jewish People*, p. 27; *idem, Paul*, p. 443.

58. Sanders, *Paul*, pp. 489-90.

59. See above, p. 78.

242   *Abraham in Galatians*

60. Betz, *Galatians*, p. 133 n. 51, notes that this type of invective is described in the rhetorical handbooks as 'frankness of speech'. See also his reference to diatribe literature (p. 130).

61. Cf. Moxnes, *Theology*, p. 209.

62. On βασκαίνω, see Delling, 'βασκαίνω', *TDNT* I, pp. 594-95; Betz, *Galatians*, p. 131; Burton, *Galatians*, p. 143. Cf. J.H. Neyrey, 'Bewitched in Galatia: Paul and Cultural Anthropology', *CBQ* 50 (1988), pp. 72-100.

63. See above, pp. 102.

64 Jewett, *Anthropological Terms*, pp. 90-100; Tyson, '"Works of Law" in Galatians', pp. 427-28.

65. Hays, *Faith of Jesus Christ*, pp. 143-46.

66. Lightfoot, *Galatians*, p. 134; Burton, *Galatians*, p. 147; Lagrange, *Saint Paul Epître aux Galates*, p. 59; Bruce, *Galatians*, p. 149; Tyson, '"Works of Law" in Galatians', p. 427. See also S. Williams, 'The Hearing of Faith: ΑΚΟΗ ΠΙΣΤΕΩΣ in Galatians 3', *NTS* 35 (1989), pp. 82-93.

67. Bligh, *Galatians in Greek*, p. 127; Mussner, *Galaterbrief*, p. 207.

68. W. Hatch, *The Pauline Idea of Faith in Its Relation to Jewish and Hellenistic Religion* (HTS 2; Cambridge, Mass.: Harvard University Press, 1917), p. 33; Bultmann, 'πιστεύω', *TDNT* VI, p. 213; Bonnard, *L'Epître de Saint Paul aux Galates*, p. 63; Schlier, *Der Brief an die Galater*, p. 122.

69. Lietzmann, *An die Galater*, p. 18; W. Schenk, 'Die Gerechtigkeit Gottes und der Glaube Christi', *TLZ* 97 (1972), p. 166; Hays, *Faith of Jesus Christ*, pp. 147-49.

70. Hays, *Faith of Jesus Christ*, p. 147.

71. Byrne, '*Sons of God*', p. 133 n. 33; Burton, *Galatians*, p. 147.

72. Hays, *Faith of Jesus Christ*, p. 199; Gaston, 'Abraham and the Righteousness of God', pp. 44, 49, 54-55; Howard, *Paul*, pp. 55-57.

73. Jewett, *Anthropological Terms*, p. 100.

74. *Ibid.*, p. 101.

75. Burton, *Galatians*, p. 153; Mussner, *Galaterbrief*, p. 211.

76. Moxnes, *Theology*, p. 209; Byrne, '*Sons of God*', p. 147.

77. See Rom. 1.7; 2.24; 3.10; 4.17; 8.36; 9.13, 33; 10.15; 11.22; 15.3, 9, 21; 1 Cor. 1.31; 2.9; 2 Cor. 8.15; 9.9. So Betz, *Galatians*, p. 140; Hays, *Faith of Jesus Christ*, pp. 199-200. It is difficult, however, to see the basis for Hays' remark that the connection with v. 5 is weakened if καθώς is taken as an introductory formula; cf. Byrne, '*Sons of God*', p. 148 n. 76.

78. Mussner, *Galaterbrief*, p. 212.

79. Bonnard, *L'Epître de Saint Paul aux Galates*, p. 65.

80. See below, 'Abraham in Jewish Literature', pp. 181-83, 187.

81. Byrne, '*Sons of God*', p. 149; Burton, *Galatians*, p. 155.

82. Mussner, *Galaterbrief*, p. 216.

83. Moxnes, *Theology*, p. 209; Beker, *Paul*, p. 48.

84. See below, 'The Opponents' Use of Abraham', pp. 170-71.

85. See below 'Abraham in Jewish Literature', pp. 187-88; Ziesler, *Righteousness*, p. 175.

86. Ziesler, *Righteousness*, p. 104.
87. Dunn, 'New Perspective', p. 115; Barclay, *Obeying the Truth*, pp. 81-88; Francis Watson, *Paul, Judaism and the Gentiles: A Sociological Approach* (SNTSMS 56; Cambridge: Cambridge University Press, 1986), pp. 69-72.
88. S. Williams, 'Review of G. Howard, *Paul: Crisis in Galatia*', *JBL* 100 (1981), p. 308.
89. Mussner, *Galaterbrief*, p. 219; Byrne, '*Sons of God*', pp. 10, 148.
90. See Ellis, *Paul's Use of the OT*, p. 149: 'his knowledge of Christ opened a new Way in which he found the true meaning of the Scriptures'.
91. See Dunn, 'New Perspective', pp. 115, 118.
92. Byrne, '*Sons of God*', p. 148.
93. Ziesler, *Righteousness*, p. 175.
94. Bruce, *Galatians*, p. 152.
95. Ziesler, *Righteousness*, p. 175; see also S. Williams, 'Justification and the Spirit in Galatians', *JSNT* 29 (1987), pp. 91-100.
96. Cf. Ziesler, *Righteousness*, p. 185: 'We should therefore maintain that in his use of Gen. 15.6 Paul combines two fundamental ideas: first that man gains acceptance with God not by anything he does, but by faith which is the response to God's grace; second, that the believer as a man in Christ is a new and righteous creature, and this (ethical) righteousness is that which is valid before God'.
97. See below, 'Paul and the Jewish Exegesis', p. 205.
98. See Sanders, *Paul, the Law, and the Jewish People*, p. 21: 'The argument is terminological. It depends on finding proof-texts for the view that *Gentiles* are *righteoused* by *faith*. Those three words are crucial, and Paul is able to link Gentiles to 'righteoused by faith' through the Abraham story. Abraham is thus the middle term, being connected with Gentiles in one proof-text and righteousness by faith in another'.
99. See below, 'Paul and Jewish Exegesis', p. 205.
100. Burton, *Galatians*, p. 159; Betz, *Galatians*, p. 142.
101. Scripture is hypostatized by Paul and treated as equivalent to ὁ θεός. See also Gal. 3.22; 4.30; Rom. 4.3; 9.17; 10.11; 11.2; cf. Schrenk, 'γραφή', *TDNT* I, pp. 751-61; Michaelis, 'προοράαω', *TDNT* V, pp. 381-82; see Str-B 3.518.
102. The phrase is interpreted in a causal manner by Mussner, *Galaterbrief*, p. 220; Byrne, '*Sons of God*', p. 150.
103. See Burton, *Galatians*, p. 161; Mussner, *Galaterbrief*, p. 220; Byrne, '*Sons of God*', p. 150.
104. *Pace* Hays, *Faith of Jesus Christ*, pp. 205-206; Gaston, 'The Righteousness of God', pp. 54-56; Howard, *Paul*, p. 57: 'Those out of faith" are not those who simply "believe" like Abraham "believed", but those who have been justified by God's grace. They are described as "those out of faith" because they belong to the faith-act of God which fulfilled the promise'. Howard explains the connection between ἐπίστευσεν (v. 6) and οἱ ἐκ πίστεως (vv. 7, 9) as an unimportant 'word connection relationship only that

serves to give a literary flavor to the flow of the argument'.
105 Hays, *Faith of Jesus Christ*, pp. 203-206.

106. *Ibid.*, p. 203.

107. Mussner, *Galaterbrief*, p. 221.

108. Σὺν τῷ πιστῷ Ἀβραάμ (v. 9) interprets the ἐν σοὶ of the quotation. The preposition σύν points back to the filial kinship expressed in v. 7.

109. Lightfoot, *Galatians*, p. 137; Burton, *Galatians*, p. 164; Lagrange, *Galates*, p. 68; Mussner, *Galaterbrief*, p. 224; Berger, 'Abraham', p. 51; Van Dulmen, *Theologie*, p. 33; Eckert, *Verkündigung*, p. 77; Longenecker, *Paul*, pp. 40-42, 124, 148; Moo, 'Law, Works of the Law', pp. 97-98; Wilckens, 'Entwicklung', pp. 167-69; Schoeps, *Paul*, pp. 175-77; Hübner, 'Gal. 3.10', pp. 215-31; Räisänen, 'Legalism', p. 77.

110. McGonigal, 'Abraham', p. 275.

111. D. Fuller, *Gospel and Law: Contrast or Continuum?* pp. 88-105, 199-204; *idem*, 'Paul and the "Works of the Law"', pp. 28-42.

112. C. Cosgrove, 'The Mosaic Law Preaches Faith: A Study in Galatians 3', *WTJ* 41 (1979), p. 147.

113. O.P. Robertson, 'Genesis 15.6: New Covenant Exposition of an Old Covenant Text', *WTJ* 42 (1980), p. 277; G. Bertram, 'ἔργον', *TDNT* II, p. 646: 'The works of the commandments (מצרת מעשי), often simply called מעשים by the Rabbis, correspond to what Paul calls the ἔργα νόμου. In Judaism the works of the law are the works required by God'.

114. Bultmann, *Theology*, vol. I, p. 264.

115. Schlier, *Der Brief an die Galater*, p. 134.

116. Betz, *Galatians*, p. 146; Mussner, *Galaterbrief*, p. 226.

117. Sanders, *Paul, the Law, and the Jewish People*, pp. 21-22.

118. Sanders, *Paul*, p. 544.

119. In an earlier work, Sanders supported the view that Paul uses this minor argument. See Sanders, 'On the Question of Fulfilling the Law in Paul and Rabbinic Judaism', in *Donum Gentilicium: New Testament Studies in Honour of David Daube*, eds. C.K. Barrett, E. Bammel, and W.D. Davies (Oxford: Clarendon Press, 1978), p. 106: 'vv. 10-12 provide a crushing refutation of the Galatians who wanted to accept circumcision. Not only would they obligate themselves to obey a law which they could not fulfill, thus falling under its curse, but following that law is in any case a way that cannot lead to salvation'. In his later work, however, Sanders rejects the view that Paul argued against the law on the basis of man's inability or failure to fulfill it. See Sanders, *Paul, the Law and the Jewish People*, p. 23. Interestingly, F.F. Bruce both accepts (*Galatians*, p. 167; *idem*, 'The Curse of the Law', p. 34) and rejects (*Galatians*, p. 160; *idem*, 'The Curse of the Law', p. 29) the use of this minor argument in Gal. 3.10.

120. Moo, 'Law, Works of the Law', pp. 97-98.

121. H. Räisänen, 'Paul's Theological Difficulties with the Law', in *Studia Biblica* 3 (1978), p. 308; cf. Sanders, *Paul, the Law and the Jewish People*, p. 23.

122. Tyson, 'Works of the Law', p. 428.

123. Byrne, '*Sons of God*', p. 151.

124. Betz, *Galatians*, p. 147; Byrne, '*Sons of God*', p. 151.

125. Cf. the use of δῆλον ὅτι in 1 Cor. 15.27; see Bultmann, 'δηλόω', *TDNT* II, pp. 61-62; H. Hanse, 'ΔΗΛΟΝ (zu Gal. 3, 11)' *ZNW* 34 (1935), pp. 299-303.

126. MT. וצדיק באמונתו יחיה
    most LXX MSS: ὁ δὲ δίκαιος ἐκ πίστεως μου ζήσεται
    LXX (A,C): ὁ δὲ δίκαιος μου ἐκ πίστεως ζήσεται.
Paul omits the personal pronoun (μου). See discussion of texts in H. Cavallin, 'The Righteous Shall Live by Faith: A Decisive Argument for the Traditional Interpretation', *ST* 32 (1978), pp. 33-34. D.M. Smith 'Ο ΔΕ ΔΙΚΑΙΟΣ ΕΚ ΠΙΣΤΕΩΣ ΖΗΣΕΤΑΙ', in *Studies in the History and Text of the New Testament in Honor of Kenneth Willis Clark*, eds., B.C. Daniels and M.J. Suggs (Salt Lake City: University of Utah Press, 1967), pp. 13-25; Kertlege, *Rechtfertigung*, pp. 89-95; Hays, *The Faith of Jesus Christ*, pp. 151-57; A. Feuillet, 'La citation d' Habacus II,4 et les huit premiers chapîtres de l'épître aux Romains', *NTS* 6 (1959-1960), pp. 52-80; Ziesler, *Righteousness*, pp. 176-77; A.T. Hanson, *Paul's Technique*, pp. 42-45.

127. So Betz, *Galatians*, p. 147; *pace* Hays, *Faith of Jesus Christ*, pp. 155-57; Howard, *Paul*, pp. 62-63.

128. Those who argue that ἐκ πίστεως is used adverbially include Lightfoot, Cavallin, Smith, and Hays. Those who take the phrase adjectivally include Howard, p. 63; Byrne, p. 152; Ziesler, p. 176; Feuillet, p. 52. The primary reasons for interpreting the phrase adjectivally are (1) the contrast between righteousness by law (v. 11a) and righteousness by faith (v. 11b), (2) the emphasis in the context (2.16; 3.6, 8) on righteousness by faith, and (3) the parallel with Rom. 1.17 where Hab. 2.4 is used to demonstrate not how the righteous live, but how they become righteous (so Feuillet, p. 52).

129. Ὁ δίκαιος in 3.11b is interpreted as a messianic reference (the Messiah, *ho dikaios*, shall live by faith) by A.T. Hanson, *Paul's Technique*, pp. 42-45; J. Bligh, 'Did Jesus Live by Faith?' *HeyJ* 9 (1968), pp. 414-19; M. Barth, 'The Faith of the Messiah', *HeyJ* 10 (1969), pp. 363-70; Hays, *The Faith of Jesus Christ*, pp. 151-54. Hays lists three possible interpretations: a) the Messiah will live by (his own) faith (fulness); b) the righteous person will live as a result of the Messiah's faith (fulness); c) the righteous person will live by (his own) faith (in the Messiah). Hays contends that 'Paul's thought is rendered wholly intelligible only if all three interpretations are held together and affirmed as correct. The ambiguity of Paul's formulation allows him to draw multiple implications out of the Habakkuk text' (p. 156).

130. Tyson, 'Works of the Law', p. 428.

131. See Hübner, *Gesetz*, p. 20: 'Grundsätzlich wäre ein Leben aus dem Tun denkbar . . . Faktisch ist dies aber nicht so'. Cf. Sanders, *Paul, the Law, and the Jewish People*, p. 54 n. 30.

132. See Hübner, *Gesetz*, p. 20: '3.12 stellt noch einmal die an sich doppelte, aber faktisch nicht doppelte Existenzmöglichkeit des Gerechten gegenüber: entweder Leben aus dem Tun oder Leben aus dem Glauben'. Also Betz, p. 147: 'Presupposed here, of course, is Paul's contrast between "doing" and "believing"'.

133. See Dunn, 'New Perspective', p. 115: 'We should not let our grasp of Paul's reasoning slip back into the old distinction between faith and works in general, between faith and 'good works', Paul is not arguing here for a concept of faith which is totally passive because it fears to become a 'work'. It is the demand for a *particular* work as the necessary expression of faith which he denies. As he puts it later in the same letter, 'In Christ Jesus neither circumcision nor uncircumcision is of any avail, but faith working through love' (5.6). Sanders, *Paul, the Law, and the Jewish People*, p. 159: 'The supposed conflict between 'doing' as such and 'faith' as such is simply not present in Galatians. What was at stake was not a way of life summarized by 'trust' versus a mode of life summarized by 'requirements', but whether or not the requirements for membership in the Israel of God would result in there being 'neither Jew not Greek".

134. See F F. Bruce, 'The Curse of the Law', in *Paul and Paulinism: Essays in honour of C.K. Barrett*, eds. M.D. Hooker and S.G. Wilson (London: SPCK, 1972), pp. 17-36; Büchsel, 'κατάρα', *TDNT* I, pp. 450-51; N.A. Dahl, 'Formgeschichtliche Beobachtungen zur Christus-Verkündigung in der Gemeindepredigt', in *Neutestamentliche Studien für R. Bultmann*, ed. W. Eltester (BZNW 21; Berlin: Töpelmann, 1954), pp. 3-9; E.G. Gordon, 'Christ, A Curse, and The Cross: an Interpretative Study of Gal. 3.13' (Ph.D. Dissertation, Princeton Theological Seminary, 1972); E.E. Ellis, 'Christ Crucified', in *Reconciliation and Hope: New Testament Essays on Atonement and Eschatology Presented to L.L. Morris*, ed. R. Banks (Grand Rapids: Eerdmans, 1974), pp. 69-75; J. Fitzmyer, 'Crucifixion in Ancient Palestine, Qumran Literature, and the New Testament', *CBQ* 40 (1978), pp. 493-513; H.W. Kuhn, 'Jesus als Gekreuzigter in der frühchristlichen Verkündigung bis zur Mitte des 2. Jahrhunderts', *ZTK* 72 (1975), pp. 1-46; D.R. Schwartz, 'Two Pauline Allusions to the Redemptive Mechanism of the Crucifixion', *JBL* 102 (1983), pp. 259-68; W. Wilcox, '"Upon a Tree"— Deut. 21.22-23 in the New Testament', *JBL* 96 (1977), pp. 85-99.

135. Sanders, *Paul, the Law, and the Jewish People*, p. 25.

136. Beker, *Paul*, pp. 50-51.

137. H.W. Kuhn, 'Jesus als Gekreuzigter', p. 33; cf. J. Denney, *The Death of Christ* (2nd edn, 1903), p. 152.

138. Hays, *The Faith of Jesus Christ*, pp. 193-237.

139. For a different explanation of the asyndeton, see B. Byrne, '*Sons of God*', p. 155 n. 75: 'the asyndeton occurs because Paul's attention is directed to the culminating διὰ τῆς πίστεως at the end of v. 14'.

140. Burton, *Galatians*, pp. 168-71.

141. Hooker, 'Interchange and Atonement', p. 351; *idem*, 'Paul and Covenantal Nomism', p. 55.

142. Beker, *Paul*, p. 54.

143. So Lightfoot, *Galatians*, p. 139; Betz, *Galatians*, p. 148; Burton, *Galatians*, p. 169; Lagrange, *Saint Paul, Epître aux Galates*, p. 71; Dahl, *Studies*, p. 132; Hays, *Faith of Jesus Christ*, pp. 116-17; A. Bandstra, *The Law and the Elements of the World: An Exegetical Study in Aspects of Paul's Teaching* (Grand Rapids: Eerdmans, 1964), p. 59; D. Schwartz, 'Two Pauline Allusions to the Redemptive Mechanism of the Crucifixion', *JBL* 102 (1983), p. 259; D. Hill, 'Salvation Proclaimed: IV. Galatians 3.10-14', *ExpTim* 93 (1981-82), p. 198; D.W.B. Robinson, 'The Distinction between Jewish and Gentile Believers in Galatians', *AusBR* 13 (1965), pp. 29-48; T.L. Donaldson, 'The "Curse of the Law" and the Inclusion of the Gentiles: Galatians 3.13-14', *NTS* 32 (1986), pp. 94-112.

144. So Bruce, *Galatians*, p. 167; Sanders, *Paul, the Law, and the Jewish People*, p. 26; Oepke, *Der Brief an die Galater*, p. 107; Schlier, *Der Brief an die Galater*, p. 136; Howard, *Paul*, p. 59; Büchsel, 'κατάρα', *TDNT* I, p. 450; Riesenfeld, 'ὑπέρ', *TDNT*, VIII p. 509; Bonnard, *L'Epître de Saint Paul aux Galates*, p. 68; Mussner, *Galaterbrief*, pp. 231-34; B. Reicke, 'The Law and the World According to Paul: Some Thoughts Concerning Gal. 4.1-11', *JBL* 70 (1951), p. 274.

145. See 1 Cor. 15.3; Riesenfeld, 'ὑπέρ', *TDNT* VIII, pp. 510-11; Hays, *Faith of Jesus Christ*, p. 85; Betz, *Galatians*, p. 26.

146. Byrne, '*Sons of God*', p. 156.

147. The curse of the law upon Gentiles is viewed by Bruce (*Galatians*, p. 167), Buchsel (*TDNT* I, p. 450), and Byrne (p. 153) in light of Rom. 2.14-15. But Paul does not present that rationale for his view of Gentiles being under the curse of the law in his letter to the Galatians.

148. So Buchsel, *TDNT* I, pp. 450-51; Lightfoot, *Galatians*, p. 139; Ridderbos, *Galatians*, p. 127; Oepke, *Der Brief an die Galater*, pp. 74-75; K. Kertelge, *Rechtfertigung*, pp. 209-12.

149. Riesenfeld, 'ὑπέρ', *TDNT* VIII, pp. 508-14; Harris, *NIDNTT* II, pp. 1196-97; Robertson, *A Grammar of the Greek New Testament*, p. 631; L. Morris, *The Apostolic Preaching of the Cross* (Grand Rapids: Eerdmans, 1955), pp. 62-64.

150. Morris, *The Apostolic Preaching of the Cross*, p. 59: 'There may be more to it than substitution, but we cannot dismiss the substitutionary aspect without doing violence to the words'.

151. Fitzmyer, 'Crucifixion', p. 511.

152. Byrne, '*Sons of God*', p. 154.

153. M. Hooker, 'Interchange in Christ', *JTS* ns 22 (1971), pp. 349-61; *idem*, 'Interchange and Atonement', *BJRL* 60 (1978), pp. 462-81.

154. 'Interchange and Atonement', pp. 470-71: 'Paul does not explain how one who is made a curse becomes a source of blessing; but since it is 'in

Christ' that the blessing comes, and since it is by being identified with the one true descendant of Abraham that Jews and Gentiles receive the promise, it is clear that the curse has been annulled—transformed into blessing. This can only be through the resurrection: the judgment of the Law—that Christ was under a curse—has been overthrown'.

155. Hays, *Faith of Jesus Christ*, p. 99.

156. *Ibid*.

157. *Ibid*., p. 114.

158. *Ibid*., p. 208.

159. See above, p. 92: Perelman, *New Rhetoric*, p. 227.

160. Bruce, *Galatians*, p. 167: 'The two *hina* clauses of v. 14 are coordinated: both express the purpose of Christ's redemptive death'. So also Burton, *Galatians*, p. 176; Byrne, '*Sons of God*', p. 156; cf. Betz, *Galatians*, p. 152: 'the second conclusion presupposes the first and is not simply parallel to it'.

161. See below, pp. 136-37.

162. Bruce, *Galatians*, p. 168.

163. See Bruce, 'The Curse of the Law', p. 30; Wilcox, 'Upon a Tree', p. 87; J. Fitzmyer, 'Crucifixion', p. 511: 'In this passage Aristotelian logic has to yield to what may be called 'rabbinic' logic—a type of interpretation of OT texts which relies on catchword bonds or free associations'.

164. Gal. 3.13; ἐπικατάρατος πᾶς ὁ κρεμάμενος ἐπὶ ξύλου Deut. 21.23 (LXX): κεκατηραμένος ὑπὸ θεοῦ πᾶς κρεμάμενος ἐπὶ ξύλου Deut. 21.23 (MT): כִּי—קִלְלַת אֱלֹהִים תָּלוּי Gal. 3.13 agrees with the LXX against the MT in the addition of ἐπὶ ξύλου; 3.13 omits the LXX phrase ὑπὸ θεοῦ. For further discussion and comparisons with Targumic and Qumran usage of Deut. 21.23, see Wilcox, 'Upon a Tree', pp. 87-90; Fitzmyer, 'Crucifixion', pp. 510-13.

165. Byrne, '*Sons of God*, p. 155.

166. Dahl, *Studies in Paul*, p. 131; Hays, *Faith of Jesus Christ*, p. 209.

167. See below, pp. 135-36.

168. Betz, *Galatians*, pp. 152-53; Hays, *Faith of Jesus Christ*, p. 212.

169. D. Daube, *The New Testament and Rabbinic Judaism*, pp. 141-50; R. Longenecker, *Biblical Exegesis*, p. 128: 'Paul is interacting with a typically rabbinic view that truth presents itself in two guises, the first and elemental form and the second a developed . . . and he is counteracting in particular the Judaizers application of this Jewish motif which argued in effect that Paul's teaching is the elemental while theirs is developed'.

170. See below, 'Abraham in Jewish Literature', pp. 187-88.

171. See below, p. 199.

172. See above, 'Rhetorical Techniques', pp. 89-90; Perelman, *New Rhetoric*, pp. 350-57.

173. O. Eger, 'Rechtswörter und Rechtsbilder in den paulinischen Briefen', *ZNW* 18 (1917-18), pp. 84-108; W.M. Ramsay, *Galatians*, pp. 349-75; Behm, 'διαθήκη', *TDNT* II, p. 129.

174. D. Walker, 'The Legal Terminology in the Epistle to the Galatians', in *The Gift of Tongues and other Essays* (Edinburgh, 1906), pp. 81-95.

175. E. Bammel, 'Gottes ΔΙΑΘΗΚΗ (Gal. III. 15-17) und das jüdische Rechtsdenken', *NTS* 6 (1959-60), pp. 313-19, who argues that the example in Paul's thought is the Jewish legal procedure of *Mattanah Beri'*. Under this arrangement, the property passes immediately into the possession of the beneficiary. This will is irrevocable; the death of the testator is not necessary to make it operative. See also W. Selb, 'Διαθήκη im Neuen Testament. Randbermerkungen eines Juristen zu einem Theologenstreit', *JJS* 25 (1974), pp. 190-92; Mussner, p. 237; Str-B, III, pp. 136-39; C.J. Bjerkelund, '"Nach menschlicher Weise rede ich"': Function und Sinn des paulinischen Ausdrucks', *ST* (1972), pp. 63-100.

176. Behm, 'διαθήκη', *TDNT* II, p. 129.

177. Against Betz, *Galatians*, p. 157; Schlier, p. 146. Διαθήκη in v. 15 clearly refers to a common legal institution, a 'will' or 'testament'; but the same term in v. 17 refers to the Abrahamic covenant and must be interpreted in the theological sense; so Burton, *Galatians*, pp. 182-83; Berger, 'Abraham', p. 54; Hartmann, 'Bundesideologie', p. 110.

178. See Hartmann, 'Bundesideologie', p. 110; Hooker, 'Paul and Covenantal Nomism', pp. 50-56.

179. Sanders, *Paul*, pp. 511-15; Käsemann, '"The Righteousness of God" in Paul' in his *Questions*, pp. 177-80; Lang, 'Gesetz und Bund', in *Rechtfertigung* (FS Käsemann), eds., J. Friedrich, W. Pohlman, and P. Stuhlmacher (Tübingen: Mohr, Siebeck, 1976), p. 305; Luz, 'Der Alte und Neue Bund bei Paulus und im Hebräerbrief', *EvT* 27 (1967), p. 318; Kennedy, 'The Significance and Range of the Covenant Conception in the New Testament', *The Expositor* 8 (1915), p. 395: 'the covenant idea as such is of subordinate value for Paul's thought'.

180. Sanders, *Paul*, p. 82; Cf. also W.C. van Unnik, 'La conception paulinienne de la Nouvelle Alliance', in *Sparsa Collecta: The Collected Essays of W.C. van Unnik* (NovTSup 29 Part 1; Leiden: Brill, 1973), p. 176: 'avant de décider si un concept est d'importance secondaire ou au contraire primordiale, il faut non pas compter mais penser les emplois du mot correspondant'.

181. Hooker, 'Paul and Covenantal Nomism', pp. 51-52: 'He is concerned to show that it is not the covenant on Mt. Sinai which brings salvation. Possibly this is why he does not make a great deal of use of Exodus typology. For the conversion of Gentiles has, in Paul's view, demonstrated the temporary nature of the Mosaic law. It is the promises of Abraham which are primary in the divine scheme'.

182. Foerster, 'κληρονόμος', *TDNT* III, p. 784.

183. The perfect tense of κεχάρισται denotes the enduring quality of the inheritance; see Byrne p. 159 n. 90; cf. Rom. 4.16.

184. See above, 'Rhetorical Techniques', p. 88; Perelman, *New Rhetoric*, pp. 201-205.

250   *Abraham in Galatians*

185. See Foerster, 'κληρονόμος', *TDNT* III pp. 779-81; J.D. Hester, 'Paul's Concept of Inheritance', *SJT* (Occasional Papers 14; Edinburgh: Oliver & Boyd, 1961); *idem*, 'The "Heir" and Heilsgeschichte: A Study of Gal. 4.1ff', in *Ökonomia: FS Oscar Cullmann* (Hamburg: Reich, 1967), pp. 118-25.

186. See below, 'Paul and Jewish Exegesis', pp. 207-208; E.E. Ellis, *Paul's Use of the OT* pp. 70-72; D. Daube, 'The Interpretation of a Generic Singular', in his *The New Testament and Rabbinic Judaism*, pp. 438-44.

187. Dahl, *Studies*, p. 130, claims that Paul's interpretation depends on an exegetical inference by analogy: 'Just as 'thine offspring' in the promise to David refers to the Messiah, so does 'thine offspring' in the promise to Abraham'. The messianic interpretation of 'your offspring' in 2 Sam. 7.12 is seen in 4QFlor 1.10-11.

188. Sanders, *Paul, the Law, and the Jewish People*, p. 160: 'He opposes Jewish particularism, but introduces another kind'.

189. Bjerkelund, 'Nach menschlicher Weise', p. 92. See also Berger, 'Abraham', p. 56: 'Die Verse 13-14a hatten gezeigt, dass Christus allein uns von dem den Segen hindernden Fluch losgekauft hat. Umgekehrt zeigen die Verse 14b-18, dass auf Christus allein die Abraham gegebenen Verheissungen hinzielen. In beiden Argumentationsreihen spielt das Gesetz eine wichtige Rolle. Nach V. 13-14a ist Christus das Eintauschobjekt gegen den Fluch des Gesetzes, so dass dessen Fluch uns jetzt nicht mehr trifft. Nach V. 14b-18 ist andererseits das Gesetz auch ohne positive Beziehung zur Verheissung. Erben Abrahams gibt es nicht auf dem Weg des Gesetzes, sondern nur auf dem Weg über die sich erfüllende Verheissung, und, da diesen Jesus zu ihrem Ziel kommt, nur im Glauben an ihn'.

190. See above, pp. 43-44.

191. See above, 'Rhetorical Techniques', p. 87-88; Perelman, *New Rhetoric* pp. 345-49.

192. Betz, *Galatians*, p. 165.

193. Cf. Rom. 4.15; 5.13, 20; 7.7-13.

194. See BAGD, p. 887; Betz, *Galatians*, p. 165; Mussner, *Galaterbrief*, p. 245; Oepke, *Der Brief an die Galater*, p. 81; Schlier, *Der Brief an die Galater*, p. 153.

195. Howard, *Paul*, pp. 59, 64; Bruce, *Galatians*, p. 180.

196. See above, 'Rhetorical Techniques', p. 92; Perelman, pp. 174-75.

197. See Byrne, *'Sons of God'*, p. 163 n. 105.

198. See Bultmann, 'ζωοποιέω', *TDNT* II, p. 874.

199. Howard, *Paul*, pp. 60-61, 64, speaks of the *suppressing* function of the law: 'the law, by its divisive power, suppressed the nations and kept Israel in isolation' (p. 64). Paul's argument in the immediate context, however, does not appear to be that the law was a divisive power which set Israel apart from other nations, but that the law 'was in fact the breaker-down of the division, the leveller of the Jews to a common solidarity in 'Gentile-sinner' status'

(Byrne, p. 164). See also the critique of the reductionistic character of Howard's position by A.J.M. Wedderburn, 'A Review Article of G. Howard, *Paul: Crisis in Galatia*', *SJT* 33 (1980), pp. 380-81.

200. See above, p. 101.

201. Paul's argument from such an understanding of salvation history demonstrates the validity of Sander's claim that Paul worked from the solution to the problem, (*Paul*, p. 443)—or, as we might say, from the fulfillment of the promise to the purpose of the law.

202. Lightfoot's claim (*Galatians*, p. 146) that there are 250-300 interpretations of this passage is reduced to a manageable list of alternatives by T. Callan, 'The Law and the Mediator: Gal. 3.19b-20' (Ph.D. Dissertation, Yale University, 1976), pp. 3-30.

203. See C. Giblin, 'Three Monotheistic Texts', *CBQ* 37 (1975), pp. 540-42.

204. See T. Callan, 'Pauline Midrash: The Exegetical Background of Gal. 3.19b', *JBL* 99 (1980), pp. 549-67.

205. *Ibid.*, p. 565.

206. T. Callan, 'The Law and the Mediator', pp. 202-203; C. Giblin, 'Three Monotheistic Texts', pp. 538-39; U. Mauser, 'Galater iii.20: die Universalität des Heils', *NTS* 13 (1966-7), pp. 258-70; Howard, *Paul*, pp. 76-81.

207. See the outline of the chiastic development in this chapter, above, p. 109.

208. See above, 'Rhetorical Techniques', p. 92-93; Perelman, *New Rhetoric*, p. 331.

209. See Mussner, *Galaterbrief*, p. 254.

210. Käsemann, *Perspectives*, p. 83: 'Gal 3.23ff. talks about the manifestation of faith in personified form'.

211. On the temporal sense of εἰς Χριστόν see below, p. 252 n. 227.

212. Betz, *Galatians*, p. 176 n. 120; see also Bultmann, *Theology* I. p. 319.

213. Lietzmann, *An die Galater*, p. 23; W. Mundle, *Der Glaubensbegriff bei Paulus* (Leipzig: Heinsius, 1923), p. 93.

214. Hays, *Faith of Jesus Christ*, p. 231.

215. *Ibid.*, pp. 229-31.

216. Mussner, *Galaterbrief*, pp. 254-55.

217. Oepke, *Der Brief an die Galater*, p. 85.

218. Dahl, *Studies*, p. 175.

219. *Ibid.*

220. See above, pp. 109-15.

221. Beker, *Paul*, p. 56.

222. Bruce, *Galatians*, p. 181.

223. Oepke, *Der Brief an die Galater*, p. 85.

224. See above, 'Rhetorical Techniques', pp. 87, 92-93.

252   *Abraham in Galatians*

225. BAGD, p. 867; the positive aspect of guarding to protect (Phil. 4.7) is not in view in this context.

226. See R. Longenecker, 'The Pedagogical Nature of the Law in Gal. 3.19–4.17', *JETS* 25 (1982), pp. 53-59; Linda L. Belleville, "Under Law": Structural Analysis and the Pauline Concept of Law in Galatians 3.21–4.11', *JSNT* (1986), pp. 53-78; David J. Lull, '"The Law was our Pedagogue": A Study in Galatians 3.19-25', *JBL* 105 (1986), pp. 481-98; N.H. Young, 'Paidagogos: The Social Setting of a Pauline Metaphor', *NovT* 29 (1987), pp. 150-76; Betz, *Galatians*, pp. 177-78; Bruce, *Galatians*, p. 182; Mussner, *Galaterbrief*, pp. 257-58; Oepke, *Der Brief an die Galater*, pp. 86-88.

227. That both of these clauses are to be taken in the purely temporal sense is supported by Betz, *Galatians*, p. 178; Mussner, *Galaterbrief*, p. 257; Byrne '*Sons of God*' p. 164 n. 110.

228. Betz, *Galatians*, p. 185. The stress on Gentile Christians in 3.26-29, however, does not mean that 3.23-25 is an exclusive reference to Jewish Christians; see Mussner, *Galaterbrief*, p. 256; Bruce, *Galatians*, p. 183; Byrne, '*Sons of God*', p. 165 n. 114.

229. See above, 'Rhetorical Techniques', p. 92; Perelman, *New Rhetoric*, p. 231.

230. The phrase ἐν Χριστῷ ᾽Ιησοῦ does not modify πίστεως since the emphasis in this section is on Christ as the sphere of salvation and since Paul uses the genitive rather than ἐν after πίστις to refer to faith in Christ (as in 𝔭46; see 2.16, 20; 3.22); so Burton, *Galatians*, p. 202; Mussner, *Galaterbrief*, p. 261; Oepke, *Der Brief an die Galater*, p. 88.

231. F. Siegert, 'Argumentation bei Paulus', p. 250: 'Gal. 3.28 ist der *ei ara* Satz die Schlussregel, die von 'In-Christus-sein' auf 'Erb-sein (der Verheissung an Abraham)' schliessen lässt. Man kann diese Stelle auch als Syllogismus wiedergeben, indem man die Schlussregel als Obersatz verwendet.
Wer in Christus ist, ist auch Abrahams Kind (v. 29a).
Ihr alle seid in Christus (v. 28a).
Darum seid ihr auch Erben der Verheissungen, die an Abraham ergingen'.

232. The epithet 'Israel of God' in 6.16, therefore, must be seen as referring to reconstituted Israel, including both Jews and Gentiles. See discussion below, pp. 212-13.

233. See Betz, *Galatians*, pp. 181-84; R. Longenecker, *New Testament Social Ethics for Today*, pp. 31-33; Brinsmead, *Galatians*, pp. 141-61; W. Meeks, 'The Image of the Androgyne: Some Uses of a Symbol in Earliest Christianity', *HR* 13 (1974), pp. 165-208; G. Brumann, *Vorpaulinische christliche Taufverkündigung bei Paulus* (BWANT, 82; Stuttgart: Kohlhammer, 1962), pp. 24, 64; D.R. MacDonald, 'There is No Male and Female: Galatians 3.26-28 and Gnostic Baptismal Tradition' (Ph.D. Dissertation, Harvard University, 1978), pp. 4-15.

234. Longenecker, *New Testament Social Ethics for Today*, p. 31.

235. Byrne, '*Sons of God*', pp. 173-74.
236. Longenecker, *New Testament Social Ethics for Today*, p. 31.
237. Betz, *Galatians*, p. 182.
238. Longenecker, *New Testament Social Ethics for Today*, p. 32.
239. Betz, *Galatians*, p. 184. It may be debated, however, as to the extent of the baptismal formula, whether it includes all of vv. 26-28 or only vv. 27-28.
240. So Mussner, *Galaterbrief*, p 266 n. 99.
241. See Betz, *Galatians*, pp. 187-88; contra Schlier, *Der Brief an die Galater*, p. 172.
242. Byrne '*Sons of God*', p. 169 n. 126.
243. See above, 'Rhetorical Techniques', p. 89; Perelman, pp. 398-405.
244. The first person plural in vv. 24-25 refers primarily, though not exclusively, to Jewish Christians; see above, pp. 122-23, 131.
245. Siegert, 'Argumentation bei Paulus', p. 283, suggests that the sacraments are used by Paul as symbols. See also Perelman, *New Rhetoric*, p. 332: 'The symbolic connection brings about transference between the symbol and the thing symbolized. When the cross, the flag, the monarch are viewed as symbols of Christianity, the fatherland, the state, these realities excite love or hate, veneration or contempt, which would be incomprehensible and ridiculous if these symbols, in addition to having a representative character, did not constitute a bond of participation. This bond is indispensable for arousing patriotic or religious fervor. Ceremonies of communion require material support on which emotion can fasten, for it is difficult to arouse and nourish emotion with a mere abstract idea'.
246. See below, p. 158. Mussner, *Galaterbrief*, p. 266: 'Der Vers zieht das Resume für das Thema, das mit 3, 7 schon angeschlagen war. Dort waren die Glaubensmenschen als die wahren Söhne Abrahams erklärt worden'.
247. Hays, *Faith of Jesus Christ*, p. 232.

Notes to Chapter 5

1. Burton, *Galatians*, p. lxxiv.
2. *Ibid.*, p. 251.
3. Betz, *Galatians*, p. 238.
4. *Ibid.*, p. 240.
5. *Ibid.*
6. F. Vouga, 'La construction de l'histoire en Galates 3-4', *ZNW* 75 (1984), p. 259.
7. *Ibid.*, p. 261.
8. *Ibid.*, pp. 261-62.
9. *Ibid.*, p. 266. Vouga's thesis is that 'les chap 3-4 ne sont pas la

confirmation de l'Evangile paulinien par une prétendue histoire du salut, mais, au contraire, la résolution du problème de l'interprétation de l'héritage juif et, par conséquent, le recadrage christologique de cette histoire' (p. 269). Now while it is true that Paul reinterprets his Jewish heritage by reframing history in the light of his Christology, I have attempted to show in ch. 4 how Paul uses his Christocentric view of salvation-history in defense of his gospel.

10. Bligh, *Galatians*, p. 378.

11. *Ibid.*, p. xiii.

12. *Ibid.*, p. 379.

13. *Ibid.*, p. 380.

14. *Ibid.*, p. 390.

15. Barrett, 'Allegory', p. 157.

16. Bligh, p. 380.

17. Barrett, 'Allegory', p. 157.

18. *Ibid.*

19. *Ibid.*, pp. 161-68.

20. See below, p. 263 n. 41.

21. Burton, *Galatians*, p. 251. Barrett ('Allegory', pp. 154-55) reviews the inability of Luther, Calvin, Schlier, and O'Neill to account for the function of the Hagar–Sarah allegory in Paul's argument.

22. A. Oepke, *Der Brief des Paulus an die Galater*, p. 110.

23. Brinsmead, *Galatians*, pp. 82-83.

24. Hays, *The Faith of Jesus Christ*, p. 233: 'The Purpose of this chapter has been to demonstrate that Paul's argument in Gal. 3.1-4.11 is a unified attempt to think through the implications of a gospel story in which salvation hinges upon the faithfulness of Jesus Christ'.

25. Hays only refers to 4.21-31 in a citation of Betz's outline of the letter (p. 222).

26. J. Beker, *Paul*, p. 374 n. 13.

27. See Betz, *Galatians*, pp. 220-21.

28. See above, p. 224 n. 80.

29. See below, p. 202-15.

30. See below, pp. 151-54.

31. See above, p. 48.

32. See above, p. 59.

33. Barrett, 'Allegory', p. 165.

34. A. Lincoln, *Paradise Now and Not Yet*, p. 27.

35. *Ibid.*, p. 28: '4.30 climaxes Paul's whole argument from Scripture and enables us to see the polemical reason for which he introduces his midrash in the first place'.

36. Paul's personal appeal (4.12) is based upon both his own example (1.13-2.14) and his exposition of Scripture (4.21-31).

37. Lincoln, *Paradise Now and Not Yet*, p. 28.

38. O. Merk, 'Der Beginn der Paränese im Galaterbrief', p. 97.

39. Bligh, *Galatians*, p. 396: 'The Greek verb 'to hear' (ἀκούειν) can also mean 'to obey'. Accordingly, v. 21 can mean: 'You who want to be under the law—why not obey the law?' Then v. 30 (its counterpart) adds: 'The law bids you send away the slave-woman and her son'.

40. Lincoln, *Paradise Now and Not Yet*, p. 28.

41. See Carl E. DeVries, 'Paul's "Cutting" Remark about a Race: Galatians 5.1-12', in *Current Issues in Biblical and Patristic Interpretation: Studies in Honor of Merrill C. Tenney*, ed. G.F. Hawthorne (Grand Rapids: Eerdmans, 1975), p. 120.

42. *Ibid.*, p. 120 n. 12.

43. Cf. Behm ('ἀνάθεμα', *TDNT*, I, pp. 354-55) who insists that the imperatives (ἀνάθεμα ἔστω) of 1.8-9 cannot refer to any act of church discipline. 'The controlling thought here is that of delivering up to the judicial wrath of God'. But surely the pronouncement of divine judgment (cf. 5.10) provides sanction for the demand for church discipline in 4.30.

44. See F.F. Bruce, '"Abraham Had Two Sons"—A Study in Pauline Hermeneutics', p. 75.

45. See above, p. 86.

46. See below, pp. 213-15.

47. Διαθήκη in this context 'amounts to a world order decreed by divine institution; it contains God's definition of the basis and purpose of human life' (Betz, *Galatians*, p. 244); cf. Behm, 'διαθήκη', *TDNT* II, p. 130. The meaning here is close to the use in 2 Cor. 3.6, 14 where the same emphasis on 'spirit' and 'freedom' is found.

48. L. Gaston ('Israel's Enemies in Pauline Theology', p. 405) argues that Paul was using a rabbinic tradition (*Mekilta, Bahodesh* 5; *Pseudo-Jonathan Tg Deut* 33.2) that the Torah was offered to the Ishmaelites and to all the nations, but was only accepted by Israel. It is important to note, however, that Paul's own perspective as expressed in Rom. 3.2; 9.4 (οἵτινές εἰσιν Ἰσραηλῖται, ὧν ἡ υἱοθεσία καὶ ἡ δόξα καὶ αἱ διαθῆκαι καὶ ἡ νομοθεσία) is reflective of the dominant emphasis on the giving of the Torah to Israel, the sons of Isaac; see Str-B III, p. 262; F.F. Bruce, *Galatians*, pp. 218-19.

49. Betz, *Galatians*, p. 244 n. 65.

50. See Mussner, *Galaterbrief*, pp. 322-25.

51. A. Lincoln, *Paradise Now and Not Yet*, p. 16.

52. *Ibid.*, p. 17; R. Jewett, 'Agitators', pp. 200-201.

53. See Gal. 3.22–4.10.

54. E.g., Burton *Galatians*, p. 262.

55. L. Gaston, 'Israel's Enemies in Pauline Theology', p. 408.

56. Lincoln, *Paradise Now and Not Yet*, p. 22.

57. The image of an eschatological Jerusalem is common in Jewish literature; see Isa. 2; 54.10-14; 60-62; Ezek. 40-48; Zech. 12-14; Tobit 13.9ff; 14.7; Jub. 4.26; Sib. Or. V, 250ff; 414-33; Ps. Sol. 11.8; Test. Levi 10.5; 1QM

256   *Abraham in Galatians*

12.13ff; 4Qp Isa. 1.7, 11; 4 Ezra 9.26-10.59; 2 Baruch 4.2-7; 6.9; 32.4; see discussion in A. Lincoln, *Paradise Now and Not Yet*, pp. 18-25; Str-B III, pp. 573-75.

58. From the 'voice' of Isa. 40.3 (=Mk 1.3; Jn 1.23) to the 'new heavens and new earth' of Isa. 65.17 (=2 Pet. 3.13; Rev. 21.1), Isaiah 40-66 was one of the most quoted sources for NT writers.

59. F.F. Bruce ('"Abraham Had Two Sons"—A Study in Pauline Hermeneutics', p. 82) suggests that 'the Christian application of Isaiah 54.1 was probably not peculiar to Paul; more probably it was part of the common exegetical stock of the church'.

60. Some lists of barren women who gave birth start with Sarah and end with Zion; see Str-B III, p. 575.

61. Isaiah sees the multiplication of the children of Jerusalem as the ingathering of the nations (cf. 44.5; 45.22; 49.6; 56.6, 7; 66.18-21) and as the work of the Spirit of God (cf. 44.3-5).

62. The discussion regarding the beginning of the parenesis is reviewed by Otto Merk, 'Der Beginn der Paränese im Galaterbrief', *ZNW* 60 (1969), pp. 83-104; D. Fletcher, 'The Singular Argument', pp. 119-140. For reasons discussed in ch. 1, I agree with Merk and Fletcher that 5.13 is the beginning of the paraenetic section.

63. See Brinsmead's review of the 'two-front theories' (*Galatians*, 15-16).

64. So W. Schmithals ('Heretics in Galatia'), who identifies the opponents as gnostic libertines.

65. So W. Lütgert, *Gesetz und Geist: Ein Untersuchung zur Vorgeschichte des Galaterbriefes* (Gütersloh: Bertelsmann, 1919), and J. Ropes, *The Singular Problem of the Epistle to the Galatians* (Cambridge, Mass.: Harvard University Press, 1929).

66. So. F.F. Bruce, *Galatians*, p. 240; F. Mussner, *Galaterbrief*, p. 367.

67. So R. Jewett, 'Agitators', p. 209.

68. See D. Fletcher, 'The Singular Argument', pp. 220-71.

69. Barrett, 'Allegory', p. 151, argues that the absence of the names 'implies that the story is already before the Galatians; they will know that the slave is Hagar, the free woman Sarah. The articles are anaphoric in this sense. The Judaizers must have continued their exegesis of the Genesis story on the same lines as Jub. 16.17f'.

70. On the importance of repetition in the development of the argument, see above, p. 92.

71. Paul appears to have adapted the text of the LXX to fit his own purposes: οὐ γὰρ κληρονομήσει ὁ υἱὸς τῆς παιδίσκης ταύτης μετὰ τοῦ υἱοῦ μου Ισαακ (Gen. 21.10 LXX).

72. D. Fletcher, 'The Singular Argument', p. 151.

73. See references above, pp. 150-51.

74. D. Fletcher, 'The Singular Argument', p. 185; J. Hawkings, 'The

Opponents of Paul in Galatia' (Ph.D. Dissertation, Yale University, 1971),
p. 150: 'I would even venture to suggest the possibility that one reason why
Paul gives a catalogue of the works of the flesh might be to remind the
Galatians that sins against charity, although they tend to think nothing of
them, are in the same category as the sins of licentiousness and revelry which
they naturally hold in abhorrence, as any Law-abiding person would'.
  75. G. Howard, *Paul's Crisis in Galatia*, p. 14.
  76. R. Jewett, *Paul's Anthropological Terms*, pp. 102-103.
  77. *Ibid.*, p. 103.
  78. Fletcher, 'The Singular Argument', p. 193.

Notes to Conclusion and Implications

  1. See below, pp. 170-74.
  2. See below, pp. 179-99.
  3. See below, pp. 202-209.
  4. See T. McGonigal, 'Abraham believed God', p. 328; Ronald Y.K.
Fung, The Epistle to the Galatians (NICNT, Grand Rapids: Eerdmans,
1988), 136.
  5. See H. Moxnes, *Theology*, p. 209; G. Howard, *Paul*, p. 57.
  6. See L. Gaston, 'Abraham and the Righteousness of God', p. 53: 'Paul's
major theological concern I understand to be not the justification of
individuals by their faith but the justification of the legitimacy of his
apostleship to and gospel for the Gentiles'.
  7. *Ibid.*
  8. See G. Schrenk, 'Was bedeutet "Israel Gottes"?' *Judaica* 5 (1949),
pp. 81-94; *idem*, 'Der Segenwunsch nach der Kampfepistel', *Judaica* 6
(1950), pp. 170-90; N. Dahl, 'Zur Auslegung von Gal. 6.16', *Judaica* 6 (1950),
pp. 151-70; P. Richardson, *Israel* pp. 74-102.
  9. So Lightfoot, *Galatians*, p. 225; E.P. Sanders, *Paul, the Law, and the
Jewish People*, p. 173.
  10. So P. Richardson, *Israel*, p. 82.
  11. G. Shrenk, 'Was bedeutet "Israel Gottes"?', p. 94.
  12. Betz, *Galatians*, p. 323.
  13. W.D. Davies, 'Paul and the People of Israel', *NTS* 24 (1977-78),
p. 10.
  14. Burton, *Galatians*, p. 358.
  15. Richardson, *Israel*, p. 82.
  16. Sanders, *Paul, the Law, and the Jewish People*, p. 174; Richardson
seems to admit that the force of the argument in Galatians might lead
readers to take the name of Israel for the church: 'The prayer is called for by
the possibility of misunderstanding Paul's intention in the letter proper.

When he reads it again and adds his own conclusion he clarifies his statements about the problem of circumcision and asserts the centrality of Christ's cross for all believers, but to prevent the Galatians from moving from this position to a new Christian exclusiveness and sectarianism, he adds his prayer for mercy on God's faithful people' (*Israel*, p. 84).

17. As he certainly does in Rom. 11; see Richardson, *Israel*, pp. 126-47.

18. See especially Burton, *Galatians*, *passim*. Also see the review and criticism of this position in F. Watson, *Paul, Judaism and the Gentiles*, pp. 1-72.

19. Against Sanders (*Paul*, pp. 513-14) who denies that the concept of covenant has any significant place in Pauline thought.

20. M. Hooker, 'Paul and "Covenantal Nomism"', in *Paul and Paulinism: Essays in Honour of C.K. Barrett* (eds. M. Hooker and S. Wilson; London: SPCK, 1982), p. 49.

21. *Ibid.*, pp. 51-56.

Notes to Appendix 1

1. Paul describes his opponents as οἱ ταράσσοντες (1.7), ὁ ταράσσων (5.10), and οἱ ἀναστατοῦντες (5.12). While his opponents are often called 'Judaizers' in contemporary literature, the original meaning of ἰουδάιζειν is 'to live like a Jew, according to Jewish customs' rather than 'to force others to become like Jews'. See Gal. 2.14. Esther 8.17 (πολλοὶ τῶν ἐθνῶν περιετέμοντο καὶ ἰουδάιζον διὰ τὸν φόβον τῶν Ἰουδαίων); Josephus, *Jewish War*, 2.454; Ignatius, *Letter to the Magnesians* 10.3 (ἄτοπόν ἐστιν Ἰησοῦν Χριστόν λαλεῖν καὶ ἰουδάιζειν). See Gutbrod, "Ἰσραήλ", *TDNT*, III, p. 383; BAGD, p. 379. Thus the real Judaizers were the Gentile believers at Galatia, who were adopting Jewish customs, not the 'agitators' themselves.

2. See surveys of various positions by Brinsmead, *Galatians*, pp. 9-22; J. Eckert, *Die urchristliche Verkündigung im Streit zwischen Paulus und seinen Gegnern nach dem Galaterbrief* (Munich: Regensburg, 1971), pp. 1-18; E.E. Ellis, 'Paul and his Opponents', in his *Prophecy and Hermeneutic in Early Christianity* (WUNT, 18; Tübingen: Mohr, 1978), pp. 80-115; J. Gunther, *St. Paul's Opponents and their Backgrounds: A Study of Apocalyptic and Jewish Sectarian Teachings* (NovTSup, 35; Leiden: Brill, 1973); G. Howard, *Paul; Crisis in Galatia* (SNTSMS, 35; Cambridge: University Press, 1979), pp. 1-19; R. Jewett, 'The Agitators and the Galatian Congregation', *NTS* 17 (1970), pp. 198-200; F. Mussner, *Galaterbrief*, pp. 14-24.

3. See Brinsmead, *Galatians*, pp. 23-33; see also J. Barclay, 'Mirror-Reading a Polemical Letter. Galatians as a Test Case', *JSNT* 31 (1987), pp. 73-93.

4. Munck, *Paul*, p. 85: 'Paul's individual letters, and the situation that forms the background of each letter, must be viewed on their own merits in

each case, and the material in the letters and behind these supposed situations may be unified only if such a procedure does not violate the individual nature of the particular letter and of the situation that lies behind it'.

5. E.g., W.M. Ramsay, *A Historical Commentary on St. Paul's Epistle to the Galatians* (London: Hodder and Stoughton, 1899); H. Koester, 'Paul and Hellenism', in *The Bible in Modern Scholarship*, ed. P. Hyatt (Philadelphia: Fortress, 1968), pp. 192-93. For a recent study of Judaism in Asia Minor see A.T. Kraabel, 'Paganism and Judaism: The Sardis Evidence', in *Paganisme, Judaïsme, Christianisme: Influences et affrontements dans le Monde Antique (Mélanges offerts à Marcel Simon)* (Paris: E. de Boccard, 1978), pp. 13-33; *idem*, 'Jews in Imperial Rome: More Archeological Evidence from an Oxford Collection', *JJS* 30 (1979), pp. 41-58.

6. E.g., 1 and 2 Corinthians do not mention the issue of circumcision, which is central in the Galatian crisis; Colossians shares a reference to τὰ στοιχεῖα τοῦ κόσμου (Gal. 4.3, 9; Col. 2.8, 20) and observance of days (Gal. 4.10; Col. 2.16), but Galatians does not include a comparable emphasis on angel-worship or asceticism and Colossians does not contain a similar attack on νόμος, ἔργα νόμου, or δικαιοῦσθαι ἐν νόμῳ. Cf. W. Schmithals's dependence upon 1 and 2 Cor. and Col. for his theory of Gnostic influence at Galatia ('Heretics in Galatia' in *Paul and the Gnostics* [trans. J. Steely; Nashville: Abingdon, 1972], pp. 30-31, 44, 47-49).

7. Brinsmead, *Galatians*, p. 24.

8. J. Tyson, 'Paul's Opponents in Galatia', *NovT* 10 (1968), p. 243; Brinsmead, *Galatians*, pp. 24-33.

9. Tyson, 'Paul's Opponents', p. 249.

10. *Ibid*.

11. *Ibid*., p. 252.

12. Brinsmead, *Galatians*, p. 25.

13. According to Brinsmead, some of Paul's terms reflect the meaning attributed to them by the opponents (e.g., ἐνάρχεσθαι-ἐπιτελεῖσθαι, ζωή, ἐλευθερία, δικαιοσύνη etc.); some of Paul's statements imply that his opponents held the opposite position (e.g., Paul said that circumcision was nothing; they must have taught that circumcision was the most important climactic sacrament [p. 141]. Paul emphasized the cross; they must have minimized its importance [p. 87]). And some of Paul's terminology is a modification of the terminology of the opponents (e.g., Paul's sacramental view of baptism is his 'dialogical counterpart' to the opponents' sacramental view of circumcision [pp. 157-61, 194]).

14. See below pp. 173-74.

15. *Pace* Schmithals, 'Heretics in Galatia', p. 39: 'he [Paul] is at a loss about the sense and reason in the practice of circumcision in Galatia'. Of course, if Paul was at a loss, then there is little hope that anyone—even Schmithals—can use his letter to discover what the opponents taught. Since,

260   *Abraham in Galatians*

however, Paul gives evidence of an intimate relationship with his Galatian converts (4.12-20), it is reasonable to suppose that his first-hand knowledge of the crisis was better than Schmithals' understanding of the situation.
16. See above, pp. 63, 87.
17. See above, p. 92; cf. also Mussner, *Galaterbrief*, p. 13.
18. See above, p. 83.
19. E.g., πίστις, οἱ ἐκ πίστεως, νόμος, οἱ ἐξ ἔργων νόμου, τοῦ ᾽Αβραάμ σπέρμα; see above, pp. 101-104, 129.
20. See above, pp. 84-85.
21. Egyptians and Arabs practised circumcision, but 'the barbaric rite of circumcision was particularly exposed to Hellenistic criticism. For both Greeks and Romans the rite was indecorous and even perverse' (Kuhn, 'περιτέμνω', *TDNT* VI, 78). Hadrian's ban on circumcision in AD 132 (*Historia Augusta*, Hadrian 14.2) put circumcision in the same category as castration, a capital crime. Both Philo (*Spec. Leg.* 1.1) and Josephus (*Ap.* 2.137) admit that circumcision was ridiculed by the Greeks and Romans. Some Jews practised ἐπισπασμός, the restoration of the foreskin, in order to avoid this ridicule in their Hellenistic environment (1 Macc. 1.15). See Moore, *Judaism*, I, p. 351: Hengel, *Judaism and Hellenism*, I, pp. 74, 262, 279, 293; Kuhn, 'περιτέμνω', *TDNT* VI, pp. 78-81.
22. Schmithals, 'Heretics in Galatia', pp. 13-64.
23. Crowfield, 'The Singular Problem of the Dual Galatians', *JBL* 64 (1945), pp. 491-500; Georgi, *Gegner*, pp. 135-36; Brinsmead, pp. 139-61; cf. R. Jewett, 'Agitators', p. 207, who argues that the circumcision message was *delivered* by the agitators from the perspective of Jewish nomism, but the message was *received* by the Galatian Christians from the perspective of the Hellenistic Mystery Religions. My criticisms of Georgi and Brinsmead in this paragraph apply to Jewett's position as well; see below, note 27.
24. Although there is considerable doubt that any of the Gnostic systems were fully developed in the first century, seed ideas for those systems were germinating in Paul's day. See R.M. Grant, *Gnosticism and Early Christianity* (New York: Columbia, 1959), p. 156; G. van Groningen, *First Century Gnosticism: Its Origins and Motifs* (Leiden: Brill, 1967); E. Yamauchi, *Pre-Christian Gnosticism: A Survey of the Proposed Evidences* (London: Tyndale, 1973); R. McL. Wilson, *The Gnostic Problem* (London: Mowbray, 1958), pp. 64-96; *idem*, 'Gnostics—in Galatia?', *SE* 4 (1968), pp. 358-67; *idem*, *Gnosis and the New Testament* (Oxford: Blackwell, 1968), p. 55 n. 42: 'The facts which led Lütgert, Ropes, Schmithals and others to see Gnosticism in some form in Galatia require explanation, but do they indicate a developed *system* or merely the raw material out of which such systems were built?'
25. E.g., E.R. Goodenough, *Jewish Symbols*; M. Hengel, *Judaism and Hellenism*.
26. The texts cited by Schmithals place circumcision in the context of Jewish nomism rather than Gnosticism (e.g. Irenaeus *Haer.* 1.26.2;

Hippolytus, *Philos.* 9.14.1; Epiphanius *Pan.* 19.5). Although Gnostic systems contained Jewish elements, the basic feature of most varieties of Gnosticism was a radical dualism which viewed the OT law as the weapon of the demonic Demiurge. Furthermore, the types of so-called Jewish Gnostic groups which advocated circumcision may not have been Gnostic at all. The Ebionites are more often classified as a deviant group of Jewish Christians (Schoeps, *Jewish Christianity*, pp. 121-30; Drane, *Paul: Libertine or Legalist*, p. 50) than as Gnostics (Schmithals, 'Heretics in Galatia', p. 36). The Elchasaites and Cerinthians may have entertained Gnostic ideas, but the fragmentary nature of the evidence precludes any clear picture of their religious systems. Klijn and Reinick's study of the same evidence brings them to the conclusion that 'patristic observations on Jewish Christianity have no great historical value' (*Patristic Evidence for Jewish Christian Sects* [NovTSup, 36; Leiden: Brill, 1973], p. 69). They also assert that 'we can now be sure that the Jewish Christianity ascribed to the Cerinthians is an invention of early Christian authors' (68). See their review of the evidence (pp. 3-19). Schmithals explains the absence of any requirement of circumcision on the part of Paul's opponents in Corinth by imagining that as the Gnostic mission advanced westward it gave up the practice of circumcision. 'Thus the church's heresy fighters cannot in fact report of any later Gnostics that they practiced circumcision'. Schmithals further admits that 'for gnosticism. . . circumcision is an unnecessary action with only symbolic significance' ('Heretics in Galatia', p. 59 n. 139). In fact, the *Gospel of Thomas* rejects the necessity of physical circumcision: 'His disciples said to him: Is circumcision profitable or not? He said to them: If it were profitable their father would beget them circumcised from their mother. But the true circumcision in Spirit has found complete usefulness' (log. 53).

27. Georgi and Brinsmead support their theory that the opponents viewed circumcision as a rite of initiation into a mystery cult be referring to E.R. Goodenough's work, *Jewish Symbols*. Goodenough describes the use of wine and the mixture of blood and wine in the traditional rite of circumcision. He claims that since the use of wine in circumcision was not authorized in the OT, and since the mixture of blood and wine was considered a powerful medium of a covenant among the Greeks and Romans, Hellenistic notions must have been incorporated into this Jewish rite of circumcision (*Jewish Symbols*, VI, pp. 142-46). However, Goodenough admits that there is no direct evidence for this view and that 'the syncretism has not altered the basic meaning of the rite' (146). Moreover, he is not able to find any Jewish sources which interpret circumcision as a rite of initiation into a mystery cult. Thus, Goodenough's work is not a solid basis for such an interpretation. See Morton Smith's review of Goodenough's work ('Goodenough's *Jewish Symbols* in Retrospect', *JBL* 86 [1967], pp. 53-68). Smith concludes that Goodnenough's 'pandemic sacramental paganism was a fantasy; so was the interpretation of pagan symbols based on it, and so was the empire-wide,

Abraham in Galatians

antirabbinic, mystical Judaism based on the interpretation of these symbols. All three are enormous exaggerations of elements which existed, but were rare, in early imperial times' (65). See also his list of other reviews of Goodenough (pp. 66-67).

Brinsmead also tries to support his theory by injecting his view of the Colossian heresy into the Galatian situation, by confusing baptism and circumcision traditions, and by reducing ἐπιτελέομαι (3.3) to a technical cultic term. On ἐπιτελέομαι see below, p. 263 n. 39.

28. E.g., Deut. 33.2 LXX; Jub. 1.29; Acts 7.53; Heb. 2.2.

29. E.g., Gen. 1.14 LXX: καιρούς... ἡμέρας... ἐνιαυτούς; Jub. 1.15; 2.9; 6.34; 1 En 75. Schoeps (*Paul*, p. 77) argues that there is a distinctively Jewish background to the terminology in 4.10.

30. Three common interpretations of στοιχεῖα (4.3, 9) are (1) 'the elementary teaching' of legal observances (Lightfoot, *Galatians*, 167), (2) 'the law and the flesh' understood as cosmic forces (A.J. Bandstra, *The Law and the Elements of the World*, Kampen: Kok, 1964), and (3) 'demonic forces' which control the cosmic elements and 'this evil age' (Schlier, *Galater*, pp. 192-93; Betz, *Galatians*, pp. 204-205). See Delling, 'στοιχειον', *TDNT* VII, pp. 670-87.

31. *Pace* Schmithals, 'Heretics in Galatia', p. 41: 'an exegesis of Gal. 3.1-5.12 would show that all the sections of this part of the epistle in which the situation in Galatia is not directly addressed (3.6-14; 3.15-18; 3.19-4.7; 4.21-31) contain current *topoi* of Paul's discussion with the *Jews* over the question of the law in which the general proof is brought forward that and why since Christ the law has lost its validity for Christians. None of these sections was conceived for the Galatian epistle'.

32. Those who argue that the opponents referred to Abraham include Barrett, pp. 158-60; Betz, p. 142, n. 29; Bruce, p. 155; Mussner, p. 217; Brinsmead, pp. 107-14; Beker, p. 43; Longenecker, *Biblical Exegesis*, p. 128; Daube, *New Testament and Rabbinic Judaism*, pp. 141, 150; Bligh p. 167; Ridderbos, p. 117; Guthrie, p. 94; Burton, pp. 153-59; Duncan, pp. 87-88. But cf. Byrne, pp. 148-49; Sutherland, p. 145; Schlier, p. 127; Schmithals, p. 41; Crowfield, pp. 495-96, 498.

33. I recognize that any use of the parallels from Jewish literature must heed the cautionary advice of Sandmel, 'Parallelomania', *JBL* 81 (1962), pp. 1-13; see also Neusner, 'Methods and Substance in the History of Judaic Ideal: An Exercise', in *Jews, Greeks, and Christians: Religious Cultures in Late Antiquity: FS W.D.Davies*, eds., Hammerton-Kelly and Scroggs (SJLA, 21; Leiden: Brill, 1976); G. Vermes, 'Jewish Studies and New Testament Interpretations', *JJS* 31 (1980), pp. 1-17; T. Donaldson, 'Parallels: Use, Misuse and Limitations', *EvQ* 55 (1983), pp. 193-210; P.S. Alexander, 'Rabbinic Judaism and the New Testament' *ZNW* 74 (1983), pp. 235-46. In this case, however, the close connection between Abraham and circumcision in Jewish literature is a genuine and illuminating parallel to the circumcision debate in Galatians.

34. See below on 'Abraham in Jewish Literature', pp. 177, 180, 195-95.

35. Borgen, 'Observations on the Theme 'Paul and Philo' in *Die paulinische Literatur und Theologie*, ed., S. Pedersen (Göttingen: Vandenhoeck & Ruprecht, 1980), p. 89; *idem*, 'Paul Preaches Circumcision and Pleases Men', in *Paul and Paulinism: Essays in Honour of C.K. Barrett* (London: SPCK, 1982), pp. 37-46.

36. Borgen 'Observations', pp. 89-90.

37. *Ibid.* Other explanations of Gal. 5.11 are (1) the opponents had in mind Paul's preconversion zeal for circumcision (Schoeps, *Paul*, p. 219), (2) the opponents actually thought that Paul still required physical circumcision since they were unaware of Paul's recent disclosure of his law-free gospel to the Jerusalem council (Howard, *Paul*, pp. 10, 29, 44), and (3) the opponents were confused by such instances as Paul's circumcision of Timothy (Schlier, p. 239; Mussner, p. 360).

38. Borgen, 'Observations', p. 93; *idem*, 'Circumcision', pp. 38-39. See below, p. 191, for references to 'ethical circumcision' in Jewish Literature.

39. See Schlier, *Galaterbrief*, pp. 123-24; Betz, *Galatians*, p. 134; Oepke, p. 68. However, the evidence cannot support Brinsmead's theory that the two verbs ἐνάρχομαι-ἐπιτελέομαι 'comprise a technical formula for progress in religious mystery from a lower to higher stage' (p. 79). According to Brinsmead's theory the opponents were defining circumcision in terms of the Hellenistic mystery religions as a mystery rite of initiation (see above). But although the term ἐπιτελέομαι was used in some cases with cultic overtones (see BAGD, 302; Delling, 'τέλος', *TDNT* VIII, p. 61 with passages listed), it was used more often in non-cultic contexts where it simply meant 'to accomplish' or 'fulfill' (see Delling, *TDNT* VIII, p. 61; especially note the frequent non-cultic use in LXX). Paul uses ἐνάρχομαι-ἐπιτελέομαι elsewhere (2 Cor. 8.6; Phil. 1.6) in a non-cultic sense.

40. Cf. Philo's apology for circumcision in *Spec. Leg.* I, pp. 1-11.

41. Barrett, 'The Allegory of Abraham, Sarah, and Hagar', in his *Essays on Paul* (London: SPCK, 1982), p. 158, argues that Paul's awkward introduction of Gen. 15.6 by the word καθώς is best explained as his response to the opponents' own use of Gen. 15.6 and the Abraham story.

42. See analysis of the argument above, pp. 109-16.

43. See references to Jewish literature below, pp. 177, 180-81, 195.

44. *Pace* Jewett, 'Agitators', p. 207; Munck (*Paul*, p. 132) draws attention to the influential role of the LXX in the Galatian churches. The authority of the Greek OT alone would have been a sufficient basis for the agitators to convince the Galatians that circumcision was necessary if they wanted to enjoy the Abrahamic blessings.

45. See above, pp. 109-29.

46. See above, pp. 129-33.

47. See below, pp. 180-98.

48. See Barrett, 'Allegory', p. 161.

49. Beker, *Paul*, pp. 43, 144; Bornkamm, *Paul*, p. 82; Bruce, *Galatians*,

pp. 229-30; Burton, *Galatians*, p. 274; Jewett, 'Agitators', p. 207; cf. G. Howard, *Paul*, pp. 14-17; Drane, *Paul*, pp. 47-48.

50. Munck (*Paul*, pp. 87-89) argues that περιτεμνόμενοι in 6.13a must refer to Gentiles in the Galatian churches who are presently receiving circumcision, since the verb is in the present tense and since the use of the verb περιτέμνω elsewhere in the epistle (5.2, 3; 6.13, 13b) means 'to receive circumcision', not 'to be a circumcised person' or 'to advocate circumcision'. See also E. Hirsch, 'Zwei Fragen zu Gal. 6', *ZNW* 29 (1930), pp. 192-97; A.E. Harvey, 'The Opposition to Paul', *SE* 4 (1968), p. 324. Against this view, Jewett ('Agitators', pp. 202-203) argues that the past tense would have implied that every person previously circumcised, even as a child, was not keeping the law. But Paul's argument is not so general; he is speaking of those who are currently advocating circumcision (6.12). Therefore, 'it is natural to use the present tense to depict their current advocacy of circumcision' (p. 203). This interpretation retains the strict sense of the present tense, while Munck and Harvey are forced by their perspective to use the past tense in describing 'the recent date' of the circumcision (Munck, p. 89) and 'the Gentiles who have recently become Jewish proselytes' (Harvey, p. 324). Jewett further suggests that the participle should be taken in the middle voice with a causative force; this is, admittedly, a rare use of the middle voice and a exceptional use of this verb, but it is grammatically possible (BDF, p. 166) and fits the context. See also P. Richardson, *Israel in the Apostolic Church* (Cambridge: Cambridge University Press, 1969), pp. 85-86; Howard, *Paul*, pp. 17-19.

51. It was widely accepted Jewish dogma that a Gentile who accepted circumcision, i.e. a proselyte, was obligated to obey the whole law (Kuhn, 'προσήλυτος', *TDNT* VI, p. 739; B.J. Bamberger, *Proselytism in the Talmudic Period* [New York: KTAV, 1968], pp. 31-37; W.G. Braude, *Jewish Proselytizing in the First Five Centuries of the Common Era* [Providence: Brown University Press, 1940], p. 8; Sanders, *Paul*, p. 206). See especially *Sifra Qedeshim* 8.3; *t. Demai* 2. 3-5.

52. E.P. Sanders (*Paul, the Law*, p. 29) suggests that 'Paul's opponents may have adopted a policy of gradualism, requiring first some of the major commandments (circumcision, food, days), a policy which was probably not unique among Jewish missionaries'. One example of the many attempts to reduce in practice the number of demands for new proselytes is the famous story in *Shabb.* 31a: 'a certain heathen came before Shammai and said to him, "Make me a proselyte, on the condition that you teach me the whole Torah while I stand on one foot". Thereupon he repulsed him with the builder's cubit which was in his hand. When he went before Hillel, he converted him; he said to him, 'What is hateful to you, do not do to your neighbor: this is the whole Torah, while the rest is commentary; therefore, go and learn it' (J. Neusner, *Rabbinic Traditions about the Pharisees before 70*, I, pp. 322-23).

53. Dunn ('The New Perspective on Paul', p. 108) calls these two requirements 'badges of covenant membership'.
54. Barrett, 'Allegory', p. 160. There is a debate in the rabbinic literature as to whether a proselyte should be called σπέρμα Ἀβραάμ or 'sons of Abraham'. Drane (*Paul*, pp. 28, 82) and Brinsmead (*Galatians*, pp. 111, 280) assert on the basis of texts listed in Str-B I, pp. 116-21 that proselytes were not given this title. See *m. Bik.* 1.4 and *Num. Rab.* 8. It appears, however, that the Str-B list is selective, Cf. Braude (*Jewish Proselytizing*, pp. 80-83, 97-99) and Bamberger (*Proselytism*, p. 67): 'Although there was some difference among the Tannaim, the view of R. Judah prevailed that in prayer converts may use the formula 'God of our fathers' (Bamberger, p. 67); 'The rabbis widened "the children of Israel" concept by renaming them children of Abraham' and bringing within the latter classification all who had heeded his summons to come and worship the one God of the universe' (Braude, 99). Also see below, p. 207-208, for discussion of Daube, 'The Interpretation of a Generic Singular' in his *NT and Rabbinic Judaism*, pp. 438-44.
55. Brinsmead, *Galatians*, pp. 111-14. See below, p. 266 n. 2, for a discussion of the sources.
56. Brinsmead points to Paul's claim that his apostleship is authenticated by a personal commission from God and to Paul's use of ἐπιτελέομαι (3.3) as evidence that the opponents presented Abraham as a prophet, inspired by God, and as the one who journeys on his religious quest (pp. 113-14). This evidence, however, does not demand Brinsmead's theory. Even if it could be demonstrated that the opponents presented these pictures of Abraham, they could have derived them directly from the biblical account without any reference to the 'apologetic' literature cited by Brinsmead.
57. See the hypothesis of R. Jewett ('Agitators', p. 205) that 'the Jewish Christians in Judea were stimulated by Zealotic pressure into a nomistic campaign among their fellow Christians in the late forties and early fifties. Their goal was to avert the suspicion that they were in communion with lawless Gentiles. It appears that the Judean Christians convinced themselves that circumcision of Gentile Christians would thwart Zealot reprisals'.
58. See above, p. 148. The distinction which Paul makes between 'you' (you Galatian believers) and 'they' (the agitators) seems to indicate that the agitators had come from outside the Galatian churches (*pace* Munck, *Paul*, pp. 87-134).

Notes to Appendix 2

1. For a survey of pre-1972 studies of Abraham in Jewish literature, see B.E. Schein, 'Our Father Abraham' (Ph.D. Dissertation, Yale Univeristy, 1972), pp. 1-18. Since 1972 the works on Abraham in Jewish literature include J.D. Mayer, 'Aspekte des Abrahambildes in der hellenistisch-

jüdischen Literatur', *EvT* 32 (1972), pp. 118-27; D.J. Harrington, 'Abraham Traditions in the Testament of Abraham and in the 'Rewritten Bible' of the Intertestamental Period', *SBL Pseudepigrapha Seminar Papers* (1972), pp. 155-64; J. Van Seters, *Abraham in History and Tradition* (New Haven: Yale University Press, 1975); E. Lucchesi, 'Nouveau parallèle entre Saint Paul (Gal. 3.16) et Philon d'Alexandrie (Questiones im Genesis)?' *NovT* 21 (1979), pp. 150-55; B. Byrne, *'Sons of God'—'Seed of Abraham': A Study of the Idea of the Sonship of God of all Christians in Paul against the Jewish Background* (AnBib, 83; Rome: Biblical Institute, 1979); E.E. Urbach, *The Sages: Their Concepts and Beliefs*, 2nd edn (trans. I. Abrahams; Jerusalem: Magnes Press, 1979); H. Moxnes, *Theology in Conflict: Studies in Paul's Understanding of God in Romans* (NovTSup, 53; Leiden: Brill, 1980), pp. 117-94; T. Dozemann, *'Sperma Abraam* in John 8 and Related Literature: Cosmology and Judgment', *CBQ* 42 (1980), pp. 345-58; H.H. Schmid, 'Gerechtigkeit und Glaube: Gen. 15.6 und sein biblisch-theologischer Kontext', *EvT* 40 (1980), pp. 396-420; L. Gaston, 'Abraham and the Righteousness of God', *Horizons in Biblical Theology* 2 (1980), pp. 39-68; T.P. McGonigal, '"Abraham believed God": Genesis 15.6 and its Use in the New Testament' (Ph.D. Dissertation, Fuller Theological Seminary, 1981), pp. 48-229; D.D. Sutherland, 'Genesis 15.6: A Study in Ancient Jewish and Christian Interpretation' (Ph.D. Dissertation, Southern Baptist Theological Seminary, 1982), pp. 6-136; J.S. Siker, 'Disinheriting the Jews: The Use of Abraham in Early Christian Controversy with Judaism from Paul through Justin Martyr' (Ph.D. Dissertation, Princeton Theological Seminary, 1988).

2. Many other features could be considered—e.g., the apocalyptic visions of Abraham, the scientific and philosophical knowledge of Abraham, the military prowess of Abraham, etc. But these features are not paralleled in Paul's portrayal of the patriarch, and so are omitted from this study. Brinsmead's (pp. 110-13) emphasis on the 'apologetic' aspects of Abraham is not germane to the study of Galatians since there is no evidence that such aspects were under discussion at Galatia.

3. E.P. Sanders (*Paul*, pp. 1-59) provides a survey of the literature on the larger issue of Paul and Judaism. The two stances mentioned here are to be understood within the context of that discussion.

4. Str.B, II, p. 186.

5. E.g., Lightfoot, *Galatians*, p. 163; Betz, *Galatians*, pp. 139, 141; Bruce, *Galatians*, p. 153.

6. Although E.P. Sanders (*Paul*, pp. 1-34) points to others (such as G.F. Moore, C.G. Montefiore, S. Schechter, S. Sandmel and W.D. Davies) who attacked the traditional thesis that Paul is the antithesis of Judaism, Sanders is certainly the chief spokesman against this thesis. I will, therefore, refer primarily to his work.

7. The literature which Sanders examines includes the Tannaitic

literature, DSS, Sirach, 1 Enoch, Jubilees, the Psalms of Solomon, and 4 Ezra.

8. Sanders, *Paul*, p. 75.

9. *Ibid.*, p. 233. Thus, for instance, Sanders will not allow for Longenecker's thesis that there was both an 'acting legalism' and a 'reacting nomism' in first century Judaism (*Paul*, pp. 56-57; cf. R. Longenecker, *Paul, Apostle of Liberty*, pp. 67-84).

10. The portrait of Abraham is not the primary subject of Sanders' work, though he makes frequent reference to it (*Paul*, pp. 28, 87, 89-93, 97-101, 109, 117, 133, 184, 191, 195-97, 201, 271, 363-65, 367, 371, 379, 389, 396, 404).

11. Most post-Sanders studies grant that Sanders' work provides a new perspective; e.g., W.D. Davies, *Paul and Rabbinic Judaism*, 4th edn, p. xxix; L. Gaston, 'Abraham and the Righteousness of God', pp. 37-41, 59; J. Dunn, 'The New Perspective on Paul', pp. 95-100.

12. Sanders, *Paul*, pp. 544, 205.

13. *Ibid.*, pp. 420-28.

14. Sanders' argument here is against the views of Weber, Charles, Bousset, Billerbeck, Bultmann, Rössler, Barrett, Ziesler, and Buchanan; see *Paul*, pp. 36-59, 183-86.

15. Sanders, *Paul*, p. 197.

16. See above, pp. 113-39, 147-50.

17. See a recent survey of the problems by P.S. Alexander, 'Rabbinic Judaism and the New Testament', *ZNW* 74 (1983), pp. 235-46.

18. G.F. Moore, 'Christian Writers on Judaism', *HTR* 14 (1921), p. 253.

19. B.E. Schein's topical approach ('Our Father Abraham'), wherein he has a mixture of references to all strands of Jewish literature, leaves the impression that all the Jewish sources are saying the same thing; the diversity of perspectives is lost.

20. Sandmel, *Philo's Place*, p. 29.

21. E.g., O. Schmitz, 'Abraham im Spätjudentum und im Urchristentum' in *Aus Schrift und Geschichte* (Stuttgart: Calwer, 1922), pp. 99-123.

22. Although the promise is presented here as a reward for obedience, the content of that promise has already been given in the call of Abraham in Gen. 12.1-3. So this is a reconfirmation on the basis of obedience. Thus the promises were not viewed as merited by Abraham's virtuous deed. *Pace* R.J. Daly, 'The Soteriological Significance of the Sacrifice of Isaac', *CBQ* 39 (1977), p. 473: 'No imagination is needed to see how important such a text (Gen. 22) would be for a theology whose basic soteriological theory centered around the idea of justification by works of obedience to the law'.

23. Westermann, *The Promises to the Fathers*, p. 75.

24. D. Sutherland, 'The Organization of the Abraham Promise Narratives', *ZAW* 95 (1983), pp. 340-41.

25. Westermann, *The Promises*, pp. 15-18.

26. See von Rad, 'Faith Reckoned as Righteousness', in his *The Problem of the Hexateuch and Other Essays* (trans. E. Dicken; New York: McGraw-Hill, 1966), p. 129: 'In a solemn statement concerning the divine purpose, it is laid down that it is faith which sets men on a right footing with God. Yahweh has disclosed his plan for the future, which is to make Abraham a great nation. Abraham has fully accepted this, has put his trust in Yahweh. ... he [the writer] says that only faith, which is the wholehearted acceptance of Yahweh's promise, brings man into a right relationship—that Yahweh "reckons" it to him'. M. Oemig ('Ist Genesis 15,6 ein Beleg für die Anrechnung des Glaubens zur Gerechtigkeit?' *ZAW* 95 [1983], pp. 182-97) and L. Gaston ('Abraham and the Righteousness of God') have attempted to counter von Rad's interpretation by their insistence that Gen. 15.6 should be translated: 'And he (Abraham) put his trust in YHWH, and he (Abraham) counted it to him (YHWH) as righteousness'. The only support that can be found for this translation, however, is a 13th century rabbi (Nachmanides, 1194-1270 C.E.). The appeal to the structure of the oracle of salvation and the phenomenon of Hebrew parallelism is not convincing, since this text does not conform in important respects to these structures.

27. See Sandmel, *Philo's Place*, pp. 31-34.

28. L. Gaston ('Abraham and the Righteousness of God', p. 47) comments on Isa. 51.1-8: 'By reference back to Abraham, Israel is urged to take comfort in and rely on the righteousness of God which is now being exercised'. As he points out, the salvation for the Gentiles is also connected with the figure of Abraham in this context (Isa. 51.4-6). These helpful insights, however, do not demand his interpretation of Gen. 15.6 (see above, note 26).

29. Moxnes, *Theology in Conflict*, p. 125: 'Thus the emphasis upon God as the guarantor of his promise ran through the various texts, as a substructure, so to speak'.

30. Nickelsburg, *Jewish Literature between the Bible and the Mishnah* (Philadelphia: Fortress 1981), pp. 55-56.

31. Sanders, *Paul*, p. 331: '"The Covenant" seems to be basically a unitary conception in Ben Sirach, and it is defined primarily as being embodied in the Mosaic Torah'.

32. Quotations are from R.H. Charles, *Apocrypha and Pseudepigrapha*.

33. So Sutherland, 'Genesis 15.6', p. 91.

34. The use of 'the covenant of Abraham' to denote circumcision is also found in Jubilees 15.9-34, *m. Aboth* 3.12, *b. Sanh.* 99a; *b. Yoma* 85b.

35. This same combination is also found in 1 Macc. 2.52, James 2.21-24, and Heb. 11.17.

36. Hahn, 'Genesis 15.6 im Neuen Testament', in his *Probleme biblischer Theologie* (Munich: Kaiser, 1971), pp. 95-96; Moxnes, *Theology in Conflict*, p. 129.

37. Sirach 44.22 states that Isaac received the promise on the basis of Abraham's merit. See Sandmel, *Philo's Place*, p. 36.

38. See Nickelsburg, *Jewish Literature*, pp. 73-80; J.C. Vanderkam, *Textual and Historical Studies in the Book of Jubilees* (HSM, 14; Missoula: Scholars Press, 1977).

39. Sandmel, *Philo's Place*, p. 49.

40. See Nickelsburg, *Jewish Literature*, pp. 114-17; Charles, *Apocrypha*, pp. 221-62; C. Dancy, *A Commentary on 1 Maccabees* (Oxford: Blackwell, 1954); S. Zeitlin, *The First Book of Maccabees* (New York: Harper, 1950), pp. 1-66. Zeitlin argues that the testament of Mattathias was added to the book after the destruction of the Temple (p. 32). However, the dissimilarity with the speech provided by Josephus and the reference to Daniel and his friends (2.59-60) are not compelling bits of evidence for his proposal. Josephus often introduces different emphases (see, for example, his treatment of Abraham below, p. 193-94) and arguments have been made for a pre-Maccabean date for Dan 1-6 (see J. Dancy, *A Commentary on 1 Maccabees*, 87). Quotations are from Charles, *Apocrypha*.

41. J. Ziesler, *The Meaning of Righteousness in Paul*, p. 104.

42. S. Zeitlin (*The Book of Judith* [Leiden: Brill, 1972] p. 28) proposes a date in the late Hasmonean period based on the many similarities to the Maccabean struggles.

43. The Psalms of Solomon were written in the middle of the 1st century B.C.E. by pious Hasidim. See Sanders, *Paul*, pp. 387-88, and the literature cited by him. Quotations are from Charles, *Pseudepigrapha*.

44. The debate regarding the date of *The Testaments of the Twelve Patriarchs* has occasioned a full-scale review: H.D. Singerland, *The Testaments of the Twelve Patriarchs: A Critical History of Research* (SBLMS, 21; Missoula: Scholars, 1977). On the one hand M. de Jonge sets their date of composition between 190 and 225 C.E. (M. de Jonge, *The Testaments of the Twelve Patriarchs: A Study of Their Text, Composition, and Origin* [Assen: van Gorcum, 1953], p. 125; *Studies on the Testaments of the Twelve patriarchs*, ed., M. de Jonge [Leiden: Brill, 1975], pp. 180-47). On the other hand, A. Dupont-Sommer argues that the Testaments should be dated early in the first century B.C.E. (Dupont-Sommer, *The Essene Writings from Qumran*, trans. G. Vermes [Oxford: Blackwell, 1961], pp. 301-305). Since the Qumran sect possessed a work very similar to our present Testament of Levi, that Testament, at least, may be dated in the first century B.C.E. Quotations are from Charles, *Pseudepigrapha*.

45. The Testament of Abraham has been described by M. Delcor as a midrashic account, written in Egypt around the turn of the era under the influence of the LXX and Palestinian Targum; see Delcor, *Le Testament d'Abraham* (SVTP, 2; Leiden: Brill, 1973), pp. 63-77. For a review of the literature, see Nickelsburg, ed., *Studies on the Testament of Abraham* SBLSCS, 6; Missoula: Scholars, 1976), pp. 9-22. Quotations are from M.E. Stone, *The Testament of Abraham* (Text and Translations: Pseudepigrapha Series, 2; Missoula: SBL, 1972).

46. *The Assumption of Moses* (= *The Testament of Moses*) in its present form is a product of the early 1st century C.E. Chapter 6 contains references to the Herodians. However, chs. 6–7 may have been added to an earlier work which was written in the early Maccabean era. See Nickelsburg, *Jewish Literature*, p. 80; Nickelsburg, ed., *Studies on the Testament of Moses*, pp. 15-52.

47. J. Bowker, *The Targums and Rabbinic Literature* (Cambridge: Cambridge University Press, 1969), pp. 30-31; Bowker dates this work in the first century C.E. shortly after the fall of Jerusalem. See also M.R. James, *The Biblical Antiquities of Philo* (London: SPCK, 1917); Nickelsburg, *Jewish Literature*, p. 265-68. Quotations are from Bowker, pp. 301-14.

48. Moxnes, *Theology in Conflict*, p. 166: 'The author was concerned to emphasize the Torah as the absolute norm for Israel. However, the crisis of year 70 had shattered the basis for confidence in God's plans and promises in the Torah. As a result, it was first necessary to rebuild trust in God. One way of doing that was to prove how God in the course of history actually had fulfilled his promises. Accordingly, when narrating Biblical history, the author sometimes inserts references to earlier promises that had now been fulfilled'.

49. Nickelsburg, *Jewish Literature*, p. 298.

50. *Ibid.*, p. 287. 4 Ezra (also known as Second Esdras in the Apocrypha) is a Jewish Apocalypse which has its fictional setting in Babylon after the destruction of Jerusalem (c. 557 B.C.E.). It was written approximately thirty years after the Roman destruction of Jerusalem in 70 C.E.

51. Sanders, *Paul*, p. 418; for a more positive interpretation, see E. Breech, 'These Fragments I have Shored against My Ruins: The Form and Function of 4 Ezra', *JBL* 92 (1973), pp. 267-74; A.C. Thompson, *Responsibility for Evil in the Theodicy of IV Ezra* (SBLDS, 29; Missoula: Scholars, 1977). See Thompson's survey of the history of research (pp. 83-120).

52. Nickelsburg, *Jewish Literature*, pp. 280-81.

53. See Sanders, *Paul*, pp. 239-328, for a comprehensive survey of the soteriology of DSS. Quotations are from Vermes, *The Dead Sea Scrolls in English*.

54. Vermes, *The Dead Seas Scrolls in English*, p. 39.

55. Moxnes, *Theology in Conflict*, p. 128.

56. Sandmel, *Philo's Place*, p. 96.

57. *Ibid.*, p. 106.

58. E.R. Goodenough (*By Light, Light: The Mystic Gospel of Hellenistic Judaism* [Amsterdam: Philo Press, 1969], p. 137-38) argues that Philo schematizes the Abraham material in terms of Pythagorean Neo-Platonism.

59. *Ibid.*, pp. 48-94.

60. Sandmel, *Philo's Place*, p. 197.

61. *Ibid.*, pp. 107-108, 191, 201.

62. *Ibid.*, p. 147 n. 221, 160; also P. Borgen, 'Observations on the Theme "Paul and Philo": Paul's Preaching of Circumcision in Galatia (Gal. 5.11)

and Debates on Circumcision in Philo', in *Die paulinische Literatur und Theologie*, ed., S. Pedersen (Göttingen: Vandenhoeck & Ruprecht, 1980) pp. 85-89.

63. The spiritual journey of proselytes is described by Philo in terms similar to those used of Abraham (*Virt.* 175-86). Philo's ethical interpretation of circumcision has raised the question as to whether he viewed bodily circumcision as a necessary requirement for proselytes. An examination of the passages seems to confirm Moore's explanation that Philo did not remove the requirement of circumcision, but he emphasized that 'what makes a proselyte is not circumcision of the flesh but the circumcison of pleasures and appetites and other affections of the soul' (Moore, I, p. 328 n. 1; Kuhn, 'προσήλυτος', TDNT VI, p. 732).

64. P. Borgen, 'Observations', pp. 86-88; *idem*, 'Paul Preaches Circumcision', in *Paul and Paulinism: Essays in honour of C.K. Barrett*, eds., M.D. Hooker and S.G. Wilson (London: SPCK, 1982), p. 39.

65. Sandmel, *Philo's Place*, p. 139.

66. Moxnes, *Theology in Conflict*, p. 160.

67. *Ibid.*, pp. 163-64.

68. *Ibid.*, pp. 155-59; Sutherland, pp. 116-35; McGonigal, pp. 126-87.

69. Sandmel, *Philo's Place*, pp. 75-76.

70. Our survey of the rabbinic traditions about Abraham does not attempt to solve the difficult problem of dating this material. Since these traditions are, for the most part, a further elaboration of traditions which we have already examined, we are simply tracing the trajectory of their development. While this trajectory enables us to see certain tendencies which may have been at work in the first century, there is no intention of anachronistically importing the fruition of these tendencies back into the 1st century context.

71. Sandmel, *Philo's Place*, p. 77-95.

72. The mishnaic reference to making void the covenant of Abraham is explained in the Gemara to mean epispasm, the restoration of the foreskin.

73. Bamberger, *Proselytism in the Talmudic Period*, p. 67.

74. Sanders, *Paul*, pp. 206-207.

75. *Ibid.*, p. 207.

76. Sandmel, *Philo's Place*, p. 95.

Notes to Appendix 3

1. D. Cohn-Sherbok, 'Paul and Rabbinic Exegesis', *SJT* 35 (1982), p. 132; J. Bonsirven, *Exégèse rabbinique et exégèse paulinienne* (Paris: Beauchesne, 1939), p. 348; H.J. Schoeps, *Paul* (Philadelphia: Westminster, 1961), p. 39: 'He [Paul] tries with the resources of traditional rabbinic logic

to gain from the text new meanings by a process of inference and combination with other texts. The methods of proof characteristic of his writings make it clear that he had learnt in the schools the seven hermeneutical rules of Hillel for the Halakha'. See also A.T. Hanson, *Studies in Paul's Technique and Theology* (London: SPCK, 1974), pp. 206-207; N. Dahl, *Studies in Paul* (Minneapolis: Augsburg, 1977), p. 175; W.D. Davies, *Jewish and Pauline Studies* (London: SPCK, 1974), pp. 176-77; E.E. Ellis, *Paul's Use of the OT* (Edinburgh: Oliver & Boyd, 1957), p. 38; D.H. King, 'Paul and the Tannaim: A Study in Galatians', *WTJ* 45 (1983), pp. 361-70.

2.   Ellis, *Paul's Use of the OT*, p. 119. See also J.C. Beker, *Paul*, p. 47, who labels Gal. 3 'the midrash on Abraham'; F. Mussner, *Galaterbrief*, p. 212: 'Paulus ist φύσει Ἰουδαῖος und rabbinisch geschult. Und so kennt er die göttliche Autorität der Schrift und ihre imfassende und normative Geltung. Er beherrscht auch die Regeln der rabbinischen Schriftauslegung, vor allem die Regeln der Kombinatorik von Schriftstellen zum Zweck eines Schriftbeweises'.

3.   See the lexical study of מדרש and דרש by A.G. Wright, 'The Literary Genre Midrash', *CBQ* 28 (1966), pp. 113-20; and G. Porton, 'Defining Midrash', in *The Study of Ancient Judaism*, ed. J. Neusner (2 vols.; New York: KTAV, 1981), I, pp. 56-58.

4.   For a history of the debate see M. Miller, 'Targum, Midrash and the Use of the OT in the NT', *JSJ* 2 (1971), pp. 36-49; G. Porton, 'Defining Midrash', pp. 55-61.

5.   A. Wright, 'The Literary Genre Midrash', p. 108.

6.   D. Moo, *The Old Testament in the Gospel Passion Narratives* (Sheffield: Almond, 1983), pp. 5-6; see also G. Porton, pp. 60-61.

7.   A. Wright, 'The Literary Genre Midrash', pp. 120-28; Many have objected that this definition of midrash is too narrow since midrashic exegesis appears in many different types of literary genre outside of rabbinic literature. See R. Le Déaut, 'A propos d'une définition du Midrash', *Bib* 59 (1969), pp. 395-413 (ET in *Int* 25 [1971], pp. 259-83); G. Porton, p. 60.

8.   D. Moo, pp. 59-66; see also D. Patte, *Early Jewish Hermeneutic in Palestine* (Missoula: SBL, 1975), pp. 319-21. In Tannaitic midrashim, haggadic and halakic midrash—the homiletical and the scholastic—are often found intermixed. See G. Porton, pp. 77-78, and E.P. Sanders, *Paul*, pp. 26-27.

9.   R. Longenecker, *Biblical Exegesis in the Apostolic Period* (Grand Rapids: Eerdmans, 1975), pp. 32-38. These three sets of hermeneutical rules are listed in H.L. Strack, *Introduction to the Talmud and Midrash*, pp. 93-98; the seven *middoth* of Hillel are found in *Aboth de R. Nathan* 37 and *tos. Sanh.* 7.11; see also the discussion in J.W. Doeve, *Jewish Hermeneutics in the Synoptic Gospels and Acts*, pp. 66-75.

10.   Bonsirven, pp. 27-32, 339-45. Cf. B. Metzger, 'The Formulas

Introducing Quotations of Scripture in the NT and the Mishnah', *JBL* 70 (1951), pp. 298-300; E. Ellis, 'How the New Testament Uses the Old', in his *Prophecy and Hermeneutic in Early Christianity: New Testament Essays* (WUNT 18; Tübingen: Mohr, 1978), pp. 148-50; *idem, Paul's Use of the OT*, pp. 48-49.

11. Ellis, *Paul's Use of the OT*, p. 48; e.g., *b. Sanh.* 2a; CD 9.8.
12. Moore, *Judaism*, I, p. 240; e.g., *b. Pes.* 81b; *b. Yeb.* 39a.
13. Moore, I, p. 240.
14. King, 'Paul and the Tannaim', pp. 365-66.
15. See the distinguishing literary features of rabbinic midrash listed by G. Porton, 'Defining Midrash', p. 79: (1) rabbinic texts are collections of independent units; (2) there is often more than one comment per biblical unit; (3) a large number of statements are assigned to a named sage; (4) the rabbinic comment may be directly connected to the biblical unit or it may be part of a dialogue, a story, or an extended soliloquy; and (5) rabbinic midrash atomizes the text.
16. Longenecker (*Biblical Exegesis*, pp. 19-20) lists four theological presuppositions common to all Jewish interpreters: (1) the divine inspiration of the Scriptures, (2) multiple meanings in the text, (3) the necessity of dealing with the plain meaning and the implied meaning, and (4) the necessity of making the text relevant.
17. See above on the hermeneutical axioms of rabbinic midrash, p. 201-202.
18. A.T. Hanson, *Studies*, p. 209.
19. G. Porton, 'Defining Midrash', p. 75: 'The pesher is essentially a running commentary with reference to eschatological events. It is the eschatological content of the pesher together with the appearance of the root *psr* which are the essential characteristics of this midrashic form'. E. Ellis, *Prophecy*, p. 190: 'Qumran pesher reflects an eschatological perspective similar to the New Testament and unlike that in rabbinic midrash'.
20. Dahl, *Studies*, p. 105: 'Paul uses exegetical methods common to the Judaism of his day. Nevertheless, he achieves results which directly contradict those which Jewish and Judaizing exegetes obtained. The reason for this is his presupposition that these passages agree with his understanding of God's act and revelation in Jesus Christ'. Cf. Longenecker, *Biblical Exegesis*, p. 104: 'Together with the earliest Jewish Christians, Paul understood the Old Testament Christologically. And he worked from the same two fixed points: (1) the Messiahship and Lordship of Jesus, as validated by the resurrection and as witnessed to by the Spirit; and (2) the revelation of God in the Scriptures of the Old Testament. But though in his own experience a true understanding of Christ preceded a proper understanding of Scripture, in his exegetical endeavors he habitually began with Scripture and moved on to Christ'.
21. So Schoeps, Cohn-Sherbok, Bonsirven, Hanson, Ellis, Longenecker, *et al.*

22. For a recent bibliography on midrash, see L. Haas, 'Bibliography on Midrash', in *The Study of Ancient Judaism*, ed., J. Neusner (New York: KTAV, 1981), I, pp. 93-99; see also W.S. Towner, 'Hermeneutical Systems of Hillel and the Tannaim: A Fresh Look', *HUCA* 53 (1982), pp. 101-35.

23. On the origin and development of rabbinic midrash, see Miller, 'Targum, Midrash', pp. 45-48.

24. See *b. Pes.* 66a; *y. Pes.* 6; *t. Pes.* 4.1-3; Longenecker, *Biblical Exegesis*, pp. 33-34; S. Zeitlin insists that Hillel should not be regarded as the initiator, but as the codifier of the *middoth* ('Hillel and the Hermeneutical Rules', *JQR* 54 [1963], pp. 161-73).

25. J. Bowker, *Targums and Rabbinic Literature*, p. 315.

26. Dahl (*Studies*, pp. 161-64) argues that this rule was originally *shene kethubim* (two passages) and was the basis for the 13th *middah* of Ishmael; see below, pp. 206-207.

27. R. Bloch ('Midrash' in *DBSup*, V, pp. 1265-66) presents the two primary characteristics of midrash as 'le rattachement et la référence constante à l'Ecriture' and 'l'adaptation au présent'. See Porton, p. 62; G. Vermes, *Scripture and Tradition*, pp. 7-9.

28. G.F. Moore, *Judaism*, I, p. 248.

29. D. Daube, 'Rabbinic Methods of Interpretation and Hellenistic Rhetoric', *HUCA* 22 (1949), pp. 239-64.

30. S. Lieberman, 'Rabbinic Interpretation of Scripture', in *Essays in Greco-Roman and Related Literature*, ed. H.A. Fischel (New York: KTAV, 1977), pp. 289-324.

31. Lieberman, p. 320.

32. Daube, p. 258.

33. P. Alexander, 'Rabbinic Judaism and the New Testament', *ZNW* 74 (1983), p. 246.

34. See M. Hengel, *Hellenism and Judaism*, I, p. 81: The educational system of the Rabbinate was probably influenced by the model of the Greek rhetorical schools'. Daube (p. 241) notes that Hillel's teachers, Shemaiah and Abtalion, are represented in the Talmud (*b. Pes.* 70b) as proselytes who had studied and taught at Alexandria.

35. Alexander, p. 246; G. Vermes ('Bible and Midrash: Early OT Exegesis', in his *Post-Biblical Studies* [Studies in Judaism in Late Antiquity (ed. J. Neusner; Leiden: Brill, 1975], p. 81) says that 'in principle, if not always in application, the *middot* of Hillel and Ishmael are commonsense rules of logic and literary criticism demanding *a fortiori* or analogical inference, confrontation of the general statute with the particular, comparison of parallel passages, and study of the context'. Daube (p. 254), however, argues that the 'naturalness' of the hermeneutical rules cannot explain the parallels between Hillel's rules and Hellenistic rhetoric. For although the ordinary person may use a rhetoical device such as the inference *a fortiori*, he will not normally be aware of the exact nature of his deduction, nor will he codify it

in a list with various other modes of deduction.

36. Ellis, *Paul's Use of the OT*, pp. 49-50; Moore, *Judaism*, I, p. 239: 'Proof-texts are often quoted in threes, a verse from the Pentateuch, another from the Prophets, and a third from the Hagiographa, not as though the word of the Law needed confirmation, but to show how the Scripture emphasizes the lesson by iteration'. E.g. *b. Meg.* 31a; *b. Ber* 18a; *b. Mak.* 16a; *b. Pes.* 7b, 8a.

37. While Paul does not strictly follow the rabbinical manner in the formation of his chain of quotations, he does emphasize and apply his thesis text by iteration.

38. See J. Fischer, 'Pauline Literary Forms and Thought Patterns', *CBQ* 39 (1977), pp. 209-33.

39. See E.P. Sanders, *Paul, and the Law and the Jewish People*, p. 21: 'We should consider how Paul chooses the quotations in Gal. 3. The argument is terminological. It depends on finding proof texts for the view that *Gentiles* are *righteoused* by *faith*. Those three words are crucial, and Paul is able to link Gentiles to 'righteoused by faith' through the Abraham story. Abraham is thus the middle term, being connected with Gentiles in one proof text and righteousness by faith in another. In the course of this argument Paul cites the only two passages in the Septuagint (LXX) in which the *dik-* root is connected with *pistis* (Gen. 15.6; Hab. 2.4)'.

40. J.W. Doeve, *Jewish Hermeneutic in the Synoptic Gospels and Acts* (Assen: van Gorcum, 1954), p. 116; D. Patte, *Early Jewish Hermeneutic*, pp. 66-67.

41. F. Hahn, 'Genesis 15.6 im Neuen Testament', in his *Probleme biblischer Theologie* (Munich: Kaiser, 1971), p. 99.

42. Ellis, *Paul's Use of the OT*, pp. 50-51; e.g., *b. Sanh* 38b.

43. Ellis, 'Midrash Pesher in Pauline Hermeneutics', in his *Prophecy and Hermeneutic in Early Christianity: New Testament Essays* (WUNT, 18; Tübingen: Mohr, 1978), pp. 177-81.

44. Paul's quotation in Gal. 3.8 agrees with Gen. 12.3 in the use of the direct address (ἐν σοί) and with Gen. 18.18 in the use of πάντα τὰ ἔθνη.

45. Cohn-Sherbok, 'Paul and Rabbinic Exegesis', p. 131.

46. Bonsirven, *Exégèse* p. 319: 'pour formuler sa thèse sur la justification par la foi S. Paul se sert des deux sentences de l'Ecriture qui expriment le principe, au concret pour Abraham (Gen. 15.6: Gal. 3.6; Rom. 4.3), et dans l'abstrait et en général (Hab. 2.4 quelque peu schématizé: Rom. 1.17; Gal. 3.11)'.

47. See above, p. 202.

48. Bonsirven, *Exégèse*, p. 298.

49. See above, p. 203-204.

50. Jeremias, 'Paulus als Hillelit', in *New Testamentica et Semitica: Studies in Honour of M. Black*, eds. E.E. Ellis and M. Wilcox (Edinburgh: T. & T. Clark, 1969), p. 93; Longenecker, *Biblical Exegesis*, p. 118.

51. Schoeps, *Paul*, pp. 177-78; followed by Drane, *Paul*, p. 30; Hübner *Gesetz*, p. 43; D. King, 'Paul and the Tannaim', p. 365. Cf. also Hays, *Faith of Jesus Christ*, pp. 218-21; Betz, *Galatians*, p. 138 n. 8.

52. Dahl, *Studies*, p. 161.

53. *Ibid.*, p. 164.

54. *Ibid.*, p. 171.

55. *Ibid.*

56. *Ibid.*, p. 172.

57. *Ibid.*, p. 175.

58. See the criticisms by Betz, *Galatians*, p. 138 n. 8; and Hays, *Faith of Jesus Christ*, pp. 218-21. They claim that Schoeps' analysis fails because the third text (Gen. 15.6) which was supposedly quoted to resolve the contradiction does not follow the two contradictory texts. They also object to Dahl's theory because verses 13-18 and 19-25 do not make any explicit reference to the texts which they supposedly explain. These criticisms appear to demand a degree of correspondence with the hermeneutical rule which would probably exclude many procedures in rabbinic literature. They also overlook Schoeps suggestion that Gen. 15.6 is recapitulated in v. 14 and Dahl's observance that the question in v. 19 is at least partially a reference to v. 12.

59. The objection that Paul does not view Hab. 2.4 and Lev. 18.5 as contradictory passages, but uses them to prove separate points in a consecutive argument (Betz, *Galatians*, p. 128 n. 8; Hays, *Faith of Jesus Christ*, pp. 218-21) fails to recognize the series of antitheses which Paul has set up in his argument and which he sharpens by the use of these two contradictory texts. See analysis above, pp. 169-72.

60. Ellis, *Paul's Use of the OT*, p. 70 n. 4; Daube, 'Generic Singular', pp. 440-44; Bonsirven, p. 298; Cohn-Sherbok, pp. 121-22; King, p. 365; e.g., *b. Shab.* 84b ('seed'); *b. Sanh.* 37a and *Gen. Rab.* 22.9 (blood).

61. See M. Wilcox, 'The Promise of the "Seed" in the New Testament and the Targumin', *JSNT* 5 (1979), 3; F. Pereira, 'The Galatian Controversy in the Light of the Targums', *IJT* 20 (1971), p. 27.

62. In a biblical context, see Gen. 4.25 (Seth); Gen. 21.12, 13 (Isaac and Ishmael); and 2 Sam. 7.12-15; for evidence in the rabbinic literature, see D. Daube, 'Generic Singular', pp. 439-43.

63. Daube, p. 441.

64. Longenecker, *Biblical Exegesis*, pp. 123-24.

65. Paul's exegesis of 'seed' is based on his understanding of the corporate solidarity of Christ and those who belong to Christ. See Longenecker, *Biblical Exegesis*, p. 124; C.A.A. Scott, *Christianity According to St. Paul*, p. 155.

66. The significance of this redefinition and restriction of the meaning of 'seed' is developed above, p. 129.

67. Jeremias, 'Paulus als Hillelit', p. 94; Longenecker, *Biblical Exegesis*, p. 118.

68. See above, p. 194.
69. Daube, 'Generic Singular', pp. 440-41.
70. See *Seder 'Olam* 3; *Mekilta Exod.* 12.40; *Gen. Rab.* 63; Josephus, *Ant.* 2.15.2; Str-B, II, pp. 668-71; Daube, 'Generic Singular', p. 440.
71. Gal. 3.6.
72. Ellis, *Paul's Use of the OT*, pp. 74-76.
73. E.g., repetition of key words, implications from the text, and interpretation by analogy.
74. Büchsel, 'ἀλλεγορέω', *TDNT* I, p. 260.
75. *Ibid.*; A.T. Hanson, *Studies in Paul's Technique and Theology*, pp. 91-95; A.T. Lincoln, *Paradise Now and Not Yet*, p. 13, points out that the present tense of the participle ἀλληγορούμενα parallels the present tense in v. 30, τὶ λέγει ἡ γραφή.
76. See Bligh, *Galatians*, p. 393.
77. O. Michel, *Paulus und seine Bibel*, p. 110.
78. A.T. Hanson, *Studies in Paul's Technique and Theology*, p. 95.
79. Schoeps, *Paul*, p. 234.
80. Longenecker, *Biblical Exegesis in the Apostolic Period*, p. 127.
81. *Ibid.*, p. 129.
82. Lincoln, *Paradise Now and Not Yet*, p. 14. See also L. Goppelt, *Typos: The Typological Interpretation of the Old Testament in the New* (trans. D. Madvig; Grand Rapids: Eerdmans, 1982), p. 140: 'In only one instance is allegorical etymology employed (Gal. 4.25a)'.
83. James Barr (*Old and New in Interpretation* [London: SCM, 1966], pp. 103-11) rejects the distinction between allegorical and typological exegesis. Barr emphasizes that allegorization does not necessarily mean a non-historical perspective. Certainly, in Paul's case, the general historical framework is preserved, but there is nevertheless, an interpretation derived from the text of Gen. 21 which goes beyond the historical account and points to a symbolic meaning. See Longenecker, *Biblical Exegesis*, p. 49 n. 111.
84. R.P.C. Hanson, *Allegory and Event* (London: SCM, 1959), p. 7.
85. A. Lincoln, *Paradise Now and Not Yet*, p. 13.
86. *Ibid.*
87. Gal. 4.29 depends on rabbinic exegesis of Gen. 21.9 in which the word 'playing' (מצחק) is interpreted in a hostile sense; see R. Le Déaut, 'Traditions targumiques dans le corpus paulinien?' *Bib* 42 (1961), pp. 37-43; Str-B, III, p. 575; *Gen. Rab.* 53.11. Paul depicts the hostile activities of the troublemakers in Galatia in Gal. 1.7; 3.1; 4.17; 5.7-10; 6.12-13.
88. A. Hanson, *Studies in Paul's Technique and Theology*, pp. 99-103.
89. A. Lincoln, *Paradise Now and Not Yet*, p. 13.
90. Longenecker, *Biblical Exegesis in the Apostolic Period*, pp. 45-47.
91. See above, pp. 189-92.
92. See *Leg Alleg* II, 244; *Cher* 3-8; *Post* 130; *Cong* 1f, 71-73, 121f; *Mut* 255; *Qu Gen* II, 21-23.

278 *Abraham in Galatians*

93. See above, p. 190.
94. Buchsel, 'ἀλληγορέω', *TDNT* I, p. 260.
95. See Clement of Alexandria, *Strom.* V. 14. 97.
96. Letter of Aristeas 150-70.
97. J.Z. Lauterbach, 'Ancient Jewish Allegorists', *JQR* 1 (1911), pp. 291-333, 503-31; Büchsel, 'ἀλληγορέω' *TDNT* I, pp. 262-63; Longenecker, *Biblical Exegesis in the Apostolic Period*, pp. 47-48; A.T. Hanson, *Studies in Paul's Technique and Theology*, p. 160; Bonsirven, 'Exégèse allégorique chez les rabbins tannaites', *RSR* 23 (1933), pp. 522-24; e.g. *Song of Songs Rabbah*.
98. See above, p. 274 n. 34.
99. Buchsel, 'ἀλληγορέω', *TDNT* I, p. 263.
100. See 1QpHab 12.3-4 where Lebanon stands for the Communal Council and wild beasts for Jews who carry out the law; cf. also 1QpMic 8-10; CD 6.2-11; 7.9-20.
101. Quotation from G. Vermes, *The Dead Sea Scrolls in English*, pp. 102-103.
102. See A.T. Hanson, *Studies in Paul's Technique and Theology*, p. 159.
103. See Ellis, *Paul's Use of the Old Testament*, p. 52 n. 4.
104. See F.F. Bruce, '"Abraham Had Two Sons"—A Study in Pauline Hermeneutics', in *New Testament Studies: Essays in Honor of Ray Summers*, eds. H. Drumwright and C. Vaughan (Waco: Baylor University Press, 1975), p. 75.
105. Barrett, 'The Allegory of Abraham, Sarah, and Hagar', p. 161.
106. Longenecker, *Biblical Exegesis in the Apostolic Period*, pp. 128-29.
107. See exegesis of Gal. 4.27 above, pp. 149-50.
108. Determination of the correct reading is complicated, but as Barrett ('Allegory', pp. 163-64) says, 'a decisive consideration in favour of the long text is that omission of Hagar leaves a bare piece of geographical information of little interest to the readers or relevance to the context: Sinai is a mountain in Arabia'. Cf. F. Mussner, 'Hagar, Sinai, Jerusalem—zum Text von Gal. 4.25a', *TQ* 135 (1955), pp. 56-60.
109. Barrett, 'The Allegory of Abraham, Sarah, and Hagar', p. 163.
110. *Ibid.*
111. *Ibid.*, p. 164.
112. See King, 'Paul and the Tannaim', p. 369.
113. See Burton, *Galatians*, p. 259; R. Hanson, *Allegory and Event*, p. 81.
114. G.I. Davies, 'Hagar, el-Hegra, and the Location of Mount Sinai', *VT* 22 (1972), pp. 152-63.
115. A. Lincoln, *Paradise Now and Not Yet*, pp. 15-16.
116. Barrett, 'The Allegory of Abraham, Sarah, and Hagar', p. 162.
117. A. Lincoln, *Paradise Now and Not Yet*, p. 14; L. Gaston ('Israel's Enemies in Pauline Theology', *NTS* 28 [1982], pp. 400-11) argues that Paul

did not equate Mt. Sinai with the present Jerusalem. He says that συστοιχεῖν should be translated 'to correspond to the opposite member of the pair in the other column (στοῖχος)'. Thus v. 25 should be translated 'It (Sinai) is in the opposite column from the present Jerusalem, for she (Hagar) serves (as a slave) with her children'. But this interpretation fails to recognize the contrast between the 'present Jerusalem' and the 'Jerusalem above'. Gaston claims that 'Paul's logic seems to make sense only if the two references to Jerusalem are somehow related, the one explaining the other' (p. 408). Cf. A. Lincoln, *Paradise Now and Not Yet*, pp. 15-32; and above, pp. 203-204.

BIBLIOGRAPHY

I. Primary Materials and Lexical Aids

Biblical Texts
Aland, K., Black, M., Martini, B.M. Metzger, B.M., and Wikgren, A., eds. *The Greek New Testament*. 3rd edn. London/New York: United Bible Societies, 1975.
Elliger, K. and Rudolph, W. *Biblia Hebraica Stuttgartensia*. Stuttgart: Deutsche Bibelstiftung, 1977.
Nestlé, E. and Aland, K. eds. *Novum Testamentum Graece*. 26th edn. Stuttgart: Deutsche Bibelstiftung, 1979.
Septuaginta. Ed. A Rahlfs. 2 vols. Stuttgart: Württembergische Bibelanstalt, 1935.

Jewish Literature
Charles, R.H., ed. *The Apocrypha and Pseudepigrapha of the Old Testament in English*. 2 vols. Oxford: Clarendon Press, 1913.
Charlesworth, James H., ed. *The Old Testament Pseudepigrapha*. Vol. 1 of *Apocalyptic Literature & Testaments*. New York: Doubleday, 1983.
Dupont-Sommer, A. *The Essene Writings from Qumran*. Trans. G. Vermes. Oxford: Blackwell, 1961.
Forestall, J.T. *Targumic Traditions and the New Testament*. SBL Aramaic Studies, 4. Chico, Ca: Scholars Press, 1979.
Friedlander, G. *Pirke de Rabbi Eliezer* (ET). New York: Hermon, 1965.
Friedmann, M. ed. *Pesikta Rabbati*. Vienna: published by editor, 1880.
Grossfeld, B. *A Bibliography of Targum Literature*. New York: KTAV, 1972.
Hass, L. 'Bibliography on Midrash', in *The Study of Ancient Judaism*. 2 vols., ed. J. Neusner. New York: KTAV, 1981. I,93-99.
James, M.R. *The Biblical Antiquities of Philo*. London: SPCK, 1917.
Josephus. Trans. H. St. J. Thackeray. Loeb Classical Library. 9 vols. London: Heinemann, 1978.
Lauterbach, J.Z., ed. *Midrash Mekilta de-Rabbi Ishmael*. 3 vols. Philadelphia: Jewish Publications Society of America, 1933-35.
Midrash Rabbah. Eds. H. Freedman and M. Simon. 10 vols. London: Soncino Press, 1939.
The Mishnah. Trans. H. Danby. Oxford: Clarendon Press, 1933.
Nickelsburg, G., ed. *Studies on the Testament of Moses*. SBLSCS 4. Cambridge: SBL, 1973.
Stone, M.E. *The Testament of Abraham*. Text and Translations: Pseudepigrapha Series 2. Missoula: SBL, 1972.

Strack, H.L. and Billerbeck, P. *Kommentar zum Neuen Testament aus Talmud und Midrasch* 6 vols. Munich: C.H. Beck. vols. 1-4, 1922-1928; vols. 5-6, eds. J. Jeremias and K. Adolph, 1956-61.

The Babylonian Talmud. General Editor, I. Epstein. 35 vols. Soncino edn. London: Soncino Press, 1935-1952.

Vermes, G. *The Dead Sea Scrolls in English*. 2nd edn. New York: Penguin, 1975.

Zeitlin, S. *The First Book of Maccabees*. New York: Harper, 1950.

—*The Book of Judith*. Leiden: Brill, 1972.

—ed. *Studies on the Testament of Abraham*. SBLSCS 6. Missoula: Scholars Press, 1976.

Greco-Roman Literature

Aristotle. *The Art of Rhetoric*. Trans. J.H. Freese. Loeb Classical Library. Vol. 22. London: Heinemann, 1975.

Cicero. Trans. H. Caplan. Loeb Classical Library. London: Heinemann, 1981.

Demetrius. *On Style*. Trans. W.R. Roberts. Loeb Classical Library. London: Heinemann, 1927.

Demosthenes. *De Corona*. Trans. C. Vance. Loeb Classical Library. 2 vols. London: Heinemann, 1963.

Plato. Trans. G. Bury. Loeb Clasical Library. 12 vols. London: Heinemann, 1914-67.

Quintilian. *The Institutio Oratio*. Trans. H. Butler. Loeb Classical Library. 4 vols. London: Heinemann, 1977.

Collections of Papyri

Ägyptische Urkunden aus den Staatlichen Museen zu Berlin, Griechische Urkunden, Berlin, 1895 ff.

An Alexandrian Erotic Fragment and other Greek Papyri chiefly Ptolemaic. Ed. B.P. Grenfell, Oxford, 1896.

Catalogue général des antiquités égyptiennes du Musée du Caire: Zenon Papyri. Ed. C. C. Edgar. Cairo, 1925 ff.

Ἐντεύξεις, *Requêtes et plaintes adressées au roi d'Egypte au IIIe siècle avant J.C.* Ed. O. Gueraud. Cairo, 1931 ff.

Fayum Towns and their Papyri. Eds. B.P. Grenfell, A.S. Hunt, and D.G. Hogarth, London, 1900.

Greek Papyri in the Library of Cornell University. Eds. W.L. Westermann and C.J. Kraemer, New York, 1926.

Griechische Papyri im Museum des Oberhessischen Geschichtsvereine zu Giessen. Eds. O. Eger, E. Kornemann, and P.M. Meyer. Giessen, 1910 ff.

Griechische Urkunden der Papyrussammlung zu Leipzig. Ed. L. Mitteis. Leipzig, 1906.

Greek Papyri in the British Museum. Eds. F.G. Kenyon and H.I. Bell. London, 1893 ff.

Papyri in the University of Michigan Collection. Eds. C.C. Edgar, A.E.R. Boak, J.G. Winter and others. Ann Arbor, 1931 ff.

A descriptive catalogue of the Greek papyri in the collection of Wilfred Morton. Eds. H.I. Bell and C.H. Roberts. London, 1948.

The Oxyrhynchus Papyri. Eds. B.P. Grenfell, A.S. Hunt, H.I. Bell and others. London, 1898 ff.

Papyri Graecae Magicae: Die griechischen Zauberpapyri. Eds. K. Preisendanz and A. Henrichs, Stuttgart: Teubner, 1973.

Catalogue of the Greek Papyri in the J. Rylands Library, Manchester. Eds. J. de M. Johnson, V. Martin, A.S. Hunt, C.H. Roberts, and E.G. Turner. Manchester, 1911 ff.

The Tebtunis Papyri. Eds. B.P. Grenfell, A.S. Hunt, J.G. Smyly and others. London, 1902 ff.

Sammelbuch griechischer Urkunden aus Ägypten. Eds. F. Preisigke and F. Bilabel. Strassburg/Berlin/Leipzig/Heidelberg, 1915ff.

Veröffentlichungen aus den badischen Papyrus-Sammlungen. Eds. W. Spiegelberg, F. Bilabel, and G.A. Gerhard. Heidelberg, 1923 ff.

Lexical Aids

Bauer, W. *A Greek-English Lexicon of the New Testament and Other Early Christian Literature.* Trans. and ed. of W. Bauer's 4th edn. W.F. Arndt and F.W. Gingrich. 2nd edn. revised and augmented by F.W. Gringrich and F.W. Danker from W. Bauer's 5th edn. Chicago: University of Chicago Press, 1979.

Blass, F. and Debrunner, A. *A Greek Grammar of the New Testament and Other Early Christian Literature.* 9th edn. Trans. and ed. R. Funk. Chicago: University of Chicago Press, 1961.

Liddell, H.G. and Scott, R. *A Greek-English Lexicon.* 9th edn. Revised by H.S. Jones and R. McKenzie. Oxford: Clarendon Press, 1940.

Moule, C.F.D. *An Idiom Book of New Testament Greek.* 2nd edn. Cambridge: Cambridge University Press, 1963.

Moulton, J.H. & Milligan, G. *The Vocabulary of the Greek Testament illustrated from the Papyri and Other Non-Literary Sources.* London: Hodder & Stoughton, 1930.

Robertson, A.T. *A Grammar of the Greek New Testament in the Light of Historical Research.* 3rd edn. London: Hodder & Stoughton, 1919.

II. Commentaries, Monographs and Articles

Alexander, P.S. 'Rabbinic Judaism and the New Testament', *ZNW* 74 (1983), 235-46.

Aris, R. 'St. Paul's Use of the Old Testament in the Letter to the Galatians', *The Journal of the Christian Brethren Research Fellowship* 17 (1969), 9-13.

Aune, David E. 'Review of Hans Dieter Betz, *Galatians: A Commentary on Paul's Letter to the Churches of Galatia*', *RelSRev* 7 (1981), 323-28.

Bahr, Gordon J. 'Paul and Letter Writing in the First Century', *CBQ* 28 (1966), 465-77.

—'The Subscriptions in the Pauline Letters', *JBL* 87 (1968), 27-41.

Baldwin, Charles S. *Ancient Rhetoric and Poetic Interpreted from Representative Works.* New York: Macmillan, 1924.

Bamberger, B.J. *Proselytism in the Talmudic Period.* New York: KTAV, 1968.

Bammel, E. 'Gottes ΔIAΘHKH (Gal. 3.15-17) und das jüdische Rechtsdenken', *NTS* 6 (1959-60), 313-19.

—'Νόμος Χριστοῦ' *SE* 3 (1964), 120-28.

Bandstra, A.J. *The Law and the Elements of the World. An Exegetical Study in Aspects of Paul's Teaching.* Grand Rapids: Eerdmans, 1964.

Barclay, John M.G., 'Mirror-Reading a Polemical Letter: Galatians as a Test Case', *JSNT* 31 (1987), pp. 73-93.

—*Obeying the Truth: A Study of Paul's Ethics in Galatians.* Edinburgh: T. & T. Clark, 1988.

284   *Abraham in Galatians*

Barr, James. *The Semantics of Biblical Language*. London: Oxford University Press, 1961.

—*Old and New in Interpretation*. London: SCM, 1966.

Barrett, C.K. *From First Adam to Last: A Study in Pauline Theology*. New York: Scribner's, 1962.

—'Galatians as an "Apologetic Letter"', *Int* 34 (1980), 414-17.

—'The Allegory of Abraham, Sarah and Hagar in the Argument of Galatians', in his *Essays on Paul*. London: SPCK, 1982.

Barth, M. 'The Kerygma of Galatians', *Int* 21 (1967), 131-36.

—'Jews and Gentiles: The Social Character of Justification in Paul', *JES* 5 (1968), 241-67.

—'The Faith of the Messiah', *HeyJ* 10 (1969), 363-70.

—*Justification: Pauline Texts Interpreted in the Light of the Old and New Testament*. Trans. A. Woodruff. Grand Rapids: Eerdmans, 1971.

Bassler, Jouette M. *Divine Impartiality: Paul and a Theological Axiom*. SBLDS 59. Chico: Scholars Press, 1982.

Bauernfeind, O. 'Die Begegnung zwischen Paulus und Kephas, Gal 1.18-20', *ZNW* 47 (1956), 268-76.

Baur, F.C. *Paul, the Apostle of Jesus Christ. His Life and Work, his Epistles and his Doctrine*. 2 vols. Trans. E. Zeller and A. Menzies. London: Williams & Norgate, 1875.

Beardslee, William A. *Literary Criticism of the New Testament*. Philadelphia: Fortress Press, 1970.

Beers, B. *Leben Abrahams*. Leipzig: Osfar Leiner, 1859.

Behm. 'ἀνάθεμα', *TDNT* I, 354-56.

—'διαθήκη', *TDNT* II, 106-34.

Beker, J.C. *Paul the Apostle: The Triumph of God in Life and Thought*. Philadelphia: Fortress, 1980.

Belleville, Linda L. '"Under Law": Structural Analysis and the Pauline Concept of Law in Galatians 3.21-4.11', *JSNT* 26 (1986), 53-78.

Berger, K. 'Abraham in den paulinischen Hauptbriefen', *MTZ* 17 (1966), 47-89.

—'Almosen für Israel. Zum historischen Kontext der paulinischen Kollekte', *NTS* 23 (1976), 180-204.

Best, E. *One Body in Christ*. London: SPCK, 1955.

—'The Revelation to Evangelize the Gentiles', *JTS* 35 (1984), 1-30.

Bertram. 'ἔργον', *TDNT* II, 635-52.

Betz, H.D. *Der Apostel Paulus und die sokratische Tradition*. Tübingen: J.C.B. Mohr, 1972.

—'Geist, Freiheit, und Gesetz. Die Botschaft des Paulus an die Gemeinden in Galatien', *ZTK* 71 (1974), 78-93.

—'The Literary Composition and Function of Paul's Letter to the Galatians', *NTS* (1975), 353-80.

—'In Defense of the Spirit: Paul's Letter to the Galatians as a Document of Early Christian Apologetics', in *Aspects of Religious Propaganda in Judaism and Early Christianity*. Ed. E. Schüssler Fiorenza. Notre Dame: University of Notre Dame, 1976, 99-114.

—*Galatians: A Commentary on Paul's Letter to the Churches in Galatia*. Hermeneia Commentaries. Philadelphia: Fortress, 1979.

Binder, H. *Der Glaube bei Paulus*. Berlin: Evangelischer Verlag, 1968.

Bjerkelund, C.J. *Parakalō: Form, Funktion und Sinn der parakalō-Satz in den paulinischen Briefen*. Bibliotheca Theologica Norvegica 1. Oslo: Universitets-

forlaget, 1967.
—'"Nach menschlicher Weise rede ich"': Funktion und Sinn des paulinischen Ausdrucks', *ST* 26 (1972), 63-100.

Black, Edwin. *Rhetorical Criticism: A Study in Method*. New York: Macmillan, 1965.

Bligh, John. *Galatians in Greek: A Structural Analysis of St. Paul's Epistle to the Galatians with Notes on the Greek*. Detroit: University of Detroit Press, 1966.

—'Did Jesus Live By Faith?' *HeyJ* 9 (1968), 418-19.

—*Galatians: A Discussion of St. Paul's Epistle*. Householder Commentaries 1. London: St. Paul's Publications, 1969.

Bloch, R. 'Midrash', *DBSup* V, 1263-81.

Boers, H.W. 'Genesis 15.6 and the Discourse Structure of Galatians'. An unpublished paper for the SBL Paul Seminar, 1976.

—'The Form-Critical Study of Paul's Letter: I Thessalonians as a Case Study', *NTS* 22 (1976), 140-58.

—'The Structure of Galatians: Rhetorical or Text-linguistic Analysis?' An unpublished paper for the SBL Paul Seminar, 1976.

Bogaert, P.M. *Abraham dans la Bible et dans la tradition juive*. Publications de l'Institutum Iudaicum Bruxelles 2. Brussels: Institutum Iudaicum, 1977.

Bonnard, P. *L'Épître de Saint Paul aux Galates*. CNT, 9. Neuchâtel-Paris: Delachaux & Niestlé, 1953.

Bonsirven, J. *Exégèse rabbinique et exégèse paulinienne*. Paris: Beauchesne, 1939.

Borgen, Peder. 'Observations on the Theme "Paul and Philo". Paul's Preaching or Circumcision in Galatia (Gal 5.11) and Debates on Circumcision in Philo', in *Die Paulinische Literatur und Theologie*. Ed. S. Pedersen. Göttingen: Vandenhoeck & Ruprecht, 1980.

—'Paul Preaches Circumcision and Pleases Men', in *Paul and Paulinism: Essays in Honour of C.K. Barrett*. Eds. M.D. Hooker and S.G. Wilson. London: SPCK, 1982, 37-46.

Bornkamm, G. *Das Ende des Gesetzes*. Munich: Kaiser, 1952.

—*Paul*. Trans. D. Stalker. New York: Harper & Row, 1971.

—'The Revelation of Christ to Paul on the Damascus Road and Paul's Doctrine of Justification and Reconciliation', in *Reconciliation and Hope*. Ed. R. Banks. Exeter: Paternoster, 1974, 90-103.

Bousset, Wilhelm. *Die Religion des Judentums im späthellenistischen Zeitalter*. 3rd edn. Tübingen: J.C.B. Mohr, 1926.

Bowker, J. *The Targums and Rabbinic Literature*. Cambridge: Cambridge University Press, 1969.

Bradley, David. 'The Topos as a Form in the Pauline Paraenesis', *JBL* 72 (1953), 238-46.

Brandt, William J. *The Rhetoric of Argumentation*. New York: Bobbs Merrill, 1970.

Braude, G. *Jewish Proselytizing in the First Five Centuries of the Common Era*. Providence: Brown University Press, 1940.

Breech, E. 'These Fragments I Have Shored Against My Ruins: The Form and Function of 4 Ezra', *JBL* 92 (1973), 267-74.

Bretscher, P.G. 'Light from Galatians 3.1 on Pauline Theology', *CTM* 34 (1963), 77-97.

Bring, R. *Commentary on Galatians*. Trans. E. Wahlstrom. Philadelphia; Muhlenberg, 1961.

Brinsmead, Bernard H. *Galatians—Dialogical Response to Opponents*. SBLDS, 65. Chico, Ca.: Scholars Press, 1982.

Brodie, C.T. 'Galatians as Art', *Bible Today* 19 (1981), 335-39.

Bruce, F.F. *Biblical Exegesis in the Qumran Texts*. Grand Rapids: Eerdmans, 1960.

—'The DSS and Early Christianity', *BJRL* 49 (1966-67), 69-90.

—'Galatians Problems 3: The "Other" Gospel', *BJRL* 53 (1971), 253-71.

—'Galatians Problems 4: The Date of the Epistle', *BJRL* 54 (1972), 216-24.

—'"Abraham Had Two Sons": A Study in Pauline Hermeneutics', in *New Testament Studies*. *FS Ray Sommers*. Eds. H. L. Downwright and C. Vaughn. Waco: Baylor, 1975. 71-84.

—'Further Thoughts on Paul's Autobiography (Gal. 1.11-2.14)', in *Jesus and Paulus: FS W.G. Kümmel*. Eds. E.E. Ellis und E. Grässer. Göttingen: Vandenhoeck & Ruprecht, 1975, 21-29.

—'Paul and the Law of Moses', *BJRL* 57 (1975), 259-79.

—*Paul: Apostle of the Heart Set Free*. Grand Rapids: Eerdmans, 1977.

—*The Time is Fulfilled*. Grand Rapids: Eerdmans, 1978.

—'The Curse of the Law', in *Paul and Paulinism: Essays in Honour of C.K. Barrett*. Eds. M.D. Hooker and S.G. Wilson. London: SPCK, 1982, 27-36.

—*The Epistle to the Galatians: A Commentary on the Greek Text*. The New International Greek Testament Commentary. Grand Rapids: Eerdmans, 1982.

Brumann, G. *Vorpaulinische christliche Taufverkündigung bei Paulus*. BWANT 82. Stuttgart: Kohlhammer, 1962.

Buchanan, G.W. 'The Use of Rabbinic Literature for New Testament Research', *BTB* 7 (1977), 110-22.

Büchsel, F. 'ἀλληγορέω', *TDNT* I, 449-51.

Buck, Charles H. 'The Date of Galatians', *JBL* 70 (1951), 113-22.

—and Taylor, Greer. *Saint Paul: A Study of the Development of his Thought*. New York: Scribner's, 1969.

Bultmann, R. 'δηλόω', *TDNT* II, 61-62.

—'ζωοποιέω', *TDNT* II, 874-75.

—'πιστεύω κτλ', *TDNT* VI, 174-228.

—*Der Stil der paulinischen Predigt und die kynisch-stoische Diatribe*. Göttingen: Vandenhoeck & Ruprecht, 1910.

—'Das Problem der Ethik bei Paulus', *ZNW* 23 (1924), 123-40.

—*Theology of the New Testament*. 2 vols. Trans. K. Grobel. New York: Scribner's, 1951, 1955.

—'Δικαιοσύνη Θεου', *JBL* 83 (1964), 12-16.

—'Christus des Gesetzes Ende', in *Glauben und Verstehen: Gesammelte Aufsätze 2*. 4th edn Tübingen: J.C.B. Mohr, 1965, 32-58.

—'Zur Auslegung von Galater 2, 15-18', 15-18', in *Exegetical: Aufsätze zur Erforschung des Neuen Testaments*. Ed. E. Dinkler. Tübingen: J.C.B. Mohr, 1967. 394-99.

Burke, Kenneth. *A Rhetoric of Motives*. New York: Braziller, 1955.

Burton, Ernest DeWitt. *A Critical and Exegetical Commentary on the Epistle to the Galatians*. ICC. Edinburgh: T. & T. Clark, 1920.

Beusiemi, A.M. 'Structura della Lettera ai Galatia', *Euntes Docete* 34 (1981), 409-26.

Bryne, B. '*Sons of God'—'Seed of Abraham': A Study of the Idea of the Sonship of God of All Christians in Paul against the Jewish Background*. AnBib 83. Rome: Biblical Institute, 1979.

Caird, G.B. *Principalities and Powers. A Study in Pauline Theology*. Oxford: Clarendon Press, 1956.

—'Review of E.P. Sanders, *Paul and Palestinian Judaism*', *JTS* 29 (1978), 538-43.

—*The Language and Imagery of the Bible.* Philadelphia: Westminster, 1980.
Callan, Terrance D., Jr. 'The Law and the Mediator: Gal 3.19b-20'. Ph.D. Dissertation, Yale University, 1976.
—'Pauline Midrash: The Exegetical Background of Gal 3.19b', *JBL* 99 (1980), 549-67.
Calvin, John. *The Epistles of Paul the Apostle to the Galatians, Ephesians, Philippians and Colossians.* Calvin's New Testament Commentaries 11. Trans. T. Parker. Grand Rapids: Eerdmans, 1965.
Campbell, K.M. 'Covenant or Testament?', *EvQ* 44 (1972), 107-11.
Cavallin, H.C.C. 'The Righteous Shall Live By Faith: A Decisive Argument for the Traditional Interpretation', *ST* 32 (1978), 33-43.
Church, F.F. 'Rhetorical Structure and Design in Paul's Letter to Philemon', *HTR* 71 (1978), 17-33.
Clark, Donald L. *Rhetoric in Greco-Roman Education.* New York: Columbia University Press, 1967.
Clark, Kenneth W. 'The Israel of God', in *Studies in New Testament and Early Christian Literature: Essays in Honor of Allen P. Wilkgren.* NovTSup 33. Leiden: Brill, 1972. 161-69.
Clements, R.E. *Abraham and David.* London: SCM, 1967.
Cohn-Sherbok, D. 'Paul and Rabbinic Exegesis', *SJT* 35 (1982), 117-32.
Cole, R.A. *The Epistle of Paul to the Galatians.* Tyndale New Testament Commentaries. London: Tyndale, 1965.
Collins, J.J. 'Rabbinic Exegesis and Pauline Exegesis', *CBQ* 3 (1941), 15-27, 145-58.
Conzelmann, H.G. *An Outline of the Theology of the New Testament.* New York: Harper & Row, 1969.
Cooper, Karl T. 'Paul and Rabbinic Soteriology', *WTJ* 44 (1982), 123-39.
Corbett, E., ed. *Rhetorical Analyses of Literary Works.* New York: Oxford University Press, 1969.
—*Classical Rhetoric for the Modern Student.* New York: Oxford University Press, 1971.
Cosgrove, C.H. 'The Mosaic Law Preaches Faith: A Study of Galatians 3', *WTJ* 41 (1978-79), 146-64.
Cothenet, E. 'À l' arrière-plan de l' allégorie d' Agar et de Sara (Ga 4.21-31)', in *De la Tôrah au Messie. FS H. Cazelles.* Eds. M. Carrez, *et al.* Paris: Desclée, 1981.
Cousar, Charles B. *Galatians.* Interpretation Series. Atlanta: John Knox, 1982.
Cranfield, C.E.B. 'St. Paul and the Law', *SJT* 17 (1964), 43-68.
Cremer, H. *Die paulinische Rechtfertigungslehre im Zusammenhang ihrer geschichtlichen Voraussetzungen.* Gütersloh: Bertelsmann, 1901.
Crownfield, F.C. 'The Singular Problem of the Dual Galatians', *JBL* 64 (1945), 491-500.
Dahl, Nils A. 'Der Name Israel: Zur Auslegung von Gal 6, 16', *Judaica* 6 (1950), 161-170.
—'Formgeschichtliche Beobachtungen zur Christusverkündigung in der Gemeindepredigt', in *Neutestamentliche Studien fur R. Bultmann.* Ed. W. Eltester. BZNW 21; Berlin: Töpelmann, 1954, 3-9.
—*Das Volk Gottes: Eine Untersuchung zum Kirchenbewusstsein des Urchristentums.* Darmstadt: Wissenschaftliche Buchgesellschaft, 1963.
—'The Story of Abraham in Luke-Acts', in *Studies in Luke-Acts.* Eds. L. Keck and J.L. Martyn. New York: Abingdon, 1966, 139-58.
—'Paul's Letter to the Galatians: Epistolary Genre, Content, and Structure'. Unpublished paper for the SBL Paul Seminar, 1973.

288   *Abraham in Galatians*

—*The Crucified Messiah and Other Essays*. Minneapolis: Augsburg, 1974.
—*Studies in Paul*. Minneapolis: Augsburg, 1977.
—'Review of E.P. Sanders, *Paul and Palestinian Judaism*', *RelSRev* 4 (1978), 153-58.
Daly, R.J. 'The Soteriological Significance of the Sacrifice of Isaac', *CBQ* 39 (1977), 45-75.
Dancy, C. *A Commentary on 1 Maccabees*. Oxford: Blackwell, 1954.
Daube, David. 'Rabbinic Methods of Interpretation and Hellenistic Rhetoric', *HUCA* 22 (1949), 239-64.
—*The New Testament and Rabbinic Judaism*. London: Athlone, 1956.
Davies, G.I. 'Hagar, El-Hegra and the Location of Mount Sinai', *VT* 22 (1972), 152-63.
Davies, W.D. *Torah in the Messianic Age and/or the Age to Come*. JBLMS, 7. Philadelphia: SBL, 1952.
—'Paul and the People of Israel', *NTS* 24 (1977), 4-39.
—*Paul and Rabbinic Judaism*. 4th edn. Philadelphia: Fortress, 1980.
—'Review of H.D. Betz, *Galatians: A Commentary on Paul's Letter to the Churches of Galatia*', *RelSRev* 7 (1981), 310-18.
—'Paul and the Law: Reflections on Pitfalls in Interpretation', in *Paul and Paulinism: Essays in Honour of C.K. Barrett*. Eds. M.D. Hooker and S.G. Wilson. London: SPCK, 1982, 4-16.
—*Jewish and Pauline Studies*. London: SPCK, 1984.
Davis, J.J. 'Some Reflections on Gal 3.28: Sexual Roles and Biblical Hermeneutics' *JETS* 19 (1976), 201-208.
Deissmann, A. *Paul: A Study in Social and Religious History*. 2nd edn. London: Hodder & Stoughton, 1926.
—*Light From the Ancient Near East*. Grand Rapids: Baker, 1978. Reprint of Hodder & Stoughton, 1909.
De Jonge, M. *The Testaments of the Twelve Patriarchs: A Study of Their Text, Composition, and Origin*. Assen: Van Gorcum, 1953.
—ed. *Studies on the Testaments of the Twelve Patriarchs*. Leiden: Brill, 1975.
Delcor, M. *Le Testament d'Abraham*. SVTP 2. Leiden: Brill, 1973.
Delling. 'βασκαίνω', *TDNT* I, 594-95.
—'στοιχεῖον', *TDNT* VII, 666-87.
—'τέλος', *TDNT* VIII, 49-87.
Derrett, J.D.M. *Studies in the New Testament*. 2 vols. Leiden: Brill, 1978.
DeVries, Carl E. 'Paul's "Cutting" Remarks about a Race: Galatians 5.1-12', in *Current Issues in Biblical and Patristic Interpretation: Studies in Honor of Merrill C. Tenney*. Ed. G. Hawthorne. Grand Rapids: Eerdmans, 1975, 115-20.
Dibelius, M. *From Tradition to Gospel*. Trans. B. Woolf. London: Nicholson & Watson, 1934.
Diedun, T.J. *New Covenant Morality in Paul*. AnBib 89. Rome: Biblical Institute Press, 1981.
Dietzfelbinger, C. *Paulus und das Alts Testament: Die Hermeneutik des Paulus, untersucht an seiner Deutung der Gestalt Abrahams*. Theologische Existenz Heute, 95. Munich: Kaiser, 1961.
—*Heilsgeschichte bei Paulus?* Munich: Kaiser, 1965.
Dion, Paul E. 'The Aramaic "Family Letter" and Related Epistolary Forms in Other Oriental Languages and in Hellenistic Greek', *Semeia* 22 (1981), 59-88.
Dobschutz, E. von. 'Wir und Ich bei Paulus', *ZST* 10 (1933), 251-77.
Dodd, C.H. *Gospel and Law*. Cambridge: Cambridge University Press, 1951.

—*According to the Scriptures.* London: Nisbet, 1952.

—'ΕΝΝΟΜΟΣ ΧΡΙΣΤΟΥ', in *Studia Paulina: In Honorem J. de Zwaan.* Haarlam: Bohn, 1953.

—*The Old Testament in the New.* Philadelphia: Fortress, 1963.

Doeve, J.W. *Jewish Hermeneutics in the Synoptic Gospels and Acts.* Assen: van Gorcum, 1954.

Donaldson, T.L. 'Parallels: Use, Misuse, and Limitations', *EVQ* 55 (1983), 193-210.

—'The "Curse of the Law" and the Inclusion of the Gentiles: Galatians 3.13-14', *NTS* 32 (1986), 94-112.

Doty, W.G. 'The Classification of Epistolary Literature', *CBQ* 31 (1969), 183-99.

—'The Concept of Genre in Literary Analysis', *SBLASP* 2 (1972), 413-48.

—*Contemporary New Testament Interpretation.* Englewood Cliffs, N.J.: Prentice Hall, 1972.

—*Letters in Primitive Christianity.* Guides to Biblical Scholarship: New Testament Series. Philadelphia: Fortress, 1973.

Doughty, D.J. 'The Priority of ΧΑΡΙΣ. An Investigation of the Theological Language of Paul', *NTS* 19 (1972-73), 163-80.

Dozemann, T. '*Sperma Abraam* in John 8 and Related Literature: Cosmology and Judgment', *CBQ* 42 (1980), 345-58.

Drane, John W. 'Tradition, Law and Ethics in Pauline Theology', *NovT* 16 (1974), 167-78.

—*Paul: Libertine or Legalist?* London: SPCK, 1975.

Dulmen, A. van *Die Theologie des Gesetzes bei Paulus.* SBM, 5. Stuttgart: Katholisches Bibelwerk, 1968.

Duncan, George S. *The Epistle of Paul to the Galatians.* MNTC. New York: Harper, 1934.

Dunn, James D.G. 'The Relationship between Paul and Jerusalem according to Galatians 1 and 2', *NTS* 28 (1982), 461-78.

—'The Incident at Antioch (Gal 2.11-18)', *JSNT* 18 (1983), 3-57.

—'The New Perspective on Paul', *BJRL* 65 (1983), 95-122.

Dupont, J. 'La Révélation du Fils de Dieu en faveur de Pierre (Mt 16, 17) et de Paul (Ga 1, 16)', *RSR* 52 (1964), 411-20.

—'The Conversion of Paul, and its Influence on his Understanding of Salvation by Faith', in *Apostolic History and the Gospel: Biblical and Historical Essays presented to F.F. Bruce.* Eds. W. Gasque and R. Martin. Grand Rapids: Eerdmans, 1970, 176-94.

Ebeling, Gerhard. *Die Wahrheit des Evangeliums: Eine Lesehilfe zum Galaterbrief.* Tübingen: J.C.B. Mohr, 1981.

Eckert, Jost. *Die urchristliche Verkündigung im Streit zwischen Paulus und seinen Gegnern nach dem Galaterbrief.* Regensburg: Friedrich Pustet, 1971.

Eger, O. 'Rechtswörter und Rechtsbilder in den paulinischen Briefen', *ZNW* 18 (1917-18), 84-108.

Ellis, E.E. 'A Note on Pauline Hermeneutics', *NTS* 2 (1955-56), 127-33.

—*Paul's Use of the Old Testament.* London: Oliver and Boyd, 1957.

—'Midrash and New Testament Quotations', in *Neotestamentica et Semitica: Studies in Honour of Matthew Black.* Eds. E.E. Ellis and Max Wilcox. Edinburgh: T. & T. Clark, 1969, 61-69.

—'Christ Crucified', in *Reconcilation and Hope: New Testament Essays on Atonement and Eschatology presented to L. Morris.* Ed. R. Banks. Grand Rapids: Eerdmans, 1974, 69-75.

—'How the New Testament Uses the Old', in *New Testament Interpretation.* Ed. I.H. Marshall. Grand Rapids: Eerdmans, 1977, 199-208.

—*Prophecy and Hermeneutic in Early Chrisianity: New Testament Essays*. WUNT, 18. Tübingen: J.C.B. Mohr, 1978.

Exler, F. *The Form of the Ancient Greek Letter. A Study in Greek Epistolography*. Washington, D.C.: Catholic University of America, 1923.

Feld, H. '"Christus, Diener der Sünde": Zum Ausgang des Streites zwischen Petrus und Paulus', *TQ* 153 (1973), 119-31.

Feuillet, A. 'Loi de Dieu, loi du Christ et loi de l'Espirit d'après les épîtres pauliniennes: Les rapports de ces trois avec la Loi Mosaïque', *NovT* 22 (1980), 29-65.

—'Structure de la section doctrinale de L' Épître aux Galates (III, 1-VI, 10)', *RevThom* 82 (1982), 5-39.

Fischel, H.A. *Rabbinic Literature and Greco-Roman Philosophy*. SPB 21. Leiden: Brill, 1973.

Fischer, James A. 'Pauline Literary Forms and Thought Patterns', *CBQ* 39 (1977), 209-23.

Fitzmyer, J.A. 'The Use of Eplicit Old Testament Quotations in Qumran Literature and in the New Testament', *NTS* 7 (1961), 297-333.

—'Crucifixion in Ancient Palestine, Qumran Literature, and the NT', *CBQ* 40 (1978), 493-513.

—'Habakkuk 2.3-4 and the New Testament', in *De la Tôrah au Messie: FS Henri Cazelles*. Eds. M. Carrez, J. Dore, and P. Grelot. Paris: Desclée, 1981, 447-56.

—'Aramaic Epistolography', *Semeia* 22 (1981), 25-57.

Fletcher, D.J. 'The Singular Argument of Paul's Letter to the Galatians'. Ph.D. Dissertation, Princeton Theological Seminary, 1982.

Foerster, 'κληρονόμος', *TDNT* III, 768-85.

Frye, Northrup. *Anatomy of Criticism*. Princeton: Princeton University Press, 1971.

Fuller, Daniel P. 'Paul and "the Works of the Law"', *WTJ* 38 (1975), 28-42.

—*Gospel and Law: Contrast or Continuum?* Grand Rapids: Eerdmans, 1980.

Fung, R.Y.K. 'The Relationship between Righteousness and Faith in the Thought of Paul, as Expressed in the Letters to the Galatians and the Romans'. Ph.D. Dissertation, University of Manchester, 1975.

—'The Forensic Character of Justification', *Themelios* 3 (1977), 16-21.

—'The Status of Justification by Faith in Paul's Thought: A Brief Survey of a Modern Debate', *Themelios* 6 (1981), 4-11.

—'A Note on Galatians 2.3-8', *JETS* 25 (1982), 49-52.

—*The Epistle to the Galatians*. NICNT. Grand Rapids: Eerdmans, 1988.

Funk, Robert W. *Language, Hermeneutic and Word of God*. New York: Harper & Row, 1966.

—'Apostolic Parousia: Form and Significance', in *Christian History and Interpretation: Studies Presented to John Knox*. Ed. W.R. Farmer, C.F.D. Moule, and R.R. Niebuhr. Cambridge: Cambridge University Press, 1967, 249-68.

Furnish, Victor Paul. *Theology and Ethics in Paul*. Nashville: Abingdon Press, 1968.

Gaston, Lloyd. 'Paul and the Torah', in *Anti-semitism and the Foundations of Christianity*. Ed. A.T. Davis. New York: Paulist Press, 1979.

—'Abraham and the Righteousness of God', *Horizons in Biblical Theology* 2 (1980), 39-68.

—'Israel's Enemies in Pauline Theology', *NTS* 28 (1982), 400-23.

Georgi, Dieter. *Die Gegner des Paulus im 2 Korintherbrief*. Neukirchen: Neukirchener Verlag, 1964.

—*Die Geschichte der Kollekte des Paulus für Jerusalem*. TF 38. Hamburg: Evangelischer Verlag, 1965.

Gertner, M. 'Midrashim in the New Testament', *JSS* 7 (1962), 267-92.

Giblin, C.H. 'Three Monotheistic Texts in Paul', *CBQ* 37 (1975), 527-47.

Goodenough, E.R. *By Light, Light: The Mystic Gospel of Hellenistic Judaism*. New Haven: Yale University Press, 1935.

—*Jewish Symbols in the Greco-Roman Period*. 13 vols. New York: Bollinger Foundation, 1965-68.

—'Paul and the Hellenization of Christianity', in *Religions in Antiquity*. Ed. J. Neusner. Leiden, 1967.

Goppelt, L. *Typos: The Typological Interpretation of the Old Testament in the New*. Trans. D. Madvig. Grand Rapids: Eerdmans, 1982.

Gordon, E.E. 'Christ, A Curse, and the Cross: An Interpretative Study of Galatians 3.13'. Ph.D. Dissertation, Princeton Theological Seminary, 1972.

Grafe, E. *Die paulinische Lehre vom Gesetz nach den vier Hauptbriefen*. Tübingen: J.C.B. Mohr, 1884.

Grant, R.M. 'Hellenistic Elements in Galatians', *ATR* 34 (1952), 223-26.

—*Gnosticism and Early Christianity*. New York: Columbia University Press, 1959.

Greenwood, David. 'Rhetorical Criticism and Formgeschichte. Some Methodological Considerations', *JBL* 89 (1970), 418-26.

Grimes, Joseph. 'Signals of Discourse Structure', *SBLASP* 8 (1975), 1.151-64.

Groningen, G. van *First Century Gnosticism: Its Origin and Motifs*. Leiden: Brill, 1967.

Gunther, J.J. *St. Paul's Opponents and their Background: A Study of Apocalyptic and Jewish Sectarian Teachings*. NovTSup 35. Leiden: Brill, 1973.

Gutbrod. 'Ἰσραήλ', *TDNT* III, 369-91.

Guthrie, Donald. *Galatians*. The Century Bible, New Series. London: Nelson, 1969.

Hall, Robert G. 'The Rhetorical Outline for Galatians: A Reconsideration', *JBL* 106 (1987), 277-87.

Hahn, F. 'Genesis 15.6 im Neuen Testament', in his *Probleme biblischer Theologie*. München: Kaiser, 1971.

—'Das Gesetzesverständnis im Römer- und Galaterbrief', *ZNW* 67 (1976), 29-63.

Halter, H. 'Gal 3, 26-29: "In Christus" Sohne Gottes und Erben der Verheissung durch Glaube und Taufe', *Freiburger Theologische Studien* 106 (1977), 108-17.

Hanse, H. 'ΔΗΛΟΝ (zu Gal 3, 11)', *ZNW* 34 (1935), 299-303.

Hanson, A.T. *Studies in Paul's Technique and Theology*. London: SPCK, 1974.

—*The Living Utterances of God: The New Testament Exegesis of the Old*. London: Darton, Longman, and Todd, 1983.

Harrington, D.J. 'Abraham Traditions in the Testament of Abraham and in the "Rewritten Bible" of the Intertestamental Period', in *Studies on the Testament of Abraham*. Ed. G. Nickelsburg, Jr. Missoula: Scholars Press, 1976.

Harrington, W.J. *Record of the Fulfillment: The New Testament*. Chicago: Priory, 1965.

Hartman, Lars. 'Bundesideologie in und hinter einigen paulinischen Texten', in *Die paulinische Literatur*. Ed. S. Pedersen. Göttingen: Vandenhoeck & Ruprecht, 1981.

Harvey, A.E. 'The Opposition to Paul', *SE* 4 (1968), 321-23.

Hatch, W.H.P. *The Pauline Idea of Faith in its Relation to Jewish and Hellenistic Religion*. HTS, 2. Cambridge, Mass.: Harvard University Press, 1917.

Haussleiter, J. 'Der Glaube Jesu Christi und der christliche Glaube; ein Beitrag zur Erklärung des Römerbriefes', *NKZ* 2 (1891), 109-45, 205-30.

Hawkins, John G. 'The Opponents of Paul in Galatia'. Ph.D. Dissertation, Yale University, 1971.

Hay, David M. 'What is Proof? Historical Verification in Philo, Josephus, and

Quintilian', *SBLASP* 17 (1979), 87-100.

Hays, R.B. 'Psalm 143 and the Logic of Romans 3', *JBL* 99 (1980), 107-15.

—*The Faith of Jesus Christ: An Investigation of the Narrative Substructure of Galatians 3.1–4.11*. SBLDS 56. Chico, Ca.: Scholars Press, 1983.

Heiland, H.W. *Die Anrechnung des Glaubens zur Gerechtigkeit*. Stuttgart: Kohlhammer, 1936.

Hengel, M. *Judaism and Hellenism*. Trans. John Bowden. 2 vols. Philadelphia: Fortress, 1974.

Herbert, G. '"Faithfulness" and "Faith"', *Theology* 58 (1955), 373-79.

Hester, James D. 'Paul's Concept of Inheritance', *SJT* Occasional Papers 14. Edinburgh: Oliver & Boyd, 1961.

—'The "Heir" and Heilsgeschichte: A Study of Gal 4.1ff', in *Oikonomia: FS Oscar Cullmann*. Ed. F. Christ. Hamburg: Reich, 1967.

—'The Rhetorical Structure of Galatians 1.11–2.14', *JBL* 103 (1984), 223-33.

—'The Use and Influence of Rhetoric in Galatians', *TZ* 42 (1986), 386-408.

Hill, D. *Greek Words and Hebrew Meanings: Studies in the Semantics of Soteriological Terms*. SNTSMS, 5. Cambridge: Cambridge University Press, 1967.

—'Salvation Proclaimed: IV. Galatians 3.10-14: Freedom and Acceptance', *ExpTim* 93 (1982), 196-200.

Hirsch, E. 'Zwei Fragen zu Galater 6', *ZNW* 29 (1930), 192-97.

Holmberg, Bengt. *Paul and Power: The Structure of Authority in the Primitive Church as Reflected in the Pauline Epistles*. ConBNT, 11. Lund: Gleerup, 1978.

Hooker, M.D. 'Interchange in Christ', *JTS* 22 (1971), 349-61.

—'Interchange and Atonement', *BJRL* 60 (1977-78), 462-81.

—*Pauline Pieces*. London: Epworth, 1979.

—'Interchange and Suffering', in *Suffering and Martyrdom in the New Testament*. Eds. W. Horbury and B. McNeil. Cambridge: Cambridge University Press, 1981.

—'Paul and "Covenantal Nomism"' in *Paul and Paulinism: Essays in Honour of C.K. Barrett*. Eds. M.D. Hooker and S.G. Wilson. London: SPCK, 1982. 47-56.

Horbury, W. 'Paul and Judaism', *ExpTim* 90 (1979), 116-18.

Howard, G. 'On the "Faith of Christ"', *HTR* 60 (1967), 459-84.

—'The "Faith of Christ"', *ExpTim* 85 (1974), 212-15.

—*Paul: Crisis in Galatia*. SNTSMS, 35. Cambridge: Cambridge University Press, 1979.

Howes, R.F., ed. *Historical Studies of Rhetoric and Rhetoricians*. Ithaca: Cornell University Press, 1961.

Hübner, Hans. 'Gal 3, 10 und die Herkunft des Paulus', *KD* 19 (1973), 215-31.

—*Das Gesetz bei Paulus: Ein Beitrag zum Werden der paulinischen Theologie*. FRLANT, 119. Göttingen: Vandenhoeck & Ruprecht, 1978.

—'Pauli Theologiae Propium', *NTS* 26 (1980), 445-73.

—'Der Galaterbrief und das Verhältnis von antiker Rhetorik und Epistolographie', *TLZ* 109 (1984), 241-50.

Hultgern, A.J. 'The *Pistis Christou* Formulation Paul', *NovT* 22 (1980), 248-63.

Hurd, John C., Jr. *The Origin of First Corinthians*. New York: Seabury, 1965.

—'Pauline Chronology and Pauline Theology', in *Christian History and Interpretation: Studies Presented to John Knox*. Eds. W.R. Farmer, R.R. Niebuhr, and C.F.D. Moule. Cambridge: Cambridge University Press, 1967, 225-48.

—'Concerning the Structure of 1 Thessalonians'. Unpublished paper for the SBL Paul Seminar, 1972.

Isaacs, W.H. 'Galatians 3.20', *ExpTim* 35 (1923-24), 565-67.

Jackson, Jared J. and Kessler, Martin, eds. *Rhetorical Criticism: Essays in Honor of James Muilenburg*. PTMS, 1. Pittsburg: Pickwick, 1974.

Jaeger, W. *Paideia: The Ideals of Greek Culture.* 3 vols. Trans. G. Highet. Oxford: Blackwell, 1945.

Jeremias, J. 'Chiasmus in den Paulusbriefen', *ZNW* 49 (1958), 145-56.

—'Άβραάμ', *TDNT* I, 8-9.

—'Paulus als Hillelit', in *Neotestamentica et Semitica: Studies in Honour of Matthew Black.* Eds. E.E. Ellis and M. Wilcox. Edinburgh: T. & T. Clark, 1969, 88-94.

Jewett, R. 'The Agitators and the Galatian Congregation', *NTS* 17 (1970), 198-212.

—*Paul's Anthropological Terms: A Study of their Use in Conflict Settings.* AGJU, 10. Leiden: Brill, 1971.

Johnson, L. 'Rom 3.21-26 and the "Faith of Jesus Christ"', *CBQ* 44 (1982), 76-90.

Judge, E.A. 'Paul's Boasting in Relation to Contemporary Professional Practice', *AusBR* 16 (1968), 37-50.

—'The Reaction Against Classical Education in the New Testament', *The Journal of Christian Education* 77 (1983), 7-14.

Jung, Peter. 'Das paulinische Vocabular', *ZKT* 74 (1952), 439-49.

Kadushin, Max. *The Rabbinic Mind.* New York: Jewish Theological Seminary of America, 1952.

Kaiser, O. 'Traditionsgeschichtliche Untersuchung von Genesis 15', *ZAW* 70 (1958), 107-26.

Käsemann, E. *Perspectives on Paul.* Trans. M. Kohl. Philadelphia: Fortress, 1971.

—*New Testament Questions for Today.* London: SCM, 1969.

Keck, Leander E. *Paul and his Letters.* Proclamation Commentaries. Philadelphia: Fortress Press, 1979.

Kennedy, George A. *The Art of Persuasion in Greece.* Princeton: Princeton University Press, 1963.

—*The Art of Rhetoric in the Roman World.* Princeton: Princeton University Press, 1972.

—*Classical Rhetoric and its Christian and Secular Tradition from Ancient to Modern Times.* Chapel Hill: University of North Carolina Press, 1980.

—*New Testament Interpretation through Rhetorical Criticism.* Chapel Hill: University of North Carolina Press, 1984.

Kennedy, H.A.A. 'The Significance and Range of the Covenant Conception in the New Testament', *The Expositor* 8 (1915), 385-410.

Kepple, R.J. 'An Analysis of Antiochene Exegesis of Galatians 4.24-26', *WTJ* 39 (1976-77), 239-49.

Kertelge, K. '*Rechtfertigung*' bei Paulus. Münster: Aschendorff, 1967.

—'*Apokalypsis Iesou Christou* (Gal 1, 12)', in *Neues Testament und Kirche.* Ed. J. Gnilka. Freiburg: Herder, 1974, 266-81.

—'Zur Deutung der Rechtfertigungsbegriffe im Galaterbrief', *BZ* 12 (1968), 211-22.

—'Gesetz und Freiheit im Galaterbrief', *NTS* 30 (1984), 382-94.

Kessler, M. 'A Methodological Setting for Rhetorical Criticism', *Semitics* 4 (1974), 22-36.

—'Inclusio in the Hebrew Bible', *Semitics* 6 (1978), 44-49.

—'An Introduction to Rhetorical Criticism of the Bible', *Semitics* 7 (1980), 1-27.

Kikawada, I.M. 'Some Proposals for the Definition of Rhetorical Criticism', *Semitics* 5 (1977), 67-91.

Kim, Chan-Hie. *The Form and Function of the Familiar Greek Letter of Recommendation.* Missoula: Scholars Press, 1972.

—'The Papyrus Invitation', *JBL* 94 (1975), 391-402.

Kim, Seyoon. *The Origin of Paul's Gospel.* Grand Rapids: Eerdmans, 1981.

King, D.H. 'Paul and the Tannaim: A Study in Galatians', *WTJ* 45 (1983), 340-70.

Kittel, G. 'ἀκοή', *TDNT* I, 216-25.

—'πίστις Ἰησοῦ Χριστοῦ bei Paulus', *TSK* 79 (1906), 419-36.

Klein, G. 'Individualgeschichte und Weltgeschichte bei Paulus: Eine Interpretation ihres Verhältnisses im Galaterbrief', *EvT* 24 (1964), 126-65.

Kleinknecht. 'νόμος', *TDNT* IV, 1022-35.

Klijn, A.F.J., and Reininck, G.J. *Patristic Evidence for Jewish-Christian Sects.* Leiden: Brill, 1973.

Kline, M.G. 'Abram's Amen', *WTJ* 31 (1968), 1-11.

Knox, John. *Chapters in a Life of Paul.* Nashville: Abingdon, Cokesbury, 1950.

Knox, W.L. 'Abraham and the Quest for God', *HTR* 28 (1935), 55-60.

Koepp, W. 'Die Abraham—Midraschimkette des Galaterbriefs als das vorpaulinische heidenchristliche Urtheologumenon', *Wissenschaftliche Zeitschrift der Universität Rostock* 2,3 (1952-53), 181-87.

Koester, Helmut. 'Paul and Hellenism', in *The Bible in Modern Scholarship*. Ed. P. Hyatt. Philadelphia: Fortress, 1968.

—*Introduction to the New Testament.* 2 vols. Philadelphia: Fortress Press, 1982.

Koskenniemi, Heikki. *Studien zur Idee und Phraseologie des griechischen Briefes bis 400 n. Chr.* Helsinki: Suomalaien Tiedeadatemi, 1956.

Kraabel, A.T. 'Paganism and Judaism: The Sardis Evidence', in *Paganisme, Judaïsme, Christianisme: Influences et affrontements dans le monde antique (Mélanges Offerts à Marcel Simon)*. Paris: Boccard, 1978.

—'Jews in Imperial Rome: More Archaeological Evidence from an Oxford Collection', *JJS* 30 (1979), 41-58.

Kuhn, K.G. 'προσήλυτος', *TDNT* VI, 727-44.

Kuhn, H.W. 'Jesus als Gekreuzigter in der frühchristlichen Verkündigung bis zur Mitte des 2. Jahrhunderts', *ZKT* 72 (1975), 1-46.

Kümmel, W.G. '"Individualgeschichte" und "Weltgeschichte" in Gal. 2.15-21', in *Christ and the Spirit in the New Testament: Essays in Honour of C.F.D. Moule.* Eds. B. Lindars and S. Smalley. Cambridge: Cambridge University Press, 1973, 157-73.

Ladd, G.E. 'The Holy Spirit in Galatians', in *Current Issues in Biblical and Patristic Interpretation: Studies in Honor of Merrill C. Tenney.* Ed. G.F. Hawthorne. Grand Rapids: Eerdmans, 1975, 211-16.

Lagrange, M. J. *Saint Paul Épître aux Galates.* 2nd edn. Paris: Librairie Lecoffre, J. Gabalda, 1925.

Lambrecht, J. 'The Line of Thought in Gal 2.14b-21', *NTS* 24 (1978), 485-95.

Lang, F.G. 'Gesetz und Bund bei Paulus', in *Rechtfertigung: FS Ernst Käsemann.* Eds. J. Friedrich, W. Pohlmann, and P. Stuhlmacher. Tübingen: J.C.B. Mohr, 1976, 305-21.

Lausberg, H. *Handbuch der literarischen Rhetorik.* 2 vols. Munich: Hueber, 1960.

—*Elemente der literarischen Rhetorik.* 3rd. edn. Munich: Hueber, 1967.

Lauterbach, J.Z. 'Ancient Jewish Allegorists', *JQR* 1 (1911), 291-33, 503-31.

—'Midrash and Mishnah', in his *Rabbinic Essays.* Cincinnati: Hebrew Union College Press, 1951, 163-256.

Le Déaut, R. 'Traditions targumiques dans le Corpus Paulinien? (Heb 11,4 et 12,24; Gal 4.29-30; II Cor 3,16)', *Bib* 42 (1961), 28-48.

—'Apropos a Definition of Midrash', *Int* 25 (1971), 259-82.

Letegan, Bernard C. 'Structural Analysis as a Basis for Further Exegetical Procedures', *SBLASP* 1 (1978), 341-60.

—'Is Paul Defending his Apostleship in Galatians?', *NTS* 34 (1988), 411-30.

Liebermann, S. *Hellenism in Jewish Palestine.* New York: The Jewish Theological

Seminary of America, 1950.

Lietzmann, Hans. *An die Galater*. HNT, 10. 3rd edn Tübingen: J.C.B. Mohr, 1932.

Lightfoot, J.B. *St. Paul's Epistle to the Galatians*. Reprint of 1865 Macmillan edition. Grand Rapids: Zondervan, 1969.

Lincoln, A.T. *Paradise Now and Not Yet*. SNTSMS, 47. Cambridge: Cambridge University Press, 1981.

Lindars, B. *New Testament Apologetic: The Doctrinal Significance of the Old Testament Quotations*. London: SCM, 1961.

Ljungman, Henrik. *Pistis: A Study of its Presuppositions and its Meaning in Pauline Use*. Lund: Gleerup, 1964.

Longenecker, Richard N. *Paul, Apostle of Liberty*. New York: Harper & Row, 1964.

—'The Obedience of Christ in the Theology of the Early Church', in *Reconciliation and Hope: New Testament Essays on Atonement and Eschatology presented to L. Morris*. Ed. R. Banks. Grand Rapids: Eerdmans, 1974, 142-52.

—*Biblical Exegesis in the Apostolic Period*. Grand Rapids: Eerdmans, 1975.

—'The "Faith of Abraham" Theme in Paul, James and Hebrews: A Study in the Circumstantial Nature of New Testament Teaching', *JETS* 29 (1977), 203-12.

—'The Pedagogical Nature of the Law in Galatians 3.19-4.7', *JETS* 25 (1982), 53-61.

—*New Testament Social Ethics for Today*. Grand Rapids: Eerdmans, 1984.

Lord, J. 'Abraham: A Study in Ancient Jewish and Christian Interpretation'. Ph.D. Dissertation, Duke University, 1968.

Lucchesi, E. 'Nouveau parallèle entre Saint Paul (Gal 3.16) et Philon d'Alexandrie (Quaestiones in Genesin)?' *NovT* 21 (1979), 150-55.

Lüdemann, Gerd. *Paul, Apostle to the Gentiles: Studies in Chronology*. Trans. F.S. Jones. Philadelphia: Fortress, 1984.

Lull, D.J. *The Spirit in Galatia. Paul's Interpretation of Pneuma as Divine Power*. SBLDS, 49, Chico, Ca.: Scolars Press, 1980.

—'"The Law was our Pedagogue": A Study in Galatians 3.19-25', *JBL* 105 (1986), 481-98.

Lund, N.W. *Chiasmus in the New Testament: A Study in Formgeschichte*. Chapel Hill: University of North Carolina Press, 1942.

Lütgert, Wilhelm. *Gesetz und Geist: Eine Untersuchung zur Vorgeschichte des Galaterbriefes*. BFCT 22. Gütersloh: Bertelsmann, 1919.

Luther, Martin. *Commentary on Saint Paul's Epistle to the Galatians*. Reprint of 1891 Highland edition. Grand Rapids; Baker, 1979.

Luz, Ulrich. 'Der alte und der neue Bund bei Paulus und im Hebräerbrief'. *EvT* 27 (1967), 318-36.

—*Das Geschichtsverständnis des Paulus*. BEvt, 49. Munich: Kaiser, 1968.

Lyonnet, S. *Les Épîtres de Saint Paul aux Galates, aux Romains*. Paris: Cerf, 1953.

Lyons, George, 'Pauline Autobiography: Toward a New Understanding'. SBL DS 73; Atlanta: Scholars Press, 1985.

Malherbe, Abraham J. 'Ancient Epistolary Theorists', *Ohio Journal of Religious Studies* 5 (1977), 3-77.

—*Social Aspects of Early Christianity*. 2nd edn. Philadelphia: Fortress, 1983.

Martyn, J. Louis. 'A Law-Observant Mission to Gentiles: The Background of Galatians', *Michigan Quarterly Review* 22 (1983), 221-35.

—'Apocalyptic Antinomies in Paul's Letter to the Galatians', *NTS* 31 (1985), 412-20.

Marxsen, W. *Introduction to the New Testament*. Trans. G. Buswell. Oxford: Blackwell, 1968.

Maurer. 'μετατίθημι', *TDNT* VIII, 161-62.

Mauser, U. 'Galater iii.20: Die Universalität des Heils', *NTS* 13 (1967), 258-70.

Mayer, J.D. 'Aspekte des Abrahambildes in der Hellinistisch—Jüdischen Literatur', *EvT* 32 (1972), 118-27.

McGonigal, T.D. '"Abraham Believed God": Genesis 15.6 and its Use in the New Testament'. Ph.D. Dissertation, Fuller Theological Seminary, 1981.

McNamara, M. *The New Testament and the Palestinian Targum*. Rome: Pontifical Biblical Institute Press, 1966.

—*Targum and Testament*. Shannon: Irish University Press, 1972.

—'"*to de (Hagar) Sinai oros estin en te Arabia*" (Gal 4.25a): Paul and Petra', *MillStud* 2 (1978), 24-41.

Meecham, H.G. *Light from Ancient Letters: Private Correspondence in the Non-literary Papyri of Oxyrhynchus of the First Four Centuries and its Bearing on New Testament Language and Thought*. London: Allen & Unwin, 1923.

Meeks, Wayne. 'The Image of the Androgyne: Some Uses of a Symbol in Earliest Christianity', *HR* 13 (1974), 165-208.

— Review of H.D. Betz, *Galatians: A Commentary on Paul's Letter to the Churches in Galatia*, *JBL* 100 (1981), 304-306.

Mendenhall, G.E. *Law and Covenant in Israel and the Ancient Near East*. Pittsburgh: The Presbyterian Board of Colportage, 1955.

Merk, O. 'Der Beginn der Paränese im Galaterbrief', *ZNW* 60 (1969), 83-104.

Metzger, B.M. 'The Formulas Introducing Quotations of Scripture in the NT and the Mishnah', *JBL* 70 (1951), 297-307.

—*A Textual Commentary on the Greek New Testament*. London: UBS, 1975.

Meyer, R. 'περιτέμνω', *TDNT* VI, 72-84.

Meyer, Paul W. Review of H.D. Betz, *Galatians: A Commentary on Paul's Letter to the Churches of Galatia*, *RelSRev* 7 (1981), 323-28.

Michaelis. 'προοράω', *TDNT* V, 381-82.

Michel, O. *Paulus und seine Bibel*. Gütersloh: Bertelsmann, 1929.

Miller, M.P. 'Targum, Midrash and the Use of the OT in the NT', *JSJ* 2 (1971), 29-82.

Momigliano, Arnaldo. *The Development of Greek Biography*. Cambridge, Mass.: Harvard University Press, 1971.

Montefiore, C.G. *Judaism and Saint Paul*. New York: Arno, 1914.

Moo, Douglas, J. '"Law", "Works of the Law", and Legalism in Paul', *WTJ* 45 (1983), 73-100.

—*The Old Testament in the Gospel Passion Narratives*. Sheffield: Almond, 1983.

Moore, George Foot. 'Christian Writers on Judaism', *HTR* 14 (1921), 197-254.

—*Judaism in the First Centuries of the Christian Era: The Age of the Tannaim*. 3 vols. Cambridge, Mass.: Harvard University Press, 1927-30.

Morris, L. *The Apostolic Preaching of the Cross*. Grand Rapids: Eerdmans, 1955.

Moule, C.F.D. 'The Biblical Conception of "Faith"', *ExpTim* 68 (1957), 157.

—'Obligation in the Ethic of Paul', in *Christian History and Interpretation: Studies Presented to John Knox*. Eds. W.R. Farmer, R.R. Niebuhr, and C.F.D. Moule. Cambridge: Cambridge University Press, 1967. 389-406.

—'Fulfillment Words in the New Testament: Use and Abuse', *NTS* 14 (1968), 293-320.

Moxnes, Halver. *Theology in Conflict: Studies in Paul's Understanding of God in Romans*. NovTSup, 53. Leiden: Brill, 1980.

Muilenburg, James. 'Form Criticism and Beyond', *JBL* 88 (1969), 1-18.

Mullins, T.Y. 'Disclosure as a Literary Form in the New Testament', *NovT* 7 (1964),

144-50.

—'Petition as a Literary Form', *NovT* 5 (1962), 46-54.

—'Formulas in New Testament Epistles', *JBL* 91 (1972), 380-90.

—'Visit Talk in the New Testament Letters', *CBQ* 35 (1973), 350-58.

Munck, Johannes. *Paul and the Salvation of Mankind*. Trans. F. Clarke. London: SCM, 1959.

Mundle, W. 'Zur Auslegung von Gal 2, 17.18', *ZNW* 23 (1924), 153.

—*Der Glaubensbegriff bei Paulus*. Leipzig: Heinsius, 1932.

Mussner, Franz. 'Hagar, Sinai, Jerusalem', *TQ* 135 (1955), 56-60.

—*Der Galaterbrief*. HTKNT, 9. Freiburg: Herder, 1974.

Neugebauer, Fritz. *In Christus: Eine Untersuchung zum Paulinischen Glaubensverständnis*. Göttingen: Vandenhoeck & Ruprecht, 1961.

Neusner, J. *The Rabbinic Traditions about the Pharisees before 70* I. Leiden: Brill, 1971.

—'Methods and Substance in the History of Judaic Ideas: An Exercise', in *Jews, Greeks, and Christians: Religious Cultures in Late Antiquity: FS W. D. Davies*. Eds. R. Hammerton-Kelly and R. Scroggs, SJLA 21. Leiden: Brill, 1976.

Neyrey, J.H. 'Bewitched in Galatia: Paul and Cultural Anthropology', *CBQ* 50 (1988), 72-100.

Nickels, P. *Targum and New Testament*. Rome: Pontifical Biblical Institute Press, 1967.

Nickelsburg, G. *Jewish Literature Between the Bible and the Mishnah*. Philadelphia: Fortress, 1981.

Norden, Eduard. *Die antike Kunstprosa*. 2 vols. Leipzig: Teubner, 1915-18.

—*Agnostos Theos. Untersuchungen zur Formen-Geschichte Religioser*. Stuttgart: Teubner, 1956.

Noth, M. 'For All Who Rely on Works of the Law are Under a Curse', in his *The Law in the Pentateuch and Other Studies*. Trans. D.R. Ap-Thomas. Edinburgh: Oliver and Boyd, 1966, 118-31.

Oemig, Manfred. 'Ist Genesis 15,6 ein Beleg für die Anrechnung Gerechtigkeit?' *ZAW* 95 (1983), 182-97.

Oepke, A. *Der Brief des Paulus an die Galater*. THKNT, 9. Berlin: Evangelische Verlagsanstalt, 1957.

O'Neill, J. *The Recovery of Paul's Letter to the Galatians*. London: SPCK, 1972.

Osiek, C. *Galatians*. New Testament Message, 12. Wilmington, De.: Glazier, 1980.

Pastor, F. 'Allegoria o tipologia en Gal 4, 21-31', *EstBib* 34 (1975), 113-19.

Patte, D. *Early Jewish Hermeneutic in Palestine*. SBLDS, 23. Missoula: Scholars Press, 1975.

—*Paul's Faith and the Power of the Gospel: A Structural Introduction to the Pauline Letters*. Philadelphia: Fortress, 1983.

Pedersen, Sigfred, ed. *Die paulinische Literatur und Theologie*. Göttingen: Vandenhoeck & Ruprecht, 1980.

Pereira, F. 'The Galatian Controversy in the Light of the Targums', *The Indian Journal of Theology* 20 (1971), 13-29.

Perelman, Chaim and Olbrechts-Tyteca, L. *The New Rhetoric: A Treatise on Argumentation*. Trans. J. Wilkinson and P. Weaver. Notre Dame: University of Notre Dame Press, 1969.

Perelmann, Chaim. *The New Rhetoric and the Humanities: Essays on Rhetoric and its Applications*. Trans. W. Kluback. Dordrecht: Reidel, 1979.

—*The Realm of Rhetoric*. Trans. W. Kluback. Notre Dame: University of Notre Dame Press, 1982.

Pilch, J.J. 'Paul's Usage and Understanding of "Apokalypsis" in Galatians 1–2: A Structural Investigation'. Ph.D. Dissertation, Marquette University, 1972.

Porton, G.G. 'Defining Midrash', in *The Study of Ancient Judaism*. 2 vols. Ed. J. Neusner. New York: KTAV, 1981, I, 55-92.

Preisker, H. 'ἐπαγγέλλω', *TDNT* II, 576-90.

—'ὀρθοποδέω', *TDNT* V.451.

Rad, G. von 'Faith Reckoned as Righteousness', in his *The Problem of the Hexateuch and Other Essays*. New York: McGraw Hill, 1966.

Räisänen, Heikki. 'Legalism and Salvation by the Law. Paul's Portrayal of the Jewish Religion as a Historical and Theological Problem', in *Die paulinische Literatur und Theologie*. Ed. S. Pedersen. Göttingen: Vandenhoeck & Ruprecht, 1980.

—*Paul and the Law*. WUNT 29. Tübingen: J.C.B. Mohr, 1983.

Ramsey, W. *A Historical Commentary on St. Paul's Epistle to the Galatians*. London: Hodder & Stoughton, 1899.

Reicke, B. 'The Law and This World According to Paul: Some Thoughts Concerning Gal 4.1-11', *JBL* 70 (1951), 259-76.

Rengstorf. 'ἁμαρτωλός', *TDNT* I, 317-35.

Richardson, Peter. *Israel in the Apostolic Church*. SNTSMS, 10. Cambridge: Cambridge University Press, 1969.

—*Paul's Ethic of Freedom*. Philadelphia: Westminster, 1979.

—'Pauline Inconsistency: I Corinthians 9.19-23 and Galtaians 2.11-14', *NTS* 26 (1979-80), 347-62.

Ridderbos, Herman N. *The Epistle of Paul to the Churches of Galatia*. NICNT. Grand Rapids: Eerdmans, 1953.

Riesenfeld. 'ὑπέρ', *TDNT* VIII, 507-16.

Robbins, Vernon K. and Patton, John H. 'Rhetoric and Biblical Criticism'. *The Quarterly Journal of Speech* 66 (1980), 327-50.

Roberson, O.P. 'Genesis 15.6: New Covenant Expositons of an Old Covenant Text', *WTJ* 42 (1979-80), 259-89.

Robinson, D.W.B. 'A Distinction between Jewish and Gentile Believers in Galatians', *AusBR* 13 (1965), 29-48.

—'"The Faith of Jesus Christ"—a New Testament Debate', *Reformed Theological Review* 29 (1970), 71-81.

Robinson, J.M. 'The Historicality of Biblical Language', in *The Old Testament and Christian Faith*. Ed. B.W. Anderson. New York: Harper & Row, 1963, 131-50.

—'Die Hodajot-Formel im Gebet und Hymnus des Frühchristentums', in *Apophoreta*. *FS E. Haenchen*. Ed. W. Eltester. Berlin: Töpelmann, 1964.

Roetzel, C. 'Judgment Form in Paul's Letters', *JBL* 88 (1969), 305-12.

Roller, Otto. *Das Formular der Paulinischen Briefe: Ein Beitrag zur Lehre vom Antiken Briefe*. Stuttgart: Kohlhammer, 1933.

Ropes, J.H. *The Singular Problem of the Epistle to the Galatians*. HTS 14. Cambridge, Mass.: Harvard University Press, 1929.

Sampley, J.P. '"Before God, I Do Not Lie" (Gal 1.20): Paul's Self-Defense in the Light of Roman Legal Praxis', *NTS* 23 (1976), 477-82.

Sanders, E.P. 'Patterns of Religion in Paul and Judaism', *HTR* 66 (1973), 458-66.

—'The Covenant as a Soteriological Category and the Nature of Salvation in Palestinian and Hellenistic Judaism', in *Jews, Greeks, and Christians*. Eds. R. Hamerton-Kelly and R. Scroggs. Leiden: Brill, 1976.

—*Paul and Palestinian Judaism*. Philadelphia: Fortress, 1977.

—'On the Question of Fulfilling the Law in Paul and Rabbinic Judaism', in *Donum Gentilicium: New Testament Studies in Honor of David Daube*. Eds. E. Bammel, C.K. Barrett, and W.D. Davies. Oxford: Clarendon, 1978, 103-26.

—*Paul, the Law, and the Jewish People.* Philadelphia: Fortress, 1983.
Sanders, J.A. 'Habakkuk in Qumran, Paul, and the Old Testament', *JR* 39 (1959), 232-44.
—'Torah and Christ', *Int* 29 (1975), 372-90.
Sanders, J.T. 'The Transition from Opening Epistolary Thanksgiving to Body in the Letters of the Pauline Corpus', *JBL* 81 (1962), 348-62.
—'Paul's Autobiographical Statements in Galatians 1-2', *JBL* 85 (1966), 335-43.
Sandmel, S. 'Abraham's Knowledge of the Existence of God', *HTR* 44 (1951), 137-39.
—'Parallelomania', *JBL* 81 (1962), 1-13.
—*Philo's Place in Judaism: A Study of Conceptions of Abraham in Jewish Literature.* New York: KTAV, 1971.
—*Judaism and Christian Beginnings.* New York: Oxford University Press, 1978.
—*The Genius of Paul: A Study in History.* Philadelphia: Fortress, 1979.
Schechter, S. *Some Aspects of Rabbinic Theology.* New York: Macmillan, 1910.
Schein, B.E. 'Our Father Abraham'. Ph.D. Dissertation, Yale University, 1972.
Schenk, Wolfgang. 'Die Gerechtigkeit Gottes und der Glaube Christi', *TLZ* 97 (1972), 161-74.
Schlier, H. *Der Brief an die Galater.* MeyerK, 7. 11th edn. Göttingen: Vandenhoeck & Ruprecht, 1951.
Schmid, H.H. 'Gerechtigkeit und Glaube: Gen 15.6 und sein biblisch-theologischer Kontext', *EvT* 40 (1980), 396-420.
Schmithals, Walter. *Paul and the Gnostics.* Trans. J. Steely. Nashville: Abingdon Press, 1972.
—'Judaisten in Galatien?' *ZNW* 74 (1983), 27-58.
Schmitz, O. 'Abraham im Spätjudentum und im Urchristentum', in *Aus Schrift und Geschichte: Theologische Abhandlungen A. Schlatter dargebracht.* Stuttgart: Calwer, 1922. 99-123.
Schneider, Norbet. *Die rhetorische Eigenart der paulinischen Antithese.* Tübingen: J.C.B. Mohr, 1970.
Schoeps, H.J. *Paul, The Theology of the Apostle in the Light of Jewish Religious History.* Trans. H. Knight. Philadelphia: Westminster, 1961.
Schrenk, G. 'γραφή', *TDNT* I, 751-61.
—'δικαιόω', *TDNT* II, 211-25.
—'Was bedeutet "Israel Gottes"?' *Judaica* 5 (1949), 81-94.
—'Der Segenwunsch nach der Kampfepistel', *Judaica* 6 (1950), 170-90.
Schubert, Paul. *Form and Function of the Pauline Thanksgiving.* Zeitschrift für die neutestamentliche Theologie, 20. Berlin: Töpelmann, 1939.
Schutz, J.H. *Paul and the Anatomy of Apostolic Authority.* SNTSMS, 26. Cambridge: Cambridge University Press, 1975.
Schwartz, D.R. 'Two Pauline Allusions to the Redemptive Mechanism of the Crucifixion', *JBL* 102 (1983), 259-86.
Schweitzer, A. *Paul and His Interpreters.* Trans. W. Montgomery. London: Black, 1912.
—*The Mysticism of Paul the Apostle.* Trans. W. Montgomery. London: Black, 1912.
Scroggs, Robin. 'Paul as Rhetorician: Two Homilies in Romans 1-11', in *Jews, Greeks and Christians: Essays in Honor of W.D. Davies.* Eds. R. Hamerton-Kelly and R. Scroggs. Leiden: Brill, 1976, 271-98.
Selb, W. '*Diatheke* im Neuen Testament. Randbemerkungen eines Juristes zu einem Theologenstreit', *JJS* 25 (1974), 190-201.
Shaw, G. *The Cost of Authority: Manipulation and Freedom in the New Testament.* Philadelphia: Fortress, 1983.

300   *Abraham in Galatians*

Siegert, Folker. 'Argumentation bei Paulus: Gezeigt an Röm 9-11'. Ph.D. Dissertation, Evangelisch-theologische Fakultät an der Eberhard-Karls-Universität zu Tübingen, 1983.

Siker, J.S. 'Disinheriting the Jews: The Use of Abraham in Early Christian Controversy with Judaism from Paul through Justin Martyr'. Ph.D. Dissertation. Princeton Theological Seminary, 1988.

Singerland, H.D. *The Testaments of the Twelve Patriarchs: A Critical History of Research*. SBLMS 21. Missoula: Scholars, 1977.

Smit, J. 'The Letter of Paul to the Galatians: a deliberative speech', NTS 35 (1989), 1-26.

Smith, D.M. 'Ο ΔΕ ΔΙΚΑΙΟΣ ΠΙΣΤΕΩΣ ΖΗΣΕΤΑΙ', in *Studies in the History and Text of the New Testament in Honor of K.W. Clark*. Eds. B.L. Daniels and M.J. Suggs. Salt Lake City: University of Utah, 1967.

Smith, M. 'Goodenough's *Jewish Symbols* in Retrospect', *JBL* 86 (1967), 53-68.

—'On the Problem of Method in the Study of Rabbinic Literature', *JBL* 92 (1973), 112-13.

Smith, Robert W. *The Art of Rhetoric in Alexandria: Its Theory and Practice in the Ancient World*. The Hague: Martinus Nijhoff, 1974.

Stange, E. 'Diktierpausen in den Paulus-Briefen', *ZNW* 18 (1917), 109-17.

Steen, Henry A. 'Les Clichés épistolaires dans des lettres sur papyrus grecques', *Classica et Mediaevalia* I, no. 2 (1938), 119-76.

Stendahl, Krister. *Paul among Jews and Gentiles*. Philadelphia: Fortress, 1976.

Stirewalt, M.L. 'Official Letter Writing and the Letter of Paul to the Churches of Galatia'. Unpublished paper for SBL Paul Seminar, 1974.

Stoike, D.A. '"The Law of Christ": A Study of Paul's Use of the Expression in Galatians 6.2'. Th.D. Dissertation, School of Theology at Claremont, 1971.

Stolle, B. 'Die Eins in Ga. 3.15-29', in *Theokratia, Jahrbuch des Institutum Delitzschianum*, vol. 2. Leiden: Brill, 1973. 204-13.

Stowers, S.K. *The Diatribe and Paul's Letter to the Romans*. SBLDS, 57. Chico, Ca: Scholars Press, 1981.

Strack, H.L. *Introduction to the Talmud and Midrash*. Philadelphia: Jewish Publication Society of America, 1931.

Stube, R. *Der Himmelsbrief: Ein Beitrag zur allgemeinen Religionsgeschichte*. Tübingen: J.C.B. Mohr, 1918.

Stuhlmacher, Peter. *Gottes Gerechtigkeit bei Paulus*. FRLANT 87. Göttingen: Vandenhoeck & Ruprecht, 1965.

—'Achtzehn Thesen zur paulinischen Kreuzestheologie', in *Rechtfertigung: FS E. Käsemann*. Eds. J. Friedrich, W. Pohlmann, and P. Stuhlmacher. Tübingen: J.C.B. Mohr, 1976, 509-25.

Sutherland, D.D. 'Genesis 15.6: A Study in Ancient Jewish and Christian Interpretation'. Ph.D. Dissertation, Southern Baptist Theological Seminary, 1982.

Sykutris, J. 'Epistolographie', in *Real-Encyclopädie der classischen Altertumswissenschaft*. Eds. A. Pauly, G. Wissowa, *et al*. Stuttgart: Metzlersche, 1931, Supplement 5.

Tannehill, R.C. *Dying and Rising with Christ: A Study in Pauline Theology*. BZNW 32. Berlin: Töpelmann, 1967.

Taylor, G.M. 'The Function of *PISTIS CHRISTOU* in Galatians', *JBL* 85 (1966), 58-76.

Tenney, Merrill C. *Galatians: The Charter of Christian Liberty*. Revised edition. Grand Rapids: Eerdmans, 1969.

Thackeray, H. St. J. *The Relation of St. Paul to Contemporary Jewish Thought*. London: Macmillan, 1900.

Thompson, A.C. *Responsibility for Evil in the Theodicy of IV Ezra*. SBLDS 29. Missoula: Scholars Press, 1977.

Thrade, Klaus. *Grundzüge griechisch-römischer Brieftopik*. Munich: C.H. Beck, 1970.

Thyen, H. *Der Stil der jüdisch-hellenistischen Homilie*. Göttingen: Vandenhoeck & Ruprecht, 1955.

Torrance, T.F. 'One Aspect of the Biblical Conception of Faith', *ExpTim* 68 (1957), 111-14.

Towner, W.S. 'Hermeneutical Systems of Hillel and the Tannaim: A Fresh Look', *HUCA* 53 (1982), 101-35.

Turner, E.G. *Greek Papyri, An Introduction*. Oxford: Clarendon, 1968.

Turpie, D.M. *The Old Testament in the New*. London: Williams & Norgate, 1868.

Tyson, J.B. 'Paul's Opponents in Galatia', *NovT* 10 (1968), 241-54.

—'"Works of Law" in Galatians', *JBL* 92 (1973), 423-31.

Unnik, W.C. van 'La Conception paulinienne de la Nouvelle Alliance', in *Sparsa Collecta: The Collected Essays of W.C. Van Unnik*. NovTSup 29. Leiden: Brill, 1973.

Urbach, E.E. *The Sages: Their Concepts and Beliefs*. Trans. I. Abrahams. 2nd edn. Jerusalem: Magnes, 1979.

Vanderkam, J.C. *Textual and Historical Studies in the Book of Jubilees*. HSM 14. Missoula: Scholars Press, 1977.

Van Seters, J. *Abraham in History and Tradition*. New Haven: Yale University Press, 1975.

Vermes, G. *Scripture and Tradition in Judaism*. SPB, 4. Leiden: Brill, 1961.

—'Jewish Studies and New Testament Interpretation', *JJS* 31 (1980), 1-17.

—'Jewish Literature and New Testament Exegesis: Reflections on Methodology', *JJS* 33 (1982), 361-76.

Via, Dan O., Jr. 'A Structural Approach to Paul's Old Testament Hermeneutics', *Int* 28 (1974), 201-20.

Vielhauer, P. 'Gesetzesdienst und Stoicheidienst im Galaterbrief', in *Rechfertigung: FS E. Käsemann*. Eds. J. Friedrich, W. Pohlmann, and P. Stuhlmacher. Tübingen: J.C.B. Mohr, 1976, 543-55.

Viertel, W.E. 'The Hermeneutics of Paul as Reflected in Romans and Galatians'. Ph.D. Dissertation, Baylor University, 1976.

Volkmann, Richard. *Die Rhetorik der Griechen und Römer in systematischer Übersicht*. Stuttgart: Teubner, 1885.

Vouga, F. 'La Construction de l'histoire en Galates 3-4', *ZNW* 75 (1984), 259-69.

—'Zur rhetorischen Gattung des Galater briefes', *ZNW* 79 (1988), 291-92.

Wacholder, Ben Zion. 'Pseudo-Eupolemus' Two Greek Fragments on the Life of Abraham', *HUCA* 34 (1963), 83-113.

Walker, D. 'The Legal Terminology in the Epistle to the Galatians', in his *The Gift of Tongues and Other Essays*. Edinburgh, 1906, 81-175.

Ward, R.B. 'The Works of Abraham', *HTR* 61 (1968), 283-90.

—'Abraham Traditions in Early Christianity', *SBLSCS* 2 (1972), 165-79.

Watson, D.F. 'The New Testament and Greco-Roman Rhetoric: A Bibliography', *JETS* 31 (1988) 465-72.

Watson, F. *Paul, Judaism and the Gentiles*. SNTSMS 56: Cambridge: Cambridge University Press, 1986.

Wedderburn, A.J.M. Review of G. Howard, *Paul: Crisis in Galatia* , *SJT* 33 (1980), 375-85.

Weiss, J. *Beiträge zur paulinischen Rhetorik*. Göttingen: Vandenhoeck & Ruprecht, 1897.

Welch, John W., ed. *Chiasmus in Antiquity: Structures, Analyses, Exegesis*. Hildesheim: Gerstenberg, 1981.

Wendland, Paul. *Die hellenistisch-römische Kultur in ihren Beziehungen zu Judentum und Christentum. Die urchristlichen Literaturformen*. Tübingen: J.C.B. Mohr, 1912.

Westermann, C. *The Promises to the Fathers*. Philadelphia: Fortress, 1980.

White, John L. 'Introductory Formulae in the Body of the Pauline Letter', *JBL* 90 (1971), 91-97.

—*The Form and Function of the Body of the Greek Letter: A Study of the Letter-Body in the Non-Literary Papyri and in Paul the Apostle*. SBLDS, 2. Missoula: Scholars Press, 1972.

—*The Form and Structure of the Official Petition: A Study in Greek Epistolographie*. SBLDS 5; Missoula: Scholars Press, 1972.

—and Kensinger, Keith A. 'Categories of Greek Papyrus Letters', *SBLASP* 10 (1976), 79-91.

—'Epistolary Formulas and Cliches in Greek Papyrus Letters', *SBLASP* 14 (1978), 289-319.

—'The Greek Documentary Letter Tradition, Third Century B.C.E. to Third Century C.E.', *Semeia* 22 (1981), 89-106.

—'Saint Paul and the Apostolic Letter Tradition', *CBQ* 45 (1983), 433-44.

Wilckens, U. 'Statements on the Development of Paul's View of the Law', in *Paul and Paulinism: Essays in Honour of C.K. Barrett*. Eds. M.D. Hooker and S.G. Wilson. London: SPCK, 1982.

—'Zur Entwicklung des paulinischen Gesetzesverständnisses', *NTS* 28 (1982), 154-90.

Wilcox, Max. '"Upon a Tree"—Deut. 21.22-23 in the NT', *JBL* 96 (1977), 85-99.

—'On Investigating the Use of the Old Testament in the New Testament', in *Text and Interpretation: Studies in the New Testament presented to Matthew Black*. Eds. E. Best and R. McL. Wilson. Cambridge: Cambridge University Press, 1979.

—'The Promise to the "Seed" in the NT and Targumim", *JSNT* 5 (1979), 2-20.

Wilder, Amos N. *Early Christian Rhetoric*. London: SCM, 1964.

Wilhelm, G. 'αλλάξαι τὴν φωνήν μου, (Gal 4,20)', *ZNW* 65 (1974), 151-55.

Williams, S. 'The Righteousness of God in Romans', *JBL* 99 (1980), 241-90.

—'Review of G. Howard, *Paul: Crisis in Galatia*', *JBL* 100 (1981), 307-308.

—'Justification and the Spirit in Galatians', *JSNT* 29 (1987), 91-100.

—'Again *Pistis Christou*', *CBQ* 49 (1987), 431-47'.

—'The Hearing of Faith: AKOH ΠΙΣΤΕΩΣ in Galatians 3', *NTS* (1989), 82-93.

Wilson, R. McL. *The Gnostic Problem*. London: Mowbray, 1958.

—'Gnostics—in Galatia?' *SE* 4 (1968), 358-67.

Winterowd, W. Ross. *Rhetoric: A Synthesis*. New York: Holt, Rinehart & Winston, 1968.

Wood, J.E. 'Isaac Typology in the New Testament', *NTS* 14 (1968), 583-89.

Wright, A.G. 'The Literary Genre Midrash', *CBQ* 28 (1966), 105-38, 415-57.

Wright, N.T. 'The Messiah and the People of God: A Study in Pauline Theology with Particular Reference to the Argument of the Epistle to the Romans'. D.Phil. Dissertation, Oxford University, 1980.

Wuellner, Wilhelm. 'Paul's Rhetoric of Argumentation in Romans', *CBQ* 38 (1976), 330-51.

—'Greek Rhetoric and Pauline Argumentation', in *Early Christian Literature and the*

Classical Intellectual Tradition. Eds. W.R. Schoedel and R.L. Wilken. Théologie Historique, 53. Paris: Editions Beauchesne, 1979.

—'Where is Rhetorical Criticism Taking Us?', *CBQ* 49 (1987), 448-63.

Yamauchi, E.M. *Pre-Christian Gnosticism: A Survey of the Proposed Evidences.* London: Tyndale, 1973.

Young, N.H. 'Paidagogos: The Social Setting of a Pauline Metaphor', *NovT* 29 (1987), 150-76.

Zahn, T. *Der Brief des Paulus an die Galater.* HKNT 9. Leipzig: Deichert, 1905.

Zeitlin, S. 'Midrash: A Historical Study', *JQR* 54 (1953), 21-36.

—'Hillel and the Hermeneutical Rules', *JQR* 64 (1963), 161-73.

Ziesler, J.A. *The Meaning of Righteousness in Paul: A Linguistic and Theological Inquiry.* SNTSMS, 20. Cambridge: Cambridge University Press, 1972.

INDEXES

INDEX OF BIBLICAL AND OTHER ANCIENT REFERENCES

OLD TESTAMENT

RABBINIC LITERATURE

PAPYRI

p46	252n230	*P. Giss.*		479.4	224n65	
P. Aml		11.4	28	500.3	224n65	
143.2	29	21.3	28	*P. Oxy.*		
P. Apoll.		*P. Grenf.*		113.19-24	36	
6.2	224n65	77.8	224n65	113.20	28, 224n65	
26.13	224n65	92.1	224n65	123.1-9	38	
29.7	224n65			123.5	224n65	
32.2	224n65	*P. Harris*		930.4	28	
63.23	224n65	157.7	224n65	932.3	29	
64.4	224n65			1070	29	
		P. Herm.		1219.1	28	
P. Baden		11	224n65	1220.23	28	
35	225n80	11.1-19	41	1223	225n80	
35.1-11	34			1223.1-22	33-37, 40	
35.6	224n65	*P. Lips.*		1223.3	224n65	
		107.2	224n65	1348	224n48	
B.G.U. 1				1666.11	28	
332	224n72	*P. Lond.*		2728.1-10	38	
423	224n72	1075	224n65	2728.5	224n65	
				2729.4	224n65	
B.G.U. 4		*P. Merton*		2783.6	224n65	
1081	224n72	28.4	224n65	3063	225n80	
		80	225n80	3063.11-16	37, 224n67	
B.G.U.		80.1-15	35	3063.11	224n65	
449.4	28	80.3	224n65			
816	28			*P. Princ.*		
846.16	28	*P. Mich. 3*		98.16	224n65	
850.1-6	34	209	224n72			
850.3	224n65			*P. Ryl.*		
984.19	224n65	*P.Mich. 8*		235.6-14	37	
1041.12	224n65	475	224n72	235.6	224n65	
1079.2	224n65	473	224n72	573.7	224n65	
		474	224n72	693.2	224n65	
P. Cairo Zen.		479	224n72			
59060.10	224n65	498	224n72	*S.B.*		
		500	224n72	6222.4	224n65	
P. Cornell				8244.3	224n65	
52.1-12	39	*P. Mich.*		9106.2	224n65	
52.5	224n65	28.16	28	9654	224n65	
		36.1	28			
P. Ent.		202.3	28	*P.S.I.*		
82.6	28	206.4	29	502.12	224n65	
		206.11	29			
P. Fay		209	28	*P. Tebt.*		
122.14	29	209.1-3	34	27.34	224n65	
		209.6	224n65	760.20	28	
P. Genev.		209.10-11	47			
57.3	224n65	209.26	41			

INDEX OF AUTHORS

JOURNAL FOR THE STUDY OF THE NEW TESTAMENT
Supplement Series